CURRENCY, CREDIT

The global financial crisis in 2008 brought central banking centre stage, prompting questions about the role of national central banks and – in Europe – of the multi-country European Central Bank. What can central banks do, and what are their limitations? How have they performed? *Currency, Credit and Crisis* seeks to provide a coherent perspective on the functions of a central bank in a small country by assessing the way in which Ireland's financial crisis from 2010 to 2013 was handled. Drawing on his experiences as Governor of the Central Bank of Ireland and in research and policy work at the World Bank, Patrick Honohan offers a detailed analytical narrative of the origins of the crisis and of policymakers' conduct during its most fraught moments.

Patrick Honohan is Honorary Professor of Economics at Trinity College Dublin, Nonresident Senior Fellow at the Peterson Institute for International Economics and a Research Fellow of the Centre for Economic Policy Research (CEPR).

STUDIES IN MACROECONOMIC HISTORY

SERIES EDITOR: Michael D. Bordo, *Rutgers University*

EDITORS:

Owen F. Humpage, *Federal Reserve Bank of Cleveland*
Christopher M. Meissner, *University of California, Davis*
Kris James Mitchener, *Santa Clara University*
David C. Wheelock, *Federal Reserve Bank of St. Louis*

The titles in this series investigate themes of interest to economists and economic historians in the rapidly developing field of macroeconomic history. The four areas covered include the application of monetary and finance theory, international economics, and quantitative methods to historical problems; the historical application of growth and development theory and theories of business fluctuations; the history of domestic and international monetary, financial, and other macroeconomic institutions; and the history of international monetary and financial systems. The series amalgamates the former Cambridge University Press series Studies in Monetary and Financial History and Studies in Quantitative Economic History.

Other Books in the Series:

William A. Allen, *The Bank of England and the Government Debt: Operations in the Gilt-Edged Market, 1928–1972 (2019)*

Eric Monnet, *Controlling Credit: Central Banking and the Planned Economy in Postwar France, 1948–1973 (2018)*

Laurence M. Ball, *The Fed and Lehman Brothers: Setting the Record Straight on a Financial Disaster (2018)*

Rodney Edvinsson, Tor Jacobson, and Daniel Waldenström, Editors, *Sveriges Riksbank and the History of Central Banking (2018)*

Peter L. Rousseau and Paul Wachtel, Editors, *Financial Systems and Economic Growth: Credit, Crises, and the Regulation from the 19th Century to the Present (2017)*

Ernst Baltensperger and Peter Kugler, *Swiss Monetary History since the Early 19th Century (2017)*

(Continued after Index)

Currency, Credit and Crisis

Central Banking in Ireland and Europe

PATRICK HONOHAN

Trinity College, Dublin

CAMBRIDGE
UNIVERSITY PRESS

CAMBRIDGE
UNIVERSITY PRESS

University Printing House, Cambridge CB2 8BS, United Kingdom

One Liberty Plaza, 20th Floor, New York, NY 10006, USA

477 Williamstown Road, Port Melbourne, VIC 3207, Australia

314–321, 3rd Floor, Plot 3, Splendor Forum, Jasola District Centre, New Delhi – 110025, India

79 Anson Road, #06–04/06, Singapore 079906

Cambridge University Press is part of the University of Cambridge.

It furthers the University's mission by disseminating knowledge in the pursuit of education, learning, and research at the highest international levels of excellence.

www.cambridge.org
Information on this title: www.cambridge.org/9781108481892
DOI: 10.1017/9781108680325

First published 2019

Printed and bound in Great Britain by Clays Ltd, Elcograf S.p.A.

A catalogue record for this publication is available from the British Library.

ISBN 978-1-108-48189-2 Hardback
ISBN 978-1-108-74158-3 Paperback

Contents

Contents

PART IV TAKING STOCK

Figures, Table and Boxes

Figures

Table

Boxes

Acknowledgements

My motivation for writing this book came from the more than six years I spent as Governor of the Central Bank of Ireland, working with an able and motivated staff to rebuild institutional morale in a constrained and often hostile environment. To provide here a comprehensive listing of all who have contributed to this effort would be impossible; to be selective seems invidious though unavoidable.

I would like to emphasize the key role played my former colleagues at the Central Bank in the 2009–13 crisis management story that is told here. Bank restructuring and economic stabilization were at the heart of the matter. The incomparable all-rounder Matthew Elderfield took the position of deputy governor for financial regulation and built on the reforms that had been initiated by Mary O'Dea. He was ably succeeded in this analytically demanding role by Cyril Roux heading a group in which Jonathan McMahon, Fiona Muldoon and Sharon Donnery served in turn with great distinction as directors in charge of bank supervision. This group included Michael Feeney, Pat Brady, Fiona McMahon, Shane O'Neill, Dwayne Price, Ed Sibley and Adrian Varley as examples of key experts who stepped into vital roles during the resolution of the crisis. Complementing the banking specialists were the economists, financial stability and monetary operations experts. Stefan Gerlach succeeded Tony Grimes as deputy governor in charge of this area and presided over a group which had to be innovative in uncharted waters. Maurice McGuire, Gabriel Fagan and Lars Frisell were, in turn, directors here, and were supported by such experts as Mark Cassidy, Rob Kelly, Rea Lydon, Fergal McCann, Yvonne McCarthy, Anne-Marie McKiernan, Gillian Phelan and Peter Sinnott, along with the legal team headed successively by Joe Gavin and Eadaoin Rock. Other areas, such as consumer protection (headed by Bernard Sheridan) and the supervision of nonbanks also had an important crisis management dimension (as will become clear), and there were many others, including those not in the category of first responder, and less in the public eye, being concerned with non-policy issues such as note and coin production, human resources, information technology and other business-as-usual tasks. I will allow myself just three more names: Liz Joyce, Human Resources Director at a time of unprecedented hiring and churn; Gerry Quinn, who, by filling the newly created position of Chief Operations Officer with considerable adroitness, ensured that the show stayed on the road; and Derville Rowland, Director of Enforcement. Without the wholehearted and enthusiastic collaboration of these and many others, as well as of the members of the Central Bank Commission (and indeed officials at the Departments of Finance and of the Taoiseach and at the National Treasury Management Agency), the story I have to tell would have had a more sombre ending.

The international central banking community might seem rarefied but it is a collegial environment and relies heavily on a sharing of opinions and conjectures. Some members of this community were very supportive in the crisis and helped me form my ideas about best solutions. Among these were Mark Carney (who made the first visit of a governor of the Bank of England to the Central Bank of Ireland) and Stan Fischer; but a full list of those from whom I received advice during the crisis would be a who's who of global central banking.

Traveling to Frankfurt twice a month for more than six years, I made some good friends and sparring partners at the European Central Bank: several members of the Governing Council are mentioned in the story that follows, but I also learnt much from others whose names do not appear below, such as Ignazio Visco of Italy and the indefatigable Erkki Liikanen, to mention just two.

Many friends helped greatly by reading and commenting on draft material for this book or through helpful discussions on particular points of relevance. In particular, I would like to thank Craig Beaumont, Olivier Blanchard, Vincent Boland, Peter Breuer, Jerry Caprio, Kevin Cardiff, Ajai Chopra, William Cline, Jeremie Cohen-Setton, Jorg Decressin, Donal Donovan, Noel Dorr, Matthew Elderfield, John FitzGerald, Nathan Foley-Fisher, Lars Frisell, Joe Gagnon, Michael Gill, Paul Gorecki, Sebnem Kalemli-Ozcan, Desmond Lachman, Philip Lane, Nellie Liang, Maurice McGuire, Ashoka Mody, Rafique Mottiar, Marcus Noland, Adam Posen, Nicolas Veron, Steve Weisman, Paul Wood and Jeromin Zettelmeyer.

I thank Thomas Conefrey for the macro-model simulations which we worked on together and which are discussed in Chapter 12.

The Central Bank archive is an invaluable resource from which I have been able to uncover some new details of the earlier history of Irish monetary matters. I am grateful to the Bank for giving me access to files on exchange rate policy in the 1990s and to my own email archive for the purpose of verifying my recollection of some of the more recent events. Nodhlag Cadden, Kate Flood, Ross Higgins and Sinéad McDonnell went to some trouble to ensure that these archival researches went smoothly.

I also want to thank Adam Posen and the Peterson Institute for International Economics for organizing a very constructive study group meeting on a draft of the book and more generally for welcoming me over the past three years into a stimulating and congenial environment of policy debate.

The book looks back to before the crisis and is based on experience and perspectives, some of which I formed many years ago, influenced by those who taught me. At University College Dublin these included Paddy Lynch (a great signpost to the library whose catholic tastes allowed him to recommend with enthusiasm both Thorstein Veblen and Friedrich Hayek) and Brendan Walsh, who became a friend and collaborator. Terence Gorman and my thesis supervisor Michio Morishima were inspiring and hugely supportive when I was a graduate student at the London School of Economics.

My indebtedness to mentors and role models in the field of central banking also goes back a long way. Renowned governor T. K. Whitaker, who was friendly with my parents, was a clear role model – he provided a character reference when I applied for my first real job, at the International Monetary Fund (IMF). I learnt so much from that two-year stint in Washington, not just about how central bankers think and talk, but also about the way in which politics and central banking are inextricably intertwined. Watching senior IMF staff members such as the late J. J. Polak and Joseph Gold advising and persuading the Fund's executive board was an education in itself. My subsequent years at the World Bank were also infused with central banking, working in a happy and productive group of financial policy specialists inspired by the leadership of Millard Long.

The Dublin economics scene has been a steady motivator for deliberating macroeconomic policy ideas with close colleagues, among whom I cannot fail to mention Eithne and John FitzGerald, Colm McCarthy,

Cormac Ó Gráda and Frances Ruane. A special word of appreciation is due to my long-time coauthor (and successor as governor) Philip Lane, who has steadily encouraged me to complete this study.

My family is less interested in central banking lore, but has nevertheless humoured me with feigned enthusiasm for numerous anecdotes and provided valuable advice and counsel: my thanks and love to Iseult and Theo.

Abbreviations

ACC	Agricultural Credit Corporation
AIB	Allied Irish Banks
BdL	Bank deutsche Länder
BIS	Bank for International Settlements
BNP	Banque Nationale de Paris
BOSI	Bank of Scotland Ireland
BRRD	Bank Recovery and Resolution Directive
C&AG	Comptroller and Auditor General
CCAR	Comprehensive Capital Analysis and Review
CEBS	Committee of European Bank Supervisors
CFD	contract for difference
CHC	Custom House Capital
CoCo	contingent capital security
DEPFA	Deutsche Pfandbriefbank
DGCOMP	Directorate General for Competition
DM	deutsche mark
DSG	Domestic Standing Group on Financial Stability
EBS	Educational Building Society
ECB	European Central Bank
ECU	European Currency Union
EFSF	European Financial Stability Facility
EFTA	European Free Trade Area
ELA	emergency liquidity assistance
EMS	European Monetary System
EMU	European Economic and Monetary Union
ERM	Exchange Rate Mechanism
ESM	European Stability Mechanism

ESRB	European Systemic Risk Board
ESRI	Economic and Social Research Institute
EU	European Union
FDI	foreign direct investment
FHLMC	Federal Home Loan Mortgage Corporation
FMS	Financial Market Stabilisation Wertmanagement AöR
FNMA	Federal National Mortgage Association
FRN	floating rate note
G7	Group of Seven
GDP	gross domestic product
GFC	global financial crisis
GNI	gross national income
GNP	gross national product
GPA	Guinness Peat Aviation
HAMP	Home Affordable Modification Program
HBOS	Halifax Bank of Scotland
HRE	Hypo Real Estate
IBRC	Irish Bank Resolution Corporation
ICI	Insurance Corporation of Ireland
IFAC	Irish Fiscal Advisory Council
ILP	Irish Life and Permanent
IMF	International Monetary Fund
INBS	Irish Nationwide Building Society
ISTC	International Securities Trading Corporation
LCH	London Clearing House
LTI	loan-to-income ratio
LTRO	longer-term refinancing operation
LTV	loan-to-value ratio
MNC	multinational corporation
NAMA	National Asset Management Agency
NCB	national central bank (in euro area)
NPRF	National Pension Reserve Fund
NTMA	National Treasury Management Agency
OECD	Organisation for Economic Co-operation and Development
OMT	outright monetary transactions
OPEC	Organization of Petroleum Exporting Countries
PCAR	prudential capital adequacy review
PMPA	Private Motorists Protection Association
PN	promissory note

PPI	payment protection insurance
PSI	private sector involvement
PTSB	Permanent-Trustee Saving Bank
PWC	Pricewaterhouse Coopers
QE	quantitative easing
RBS	Royal Bank of Scotland
RSA	Royal and Sun Alliance
SAREB	Sociedad de Gestión de Activos Procedentes de la Reestructuración Bancaria
SGP	Stability and Growth Pact
SMP	Securities Market Programme
SRB	Single Resolution Board
SSM	Single Supervisory Mechanism
SVR	standard variable rate
TARGET	Trans-European Automated Real-time Gross Settlement Express Transfer System
TARP	Troubled Asset Relief Program
TCD	Trinity College Dublin
TFEU	Treaty on the Functioning of the European Union
TLTRO	targeted longer-term refinancing operation
UBS	Union de Banques Suisses/Union Bank of Switzerland
UCD	University College Dublin
USC	universal social charge
WaMu	Washington Mutual Savings Bank

Banking Dramatis Personae

Name changes and mergers among banks complicate the story. To help the reader keep track we provide a simplified and informal list here in alphabetical order of the most important banks involved.

ACC Bank. Formerly the government-owned Agricultural Credit Corporation, ACC Bank was a subsidiary of the Netherlands-based Rabo Group. It quit the market in 2013.

Allied Irish Banks (AIB). One of the two largest banks active in the Irish market, AIB must not be confused with Anglo Irish Bank. It has sizable operations in Northern Ireland (through its First Trust subsidiary). It sold its sizable and profitable subsidiary in Poland during the crisis to help boost cash and strengthen its capital.

Anglo Irish Bank. Grew to be the third largest domestic bank with a total asset size of about €100 billion, of which almost 40% was lost in bad loans. It was Anglo's liquidity position that triggered the guarantee of September 2008. Anglo is not to be confused with AIB. In 2011 Anglo was merged with INBS and the group renamed IBRC.

Bank of Ireland. Once Ireland's central bank, and sometimes appearing weighed down with an awareness of its 235-year history, Bank of Ireland vies with Allied Irish Banks for first place in size. It has long had sizable activities in Great Britain and Northern Ireland.

Bank of Scotland Ireland (BOSI). Formerly the government-owned Industrial Credit Company, BOSI was a subsidiary of the UK-based Lloyds Banking Group, and previously of HBOS. It pulled out of Irish banking at the end of 2010, repaying all of its liabilities.

Danske Bank. This Danish group operated a sizable branch in Ireland, formed from National Irish Bank, previously Northern Bank.

(cont.)

Depfa. Formerly Deutsche Pfandbriefbank, it had the largest balance sheet of any bank operating in Ireland, but was essentially an offshore German bank, established in Dublin's International Financial Service Centre doing mainly international business. Bought by another German bank, Hypo RE, in 2007, Depfa's liquidity situation in September 2008 helped bring down Hypo (which had its own loan-loss problems), triggering a rescue by the German federal authorities.

Educational Building Society (EBS). A mortgage lender. At the behest of the Troika it was merged with AIB in 2011.

Irish Bank Resolution Corporation (IBRC). Created in 2011 from the merger of Anglo and INBS. IBRC was liquidated in February 2013.

Irish Life and Permanent (ILP). Formed from the merger of a building society and a life insurance company, ILP's lending activities were mainly in retail mortgages. After the crisis, the life insurance firm was spun off and the bank renamed Permanent TSB (PTSB).

Irish Nationwide Building Society (INBS). A small mortgage lending institution whose venture into property developer lending went sour on an unsurpassed scale. INBS was merged with Anglo in 2011 to form IBRC.

KBC Ireland. A subsidiary of the Belgian group, it was previously known as Irish Intercontinental Bank.

Permanent TSB (PTSB). The surviving banking arm of ILP.

Ulster Bank. A subsidiary of Royal Bank of Scotland, Ulster Bank has long been a full-service bank with a sizable market share on both sides of the border on the island of Ireland.

Introduction

It would be an understatement to say that Ireland's economic and financial condition in late 2010 was extraordinarily stressed. Numbers at work had fallen by about 15 per cent. The government's borrowing requirement had been reported at the astonishing equivalent of more than a third of annual national income. Every one of the country's main banks needed a capital injection in order to avoid insolvency.

Official efforts to get to the bottom of the banking losses, and to consolidate the public finances, had so far not been sufficiently fast or thorough to convince the markets. In the absence of supportive messages from official European voices, investors had lost confidence that they would be repaid in full and on time. Billions of euros were flowing out through the banks each week. Week-by-week the yield on Irish government bonds was rising to unaffordable levels.

A sense of economic panic began to seep through Irish society, especially as the government began to project an impression of indecision and drift.

The role of the Central Bank of Ireland in this situation was multidimensional. Responsible for the prudential supervision of banks, it had clearly failed to prevent their reckless property-related lending during 2004–7 that had now gone so sour. The government's two-year old attempt to backstop the banks with a blanket guarantee had failed, with the result that the Central Bank was now lending unprecedented sums totalling more than the equivalent of one year's gross domestic product (GDP). Without these loans the banks would have been unable to meet withdrawals from international and local depositors, and would have collapsed, triggering (thanks to the guarantee) cash calls on the government – which would have forced it too into default. The Central Bank could make these loans because of Ireland's membership of the euro area, but the loans were only short term, and could be renewed only with the acquiescence of the European

1

Central Bank (ECB) – and the ECB was becoming increasingly perturbed at the scale of borrowing.

In November 2010 a term loan of tens of billions of euros was offered by the International Monetary Fund (IMF) and Europe as a means of restoring confidence and providing time for Ireland to prove its commitment and ability to bring the situation under control. At first, the loan's financial terms were too onerous, and there were missed opportunities in its design, not least because of the de facto prohibition on bailing-in unguaranteed senior bank bond holders. But that loan, and the seal of approval it provided to the stabilizing policies of the Irish public authorities, did the trick (especially with improvements in the financial terms on the various sums borrowed). It enabled Ireland to return to a sustainable path of employment growth, though not without wrenching disruptions: despite best efforts, these were unavoidable, given the pre-crisis excesses.

THE BOOK

The story of Ireland's spectacular financial crisis of 2008–13 is told in this book from the viewpoint of a central banker.

But I also want to place the account in a wider context, both historical and institutional. I want to describe what Ireland's monetary and central banking arrangements looked like in the earlier decades of independence before euro membership; this goes some way to explaining why Ireland signed up for the euro with apparent enthusiasm. I want to give my perspective on the basic question of what central banks are for, what they can realistically hope to achieve, and what is in practice beyond their reach.

A reader interested primarily in the crisis narrative can turn straight away to Chapter 7.

The Irish crisis raises many questions for monetary and financial policy in small countries. Was the euro exchange rate regime simply wrong for Ireland? If not, how could it have been better managed? What about banks: can they be better controlled, given the international context in which they now typically operate? And as to the international official partners, should they have done more to steer Irish policymakers away from the abyss, or to shoulder more of the burden when the catastrophe struck?

At the heart of each of these questions is the role of central banking. Scarcely noticed by the general public in the years before the crisis, whether in Ireland or elsewhere, the world's central banks took centre stage in economic policy from 2008. This reflected both their collective failure to prevent the crash and their ability to take unorthodox action to bring the main elements of the financial system back into working order. If central banks were too reliant on passive and mechanical strategies before the crisis and controversially aggressive in their response to it, it seems that central banking remains an art rather than a science. Central banks are inherently limited in their ability to advance the quality of national economic performance. Over-enthusiastic central banking actions have often been the cause of distortions and distress; but passivity in the face of excess and crisis is also to be avoided.

Much has been written about the conduct of monetary and financial policy in large economies. But most countries are small. This book seeks to provide a coherent perspective on the functions of a central bank in a small European country. It takes a historical approach, noting alternative policy choices that have been made by Ireland in the past and by other countries in similar circumstances. Ireland's recent experience is seen to have deep roots and, while the scale of the boom and the subsequent collapse were certainly very large by global historical standards, they were certainly not unprecedented in their shape.

My own qualifications for considering these issues draw on three different strands of my professional experience. Most obviously, as the Central Bank Governor from September 2009, I was assigned the task of pulling the Irish financial system out of the slump. In addition, earlier in my career as an economist in Ireland I was lucky enough to have ringside seats at several turning points in Irish financial policy such as the breaking of the Irish pound's one-for-one link with sterling in 1979 and the devaluations of 1983 and 1986. Finally, through my research and policy work at the World Bank 1987–90 and 1998–2007, I learnt much that is relevant from successes and failures with financial crises and financial policy, both historical and contemporary, in a wide variety of other countries.

With the benefit of hindsight it is easy to see many things that could (and should) have been done far better in the two decades of Ireland's euro membership. Domestic macroeconomic management should have been better adapted to the exchange rate regime. In particular the fiscal authorities should have recognized the transitory nature of the revenue boom which masked the fact that fiscal policy was on as damaging a path by 2005 as it had been in 1977. Prudential policy should have been less passive. There should have been a more inclusive European approach to crisis management exhibiting more solidarity.

What is surprising is that this crisis happened after a century during which Ireland had had long experience of a fixed exchange rate regime (before 1979) and during which its banks became well accustomed to operating in an international environment and through periods of weak economic performance without suffering more than trifling loan losses. To an extent it may have been the very stability that had marked the first half century of Ireland's independence that lulled policymakers into a false sense of security.

High finance may seem abstruse, and there are indeed elements of complexity. But what emerges from Ireland's experience is the importance of what might be termed common sense – or at least a number of widely accepted pragmatic principles – relative to ideology, political preferences or doctrinal fashions, in ensuring that finance performs adequately in supporting economic prosperity. Common sense, informed by an awareness of the lessons of financial history, should have been sufficient to alert informed participants that Ireland's banking system had embraced the global wave of financialization to excess. Common sense and an instinct for self-preservation should have prevented politicians from driving Ireland's public finances over a cliff twice in a generation. Designing and implementing recovery demanded on both occasions a practical sense of what is and is not possible in dealing with economic and financial relationships. Most Irish people, being residents of what is perhaps the most globalized economy in the world, have that common sense, even if they have sometimes lost sight of it. The speed with which Ireland recognized the severity of the crash, and the scale of the adjustment that would be required, helped speed the adjustment. International partners helped more in the end than they were willing to at first.

Despite the depth of the recent economic downturn, the second half-century of Ireland's independence has seen a sustained growth in economic prosperity. Unlike what has prevailed in other countries, finance has not been a conspicuous contributor to that prosperity. And this is regardless of the exchange rate regime in effect. The financial sector's performance has been at best mediocre; it has been an obstacle during several significant episodes. Ireland needs to manage finance better over the decades to come, through the informed and strategic application of common sense.

THE IRISH MACROFINANCIAL CRISIS

The Irish downturn is rightly seen as a central element in the euro area crisis, itself a key strand in the global financial crisis of those years. But Ireland was hit particularly hard by these events because Ireland had generated its own home-grown macrofinancial crisis which was only brought to a head by the global events and deepened by the problems of the euro area. Though straightforward, it is worth summarizing here the bones of the Irish story.

In recent decades Ireland has built its economic growth model around an effective embrace of globalization. Successive governments have crafted economic and social policy in a manner designed to attract inward direct investment by the most innovative multinational corporations in such sectors as pharmaceuticals, information and medical technology and software. Money and banking policy has hewed closely to the prevailing international doctrines and fashions. After half a century of relative economic stagnation punctuated by sharp recessions, adoption of this policy approach began to yield tangible results. Employment and income growth accelerated, especially from the mid-1980s, generating a degree of euphoria and complacency as the economy approached full employment in the late 1990s.

At that point the global surge in financialization seemed to be the next wave for Ireland to join. Irish banks, most of them with historic roots dating from when Ireland was part of the United Kingdom, and reliant for many subsequent decades on the London money market for their wholesale activities, were no strangers to international finance. They jumped on this bandwagon with enthusiasm. Poorly managed and weakly supervised, they had easy access to funding in the world's capital markets and took their cue from the innovations of British banks in what became, by the early 2000s, an out-of-control expansion of mortgage credit and lending for property development. Lower interest rates, ensured by adoption of the euro in 1999, helped underpin loan demand. Acceleration of credit pumped up house prices and convinced many people that property investment was not only profitable but also essential. The property price and construction bubble boosted tax revenue, encouraging government to reduce income tax rates, increase benefits and salaries and generally expand spending as if the boom would last forever.

Irish house prices had already peaked before the global financial crisis hit and Irish banks, with their large exposure, especially to property developer loans, began to seem vulnerable long before the Lehman Brothers bankruptcy. As their international funders withdrew, and as they ran out of collateral eligible for borrowing at the ECB, the Irish banks suddenly found themselves on the brink of failure. An improvised blanket guarantee of the banks' liabilities announced by the government in September 2008 provided temporary relief, but the damage had been done. With the economy now hit by the global economic downturn on top of the collapse in construction and a contraction of consumer spending, job losses multiplied during 2009. The evaporation of boom-related revenue now meant that the budget deficit was sure to balloon, making nonsense of the Ireland's AAA rating. The government recognized the need to dial back its spending and restore the cuts that had been made to income tax rates.

As property prices continued to fall, the banks risked being over-whelmed by the challenges of managing a huge non-performing property-backed loan portfolio. The government attempted to stabilize the situation by carving out the large property-related loans, obliging the banks to sell them at long-term economic value to a purpose-created asset management body, National Asset Management Agency (NAMA). The huge losses thus crystallized wiped out almost all shareholder value, alarming investors not only about the banks' assets but about the creditworthiness of the Irish government, as the latter had guaranteed to cover losses not met by share-holder funds. With the banking system now relying heavily on emergency liquidity from the Central Bank, and the government faced with prohibi-tive interest costs on its borrowing, the only safe course was to seek the assistance of the so-called Troika (effectively the IMF plus European lending facilities coordinated by the European Commission, in association with the ECB), to provide financial support while it proved its determina-tion to restore balance to the public finances.

The financial terms on which the assistance came were at first unfavour-able. The interest rates on the official funds being borrowed were danger-ously high. Even though the large and still uncertain banking losses were a major factor in weakening market confidence in Ireland, the official lenders had also said no to both of two obvious steps that could help put an end to such uncertainty. Thus they refused either to countenance a bail-in of the unguaranteed senior creditors of the failed banks or to absorb some of the risks by directly recapitalizing the other banks. Later, though, the interest rates on the European loans to Ireland were lowered, and their maturity extended, and the liquidation of the failed banks was carried out in a way that limited the net financial cost to Ireland.

The economic and fiscal projections made at the time the programme of assistance was negotiated proved to be sufficiently accurate for market confidence to be gradually restored. Aggregate economic recovery was under way by mid-2012. Unemployment, which had soared from below 5 per cent in 2007 to 16 per cent five years later (despite emigration), began to fall steadily, dropping below 6 per cent in 2018.

Many scars remained and many households had suffered greatly. Indebtedness of households remained high, with unresolved non-performing mortgage loans. Aggregate real household spending regained its pre-crisis level only in 2016 (despite population growth), while current public spending remained below the peak after a decade (in real terms, including higher interest costs and despite an increasing population). Likewise, it was 2018 before the total numbers at work matched the previous peak. But the worst was over.

POINTS OF CONTENTION

Although these main outlines of the Irish macro-financial crisis of 2008–13 may be well known, it will become clear in the chapters that follow that many details are little known; some aspects remain disputed and some misunderstood. The following are among the most significant examples.

The main cause of the crisis was certainly the wave of reckless bank lending, but most of the fiscal austerity measures did not go to pay for the bank losses. Even without the bank losses, measures were going to be needed to make up for the large hole that had opened up in the public finances when the flow of tax revenue from the property bubble suddenly ceased, revealing that the reductions in income tax and the spending increases that had been embarked over the previous few years were not sustainable.

Where the banking losses had a big impact was in accelerating the need for the government to adjust its budget. The income tax and levy increases, the cutbacks in public services and the public servant salary reductions could have been spread out over a longer adjustment period if investor confidence in Ireland had not been tipped over by the progressive disclosure of such heavy banking losses.

Likewise, the Troika programme did not cause Ireland's austerity; it eased it. Ninety per cent of the job losses had happened by the time the Troika arrived. By providing loans when the private market would not, the programme allowed the government to make the fiscal adjustments in a more orderly and gradual manner. The choice of what taxes and spending measures to target was largely one for the government. The Troika had suggestions, some of which they pressed vigorously, but for the most part they were content with any reasonable choice of measures as long as the net impact on the government's deficit was sufficient.

While it is easy to point to design shortcomings in the euro, the Irish crisis cannot be blamed on membership in the euro area. As with previous exchange rate regimes, economic performance depended on the accompanying fiscal and regulatory policies being well adapted to the new regime.

Ireland's fiscal and regulatory policies in the first decade of the system fell far short of what was needed to stay safe.

But management by Europe of the crisis was also poor. Even governments with sufficient headroom terminated their countercyclical fiscal spending too soon. The ECB's response, though vigorous, failed at first to recognize and fully understand the severity of the unfolding crash. The actions taken both by the ECB and the Eurogroup Ministers lacked clarity and persistence. In many cases censoriousness and lack of trust permeated the approach from officials on the creditor side. At first, the official lending to Greece, Ireland and Portugal was at rates of interest that did not make sense. Only later was a more reasonable approach adopted.

After the expiry of the initial bank guarantee, the Irish government would have willingly seen losses imposed on the unguaranteed senior debt of the failed, gone-concern banks Anglo and INBS. As several participants subsequently realized, it was wrong-headed of the ECB to prevent this (and inconsistent with the general policy on bank resolution subsequently adopted in Europe). They likely hope that their acquiescence in the complex financing arrangements around the subsequent liquidation, which have worked for Ireland even better than hoped, has made amends.

As in other countries, crisis management brought the Central Bank of Ireland, long accustomed to a largely passive role, into unfamiliar territory. For a while it assumed a much greater prominence in the economy and society. Ensuring that the country would not slide further into a semi-permanent slump of over-indebtedness was the first priority. No longer deferential to the banks, the Central Bank nevertheless found, as in other countries, that it was a difficult and slow job to get the banks to acknowledge the scale of their prospective losses; to deal with non-performing borrowers in a fair, sensitive and sustainable manner; and to eliminate sharp practice and worse vis-à-vis their customers – behaviour engendered by a long-standing culture of corporate entitlement.

The recent macro-financial crisis was the most dramatic and probably the worst in the history of the Irish State, though it is close run by that of the 1980s. Understandably, successive crisis-period governments sought to recover as much as possible of the prosperity that the globalized Irish economy had enjoyed before the property bubble. This was not going to be fully possible, and choices had to be made. In large part, though, governments chose not to radically reimagine any significant aspects of the Irish economy as they coped with the downturn: surely a missed opportunity.

WIDER IMPLICATIONS FOR CENTRAL BANKING

When the euro began, some had asked: why does Ireland need its own central bank? It was a fair question. Central banks are about money and credit, and these aspects of the Irish economy have long been globalized. But the euro did not make national central banks redundant. Instead, Ireland's experience, both before the euro and during the past twenty years, provides an instructive case history or what central banks are for; what they can and cannot do (in Ireland's case both at the national level and as part of the Eurosystem). The Central Bank of Ireland has been close to the heart of much of the crisis story, both in regard to the macroeconomic aspects, seeking to ensure that economic recovery could be attained and the costs of the crisis minimized, and in regard to the microeconomic challenges of supervising the conduct and risks of the banks.

If, in previous decades, a consensus had been growing that central banks should have an aggressively independent and exclusive focus on ensuring price stability through the application of simple policy rules, the crisis has shown the inadequacy of such a limited concept. While this is nowhere more evident than in Ireland, the lesson is a global one.

Around the world, the ambitions of, and general expectations for, national central banks grew dramatically in the recent crisis. Central banks have greatly expanded their balance sheets. Many of them have been assigned new responsibilities for the regulation and supervision of banks and have adopted a greater degree of intrusiveness in these activities.

In an increasingly complex and evolving financial environment, it is unlikely that this deeper engagement will or should be simply a transient phase, to be succeeded soon by a return to the more passive and mechanical mode that had become fashionable.

For, by the second half of the twentieth century, a caricature had emerged of the sound central banker as one who would be sparing and terse in his or her communication. Central bank independence was sometimes interpreted as entailing a relationship with government that should verge on hostility. As to the control of banks, these were often seen as best run by those who had a financial stake in their profitability and as requiring only relatively light official supervision of their governance structures.

Countries whose central banks did not comply with these constraints were warned that they would be bedevilled by high and volatile inflation, growth-sapping distortions of the allocation of credit, and periodic crises of banking insolvency.

Although historical examples of such failures can be multiplied, our narrative here illustrates the degree to which the narrow ideal of central banking needs to be qualified. The crisis has exposed the inadequacy, even for the central bank of a small country, of that jaded caricature of an isolated, rule-bound central bank reluctant to interfere in a smoothly functioning market mechanism where financiers can be relied on for prudence and fair-dealing.

That is not to deny the attraction of a regime in which central banks were encouraged to focus on simple rule-based policies – fixed exchange rates, steady monetary growth paths and mechanical interest rate rules. Poorly crafted monetary activism risks being punished by the financial markets.

The experiences described in what follows provide evidence that the effective central bank is increasingly an active and intrusive body, willing to innovate in its response to critical situations, and prepared to cooperate with, but not accept dictation from, government.

Thus, a central bank's independence from government does not mean its indifference to national economic performance and to the ability of the national government to pursue a coherent macroeconomic policy. The central bank is an arm of the state, albeit not of the government. There are occasions, especially during crisis, when the central bank needs a deep understanding of the policy and capacity of the government, so that it can act as a trusted policy adviser and, without pandering to political short-termism, can cooperate with government policy to achieve its man-dated objectives more effectively. This applies also within the euro area, where the potential conflicts of objectives can require careful management.

Clearly, the central bank in a small country must understand that it is constrained by market forces and international conventions. All too often, defiance of these constraints results in a whiplash. But this implies that success in achieving a central bank's national goals must be sought by active manoeuvring within these constraints and working with the grain of market functioning and international financial diplomacy.

The effective central bank, however small, will not be passive. Maintaining price stability, whether or not it is underpinned by an exchange rate peg, requires determination and vigour in acting against public or private actions that put that goal at risk. Insufficiently forceful or consistent central bank actions can allow the emergence of damaging bubbles and other spending excesses.

This means that, even in a small country, macroprudential and micro-prudential policies must be pursued actively to ensure that banks do not create havoc. Powerful though modern financial markets may be, no one now imagines that markets are omniscient. Markets can allow the emergence of significant and dangerous imbalances – even ones confined to a small economy when the rest of the world is more stable. In this respect the adage that banks are global in life but national in death needs to be qualified. Banks can facilitate or even stoke up a national bubble despite globalization. And the experiences documented in what follows confirm the correctness of the great global shift towards ensuring that banks have sufficient bail-inable liabilities and a plan for resolution to ensure that reckless bank mismanagement does not have an immediate knock-on to the public finances.

Consumer protection too is primarily a matter for national jurisdiction: no global or international influences are likely to effectively impede a bank that is willing to mistreat its customers in the interests of short-term profit gain.

Finally, even if the central bank's ultimate function is to protect the monetary system from being looted by extravagant provision of liquidity, it must also know when to be open-handed in accommodating and facilitating a recovery of aggregate demand in a fear-driven recession.

In managing crises and in guarding against the emergence of future crises, then, central banks (and other financial authorities) need to be much more active than was conventional in the past. Clarity and persistence in pursuing attainable goals consistent with the legal mandate must be the hallmark. At the same time, they have to respect the limitations of their mandates: they cannot arrogate to themselves the role of government, but have to work with government. These lessons are in large part applicable to central banks in small countries whether or not they are part of the euro area. It is by elucidating the experience of Irish central banking in Europe that this book seeks to illuminate these lessons.

STRUCTURE OF THE BOOK

The book is divided into four parts. The central topic is Ireland's navigation of the crisis that broke out in 2008 with recovery only fully under way by 2013. The stages of this crisis are narrated in Part III, to which the impatient reader can turn. But a fuller understanding requires widening the focus, both historically and in terms of fully understanding the role of a central bank.

The chapters in Part I are linked by their exploration of the choice of currency regime and the economic performance associated with that choice. Now part of the euro area, Ireland has had a chequered record with different types of currency regime from fixed to floating and back again.

Beginning with a look at the sterling link which prevailed well into the second half-century of Ireland's independence and at the adjustable rate period which followed, Chapter 1 argues that the choice of regime matters less than the quality of the accompanying policies. The Irish history throws light on how things can go well or badly under either fixed or more flexible exchange rate regimes. In both types of regime Irish policymakers have often failed to draw the lessons for the discipline needed for successful adherence to a stable currency.

The decision to join the euro area is the topic of Chapter 2. Politics was the driver of this choice, with the economic arguments more finely balanced. With the benefit of hindsight, would another decision have worked out better? The main mistake lay not in the decision to join but in how the macroeconomic and prudential economic policy was conducted after joining. The discussion suggests that Ireland has probably done as well in the system as it would have outside.

But Ireland's crisis was embedded in the global financial crisis, of which the euro area crisis was a particularly severe strand that separated itself in early 2010. Chapter 3 dissects the euro area crisis, asking what made it so severe. Two alternative and diametrically opposed approaches to the euro area crisis are considered; if adopted early enough either might have worked better overall than the path followed. As far as the banking losses and the Greek government debt are concerned, a single-minded policy either of default or of collective socialization at the European level might have allowed a speedier and less costly recovery from the crisis than the compromise middle course that was adopted.

Before plunging into an account of the financial crisis in Ireland, I pause in Part II of the book to reflect on the overall performance of the financial sector in Ireland in contributing to national economic prosperity and what the role of the Central Bank in improving that performance has been and can be.

Banking is inherently a fragile activity but, for a century, Irish banking had been largely stable and prudent in its business decisions, albeit with some worrying missteps from the 1980s. The banking stability that had marked the first half century of Ireland's independence may have lulled policymakers into a false sense of security. Chapter 4 explains how, influenced by global trends, the Irish banks got caught up in a construction and property bubble which, largely unchecked by financial regulation and supervision, led to collapse. While financial regulators in many countries performed poorly in checking the excesses of the early 2000s, the Irish regulators allowed excesses to cumulate to the point where they could threaten the solvency of the Irish state.

Remaining solvent should be considered a low bar for the performance of a financial intermediary. Chapter 5 explores more broadly the contribution of banking and finance to economic wellbeing in Ireland including issues of pricing and fair dealing. Irish banks have not stood out as important contributors to Irish economic growth. The record is at best mediocre. Banking has displayed cost inefficiency and (as in other countries) there have been notable instances of sharp practice (such as the tracker mortgage debacle). The glacial pace of the banks' post-crisis dealings with non-performing loans, albeit better than in some other countries, is also disappointing. Although bringing the problem of non-performing loans under control took much longer than hoped for, it remains unclear what effective policy measures could have speeded things up. This chapter also digresses to consider whether a government-subsidized debt relief scheme could have helped. Other important subsectors of Irish finance are also described, both those catering to the local market – including insurance (with its own chequered history) and credit unions – and the financial export sector.

The state's chief bank, the Central Bank of Ireland, is part of the euro system but is also the main regulator of the rest of the financial sector. The crisis has brought a reassessment of the extent to which the resources and powers of a central bank could be employed more effectively to improve the soundness and conduct of the financial sector. A long-tail of post-crisis shortcomings of that sector is still in the process of being resolved. Recent central banking innovations that push the boundaries of central banking, replacing an excessive passivity of the past, are discussed in Chapter 6.

Part III turns to the years of crisis management, 2008–13.

Chapter 7 is devoted to the iconic event of the crisis, the notorious bank guarantee – whose importance has, however, been generally exaggerated. Nothing that could have been done as late as the end of September 2008 would have prevented the meltdown that was already under way. While the Irish authorities moved quickly in both banking and fiscal policy to try to staunch the ensuing haemorrhage, the following two years saw a slow-motion unfolding of the scale of the problem to the point where financial markets lost confidence.

Chapter 8 recounts the evolution of banking policy as the Irish authorities sought to stabilize the banks by carving out the big property loans and injecting capital where needed. It describes the asset management agency NAMA whose innovative design, while not perfect, avoided many pitfalls.

Growing international awareness of the deteriorating fiscal situation, side-swiped by the scale of losses uncovered in the NAMA loan purchases, led inexorably to the application for financial assistance from the European Union and IMF. Early entry into a programme of support was the key to correcting the financial and economic slide. The conduct of the initial negotiations for this programme is described in Chapter 9. The high interest rate and lack of a risk-sharing element cast doubt on the viability of the initial programme.

Chapter 10 details the work of cleaning up the banking system which was the necessary complement to the tight but unavoidable fiscal control delivered by the government in line with what had been agreed for the EU–IMF programme. Injecting enough capital to meet a much more demanding – and (because granular) credible – stress test helped restore international confidence in the continuing banks. Being so close to the fiscal cliff edge had hitherto ruled out any idea of the government investing cash in the banks on such a scale. Besides, if the sovereign's debt was unsustainable, the banks, no matter how well capitalized, could not recover their ability to function in the market. Removing the two weakest banks – while ensuring acceptable financing conditions for their losses – was another key component of banking policy. Success in lowering the government's debt servicing costs and extending maturities of the official loans helped enable on-time exit from the programme. Thus, protected in the end by support from official foreign partners, implementation of sufficiently effective banking and fiscal measures ensured that the economy was stabilized and restored to a growth path over the following three years.

The concluding Part IV steps back to take stock.

Chapter 11 takes a wider look at what has been a decade of banking crises in Europe. Ireland's experience was on the extreme end resulting in a collapse in market confidence in the economy as a whole, as also happened in Cyprus and Iceland. But twenty or more European countries experienced systemic banking crises. If the causes and aetiologies of these crises were diverse, the policy responses were just as varied. The willingness of public authorities to stabilize banking through emergency liquidity and to bail out creditors of failing institutions varied from country to country and over time. In the end, a new, albeit fragile, consensus had emerged, both in Europe and more widely, around an approach which insists on much more equity capital and envisages bail-in of wholesale creditors where necessary. Application of such an approach in Ireland back in

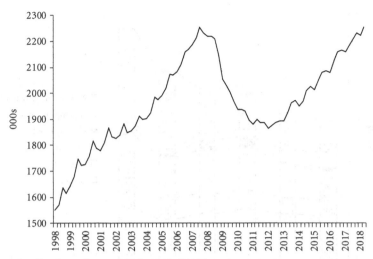

Figure I.1 Total numbers at work, 1998–2018.
Source: Central Statistics Office.

2008 would have avoided budgetary outlays to make bank creditors whole, and, if applied in compliance with a Europe-wide rule-book, would not have implied the kind of national reputational damage that would have resulted from an unilateral bail-in by Ireland of the creditors of banks that had fuelled several years of transitory prosperity. It remains an open question as to whether such an approach, had it been applied from the start on an international basis, would have increased or reduced the severity of the crisis in Europe as a whole.

Chapter 12 moves beyond the financial sector to consider the overall macroeconomic scale and impact of the crisis and the recovery, including issues of income and wealth distribution, and compares this experience with previous macroeconomic setbacks. Relative to the previous fiscal crisis of the 1980s, corrective policy was both prompt and more decisive, speeding the process of recovery. While Ireland's economic collapse was one of the most severe in the crisis (cf. Figure I.1), this partly reflects the scale of the previous imbalances. A steady recovery brought total employment in Ireland by mid-2018 back to the peak level reached a decade before and more than 40 per cent above where it had been twenty years before on the eve of euro membership, one of the biggest net changes in Europe. Indeed, despite the severe setback 2008–13, which had a devastating impact on many households, Ireland has experienced a stronger aggregate economic performance in this generation than in any previous period of comparable length (cf. Figure I.2).

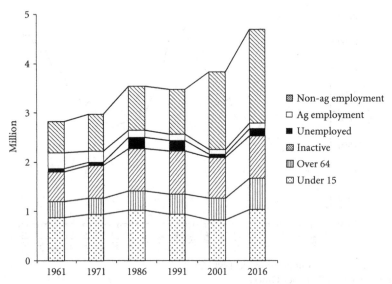

Figure I.2 Distribution of population, 1961–2016.
Source: Central Statistics Office.

The concluding Chapter 13 reviews some of the key lessons that have been learnt. The banking and policy errors that led to the crisis caused severe damage, especially to those who lost their jobs or who had been persuaded to buy over-priced property as well as to those dependent for retirement income on property income that dried up. Many public services have also been acutely constrained. The catastrophe has left lasting scars. Avoiding a recurrence requires a strategic approach to macroeconomic and prudential policy that avoids the build-up of dangerous imbalances. And if things do go wrong, Ireland's experience points to the importance of prompt recognition by the central bank of the scale of an incipient financial crisis and of sufficient front-loaded corrective action, supported if necessary by recourse to international official financial assistance.

The degree of economic policy integration in the euro area is not yet close to the point where the abolition of national central banks could be safely envisaged. But centralizing reforms in bank supervision and resolution have already helped to address some of the most serious architectural gaps in the system's design: it is essential that these be kept operational and fully enforced. More is needed and could be achieved in the euro area despite the wider policy challenges faced by the European Union. Better intergovernmental risk-sharing mechanisms should be created, and this can be done without creating undue moral hazard. And monetary policy must not be hijacked by fundamentalist dogma.

* * *

The central bank sets the tone of a country's approach to the world of finance. By its analysis, its communication and its actions, a successful central bank will not only ensure domestic price stability, but will also limit the impact of financial instability, whether home-grown or imported from abroad. Central banks are often charged with supervising the banks and other financial intermediaries, seeking to ensure that they are managed prudently and with due regard to the interests of their customers.

The global reach of finance means that the goals of a national central bank can be achieved only if it is effective in negotiating with and manoeuvring around the international centres of financial power. The chapters that follow illustrate how this challenge has been tackled in Ireland's dealings with and among its European counterparts.

As we approach the second century of Ireland's independence, it is impossible to foresee with precision the nature of the crises that will, no doubt, be faced in the future. The withdrawal of Ireland's main trading partner from the European Union, and international pressures on the long-standing corporate taxation policies of Ireland, are only a couple of the more obvious of the challenges in early prospect. But understanding how the varied conditions of the past century have been dealt with should help in coping with the unexpected.

PART I

CURRENCY

1

Currency Choices

Handling cash in Ireland when I was a small boy offered more variety and distraction than it would have in most other countries. Everyone loved the Irish coins, with their striking images of farmyard and countryside animals. My favourite was the pig on the ha'penny piece – actually six pigs (a sow and five piglets), though I'm not sure that I ever counted them. The sow looked weary but determined, in contrast to the haughty hen (with her three chickens) that dominated the much larger bronze penny. Two of these were needed for the bus fare into the city centre school that I attended and one for the trip home for lunch.

In the static Irish economy of the mid-1950s, though, money and banking remained a postcolonial throwback. The penny and the ha'penny exemplified this by being exactly the same size as their English counterparts, and one was almost as likely to find the head of a British monarch, whether Elizabeth, George, the lugubrious Edward or a heavily worn Victoria in one's pocket as to find the hen. Differences emerged in some of the higher denominations. The florin and half-crown were the same size and colour as their English counterparts and, of course, had identical values. But why was the English threepence much larger than the Irish one (and not even round)? And why was the English tanner so much smaller than the Irish sixpence? Nobody knew. What was clear, though, was that, independent Republic or not, not much had changed in Ireland's money and banking and not much seemed likely to change.

It would not have been easy in the 1950s to foresee the successive waves of change that swept over Irish finance in subsequent decades. The certainties of the 1950s – certainties that conveyed economic stagnation as much as nominal stability – were progressively dismantled, and the dominance of the post-colonial financial connection was gradually eroded and replaced by engagement in a wider European, transatlantic and global financial universe.

Fascinated by the titles of textbooks that lay untouched on my father's bookshelves, with names like *The Art of Central Banking, Monetary Theory and the Trade Cycle* and *Clare's Money Market Primer*, I began to become more and more interested in the question of how governments should manage monetary and banking affairs in a small economy. And I have been fortunate to have had a close-in view of how this question has been addressed both in Ireland and in many other parts of the world over the years.

It turns out to be a question with few pat answers. Simple rules can help provide a framework, but unforeseen events repeatedly call for discretionary actions whose successful design depends on interpreting developments in the light of historical patterns. And so it was in the great financial crisis.

Though triggered by the sudden freezing of the global financial markets in 2008, then deepened by the euro area crisis of 2010–12, and manifested most clearly in the comprehensive failure of the banking system, the origins of the financial crash in Ireland and the evolution of its aftermath can be properly understood only in terms of national institutions and national policy actions. For both banks and policy, there is an intriguing back-story.

Part of the story is about the banks: how they drifted over the years from prudence to uncontrolled liberality, and about the deferential approach adopted by the public authorities vis-à-vis the banks throughout. Such a regulatory attitude may have been harmless in previous decades when the banks had conducted themselves with almost excessive caution, but was woefully misplaced when overconfident, buccaneering bankers took over. The influence of international exemplars and fashions was very strong in this story. Banks and regulators took their cues mainly and almost slavishly from developments in Britain, whose banks also moved from caution to free-wheeling extravagance.

An important part of the story, and in particular that of the influence of international developments, has to do with Ireland's evolving currency regime. Currency regime choice is at the heart of any country's domestic and international financial environment. As we will see, Ireland experienced several varieties of currency regime, as it moved from dependence on Britain to the wider and more promising horizons of European integration. In this process it suffered several reversals that can now be seen as reflecting failures to adhere to the discipline needed if the economy is to flourish with a stable currency. The obvious lessons were either not well learnt or too soon forgotten. Indeed, it seems fair to say that, to most contemporary observers, Ireland's currency and central banking experience had throughout most of the twentieth century seemed sufficiently benign that the need for financial and fiscal discipline in adhering to a firm monetary anchor was never fully appreciated.

The most obvious of the consequential mishaps was the analytical and political failure in the early 2000s to recognize that the huge surge in government revenue resulting from the property boom was going to be transitory. But Ireland had form here: an error of comparable magnitude had been made a quarter century earlier. And a more subtle error had been made mid-century when the Irish pound was still pegged to a sterling link.

Leaving most of the discussion of matters concerning banking to later chapters, we begin this chapter by exploring the currency regime choices before the euro. Ireland dodged some bullets that felled other countries in this regard, avoiding both hyperinflation and egregious overvaluation. But some of the weakest episodes in Ireland's economic history in the twentieth century, including the recession of the mid-1950s and the high interest rates of the 1980s, owed more than was recognized to failures to integrate other policy dimensions with the currency regime.

CURRENCY CHOICES: FIXED OR FLOATING?

Ambiguous Theoretical Predictions

Currency arrangements come in two main flavours: fixed and floating. But which is best? This question has generated an endless and often confusing debate. (For a balanced summary, see Klein and Shambaugh [2012] and for a more recent discussion, see Gopinath [2018].) Over time and across countries, the choices made have varied, with Ireland's experience being more varied than most.

From a theoretical point of view, the main advantage of a fixed regime, in which the currency is maintained at a fixed value against some other currency or commodity, is that it can give a degree of price certainty which may be helpful in reducing the risks of foreign trade and may help keep interest rates low. Floating regimes can allow import and export prices to adjust smoothly in response to shifting external or internal conditions. But each type of regime also has its drawbacks.

Having the capacity to create the national currency, a country's central bank can, within limits determined by its stock of foreign exchange reserves, maintain the value of that currency in the market by buying and selling foreign currency. But fixed exchange rates may prove impossible to sustain indefinitely. They are vulnerable to large supply disturbances or international price shocks, to lax monetary or fiscal policy and to financial market speculation. The life of an unsustainable peg may be prolonged by high interest rates or controls on capital movements or other foreign exchange transactions. But high interest rates can damage the domestic economy, and capital controls tend to develop leaks and become themselves unsustainable. (This is what is often called the fixed exchange rate policy trilemma, wherein no country can have all three of the following: a fixed exchange rate, freedom of international capital movement and the ability to set interest rates at the right level for maintaining full employment.)

Floating regimes do not present an easy target to speculators. But, lacking any price anchor, they can experience much volatility and result in large price uncertainty. In floating regimes, undisciplined monetary and fiscal policies tend to translate into large exchange rate movements and surges in inflation. Such movements can also damage economic wellbeing.

Fixed and floating regimes come in several varieties. If there is to be a peg, the choice of peg may be easy if the country's external transactions are predominantly with a large trading partner (such as Ireland's trade with the UK in the first half of the twentieth century). Otherwise pegging to the value of a basket of currencies of several of the country's main trading partners can be imagined. A peg can be adjustable, perhaps frequently, as with a so-called crawling peg. A float can be managed, as when the central bank intervenes in the foreign exchange market to moderate sharp movements or to lean against a trend.

If the rate is to float, monetary policy needs to be guided by an alternative policy goal or set of goals, and these days price stability is usually one of the primary goals set for central banks that operate floating exchange rate regimes.

The proportion of countries choosing one or another of these different schemes has changed quite substantially over the past 100 years, suggesting that the relative advantages may also have been evolving. Fixed exchange rates may work better for countries with relatively undeveloped financial markets; floating or adjustable rates may be better for countries that are vulnerable to big shocks in their export markets. At the most recent count, about one in two countries has a fixed exchange rate regime, but most of them are small countries.

Over the years, independent Ireland chose a sequence of contrasting currency regimes. In the past 100 years Ireland has (1) employed a foreign currency (sterling); (2) used a domestic currency pegged to sterling at one-to-one; (3) participated in a multi-country adjustable peg system (the so-called Exchange Rate Mechanism [ERM]); (4) operated a de facto floating exchange rate; and (5) adopted the common currency of the multi-country European Monetary Union.

One way or another, then, almost every type of exchange rate regime has been tried in Ireland. Each choice has taken place against the background of wider trends in monetary and exchange rate systems in the rest of the world. The experience has been not only varied but in many respects also paradoxical and not conducive to drawing a simple conclusion, unless that conclusion be that each type of exchange rate regime requires accompanying fiscal policies and wage-setting institutions that are well adapted to the regime and to the prevailing wider international context.

The Global Context

It was in the first decades of the twentieth century that governments around the world moved decisively from basing their monetary systems on gold and silver to paper and from reliance on precious metals to the control of the state. Admittedly, neither government influence nor paper was previously unknown in matters of money or financial contracts. Waves of inflation and deflation were endemic, but gold and silver had always represented the bedrock of payments systems to which societies had previously returned after episodes of monetary disruption. After World War I, the newly established nations, and those recovering from wartime devastation, or just from the inflationary consequences of war, did not put in place a lasting return to commodity-based money.

The early years of this new world of managed (or mismanaged) currencies were little short of disastrous in many cases. The famous German hyperinflation of 1922–3 was only the most extreme of a wave of hyperinflations that also swept through Austria, Hungary, Poland and Russia in those years.

Also disruptive, albeit on a lesser scale, and in sharp contrast, Britain suffered the consequences of the opposite extreme, a misguided attempt to force prices and the exchange rate back to where they had been before the war. Industrial unrest and a deep recession were the result, before the effort was abandoned. French governments flip-flopped between tight and lax currency phases in the 1920s and 1930s (cf. Schuker 1976). The United States stayed with gold longer than most, but abandoned it in 1933 also following the election of Franklin D. Roosevelt and as part of his sweeping

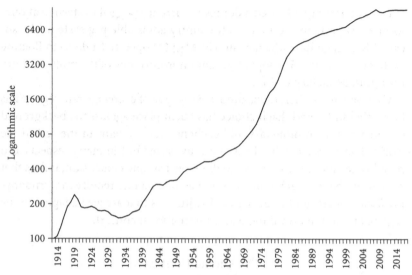

Figure 1.1 Consumer prices in Ireland, 1914–2018.
Source: Central Statistics Office, except annual changes 1914–22 interpolated from British Cost of Living Series.

measures to cope with the Great Depression. Indeed, the Federal Reserve's overly rigid policy designed to maintain the gold standard in orthodox fashion had contributed much to the depth of the Great Depression in the United States (Eichengreen 2015).

Fortuitously, Ireland largely escaped the currency turbulence which characterized the 1920s and 1930s for many countries. By choosing sterling at first, Ireland did not fall into the high inflation trap that enveloped many European states new and old in the early 1920s. Furthermore, its close trading links with Britain meant that the impact on Ireland of the economic turmoil triggered by sterling troubles in the 1920s and 1930s was indirect and less severe than the impact on British export sectors. (Figure 1.1 shows the trend of Irish consumer prices over the past 100 years; the scale is logarithmic so that the slope of the line indicates the inflation rate.)

After the chaos of World War II, the major powers made a concerted effort to return to a regime of fixed exchange rates, this time anchored on the US dollar as much as on commodity gold. The attempt, known as the Bretton Woods exchange rate system, survived for a quarter century of economic recovery and progress now recalled with nostalgia as a golden age.

For Ireland, though, while this period continued to be one of currency stability, it was no golden age but instead a period of economic stagnation and recession.

Despite the collapse of the Bretton Woods system in 1971, Ireland kept its peg with sterling at first but, again paradoxically, this no longer delivered price stability; instead, high inflation was imported through the fixed exchange rate.

Partly in response, Ireland then signed up to what was billed as a zone of monetary stability in Europe. This was the European Monetary System (EMS), designed to recover some of the currency predictability of the discarded Bretton Woods system. But for Ireland there was again a further irony, as it proved to be anything but a zone of stability: there followed a period of maximum currency instability for Ireland.

A final pre-euro counter-intuitive currency experience came when Ireland moved to a floating regime in the early 1990s – a time free of the kinds of shocks for which such regimes are thought to be advantageous – and suffered no acceleration of inflation despite the regime having no evident anchor for the price level beyond the expectation at least from mid-decade that there would be a transition into the single currency.

It was the disappointments of previous currency regimes that convinced the European Union to construct a single currency. Ireland joined this from the outset, not so much for the economic advantages which had driven its creation, but as a perceived political and diplomatic imperative.

The Choices Made

Currency regime choices in Ireland thus followed a zig-zag route in terms of stability. What did Irish policymakers hope from the currency regimes they chose at different points in time? Overall, stability, predictability and maintenance of Ireland's price and wage competitiveness were constant themes in public discussion down the years. But it would be a mistake to see the adoption of any of these four quite different regimes as having been the result of voluntarist policy action. Instead, Ireland's shifting exchange rate regimes during the past 100 years reflected a largely passive approach to shifting external norms initiated by Ireland's economic and political partners in Europe.

That is not to say that these were bad choices. Indeed each regime could have permitted a good economic performance: the choice of currency regime is less decisive for economic performance than is often supposed. But each currency regime requires that the remainder of the government's

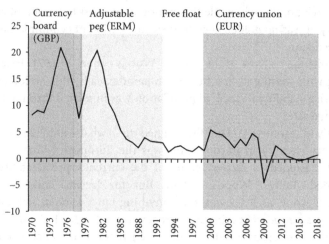

Figure 1.2 Nominal anchor: Alternative exchange rate regimes, 1970–2018. Ireland CPI inflation.
Source: Central Statistics Office.

policy package is consistent with the implications of the regime. Irish government policy was not always conducted in such a consistent manner, above all in the early 2000s, but not only then.

At only a few points did the currency regime confront the Irish political system with tough decisions. For example, if Ireland had stayed with sterling into the early 1980s, it would then have suffered a sharp loss of competitiveness when sterling surged, boosted by North Sea oil and by a tight monetary policy. But that did not happen, as Ireland stepped into the new EMS just in time to avoid the appreciation of sterling.

Then again, contrary to expectations, joining the EMS, with its freedom to make frequent devaluations where necessary, substituted a weaker regime than sterling would then have provided, but still enabled Ireland to enjoy a declining rate of inflation (cf. Figure 1.2).

When the currency regime did present a tough decision in the mid-1950s, the problem was misdiagnosed and policymakers failed (even after the event) to see how neglect of the discipline needed to adhere to a fixed exchange rate had contributed to the stresses of the time.

The cumulative result of these accidents and paradoxes was that Irish governments were never sufficiently faced with the realization that maintaining a currency regime that ensures stable prices involves discipline if it is not to have severe side effects. Neglect of this home truth was to have heavy consequences in the new century.

Which of the regimes has been the best for Ireland? Let us look more closely at the experiences of each regime. We will find that it is hard to provide an indisputable answer to this question.

THE STERLING LINK

The Currency Board

The link with sterling was long standing. Indeed, although it had previously had a separate existence, with considerable volatility during and after the Napoleonic Wars, the Irish pound was unified with the pound sterling, itself anchored to gold, as long ago as 1826.[1] And for the first years of Ireland's independence in the early 1920s, the pound sterling remained the currency in use even in terms of notes and coin. Most importantly, the pound sterling continued to be the unit of account in which all prices were quoted. The same banks that had emerged during the previous century and a half, some of them headquartered in London or Belfast, continued to operate much as before. This monetary and banking continuity clearly represented the stable and conventional option, given that almost all of the new state's exports (mainly live animals or in the category of food, drink and tobacco) went to Britain, which was also the chief source of imports, and also given sterling's still leading role among currencies of the world.

But politics called for something more than a convenient foreign currency. An American expert, Henry Parker Willis, was invited to chair a commission to look into the whole question of currency, credit and banking for the new state.[2] Based on the commission's report, and seen as emblematic of sovereignty, a national currency was introduced in 1927. Known at first as the Free State pound or Saorstát punt, later as the

---

[1] Before being pegged in 1826, the Irish pound had fluctuated in value, especially during the Napoleonic period; for much of the eighteenth century, it was fixed at thirteen Irish equals twelve sterling pounds.

[2] Willis, a professor at Columbia University in New York, was just the man for the job: he had been one of the designers of the legislation for the Federal Reserve System and was the first secretary, and later director of research, of the Federal Reserve Board; he was also editor of the well-known US business newspaper *Journal of Commerce* from 1919 to 1931. Reflecting the conservative cast of the government of the time, four of the other seven members of the Willis commission were serving directors of Irish banks. Not surprisingly, these were not keen on much change in Ireland's currency and banking arrangements. For more on the international context within which the Willis commission was working, see Drea (2015). (Incidentally, although much of the Irish literature refers to Parker Willis as if this was a double-barrelled family name, Parker was in fact a second given name, and the one by which Willis was generally known.)

Irish pound, it was launched with the animal image coins mentioned earlier.[3] Following the recommendation of the Willis commission, two distinctive series of national banknotes were introduced.[4] More important was the decision, also recommended by the Willis commission, to maintain equal value with sterling. The Irish pound notes were to be exchangeable one-for-one with sterling.[5] This decision coloured Irish financial and economic developments for the next half-century.

There could be an irony in Ireland choosing as a stability option to link with sterling at a time of considerable tension around the role and stability of sterling itself. Sterling's role as the unquestioned core of the global financial system was challenged for the first time in the late 1920s by the US dollar and, although it recovered some of its relative standing in subsequent years, this was the beginning of the end of UK global financial dominance.

The 1925 decision of the British authorities to deflate the economy and restore the old pre-war parity of sterling with gold is generally thought to have been misguided, especially given the considerable inflation which had occurred during the war years. For one thing, it resulted in an economic recession in Britain. Would the deflation entailed by return to the old gold parity spill over into a damaging effect for Ireland? This risk was

---

[3] The design of these coins was chosen by a committee, chaired by the poet William Butler Yeats. The best account of the selection process is by Yeats himself in a pamphlet entitled 'What we did or tried to do' in which he describes his embarrassment at having over-promised one of the artists that at least one of his designs would be used. He also notes his annoyance at some technical corrections to the drawings that were insisted upon by the Irish Department of Agriculture: "I sigh, however, over the pig, though I admit that the state of the market for pig's cheeks made the old design impossible. A design is like a musical composition, alter some detail and all has to be altered. With the round cheek of the pig went the lifted head, the look of insolence and of wisdom, and the comfortable round bodies of the little pigs." The image of a harp on the obverse of each of the coins has been retained for the Irish euro coins today.

[4] Each bank was permitted to issue 'consolidated' notes, colloquially known as 'ploughman notes' in reference to the evocative image on the face of each note. This was an innovation, probably dreamt up by Willis, as it partially paralleled the system of 'national bank notes' that had been introduced in the USA some sixty years before. It was designed to enable the private Irish commercial banks to continue to benefit in the new state from the note-issuing privileges they had enjoyed for decades under British rule. Each note was the responsibility of one of the banks, but backstopped also by a guarantee of the Currency Commission and denominated in the new national currency. The bankers were foiled, however, by the new Fianna Fáil government's imposition in the early 1930s of such high taxes on outstanding consolidated notes that there was little or no advantage for the banks in issuing more of them. Thus it was the new Currency Commission notes (later evolving into Central Bank notes) that soon dominated.

[5] The Irish currency was freely convertible at one-to-one without any margins or spread.

recognized at the time, but the idea of launching an autonomous Irish currency depreciated against sterling was unattractive in the cautious Irish political and business atmosphere of the 1920s. As it turned out, sterling's adherence to gold survived less than half a dozen years before having to be abandoned in favour of a floating exchange rate regime during the Great Depression.

Ireland was not alone in searching for a reconfigured currency system in the years after World War I. Before the war, convertibility of paper currencies into gold (or in a few places silver) defined most currency arrangements. But wartime finance in many countries had been based on inflationary issues of paper not convertible to gold. As mentioned, many countries failed to reintroduce currency stability at first. Reflecting the new dominance of paper currency, British colonies and dominions began to introduce official agencies, including currency boards and central banks, to regulate currency matters in this new era. The currency board was the least ambitious of such arrangements. A currency board was introduced in the West African colonies as early as 1913 and the practice spread widely in the British colonies. Compared with simply using Bank of England notes, it offered the colonial administration the advantage of ensuring local availability of coin and notes while the board could earn interest in London by investing the sterling that had been acquired by the board in return for the newly issued local currency.

The limited powers of a currency board ensured that this, the option that was adopted for Ireland with the title of Currency Commission, was a conservative and minimal institutional initiative.[6] Unlike a central bank, a currency board did not have the power to lend locally, even to commercial banks or the government, and had no resources to influence local interest rates or the rate of exchange vis-à-vis London. The Irish bankers, at least some of whom made it clear they would have preferred the business of providing notes to be left with them,[7] were reasonably happy

---

[6] I have no explanation for the ambiguous overuse of the term 'Commission' in Irish banking matters. There were the two early commissions of inquiry, similar to 'Royal Commissions' in the UK, namely that chaired by Henry Parker Willis, reporting in 1926, and that chaired by Joseph Brennan, generally known as the Banking Commission, reporting in 1938. Then there was the Currency Commission, a standing body which actually managed the currency from 1927 to 1943 and which Joseph Brennan also chaired throughout that period. Finally, what is effectively the board of directors of the Central Bank has been called the Central Bank Commission since the reform legislation of 2010.

[7] Andrew Jameson, de facto the Bank of Ireland's representative on the Willis commission, asked rhetorically what justification there could be for destroying the existing system of banking by creating the new Currency Commission note issue (Moynihan 1975: 54).

that continuity with the past would thus be preserved, despite the creation of a national currency.

A Central Bank?

More advanced nationalist thinking on currency and credit matters was not yet silenced, though. Why could Ireland not have a central bank to better animate the financial aspects of the economy? After all, the establishment of national central banks had been recommended in several international fora.

Ironically, some of this international enthusiasm for central banks was driven by the ambition of Montagu Norman, who served as Governor of the Bank of England for a record quarter century (1920–44). He wanted to preside over what might be thought of as a neo-colonial international network of like-minded monetary officials with whom he could deal on financial issues without having to work through governments. It is not clear whether the leading Irish nationalist financial mandarins Joseph Brennan and J. J. McElligott realized that their ambitions to create an Irish central bank played into this goal.[8]

The objective of the second commission of inquiry set up by the more radical Fianna Fáil government that came into power in 1932 was to see what needed shaking-up in Irish banking. This Banking Commission met 150 times from 1934 to 1938. Despite evident scepticism on the part of the Irish banks, the Commission did, albeit with little apparent enthusiasm, recommend the creation of a central bank.[9]

The close continuing banking ties between London and Dublin at this time – a decade and a half after independence – cannot be illustrated better than by an astonishing letter of December 1937 in the archives of the Bank of England. It was written to Sir Otto Niemeyer, a senior Bank of England official, by Per Jacobsson, who, as Economic Advisor at the Bank for International Settlements, had been appointed by the Irish Government to the Banking Commission (on the recommendation of the Bank of England).[10] The letter gives Niemeyer an account of the most recent

---

[8] Brennan had been Secretary (most senior official) of the Irish Department of Finance 1923-7 before being chosen to head the new Currency Commission; he was succeeded in the Department by McElligott.

[9] As expressed in his addendum to the report of the Commission of Inquiry into Banking Currency and Credit (to give its full title), the view of Charles Campbell (Lord Glenavy), a director of the Bank of Ireland, was that 'nothing whatever is wrong with the system . . . of currency, banking and credit'.

[10] The Basel-based Bank for International Settlements (BIS) had been set up chiefly to manage the German legacy debts relating to World War I. It was to become host to the

discussions of the Banking Commission and makes it clear that Jacobsson had made a practice of calling into the Bank of England on his way back to Basel after the meetings in Dublin to keep Niemeyer informed of the proceedings of the Commission. This looks like both an extraordinary breach of confidence and a revelation as to the perceived role and standing of the Bank of England in relation to Irish affairs.[11] One wonders whether the other members of the Banking Commission in Dublin would have been surprised to learn of this channel of communication to London.

But if London kept closely in touch with Dublin bankers, the latter nevertheless did not have as much access to the Bank of England as they imagined. This was forcibly brought home to them on the outbreak of war in September 1939 when an inquiry from the Bank of Ireland as to the availability of credit if needed in this emergency was met with a negative response. Montagu Norman's diary records him advising the Dubliners that "Eire is a Dominion and we in London cannot provide Emergency needs" (cf. Ó Gráda 1995).

Perhaps the Irish banks had thus been wrong in assuming that the existing regime was adequate to all their needs. After all, Ireland was no longer part of the UK (and indeed remained neutral in the war). Perhaps the banks really did need something more than a currency board. It was not long before the legislation necessary to create a central bank was enacted.

For many years after the 1943 establishment of the Central Bank of Ireland, though, little actually changed. It was led first by Joseph Brennan, transiting seamlessly from chairmanship of the Currency Commission. Brennan retired in 1953, having become disenchanted with the dismissive manner in which politicians pushed back his conservative advice on fiscal policy. He was succeeded by J. J. McElligott, who, after a quarter century as Secretary of the Department of Finance, was by now equally conservative. The fixed one-to-one peg with sterling remained unquestioned. Essentially no attempt was made to use the Bank's new powers. The commercial banks continued to place surplus funds and hold their main cash reserves in London.

international club of central bankers conceived by Montagu Norman, and continues to fill that role today. Per Jacobsson was later Managing Director of the International Monetary Fund (IMF).

[11] Willis too had paid 'unofficial and private' visits to the Bank of England when Chair of the 1926 Commission. Niemeyer's view of Irish financial officials was that "They will, therefore, require a good deal of bottle holding ... if they are to conduct their operations without being a nuisance both to themselves and to us." Later he remarked "I also imagine the trouble with the Irish is that they have the vaguest ideas as to what banking means, though very practical ideas on the subject of getting tick" (Drea 2013).

Indeed, the main achievement of currency policy in the fifty years of the sterling link was to have managed to avoid any speculative or international payments pressure that could have brought the peg into doubt. And it was an achievement, given how many other countries, including countries that operated currency board systems until independence, quickly lost or abandoned price and exchange rate stability as they embraced the freedoms of national independence and tried to employ central banking to generate economic growth through accelerated provision of credit. Many, perhaps most, of the small countries who abandoned their pegs against sterling, the US dollar or the French franc, came to regret the period of financial instability that followed, unaccompanied by the hoped-for acceleration in growth.

What else might one realistically have expected from a central bank bound to adhere to a fixed exchange rate? Surely less than some imagined. Extensive provision of credit to government would quickly have generated inflation undermining the currency peg. Given the continuing close business connections between Dublin and London, there was no evident strong need for the development of a local money market in which banks and other large firms could borrow and lend to smooth out short-term fluctuations in their liquidity. Only if it was considered as a stepping stone to an autonomous currency would a separate market be needed.

The timeless truth is that, while a stable monetary system is needed as a platform for economic activity, sustained growth can be built only by using the essential ingredients of saving and investment in human and physical capital.

Besides, there was no significant public demand for a change in the currency arrangements. To be sure, the currency peg meant that Irish inflation would track UK inflation quite closely (with transitory exceptions as during World War II), and this was a source of occasional discontent, for example at the time of the sterling devaluations of September 1931[12] and September 1949,[13] and especially in the high-inflation period of the mid-1970s. The average annual consumer price inflation rate over the period of

---

[12] The Irish authorities were not given much advance notice of the 1931 suspension of sterling convertibility into gold (which was followed by a sizable depreciation). It was one of the commercial Irish banks (the National) that first learnt of the decision, which had already been communicated to the French and US ambassadors (Moynihan, 1975: 169–70). For the Irish pound not to follow sterling down on that occasion would have rendered the Irish banks balance sheet insolvent (that is, their total assets would be less than their total liabilities), as their liquid reserves were held in London and denominated in sterling, but the bulk of their deposits was presumably denominated in Irish pounds.

[13] The 1949 devaluation was widely expected in advance, but the idea of taking some precautionary action was dismissed for fear of the loss of British goodwill that would

the sterling link 1927–78 was 4.8 per cent; the highest 20.9 per cent in 1975; prices *fell* by 6.6 per cent in 1931. Clearly this variability was not a great success by subsequent standards of achieved price stability. Exchange rate stability was ensured vis-à-vis the main trading partner, but by no means more widely.

Less was heard about the merits of having a weaker currency in the years of the sterling link, possibly in part because sterling was not a strong currency during that period, falling as it did from 4.8 US dollars in 1927 to 2.8 by October 1949 and to 2.4 in November 1967, later dipping below 1.6 in October 1976.

The Crisis of 1955–6

The sterling link did impose constraints on Irish economic policy, especially in regard to interest rates. Often thought of as a key enabler of economic growth, wholesale interest rates in an open financial system have to be consistent with financial market opportunities and expectations.[14] Having a central bank is not sufficient to alter this truism but it was not always fully recognized. The unquestioned sterling link combined with the traditional freedom to make and receive payments vis-à-vis Britain implied that Irish interest rates could not be pushed below those in London for long.[15] An attempt to do so in the mid-1950s had severe consequences.

In fact it seems that the severe macroeconomic crisis of 1955–6 in Ireland may be indirectly attributable – at least in part – to the failure of the Irish banks to match the 150 basis point (1½ percentage point) increase in the Bank of England's policy rate in the early months of 1955. At the time (and until the 1980s) the Irish banks operated as a cartel in setting interest

result (Moynihan, 1975: 354–5). But it was surely not necessary to convert a large block of US dollars received from Marshall Aid into sterling so close to the date of devaluation. This transaction had the effect of losing value amounting to about 1 per cent of Ireland's GDP at that time. I came across this little known fact in 1970 when, as a summer student intern in the Central Bank, I was assigned to assemble external reserves and monetary statistics going back to the start of the Currency Commission from dusty files. The series that I prepared appeared in the Statistical Appendices of Moynihan's institutional history (1975).

[14] This kind of argument is, however, sometimes distorted into a defence of wide and highly profitable spreads on retail lending rates.

[15] Indeed, the banks, operating as a cartel, had printed on cardboard a ready-reckoner schedule allowing their managers to read off the interest rates to be charged on different classes of loan and paid on deposits in Ireland for each level of the London Bank Rate ranging from 2 per cent to 8 per cent. The mapping between the banks in 1922 was still being used more than a decade later.

rates for their borrowing and depositing customers. But it was the newly appointed Minister for Finance, the energetic Gerard Sweetman, who, by means of threatening legislation, prevailed on the banks to hold their rates.[16] The consequence of the unusually wide spread that opened up as a result between London and Dublin rates was a deterioration in the overall balance of payments and a decline in the net foreign assets of the banking system by almost a fifth.[17] Not fatal in itself, this deterioration triggered an inappropriate and damaging response in the form of heavy supplementary import duties: a dose of misplaced austerity which contributed to a sharp recession and a surge in emigration.

This was an own-goal created by the government over-reacting to a net drain of funds at least partly caused by its own action in capping interest rates (Honohan and Ó Gráda 1998).

There was a happy ending to the story of the 1955–6 crisis in that it triggered a re-examination of the whole approach to economic policy in Ireland and the adoption of the more open outward-looking approach, which has characterized the Irish economy ever since. Exports and inward foreign direct investment were encouraged, and later free trade was embraced, first with Britain and then in the European Community.[18] The seemingly inexorable population decline that had

---

[16] Government pressure on the banks regarding their interest rates was a recurrent feature of the 1950s – and later. In the early decades the position of the Central Bank in such matters was compromised by the presence of bank directors on its Board of Directors. This no doubt weakened the influence of the Central Bank with Government. A reading of what documentation can be found for these years in the Bank's archives (which gives greater attention to the question of bank profits than to that of macroeconomic stability) suggests that Governor McElligott found himself attempting to reason with both sides, but having little effect on either. Still, a less than aggressive approach of the Central Bank is suggested by the laconic account provided by a later Governor, Maurice Moynihan, of the 1955 episode. The banks, he wrote, 'were left with the feeling that the course which they had been persuaded to follow was not entirely the appropriate one. The Central Bank on the whole sympathised with them, and representations, both oral and written, were made to the Minister by the Governor in February and March 1955 and were renewed from time to time.' (Cf. Moynihan 1975: 421–2; see also Meenan [1970], who like Moynihan was on the Board of the Central Bank at the time, for a comparable account.)

[17] Behind the scenes, there was a scramble for liquidity over the following months to protect the banks' liquidity and to try to alleviate a tightening credit squeeze. This was partly met by the Central Bank, which for the first time rediscounted bills, albeit on a small scale (about £1 million of bills of the private tea importing consortium and about £3 million of Exchequer Bills in 1955, more later), and to a much larger extent by various government departments cashing in their sterling balances held in London (which fell from £32 million at the end of 1954 to less than £14 million at the end of 1956).

[18] T. K. Whitaker, then a path-breaking Secretary of the Department of Finance (and only later a Governor of the Central Bank), is generally seen as the main architect of the shift

begun more than a century before was stemmed and then reversed, and eventually per capita economic growth began to accelerate – and not only with respect to an underperforming UK economy (Honohan and Walsh 2002; O'Rourke 2016).

A wider question is whether the sterling link constrained Irish economic growth. That it might have was sometimes argued on the ground that the link's existence made trade with the UK relatively easy, thereby distracting exporters from entering into the more economically dynamic markets further afield. Certainly, even as late as 1980, more than a half of merchandise imports still came from the UK, a percentage which had not fallen for more than twenty years; whereas by 1998, after twenty years of an independent currency, the share had fallen to one-third. On the other hand, the more significant trend relates to exports, and here, although the UK share was still about three-quarters in 1961, it fell rather steadily in the following years to 55 per cent in 1973 (year of European Economic Community [EEC] membership), 46 per cent in 1979 (end of sterling link) and 20 per cent by the end of the century.

THE EMS: A ZONE OF MONETARY STABILITY?

Europe Offers an Alternative Currency Regime

Gradually, especially with T. K. Whitaker as governor (1969–76), the Central Bank exercised more and more of its powers, effecting a transfer of the commercial banks foreign reserves to the Central Bank and facilitating the emergence of a Dublin money market.[19] Quietly, the

---

towards an export-oriented economic policy. But his views on the need for a new intellectual climate were already shared within the Central Bank as evidenced in a 1957 letter from Governor McElligott to University College Dublin (UCD) History Professor Desmond Williams in which he noted that UCD had 'one professor of economics and seven professors of Irish of one kind or another ... and yet we wonder why we are not making more progress in the development of our industry and our agriculture'.

[19] Judging from his unpublished memoir, maintained in the archive of the Central Bank, Whitaker's years at the Central Bank seem to have been dominated by the provision of advice to the Minister for Finance on issues of fiscal policy, incomes policy and competitiveness. He now also found himself having to resist the Department of Finance's renewed attempts to prevent market increases in interest rates emanating from London. The mistake of 1955–6, which he had witnessed at first hand, would not be repeated. Whitaker was influential in Irish central banking even before becoming Governor. His memoir notes his role, when at the Department of Finance, in encouraging such innovations as the acquisition of US dollars in 1954 to diversify the currency composition of the Central Bank's foreign exchange reserves, and the first use of bill discounting (1955).

institutional prerequisites for a change in the currency regime were also put in place, even though no such proposal was officially in the cards. Certainly, there was no willingness to devalue.[20]

By the 1970s, the suspicion was growing that the sterling link was indeed having the effect of limiting the ambition of Irish exporters to what had, by the 1960s, become an underperforming UK market. True or false, such ideas were beginning to gain traction in policy circles. In addition, recurrent bouts of sterling weakness continued to encourage some waves of support for a stronger Irish currency regime. High imported inflation and the sterling crisis (with apparent adverse knock-on effects on the prices that Irish farmers would get for their export produce) was prompting some consideration of an upward shift in the value of the Irish pound.[21]

This happened notably in 1974/5, when the prospect of Britain leaving the EEC came into focus in the lead-up to the first British referendum on that topic, which took place in June 1975. The possibility of a change resurfaced actively in government circles during the sterling crisis of late 1976, as the deutsche mark (DM) soared from 19 pence to more than 26 pence.

Quite detailed contingency plans were prepared in Dublin in advance of the 1975 referendum. This included preparation for introducing exchange controls vis-à-vis the UK as well as consideration of alternative exchange rate regimes. But officials cautioned against a move even if the referendum was lost.[22]

After all, what alternative currency regime would represent an improvement? One possibility would be to establish a new peg against sterling at a higher rate. Revaluing to a new fixed rate against sterling would in itself provide only a temporary relief against imported inflation. Besides, any

---

[20] Pre-emptively assembling some arguments against devaluation, which he feared could become a policy option given his assessment of the deterioration of competitiveness and in the fiscal position, Whitaker felt the need in April 1970 to have recourse to rhetoric such as 'it would not be a source of national pride to have to admit that the Irish pound could no longer look even a depreciating pound sterling in the face' (Whitaker 1979: 38).

[21] "We have tied ourselves to a currency which 'floats' like a stone" wrote economics professor Louis P. F. Smith.

[22] A revaluation would not have required parliamentary approval since a 1971 change in Irish law to align with IMF membership requirements that 'par value of the currency of each member shall be expressed in terms of gold' and not adjusted 'except to correct a fundamental disequilibrium . . . and only after consultation with the Fund' rather than being defined in law as equal to the pound sterling. Ironically, the new law had been enacted just before the IMF's gold-based exchange rate system effectively collapsed when Richard Nixon took the US dollar off the system in August 1971. I remember these events well as I had just accepted a job offer from the IMF – my first permanent job. It is amusing to recall the concerns of my prospective father-in-law that Nixon's action might threaten his daughter's financial security. The IMF survived, however.

new peg would obviously be seen as subject to further adjustments and perhaps the target of speculative pressures.

There was no enthusiasm for a floating exchange rate. The example of Canada notwithstanding, floating was seen as something only undisciplined countries would have recourse to: sinking was more likely than floating. Besides, into the 1970s and 1980s more than three-quarters of the currencies in the world had some form of pegged regime.

Finding more adherents was the option of a basket peg, as had been adopted in New Zealand during 1973. The main idea here was that overall stability might be improved by adjusting the rate against other currencies up or down – perhaps on a daily basis – to maintain a stable average exchange rate against a basket of currencies. The average value of the Irish pound vis-à-vis its main trading partners was being tracked and published regularly from the early 1970s. If there had to be a move from the sterling link, stabilizing this 'effective exchange rate index' was the alternative eventually favoured by the Central Bank and the Department of Finance, if a change was to be made.[23]

Britain was still Ireland's leading trading partner: a basket peg would introduce fluctuations against each individual currency including that of the main trading partner.

Lacking an obvious alternative, the status quo was maintained: no change was made to the sterling peg regime. It would take an external push to move to a different regime.

But when the EEC (of just nine member states at the time) came up with a proposed new exchange rate regime defining a 'zone of monetary stability' in Europe, Ireland was suddenly presented with a ready-made plausible alternative exchange rate regime. And, thanks to the preparations that had been made over the years, Ireland's membership could be imagined even if Britain did not want to join.

At first Britain was involved in the preliminary planning of the EMS.[24] But it quickly decided to stay outside of the Exchange Rate Mechanism (ERM) which was the heart of the system.[25]

---

[23] Another variant favoured by some was to peg against the European Unit of Account. In 1975 there were also adherents of Ireland joining the European 'snake' joint float.

[24] Little effort had been made, though, to involve the Irish government in the preparation and planning of the EMS initiative. The German and French members of the 'Group of Three' experts doing the planning behind closed doors had expected their British counterpart to keep Ireland informed, but he did not do so, a discourtesy that caused considerable annoyance in Dublin (Honohan and Murphy 2010).

[25] Britain opted in to a few peripheral elements of the institutional collaboration and was therefore regarded as a member of the EMS, even though it did not join the currency arrangement until a decade after it got under way.

The ERM was a regime of fixed but adjustable pegs or 'parities' between the member states, together with an allowed margin of fluctuation.[26] Each participant would intervene to prevent their currency from exceeding these margins. Adjusting the parities would be by agreement: any participant could request a meeting to decide on what became known as a 'realignment'.[27]

Without Britain, the ERM was never going to be an ideal exchange rate regime for Ireland, given the still close trading relations. But Europe was the future; to turn Ireland's back on the new exchange rate regime would be a major political step back from full engagement with the Community. Besides, there was the disappointing weakness and instability of sterling.

Lured also by an attractive financial package of assistance from Europe, designed to pay for measures that would help Ireland cope with what was expected to be a stronger currency regime, the Irish government decided to join up.

The EMS start date was set for 13 March 1979 and the Governors of the EEC Central Banks scheduled a special meeting during the routine bimonthly meetings of central bank governors at the BIS in Basel to take the final operational decisions and start up the new system.[28] Within days, sterling weakened to the point where the one-for-one link quickly became incompatible with the permissible range of fluctuation of the Irish pound vis-à-vis the other member currencies.[29] The sterling link was at an end.

---

[26] The fluctuation limits were 2¼ per cent above and below each bilateral parity. In 1978 I was one of a handful of young economists in the Central Bank tasked with preparation for the new regime. I participated in the 'expert group' drawn from each of the national central banks of member states charged with the details of the system's elaborate rules. I recall having had a hand in designing the formula for the 'divergence indicator' which was designed to ensure that all outlier countries, whether debtor or creditor, should have to adjust imbalances in their economies. In practice, though, like the mutual obligations to intervene in unlimited amounts to maintain their currencies within the allowed margins, these divergence indicator rules were ineffective in constraining the strong currencies, especially the DM (James 2012).

[27] There were other features, including the definition of a new composite currency unit of account called the European Currency Unit (ECU); this was replaced in 1999 at par by the euro. These were also some short-term financing facilities to ensure that each participant had the cash wherewithal to ensure that the fluctuation limits were being observed.

[28] What fun it was for Padraic O'Connor and myself, then the Central Bank's technical specialists on the topic, to fly out to this meeting in a private plane with Governor Charlie Murray. Exemplary parsimony dictated a propeller plane, chartered one-way-only: we returned in economy class on a scheduled flight. I am not aware of the Central Bank ever chartering an aircraft before or since.

[29] Senior officials at the Central Bank hoped that exchange rate fluctuations would be sufficiently small to allow us to maintain the sterling link for a good while even though

Fiscal Correction and Recession

Ireland's early years in the EMS coincided with the onset of the deep recession of the 1980s, a searing event which was generated by the fiscal contraction needed to correct imbalances that had opened up in the late 1970s as a result of a poorly judged fiscal expansion designed to achieve full employment through government spending.

Like many other countries, Ireland had tried to spend its way out of the earlier stagflation period triggered by the oil price hike of 1973. But even a sharp rise in the fiscal deficit was unable to limit the rise in unemployment, given the close labour market links across the Irish Sea. Unsurprisingly, given the exchange rate peg, Irish inflation also tracked the UK experience, briefly approaching 25 per cent per annum in 1975. But, after a brief budgetary retrenchment in 1976 which cost the government of the day the next election, the new government doubled-down on fiscal expansion. The financial markets were not impressed by the scale of borrowing. High nominal and – by the early 1980s – real interest rates together with record unemployment levels (paralleling those in the UK of the Thatcher government) meant that Irish government debt was, by 1981, on an up-escalator requiring a degree of austerity which no politician could at first stomach. Tax increases sufficient to hold the fort discouraged investor and consumer spending. It was not until 1987, following the fourth General Election in six years,[30] that a government screwed-up its courage (helped by a constructive position by the political opposition) to accomplish adjustment on the necessary scale.

Given the severity of the 1980s recession (to which we return in Chapter 12) it is remarkable that mistakes of fiscal excess were repeated less than two decades later.

Realignments of the Irish Pound in the ERM

In the event, the ERM did not prove to be an especially strong exchange rate regime for Ireland. For one thing, sterling started to appreciate against the DM especially from early 1980, thanks in part to North Sea Oil but also

we were entering the new system. However, I made a few calculations, based on experience with daily exchange rate movements, and reported to top management that the sterling link was likely to last only a few weeks. (My estimate was for an expected value of 6 weeks.) It was gratifying to see the accuracy of this advice so quickly confirmed.

[30] Simplifying slightly, governments alternated between Fianna Fáil (1977–81; 82 [Feb–Nov]; 87–9) and a Fine Gael–Labour coalition (1973–7; 81–2; 82–7).

to the deflationary policies of Mrs Thatcher's government. Ireland was spared what could have been a very damaging currency appreciation at a difficult time of economic downturn.[31] By early 1981 the Irish pound was worth only about 75 pence sterling.

The scale as well as the direction of this movement against sterling was against expectations. The Central Bank still had the idea that maintaining a stable average value (effective exchange rate index) of the Irish pound should be the guiding principle for Ireland whenever the opportunity arose for a realignment in the currency.[32] This average value had declined sharply in the winter of 1980–81, reflecting movements in the US dollar as well as sterling. Perhaps Ireland should call for an upward realignment of the Irish pound? Tellingly, the Central Bank made this suggestion to Department of Finance officials at a high-level meeting held on 11 June 1981, the very day of a general election. (Civil servants could expect little interruption from their political masters on that day!) In Ireland, as in most countries, policy on exchange rate realignments was decided by the government, however, and not by the Central Bank. Unsurprisingly (given the rapidly rising unemployment against which the weak currency provided at least some protection) the department's officials demurred at the suggestion of a currency appreciation, but they did accept the general principle being proposed by the Central Bank, namely that the opportunity should normally be taken at general realignments to seek to undo recent sharp movements in the average value (effective index) of the Irish pound. "Government must be made aware that, in certain circumstances, by avoiding a realignment in the EMS, they may not be achieving the best exchange rate objective." Although not made public, this general

---

[31] Escaping from the sterling link just before it would have dragged Ireland into an even more severe loss of competitiveness was a piece of luck. Indeed, an *Irish Times* opinion column (by Bill Murdock) entitled 'Even Outside EMS Sterling Link Might Have Gone' that appeared just after the break occurred made exactly that point. "Taking the long-term view," Murdock wrote "it may be better to be part of the EMS now rather than being forced to part company with sterling – outside the system – later." I remember this column because he cited a paper that I had published the year before in the *Economic and Social Review* highlighting the risk that North Sea oil could result in an increase in the value of sterling. It is interesting to see in the recently declassified files the bureaucratic manoeuvring which was necessary for me to persuade my superiors at the Central Bank in 1977 not to forbid the publication of that article – my very first academic publication. The question of publication was considered right up the organization even reaching the desk of Governor Charlie Murray, but in the end it was not blocked, 'but only' the Deputy General Manager wrote 'because I don't think we have the right to stop him'.

[32] I myself had a hand in preparing the staff papers elaborating this policy in those years.

policy approach was agreed by the government in December 1981 (Central Bank file 276/82 part 2).

The effective index policy was not closely adhered to in subsequent years, but taking one year with the next, actual decisions around realignments could be said to have been broadly in line with this policy. Thus, when sterling fell back from 1981, a series of currency realignments allowed the Irish government to *devalue* against the DM about once a year on average without that attracting adverse political attention.

The largest of these realignments was in March 1983. The main international focus at the time was on the French franc, which was under pressure for weeks, but markets accurately foresaw that the Irish pound would also be devalued, given how weak sterling had become over the past several months, thus increasing the average (index) value of the Irish pound – though the Irish pound was still far below its old parity with sterling.[33] Reluctant to initiate the realignment, Ireland battled sizable outflows of funds, as holders of Irish pounds accelerated their acquisition of foreign exchange in order to escape the anticipated devaluation. Even though wholesale interest rates were increased in several steps to 17 per cent, the Central Bank had to make substantial foreign exchange interventions: US$700 million in the final three weeks alone. That represented a considerable amount of the country's foreign exchange reserves sold in exchange for soon-to-be-devalued Irish pounds. At last the realignment was called and Ireland took the opportunity to devalue against all the other members. It was a sizable devaluation: by 8½ per cent against the DM, thereby depreciating by one percentage point more than even the French franc. The policy of undoing sudden changes in the effective index had been broadly adhered to: immediately post-realignment, the index was within 1 per cent of its average value during 1982 – but still far below where it had been when the sterling link was broken.

The 1986 Unilateral Devaluation

Although the opportunities offered by realignments were thus actively seized by Ireland to prevent currency strength adding headwinds to an economy stressed by fiscal adjustment, this amounted to achieving

---

[33] The weight of sterling in the Central Bank's effective exchange rate index at the time was greater than 45%, with the US dollar at 14%, the DM at less than 12%, the French franc at about 8%, the Netherlands guilder at 5%. The ERM currencies taken together accounted for something over a third of the index.

currency weakness by stealth. Only once did Ireland initiate a specific realignment to devalue the Irish pound. This was in August 1986 and followed a period of further weakness of sterling. (As Taoiseach Garret Fitz Gerald's economic advisor, I had a hand in this devaluation myself.)

The economy was in the doldrums, flattened not only by the protracted period of domestic fiscal adjustment, but also by the contemporary retrenchment in the UK. Now it looked like the private sector could face difficulties from the depreciation of sterling. Sterling was falling partly in sympathy with the US dollar, whose protracted overvaluation up to 1985 was being reversed; sterling's weakness also reflected the sharp fall in oil prices following a strategic policy shift by OPEC.

As a result mainly of the sterling movements, and despite a general realignment in April of 1986, Ireland's overall wage competitiveness against its main trading partners was deteriorating relatively rapidly. Even if there was no further sterling movement, Ireland's wage competitiveness for 1986 was heading for an average value of 5½ per cent worse than the previous year, having stayed within a relatively tight range since 1982. I persuaded Garret that devaluation was needed to head off what would have been a further contractionary impulse coming from this loss of competitiveness. He took the matter up with Finance Minister John Bruton (later himself to become Taoiseach), who at first expressed opposition. Soon, though, and following a new bout of sterling weakness (bringing sterling to its lowest value against the DM), the minister had brought his officials to see that the balance of advantages favoured a devaluation, even though it would have to be an unilateral realignment called by Ireland. The European partners agreed and a devaluation of 8 per cent against each of the other currencies was decided – unusually by telephone and without the need for a physical meeting. The planning had been quick and confidential, and there was less pre-realignment foreign exchange market speculation than in 1983.[34] A textbook implementation of a needed exchange rate adjustment, we felt.[35] The 1986 devaluation is often seen as having helped underpin the export-led recovery of the Irish economy

---

[34] For example, the aggregate value of exchange market intervention by the Central Bank on the day before the devaluation was a routine US$28 million. In the 1980s, much of Ireland's large balance of payments deficit was financed by government foreign borrowing. Since the foreign currency proceeds of this borrowing were placed with the Central Bank in the first instance, there was a steady requirement for the Central Bank to enter the market as a seller of foreign exchange.

[35] Only one of eighteen other ERM crisis events was accompanied by less of an effect on interest rates and reserves, according to the calculations and approach of Eichengreen et al. (1996).

from 1988, especially as the effect was boosted by a period of sterling strength from early 1987, and because the weak employment conditions militated against wages being pushed up unsustainably to offset the competitiveness gain.

Assessment of the ERM

Apart from the escape it offered from sterling's 1980s strength, the ERM did not have much to recommend it as an exchange rate regime. Despite all of the realignments it eventually proved to be no stronger or weaker *on average* than the sterling link would have been in the end. It provided no greater degree of price stability than had the sterling link: Ireland's inflation rate averaged 7.7 per cent per annum in the ERM and had reached 20.3 per cent in 1981. However, by the time it fell apart in the summer of 1993, the Irish pound was back to 98 pence sterling.

But, above all, the ERM contributed to Ireland's high interest rates in those years. In short, the market uncertainty created by the relatively frequent devaluations, combined with the fiscal crisis of the 1980s, resulted in Ireland – an over-indebted country in recession – being faced with high interest rates during the ERM period. It is no surprise that Irish interest rates were higher than those in the ERM's core country, Germany. A premium would have been needed to compensate the fall of more than a third in the value of the Irish pound against the DM from 1979 to 1993. But the interest differential was much higher than the actual depreciation would imply. In net terms, Irish assets yielded over 2½ percentage points (250 basis points) per annum higher after allowing for the exchange rate movements. That accumulates to a more than 40 per cent profit from holding Irish pound assets over that fourteen-year period relative to holding DM-denominated assets – evidently an extra cost for a borrower. The reason was clearly the risk aversion of speculators and their assumption that an even weaker exchange rate policy would be pursued. No doubt the fiscal crisis of the time made such speculation even more plausible.[36] As a result, whenever sterling weakened, there was a tendency for Irish money market interest rates to rise, reflecting some speculation about a future realignment (Honohan and Conroy 1994). Official rates typically

---

[36] Indeed, as late as 1988, legendary international macroeconomist Rudi Dornbusch was advocating a debt restructuring for Ireland (Dornbusch 1989). As fears of restructuring would likely have shown up in foreign currency borrowing rates as well, and did not, it is not clear that the Irish pound interest rates embodied a distinct credit risk component.

followed. This vulnerability to speculation was an increasingly problematic feature of exchange rate regimes with fixed-but-adjustable pegs. Could Ireland do better with a more flexible regime?

The ERM Crisis

As it turned out, this was to be tested sooner than expected. The ERM disintegrated dramatically in the winter of 1992–3. The problem was the appreciation of the DM which resulted from the configuration of monetary and fiscal policy actions taken by the German authorities on reunification of that country. The UK (which had joined the ERM only in 1990) was (along with Italy) suddenly forced out by the pressure of speculation in the famous currency collapse of Black Wednesday September 16, 1992. (This was the day the investment fund controlled by George Soros is said to have made €1 billion by taking a position against sterling.) Could or should Ireland follow suit? After all, the economy was stronger now, having made a good start to its recovery from the fiscal doldrums of the 1980s; perhaps it did not need to follow sterling – at least this was one view held in policy circles.

But the Irish pound, which had been trading between 90 and 94 pence sterling before September suddenly found itself at an unprecedented premium against sterling, approaching £1.10. It had also been appreciating (with the DM) against other currencies (including ERM members Portugal and Spain). But it was these record values against sterling that were politically decisive. Markets immediately foresaw a likely devaluation. Indeed on the day after Black Wednesday alone the Central Bank sold US$1.67 billion to defend the currency – a record daily intervention; total foreign exchange market intervention by the Central Bank in September 1992 came to US$4 billion.

With further sizable outflows, especially after the Swedish and Iberian devaluations in November, weeks of record interest rates followed. These, designed to make speculation too expensive, mainly hit ordinary business and personal borrowers. A devaluation at the first opportunity would have been suggested by the 1981 policy approach approved by the government, given how high the effective index of the Irish pound had moved as a result of sterling's exit. But policy hesitated (notably reflected in what was interpreted by the market as an equivocal statement by Finance Minister Ahern in the first week of January 1993). With UK monetary policy easing later that month, further outflows prompted the Central Bank to lift its overnight lending rate to the banks to an all-time record of 100 per cent per annum. But it was in vain. Indeed the massive currency interventions which had been undertaken over more than four months resulted in sizable economic losses to the Central Bank when a 10 per cent devaluation was finally decided on at the end of January.[37]

Somewhat inauspiciously, the devaluation was announced just as the Bank commemorated the fiftieth anniversary of its foundation. Schadenfreude prevailed among many of the invitees at a grand and formal concert two days later in Dublin's National Concert Hall to mark the anniversary (and inevitably dubbed the 'devaluation disco' by wags).

The new Irish central exchange rate in the ERM would not have a lasting significance. Within a few months of further speculation against other currencies in the system, the ERM narrow band of fluctuation was abandoned. Although a new wide band of plus or minus 15 per cent was established in its place, this was so wide as to be irrelevant and the ERM was, for most practical purposes, at an end.

* * *

Ireland allowed politics and the prevailing conventional wisdom to determine its currency regime in the first seventy-five years of independence. Two sharply contrasting regimes were pursued in this period. The initial one-for-one link with sterling remained unquestioned until succeeded by the politically motivated shift to the adjustable peg regime of the EMS. Neither regime was demonstrably superior to the other. Errors in macroeconomic policy management in each regime caused severe economic crises; but strong recovery was also shown to be possible in each. Britain remained by far the most important trading partner, but its dominance was already being eroded as a consequence of EU membership long before the sterling link was abandoned. Currency choice in Ireland seems to have been largely incidental to the long-term evolution of Irish economic

---

[37] Losses were not recorded in the annual accounts, however, as these accounts were naturally maintained in the depreciated Irish pounds. Such issues are more clearly seen by making calculations in foreign currency. The same is true in advance of a devaluation. For example, one of the reasons given for being slow to devalue was the optical illusion that Ireland's foreign debt would increase by the amount of the devaluation. Not so: as I repeatedly advised in those years, in the unchanged international prices, there would be no change in the value of foreign currency denominated debt; Irish pound denominated debt would fall in value and the country's ability to generate the export earnings to service foreign debt would increase (cf. Honohan 1993). I later published an estimate of the sizable economic losses incurred by selling such a large quantity of foreign exchange reserves at a price 8 per cent below what they became worth the day after the devaluation (Honohan 1994). The lesson: don't hold on to an untenable and costly policy.

wellbeing, characterized by stagnation until the mid-1950s, followed by a tentative improvement in 1960s before setbacks impeded a long overdue convergence towards the living standards that had been attained in the more advanced European economies.

The worst of these setbacks was the self-imposed fiscal crisis and budgetary-induced contraction of the 1980s. Eventually, politics allowed a decisive correction and this, accompanied by an improvement in competitiveness partly driven by exchange rate policy, heralded a vigorous recovery.

From a wider historical perspective, the first fifty years of Central Banking in Ireland (from 1943 to 1993) falls into two neat halves: first a period of postcolonial quiescence where the UK was the dominant reference point; second, a period of monetary instability and turbulence, both in the final years of the sterling link and then in the EMS. The next quarter century would be defined by Ireland's chequered but, on balance, largely successful effort to cope with the forces of financialization and hyperglobalization.

This brought with it a sharp improvement in aggregate economic performance in terms of employment and output growth – the Celtic Tiger. Its start coincided with the temporary abandonment of any binding exchange rate peg in 1993. But already the course had been set for euro membership with the adoption, by a majority of 69 per cent of the voters in a June 1992 referendum, of the Maastricht Treaty ushering in the single currency.

2

Towards the Euro

If the devaluation of January 1993 was seen at the time as a major setback for Irish exchange rate policy and for the Central Bank in particular, what ensued was a pleasant surprise. Well placed as a result of the fiscal reforms, the wage restraint, and the sensible decision not to hold onto an unrealistic peg, the economy seemed to defy gravity in the following years as it awaited the creation of the euro. It was now that the economy became characterized as a 'Celtic Tiger'. The analogy was with the fast-growing emerging economies in Asia which were already being described (with more geographical justification) as tigers.

Indeed, the effective abandonment by Europe of the narrow-band of the Exchange Rate Mechanism (ERM) a few months after the devaluation marks the start of what was certainly the most successful period in Irish economic history. It brought average Irish living standards at last close to the frontier of European levels. And the expansion of economic activity and employment was a solid one, based on competitive pricing and on growing exports into the world economy. The public finances benefited from the flow of revenue and from the reduced needs for unemployment assistance. Government borrowing declined and the debt ratio dropped steadily. This was a sustainable achievement.

But success bred complacency. The drivers of the good economic performance were not fully understood. Pundits imagined a new era of permanently high growth rates, driven by success in the new technological economy and offering a steady increase in jobs that would reverse the historic migration flows. Some politicians and business people and bankers became so used to success that they no longer stress-tested their plans. Gradually the elements that had driven the sustainable growth were overtaken by transitory and evanescent components.

And complacency proved lethal in the liberalized financial environment of the new century, perhaps exacerbated by the removal of exchange risk with the creation of the euro. As financial markets relaxed their vigilance, spending and borrowing became easy and a trap for the unwary, as Irish decision-makers had become. When the huge imbalances that were generated by these excesses were eventually recognized, confidence was suddenly lost, resulting in the crash, followed by a painful and protracted correction of the imbalances.

THE FLOATING RATE PERIOD AND ITS AFTERMATH

For almost six years, from mid-1993 to the end of 1998, the exchange rate regime that prevailed amounted to a floating exchange rate for the Irish pound given that the formal intervention margins had been widened to plus or minus 15 per cent. It is somewhat paradoxical that this unparalleled flexibility prevailed while the already-agreed-upon European Monetary Union was being put in place – a regime that would permanently remove all currency flexibility.

Floating was something not experienced in Ireland for two centuries. How would the Irish economy cope? Surprisingly well, it seems. During this period, a largely passive monetary and exchange rate policy seemed to result in an acceptable degree of stability – partly underpinned by the growing expectation of euro membership. Inflation hovered around 2 per cent per annum (which can be compared with the hundred-year average of between 4 and 5 per cent, and was much better than during the ERM; see Figure 1.2). And the exchange rate was more stable than during the ERM: the standard deviation of the trade-weighted average exchange rate against Ireland's main trading partners was halved; even against sterling, the Irish pound was a little more stable than it had been.

The floating rate period was also one of rapid economic growth and falling unemployment. Led by export expansion, aggregate economic activity grew rapidly adding to total numbers at work, reducing unemployment from record high levels to rates lower than ever previously recorded. Was it a coincidence that the years of exchange rate flexibility proved to coincide with the most successful years of Irish macroeconomic performance?

Why did the economy grow so strongly and sustainably in the 1990s?[1] One global factor was the generally strong and almost uninterrupted

---

[1] Honohan and Walsh (2002) provide a fuller account.

economic growth of most of Ireland's trading partners in this period of increasing globalization. After the turbulence of previous decades, this was becoming known as the era of 'great moderation'.

But domestic factors must also have been at work. One prerequisite was the absence of ill-conceived macroeconomic policy activism (such as the interest rate blunder of 1955 and the pro-cyclical fiscal over-expansion of the late 1970s) and the return by the late 1980s to a sustainable debt and deficit path. With the disruption that had been caused by policy mistakes of this type removed, forces of convergence could assert themselves and bring Ireland towards the international frontier.

Many of the institutional prerequisites for national economic success were already in place such as effective legal and administrative systems. Enlightened structural policies of earlier decades now bore fruit, notably the sharp increase in the provision of free secondary education and the expansion of third level, equipping each new generation to prosper provided sufficient jobs materialized.

And the jobs came. Well positioned within the European Union's single market, and with a low corporate tax rate effectively protected by tax treaties, Ireland was being energetically promoted by an effective Industrial Development Authority as a destination for inward direct investment especially from US multinational corporations (MNCs) (though the employment content of most of this inward foreign direct investment [FDI] was much lower than its contribution to exports and gross domestic product [GDP]).

All the way through the 1990s, average wage rates, influenced by negotiated national wage agreements, showed a moderate trend, though after-tax wages rose more rapidly reflecting reductions in the income tax schedule. Indeed, income tax concessions were a key part of the wage agreements. The result was a steady improvement in measured international wage competitiveness (Figure 2.1). Despite the tax cuts, the public finances, strengthened by revenue buoyancy and a falling dependency rate thanks to demographic trends, moved into surplus and debt ratios shrank as the economy grew. The availability of 'structural fund' grants from the European Union, starting in 1988, and reaching more than 3 per cent of GDP in some years, helped boost public investment.

It is important to recognize that the growth surge in the Celtic Tiger years was one of employment, not of productivity. Average labour productivity growth in the economy as a whole was indeed strong at about 2 per cent per annum (when the raw data are adjusted to remove several

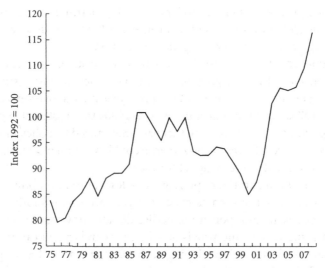

Figure 2.1 Relative hourly earnings, 1975–2008. Ireland vis-à-vis main trading partners.
Source: Central Bank of Ireland.

distortions), but not miraculous.[2] But the unemployment rate fell sharply; participation rates, especially of women, increased; the move out of under-employment in the agriculture sector was steady; and significant net inward migration was present for the first-ever sustained period.[3]

Rather absent in explanations of the Celtic Tiger is the banking sector. True, special efforts had been made by the government to create a kind of offshore financial services centre in Dublin. Enhanced fiscal inducements were, at first, part of the package, and the Centre was a success, especially in generating tax revenue despite the low rates. But its employment contribution was on a modest scale relative to overall job creation record of the 1990s.

[2] That the activities of high-profit MNCs severely distort Irish macroeconomic statistics should by now be well known. Irish manufacturing output and exports and productivity have been greatly flattered by the published numbers which need to be significantly adjusted before making comparisons with other countries. A paper that I prepared for the Central Bank in 1984 pinpointed the nature of the problem, and earned me a certain notoriety when this paper was leaked to the media. These misleading numbers tended to lower policymakers' guard against vulnerabilities. In the years since then, as discussed in Chapter 12, the difficulties in interpreting some Irish macroeconomic statistics have only become worse.

[3] As in previous decades, Irish unemployment fluctuations paralleled those in the UK, but this time the fall in Irish unemployment was much faster and by 2000 brought Irish rates below those in Britain for the first time on record.

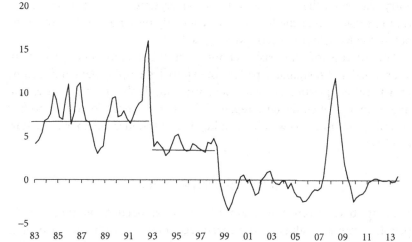

Figure 2.2 Real interest rates, 1983–2013. Per cent per annum; interbank rates deflated by four-quarter future inflation.
Source: Author's calculation from Central Bank and Central Statistics Office Data.

And the banks were certainly not increasing their emphasis on provision of credit to firms. MNCs relied on their foreign parents for funding, and government grants played a sizable role for both foreign and Irish-based business expansion. Instead, the banks, as in other countries, were increasingly emphasizing property-based lending. While the figures for the two years are not strictly comparable, the share of bank lending going to property seems to have more than doubled between 1984 and 1999 (and would continue to grow vigorously thereafter). Reflecting this expansion of credit, residential construction contributed much of the growth in domestic capital formation from 1993 on. This banking sector was not a locomotive of employment growth in the export sectors.

Was the approach of the euro a factor in promoting growth? One dimension is interest rates. But while the floating rate period did see a step-like reduction in the average level of interest rates and the spread between Irish and German interest rates, the really big reduction did not come until the last few months before the euro began (Figure 2.2).

Some observers did subsequently attribute the increasingly comfortable fiscal numbers to successive governments' efforts to meet the Maastricht criteria with their guidance on the ratios to GDP of General Government Borrowing (3 per cent) and the Gross Government Debt (60 per cent) as entry criteria for the euro area. But such an argument is not persuasive; the timing suggests that the finances were already on target for this outcome before the Maastricht criteria were agreed.

The success of the Irish economy in the floating-rate years with a sustained and sustainable pattern of export-led employment and income growth raised questions in some observers' minds about the pressures that might emerge when the euro replaced the Irish pound. Would Ireland fare as well in the euro area which it would join as a founder member at the start of 1999?

WHY JOIN THE EURO?

Looking back from the years of crisis, associated as they are in people's minds – albeit not entirely accurately – with the euro, it is natural to ask how it was that Ireland decided more than a quarter century ago to join this exchange rate system and adopt the common currency. One million voters cast their vote in favour of the Maastricht Treaty in the referendum held in June 1992, shortly before the ERM crisis.

Even before the ERM collapsed under the combined pressure of the UK's belated participation and the German fiscal adjustments to pay for national reunification, its relatively disappointing record had induced European leaders to push forward with an ambitious plan for monetary unification, replacing national currencies by a single currency, the euro, which would be managed by a supranational and politically independent European Central Bank (ECB).

Across the European Union various advantages were seen for the single currency. Some of these related to microeconomic aspects. Removal of foreign exchange transactions costs would be a clear gain for economic efficiency. Elimination of exchange rate fluctuations would make the costs and benefits of cross-border investment and trade more predictable. Other foreseen advantages were more macroeconomic in character. Inflation would be kept under control by generalizing the independence and discipline operated by the Bundesbank by designing the same features into the ECB. Furthermore, the temptation for some countries to gain competitive advantage through devaluation would be neutralized. There were also arguments relating to the international division of political power among EU member states. Despite Germany's fear of surrendering autonomous control over its own monetary stability, this was conceded, in part as a means of redressing the power imbalance within the Union that had been generated by German reunification.[4]

The quantitative importance of these advantages could be and was extensively debated (see e.g. Rose 2000). Some of the largest estimates of the potential growth in cross-border trade were found in studies that looked at the mirror image of formation of a currency union, namely postcolonial trade shrinkage following the dismantling of currency links such as the Irish one with sterling. The effect of formation of a currency union might not be symmetrical with that of its disintegration. Besides, might not the importance of exchange risk and transactions costs diminish anyway with the growth of financial innovations and computerized payments systems?

To be set against the touted advantages of creating a currency union were the risks of asymmetric shocks. The monetary policy response to disturbances that hit some member countries but not all might suit some, but inevitably not all. Having exchange rate flexibility gave countries a convenient tool to insulate themselves against the disruption of some forms of economic shock that hit them but not their trading partners (or vice-versa). Losing this adjuster would be of little consequence if wages, prices or labour mobility were sufficiently flexible to do the necessary adjustment to such shocks. Otherwise the so-called theory of optimal currency areas (which emphasizes international labour mobility and wage flexibility among the prerequisites for a smoothly functioning currency union) cautioned against their creation. Not everyone was convinced by the arguments of some that shocks affecting the different member states would become increasingly synchronized as the currency union deepened economic integration between the members.

Still, although many observers questioned whether a common currency should precede the creation of a federal European state, the outsourcing of currency policy to a non-governmental agency offered to others the large prize of an escape from the turbulence and inflationary bias of European currencies in the previous decades.

Ultimately, the most important driver of the euro project was undoubtedly the political one of moving forward to an ever-closer union. But little account was taken of the possibility, evoked in a farsighted contribution by Feldstein (1997), that the strains of adjusting to a major asymmetric shock

---

[4] The prehistory of the euro is analysed in detail in James (2012). See also Brunnermeier et al. (2016), Eichengreen (2011) and Mody (2018).

could lead to acute political tensions – even war, he said – between member states of the new currency area.[5]

What of Ireland's decision to join? This too was largely political. Despite dissatisfaction with both the sterling link and the ERM which succeeded it, Irish public policy with regard to the exchange rate regime continued in the 1980s to be reactive to European policy proposals. The alternative was for Ireland to strike out on its own, and the practical options in that respect were as limited as ever.

Ireland had prospered from its membership in the European Union. The boost to farm income from the start; the diversification and expansion of industry, driven by expansion into the wider and more dynamic continental economy; and latterly the very sizable expansion in structural funds were all clear positives. Most influential analysts felt that, in order not to lose its hard won place in the dynamic inner circle of the Union, Ireland should adopt the common currency even if Britain stayed out, as always seemed likely.

With such strategic issues dominating, the economic arguments took a back seat in this debate. Rather late in the day, indeed almost three years after the Maastricht referendum, the Irish government commissioned a study of the likely economic impact of EMU membership for Ireland. With colleagues John FitzGerald and the late Terry Baker, I was part of the team of researchers from the Economic and Social Research Institute (ESRI) leading this effort. While the study (Baker et al. 1996) was wide-ranging in its coverage of different sectors, the key central question that had to be asked related to the macroeconomic conundrum: would the risks of asymmetric shocks outweigh the benefits of reduced currency instability? In our view the answer was by no means clear. Clearly euro membership would remove a degree of flexibility (not least with respect to the movements of sterling, assuming it stayed out). With Britain still such an important trading partner, Ireland had a built-in generator of asymmetric shocks: for example, depreciation of the pound sterling would not be anything like as significant for other euro area countries as it would be for Ireland. Indeed, the dominance of the UK in our trade meant that the euro area would have a lower share of Ireland's trade than that of any of

---

[5] Feldstein, based in the United States, was not the first economist to question the goal of a single currency on grounds that it could exacerbate tensions between member states. Mody (2018) reminds us of the much earlier critiques along these lines from two of the leading British academics of the 1970s, both eurosceptics but with sharply contrasting political outlooks: the left-leaning Cambridge don Nicholas Kaldor, and Margaret Thatcher's advisor from the London School of Economics Alan Walters.

the other members. On the other hand, our long experience with the high interest rates that were driven both by expected devaluations and by an additional exchange rate risk premium should be at an end. This interest rate wedge that had imposed a higher cost of capital, thereby discouraging investment, could be removed. In the end, model calculations suggested a net advantage so slight for membership that it was well within the margin of error and of model uncertainty. In other words, the promise of low interest rates, resulting from the removal of exchange rate risk, was seen as largely offsetting the threat of a loss of competitiveness vis-à-vis the UK.

There was a vigorous national debate (recalled in Barry 2017). While majority opinion among economists probably sided with the conclusion of the ESRI, several highly respected figures took the opposite view. They felt that the net economic argument was unfavourable to membership. They expressed doubts that interest rates would converge, and pointed out that, even if they did, low interest rates would not always be ideal for macroeconomic conditions in Ireland. On the first point (interest rate convergence) the doubters proved to be totally wrong for almost a decade and then, suddenly and dramatically, right. They were also right in their implicit doubts that the fiscal and prudential policies needed to contain the risks that might be stoked by very low interest rates would in fact be implemented in Ireland. If domestic policy had been better, neither of the doubters' concerns would have materialized.

Ireland was not, of course, the only country wrestling with the pros and cons of euro area membership. Perhaps ironically in view of subsequent events, it was the Mediterranean countries with weaker track records of macroeconomic stability and fiscal discipline that displayed most enthusiasm for joining: they sought the stability that the Bundesbank had brought to Germany's monetary and financial system, and they worked hard in a variety of ways to make sure that they passed the Maastricht qualifying criteria for early membership.[6] These criteria aimed to ensure that prospective members had achieved sufficient convergence towards fiscal balance, inflation and interest rates.

The UK, still operating Europe's largest financial centre, and still smarting from its disruptive and humiliating failure in the 1992 ERM crisis, displayed less enthusiasm; Chancellor of the Exchequer (later Prime

---

[6] Including, in the case of Greece (as became clear only much later), the use of non-transparent derivative contracts to make their fiscal accounts look stronger than they really were.

Minister) Gordon Brown defined five tests – very sensible and much broader in scope than the Maastricht criteria – that would need to be satisfied before Britain would abandon reliance on the derogation it had negotiated to stay out. Among the Brown tests, the key stumbling block was the need to be sure that the new system had the flexibility to deal with problems that might arise. As he did later in October 2008 (when he identified the urgent need for large injections of public capital into banks), Brown had put his finger on the key missing policy ingredient.

Germany, later to be seen as a major beneficiary of the system, also had its fair share of sceptics when the euro was launched. The Bundesbank had done a fine job, such sceptics emphasized, by maintaining price stability: many in Germany doubted that its successor would have the backbone to do the same.

With the Bundesbank seen by all sides as the model to be emulated, it was probably inevitable that the ECB would establish its headquarters in Frankfurt am Main – not far from its exemplar.[7] Henceforth monetary policy decisions for Ireland would be taken in Frankfurt rather than in Dublin. The Governing Council of the ECB, made up of six executive board members appointed by the European Council (the heads of government of the European Union's member states), together with the governors of the national central banks of each of the euro area members, is the deciding body for all such decisions.

IRELAND IN THE EARLY YEARS OF THE EURO: THE EMERGENCE OF THE PROPERTY BOOM

The replacement of the Irish pound by the euro took place formally from the start of 1999, though Irish notes and coin continued to circulate until the start of 2002 when they were replaced in a smooth and well-prepared operation by the new euro notes and coin. Exchange rate and monetary policy was now mostly removed from domestic debate. Furthermore,

---

[7] Various other locations were seriously considered, including a French suggestion of the banks of the Rhine at Strasbourg. If it could not be Frankfurt, one German suggestion was historic Mainz, a discreet 45 km from Frankfurt. But why was the Bundesbank in Frankfurt? Old-timers recall the post-war debates over where the central bank's precursor (the Bank deutscher Länder BdL) should be located. Banks pushed for Frankfurt or Berlin, but the occupying American powers would not have favoured the latter. Adenauer is said to have favoured Dusseldorf, as he saw Frankfurt as a city of commerce, rather than democracy and government. Influential Bavarian interests pushed for Munich. In the end the choice of Frankfurt for the BdL was, they say, as much a political compromise between Rheinlanders and Bavarians as anything else.

macroeconomic pressures generally seemed to recede, especially as the strong growth in economic activity and employment, with reductions in the debt ratio and falling unemployment, despite substantial inward migration, continued into the new millennium.

Unfortunately, this Celtic Tiger experience fomented a degree of complacency and overoptimism. Public and private sectors began to behave as if boom conditions would continue indefinitely. Some observers detect a change of gear around 2002 or 2003. The government made further reductions in the schedule of income tax, and increased public spending programmes including higher rates of public servants' pay, and of social benefits. Wage rates increased in the private sector also, albeit somewhat more slowly, so that from 2000 to 2008 wage competitiveness deteriorated vis-à-vis Ireland's trading partners by as much as 36 per cent. Some of this deterioration was vis-à-vis partners also using the euro, so cannot be wholly attributed to the appreciation of the euro. The private sector built and bought residential and commercial property at home and abroad, fuelled (as we will discuss in much more detail later) by aggressive credit expansion by the banks, which in turn had ready access to foreign funding, thanks to the contemporaneous surge in global financial intermediation.

Rapid economic growth and increases in employment continued up to 2007, helped by continuing inward migration. But the character of the growth had changed. Instead of being based on cost-effective production for export, the growth engine was now construction. As a share of total employment, building and construction soared from the normal 6 to 7 per cent to take over 13 per cent by 2007. Many more were engaged in ancillary and indirect activities spinning off the construction boom. And despite the increased supply, housing prices continued to soar, reaching 540 per cent of their 1994 values by 2007 – 360 per cent in real terms, deflated by consumer prices. Unless one believed in the vision of an unending flow of large-scale inward migration with Ireland taking an ever-increasing share of a growing global economic market, this boom was sure to end. After all, from about 2000, Ireland was no longer increasing its share of global trade in goods and services, apparently contradicting the premise of such a vision.

The transitory nature of much of the growing Irish tax receipts in the early years of the euro area was not sufficiently recognized by analysts who tended to take the measured government surpluses as readily sustainable. In fact, however, tax revenue was doomed to collapse as soon as the property and construction bubble burst: the huge volume of transactions in the housing market was boosting the revenue from the high tax rate (known as stamp duty) on these transactions. Furthermore, the rise in property prices was generating additional tax receipts from capital gains and corporation profits. As soon as the property market returned even to normal functioning, these exceptional revenues would dry up: more so if the boom turned to bust. These revenues were being used in part to reduce the government's debt ratio, but also to lower income tax rates, and to increase the rates of public sector pay and social benefits, as well as to finance increases in other government spending programmes. Given the artificial and transitory nature of these and other revenue sources in the boom, it should have been evident that measured government borrowing requirements were being artificially and temporarily suppressed by the boom. A proper calculation of the underlying trend in the deficit (when the transitory impact of boom-time receipts was netted out, revealing the impact of the lower tax rates and higher public service costs) would have shown that it was alarmingly high. All too soon this hidden underlying deficit became a reality.

That the Irish public finances would move so suddenly into crisis was remarkable in three different ways. First, the severe fiscal crisis of the 1980s had been raging barely two decades earlier: how could institutional memory in the Irish public service have been so short as to have allowed the public finances to be exposed to a comparable risk again? Second, why did international surveillance by such entities as the Organisation for Economic Co-operation and Development (OECD) and International Monetary Fund (IMF) largely fail to warn sufficiently of the potential imbalances that were building? And third, how was it that rules and analyses of the European Commission and ECB failed too to guard against the disaster? It seems that macroeconomic surveillance was tainted by the vague notion that single currency, combined with the simple budgetary rules of the Stability and Growth Pact (often criticized for being too strict), would put paid to any aggregate financial crises. The huge financial stocks and flows related to the offshore activities of the Dublin International Financial Services Centre certainly complicated analysis and masked the degree to which the property and construction bubble was being financed by bank borrowing from abroad.[8] Besides, the current account deficit in

---

[8] At the 2006 Annual Conference of the Dublin Economic Workshop in Kenmare, Co. Kerry, I pointed out that credit institutions had recently become net importers of funds to Irish residents on a huge scale: 41 per cent of GDP by the end of 2005. The reaction of most participants was surprise and some doubt as to the reliability of the figure. Unfortunately there had been no mistake in my calculation.

the balance of payments, if anyone did pay attention to it, had only recently moved into a zone that would trigger concern.

To the casual observer, the Irish boom that was sustained into most of the first decade of the euro seemed miraculous.[9] But whereas the expansion that had preceded euro membership was largely sustainable, that which followed carried the seeds of its own destruction.

The scale of the employment and activity downturn which ensued was larger than in most other countries. This can be attributed in part to the degree to which the economy had been skewed in the direction of construction: the collapse of the construction sector meant the loss of a much higher proportion of employment than would normally be the case. That it coincided with a global downturn meant that new alternative employment opportunities from switching to export activity were not readily available. And the decline in the international value of sterling vis-à-vis the euro undermined competitiveness in the closest, and still the largest single, trading partner. The fact that the threat to sustainability of the public finances limited the possibility of a countercyclical fiscal impulse (beyond the automatic stabilizers already built into fiscal policy) added to the pressures.

THE COUNTERFACTUAL: WHAT IF IRELAND HAD NOT JOINED?

What might have happened had Ireland not joined the euro area? I will not spend time talking about the wider political economy dimension to this – already evoked in some of the debate of the 1990s – including the impact non-participation would have had on Ireland's ability to influence and prosper in general within the EU, and where Ireland would find itself now vis-à-vis Brexit.

Counterfactual Celtic Tiger

But how might the Irish macroeconomy have performed in the period 1997–2007 outside the euro area? That, of course, depends on many imponderables, starting with the question of what alternative exchange

---

[9] Indeed, so much so that as late as 26 June 2008, a seminar was held in Brussels under the auspices of the European Commission on the topic 'Ireland's economic transformation: Miracle or Model', at which economic experts on Ireland from home and abroad were invited to review Ireland's economic success for the edification of Commission staff.

rate regime might have been followed. Advocates of staying out felt that continuation of the exchange rate regime that had been in effect since the effective collapse of the narrow bank ERM would be the best arrangement: after all, this was, in Leddin and Walsh's 2003 view, Irish exchange rate policy's 'finest hour' (cf. Barry 2017). Actually it is not easy to define just what that regime was.

It is possible to detect an apparent influence of both sterling and the deutsche mark on movements of the Irish pound in this period. For instance a decline in either of those currencies against the US dollar tended to be correlated with Irish pound weakness. This is consistent with Barry's (2017) characterization of a path 'co-determined by movements of sterling and the deutsche mark'. But exchange rate policy was never explicitly detailed in those years, either by the Central Bank or by the Minister for Finance. (Strictly speaking, exchange rate policy was a matter for the government, and not for the Central Bank.)

The stated objective of monetary policy in the floating period was price stability 'predicated on maintaining a firm exchange rate vis-à-vis other low inflation countries.' This carries echoes of the 1980s ERM policy of seeking to stabilize the trade-weighted average value of the currency – the effective index. Indeed, in November 1993 the Central Bank Board endorsed a policy of loosely targeting the effective index, though there was to be secrecy about the target range, and even the Board does not appear to have been told – at least in writing – what the range would be.[10] Note also that price stability was not publicly defined in terms of any particular range of the inflation rate. Instead, the idea was that if the effective index remained stable, Irish inflation would tend to the same as the average inflation rate of our trading partners.[11] What was proposed envisaged a great deal of management discretion in the operation of this exchange rate policy as to how much tolerance there should be for deviations of the effective index around the target. Interest rate increases rather than exchange market intervention were seen as the main policy tools.[12]

---

[10] The reluctance to reveal a target range undoubtedly reflected the Bank's fear that such information would strengthen the hand of currency speculators. The Bank's ability to defend the currency against speculative activity was limited by the scale of its foreign exchange reserves. The optimal size and composition of these reserves was a perennial source of debate and analysis at the Bank until the arrival of the euro (see Box 2.1).

[11] This idea was perhaps overstated: the underlying theory of 'purchasing power parity' does not really work as smoothly and thoroughly as might be supposed.

[12] "In summary, the strategy for management of the exchange rate would be to resist pressures resulting in a decline in the [effective rate] where it is possible to do so but to accept some decline in the case of persistent pressures; it would also be desirable to signal

Figure 2.3 Nominal effective exchange rate, 1979–2008.
Source: Central Bank of Ireland.

However, the actual volatility of the effective index (Figure 2.3) around a gradual depreciating trend during the floating rate period casts some doubt on whether the stated policy was actually pursued with any vigour. It seems that the Central Bank acquiesced for the most part in exchange rate movements for the Irish pound that were chiefly determined in the private market, whenever they did not seem to pose competitiveness difficulties for Ireland.

Projecting the 'finest hour' exchange rate trend into the new millennium would have given a weaker rate than actual. This could have averted the loss of wage competitiveness that actually occurred (Figure 2.1). It would also have fuelled stronger external demand (as well as higher inflation).

Given 'when you have it you spend it' fiscal policy and a prudential banking policy that in all important respects was largely passive, to what extent would the Irish economy have avoided the excesses of the bank-driven property and construction bubble that actually occurred?[13]

Certainly, 'monetary union gave Irish and other periphery banks access to much broader eurozone capital markets' (Barry 2017; Honohan 2000,

by interest rate increases a reluctance to accept this depreciation and a willingness to see a subsequent recovery in the exchange rate." ('Managing the Exchange Rate within the Wider ERM bands, Central Bank Board paper 18 November 1993. File 276/82.)

[13] Defending spending cut-backs in the face of less buoyant tax revenue in November 2001, Charlie McCreevy, finance minister between 1997 and 2004, famously remarked 'when you have it, you spend it', an advocacy of pro-cyclical fiscal policy which was much criticized.

2006). Still, it is equally likely the extraordinary surge of cheap loanable funds that swept across the advanced economies in the 2003–6 period would not have passed Ireland by. Ireland was seen as a good risk: even before euro area membership, the Irish government's credit rating was already pitched just one notch below AAA (since October 1994 by Fitch, since February 1997 by Moody's) so a low cost of sovereign funding in foreign currency would not have required euro membership. To be sure, a currency risk premium would still have been present as far as domestic currency interest rates were concerned. This would plausibly have dampened the appetite of households for borrowing in local currency.

But it is less clear that a local currency risk premium would have sufficiently insulated Ireland from the temptations created by the global credit surge. The Celtic Tiger period of 1994–2000 had created a plausible boom-narrative which could have been as seductive for foreign investors as for national policymakers.

One corrective mechanism could have been an appreciation of the national currency in those years. An appreciation could have been driven by the capital inflows and it would have had a dampening effect on export demand, led to import substitution and generally imparted a deflationary impact. Whether this would have occurred, what the monetary policy response would have been, and whether it would have been sufficient to offset the euphoria of a property boom in time to prevent its excesses is hard to assess.[14]

The lack of a clear alternative explanation of Ireland's rapid growth experience in the Celtic Tiger years allowed the emergence of this flawed narrative asserting some new and quasi-permanent ability of the Irish economy to outperform other countries in output, employment and population growth. Belief in this narrative during the late 1990s and early 2000s justified, for many, the heavy borrowing to build and buy property.

One wonders whether, against this background, prudential regulation would have adequately discouraged foreign currency mortgage borrowing if a floating exchange rate had been maintained into the 2000s. After all, many other countries were doing such borrowing. And the big developers would have been happy to finance their ventures in foreign currency. Would a non-euro Ireland really have sat out this tidal wave, or would it

---

[14] After all, some of the funds imported through the banking system were channelled bank by the borrowers into property investment abroad; that would have reduced the upward pressure on the national currency. Besides, with strong growth in wages and prices, the *real* exchange rate did actually appreciate in the boom.

have tried to surf it as Iceland and Latvia did, to take two very relevant examples?

Given the euphoric global financial environment of the time, it is not hard to imagine an outsize property boom even in a non-euro Ireland of the early 2000s. After all, as we will see, UK-owned banks were to the fore in the aggressive introduction of risky loan products turbocharging the Irish mortgage market in those years.

Counterfactual Crisis Management

At the risk of anticipating the more detailed discussion of Irish crisis management in later chapters, it is worth addressing here also the other part of the counterfactual or 'what if' question: namely how different would the challenge of crisis management have been if Ireland, outside the euro area, had been faced with the 'sudden stops' of 2008–10, its banking system having accumulated a large volume of foreign currency-denominated debt?

Here the obvious comparator to look at is Iceland. Much discussion focuses on the different treatment of bank debt as between Ireland and Iceland, and we return to this issue in later chapters. But arguably the more important difference lies in the response of the real exchange rate to the crisis. Iceland experienced a sharp nominal depreciation of its currency when the sudden stop occurred as the foreign exchange market sought a new equilibrium given the limitation of new borrowing. Accordingly real wages fell sharply in Iceland (Figure 2.4). Ireland remained with the euro: on average real wages did not fall until 2010 and then, despite reductions in many public service salaries, only moderately. Instead, given the compression of demand especially – but not only – in the construction sector and from the fiscal correction, the consequence was a sharp fall in Irish employment.

If Ireland did not see as large a real exchange rate adjustment as Iceland, even relative to other euro area countries, how was the emerging payment deficit covered? The answer is that, at first, the gap was filled by very heavy borrowing from the central bank, that is to say, the Eurosystem.[15] Thus, whereas some of the contributors to the EMU membership debate of the

---

[15] The Eurosystem is a term denoting the European Central Bank plus the national central banks that are members of the euro area. As we will see, it was from the Central Bank of Ireland that the commercial banks borrowed; but these funds were ultimately sourced from the rest of the Eurosystem.

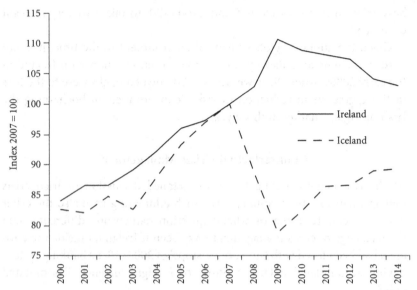

Figure 2.4 Ireland and Iceland: Real wages, 2000–14. (Constant 2015 prices national currency units.)
Source: OECD Statistics.

1990s feared the absence of a lender of last resort for the banking system (Barry 2017), in the end this proved to be a largely misplaced fear. As we will see later, the years of crisis saw last resort loans provided to the Irish banking system on a prodigious scale – with more than 100 per cent of GDP being borrowed from the central bank by early 2011. (That said, an indefinitely large expansion of such finance could not be relied on indefinitely, as also became clear.)

In the financial markets, then, the experience of Iceland is also instructive as to what would likely have happened to Ireland outside the euro. Regardless of whether or not the Irish government in such circumstances would have guaranteed banking debt (relatively much smaller than that of Iceland), it can safely be assumed that, absent a central bank with the ability to lend *à l'outrance* the borrowed currency, the sudden stop of 2008 would have faced Ireland with a financial melt-down triggering an even speedier recourse to the IMF.

SHOULD WE BLAME THE EURO FOR IRELAND'S CRASH?

The European Economic and Monetary Union – to give it its full name, even though the single currency and the central bank were and are still the heart of the regime – entailed something much more than a fixed exchange rate system. And it involved much more than simply an exchange of banknotes and coin. By enacting national laws that redenominated all local currency claims into euros, it drastically raised the bar against any national tinkering with currency values.

And it worked to convince the markets that exchange rate risk between member countries had been eliminated. After all, bond yields in different currencies had differed widely in the decades before the euro began and that was mainly associated – as we saw for Ireland – with exchange rate risk. But as the start date approached, bond yields of member governments converged to a tight band reflecting nothing more than transactions costs. And this tight convergence held through the first decade of the system.

The lack of a risk premium in the interest yield on bonds of countries that had traditionally had difficulty in maintaining internal monetary and fiscal discipline (including Ireland) implies that financial markets held one of two quite different beliefs. Market participants may have believed that those countries would recognize that policy had to be different in this new and tougher exchange rate regime. Or they may have assumed that, despite its uncompromising wording, the EU Treaty prohibition on bailouts of distressed national governments would be bypassed. In other words they may have assumed that, if a country became over-indebted, some form of transfer of resources from other member states would be engineered to make sure that the creditors were repaid on time.

When bond yields diverged again (from late 2008), it was because credit (or default) risk – hitherto almost unknown for EU government bonds – had emerged in response to the crisis.[16] The scale of the global financial crisis; the extent to which it was an asymmetric shock affecting different countries to differing degrees; and the sharp increase in government debt ratios that occurred as governments responded to the recession with appropriately Keynesian measures ensured that spreads widened not just for Greece but for more than half of the original member states including, of course, Ireland, driven by credit risk. And with credit risk came, for a while, a degree of regime break-up risk. Ireland was not immune from these risks.

The fact that Ireland managed to recover most of the lost ground in terms of bond spreads post crisis (with Irish government bonds trading at less than a percentage point above Germany already by the autumn of 2014, and lower later on) shows that the narrowing of interest rate spreads

---

[16] This important shift in the market's expectation was soon validated by the Greek debt restructuring of 2012.

anticipated before membership has not been permanently lost in the crisis.[17] The lesson for me is not that the euro was fatally unsuitable for Ireland to join, but that its introduction was not accompanied by the necessary discipline in national policies.[18] We return in Chapter 12 to the question of how Ireland would have performed had more intrusive bank supervision prevented the property bubble.

Some of the architectural flaws in the design of the euro area now pointed to as culprits are therefore not necessarily to be blamed for the disappointing performance of Ireland in the euro system. Yes, it would have been better if banking supervision had been centralized from the outset (a point already made in Honohan 1991). But it is a stretch to suppose that a central supervisor would have ensured that Ireland (or indeed other euro area countries) remained untouched by a wave of banking failures which swept across the USA, UK, and Switzerland, among others, at the same time. Considering how positive the IMF's 2006 assessment of Ireland's prudential arrangements was, it is easy to imagine that a euro-area supervisor might also not have been sufficiently intrusive to prevent the Irish banks from indulging in excesses.

Above all, it is vital to recall that the supposed solution which is precluded by the existence of the single currency, namely currency devaluation, was used repeatedly by the stressed countries in the past engendering recurrent waves of inflation rather than growth.

The design of the euro area which Ireland joined was robust to the kinds of moderate shock that had been experienced in the decade before it was created. It was hit by a shock which better national policies could have averted and for which the architecture was not sufficient. In particular, as discussed in more detail in the next chapter, a shock of this scale required more collaborative, trusting and collegial action as well as faster and better collective crisis management. Despite these shortcomings, Ireland has survived a turbulent second decade in the system, and ended with employment back at its highest-ever level.

Ireland has probably done as well in the system as it would have outside. Employment growth in the past twenty years was as fast as in the previous twenty. With better domestic policies before the crisis it could have weathered the second decade more effectively, with less of a legacy of personal

---

[17] The average *yield* on 10-year Irish government bonds during 2015–8 was 0.92 per cent.
[18] Fiscal discipline is now more firmly hardwired into the system through the mechanisms developed around the Fiscal Treaty of 2011; indeed, the risk now is that these could prove to be enforced with too much rigidity. Banking supervision has been enhanced with the creation of the Single Supervisory Mechanism.

BOX 2.1 **Foreign Exchange Reserves**

Before turning to the operation of the euro area and its crisis, it is worth making a short digression on the smaller issue of foreign exchange reserves policy over the years. This also serves as a back story to the nationally vital questions that arose about the Central Bank's asset portfolio and the credit and market risks it was taking during the recent crisis. Eventually (as we will see in later chapters) the Central Bank ended up holding a very large block of long-term and very long-term Irish government bonds as a result of the ECB asset purchase programme (QE) and the liquidation of IBRC/Anglo Irish Bank.

The lack of a clear view internationally – beyond rules of thumb such as those used by the IMF for assessing reserve adequacy (IMF 2015) – on optimal foreign exchange reserves policy continues to hamper the development of an agreed and systematic policy in this area. How big should the gold and foreign exchange reserves of a central bank be? What should be the currency composition of the portfolio? Fashions have changed over the years, with an earlier downward trend in the relative size of national reserves sharply reversed after the East Asia crisis of 1997–8, when affected governments decided to reduce their exposure to a sudden stop of capital flows by building up very large foreign exchange reserves.

The size and composition of external reserves was long a central focus of the Irish monetary authorities.

Size

In the early days, the 100 per cent backing of the currency board issues determined minimum holdings of foreign currency. Throughout the sterling link period the Central Bank's foreign assets exceeded the sum of Irish currency outstanding and its liabilities to the banks. During the 1970s, though, policy discussions on reserve adequacy tended to look more at ensuring that the stock of reserves would provide adequate cover for several months of imports. On average, reserves were a bit more than 3 months' cover in those years, drifting lower during the ERM period to about 2 months' imports (in part reflecting the higher share of imports in an increasingly globalized economy).

Adoption of the euro altered the Central Bank's strategy for holding external assets. Having joined a currency union, there was no longer any

BOX 2.1 (cont.)

evident currency-pegging purpose for national central bank holdings of foreign exchange reserves. Some of these were to be assigned to contribute to the Eurosystem's collective external reserves, but the remainder would form an investment portfolio for the Central Bank, generating income to cover operational expenses, as well as a sizable contribution to profits (accruing to the shareholder, namely the government).

Ultimately, this investment portfolio, the evolution of whose overall size is restricted in the euro area by Eurosystem agreements, would prove (as we will see) to be a valuable source of revenue offsetting a sizable part of the direct costs of bailing out the banks.

Composition

In the era of the Currency Commission, external reserves were at first held exclusively in the form of sterling investments.

The diversification of the currency composition of Irish reserves over subsequent decades seems to have been driven primarily by episodes of heightened risk and opportunity.

A modest amount of gold was acquired as war approached and at one point gold holdings amounted to more than a quarter of the official sector's external reserves, though the accumulation of foreign exchange resulting from wartime and subsequent surpluses soon reduced this proportion below 10 per cent. During the war a small amount of US dollars was borrowed in New York and placed on deposit as a reserve in case of need (Moynihan 1975: 245).

The next move towards expanding the range of currencies held by the Central Bank was in 1954, and it was not until 1957 that any significant net amount of non-sterling foreign currency assets were acquired, and indeed until 1968 this segment (at first mainly US dollars) scarcely exceeded 10 per cent.

A larger amount of gold was purchased by the Central Bank in 1968. According to Whitaker (1980) this reflected not so much the widespread speculation about changes in the official US$ price of gold at that time, but was more a reaction to the sterling devaluation of 1967 and fears of further slippage in the value of sterling. The purchases were made by running down sterling investments; some of the proceeds of sterling

BOX 2.1 (cont.)

sales were also used to acquire other foreign assets. Purchases ended when the Bank of England offered a US$ guarantee on official sterling holdings (in what were called the Basle arrangements). To benefit from this guarantee, a sizable block of sterling assets of the commercial banks was acquired by the Central Bank in November 1968, and again the following year. The guarantee was renewed several times and the Central Bank received some £11 million in payouts from the Bank of England before the scheme expired in 1974.

The gold that had been recently bought was subsequently sold during 1969–70, and at the official rate of US$35 per ounce, as the Central Bank adhered to the international agreement to refrain from selling official gold on the open market despite the higher prices there. Whitaker claimed that it had always been the intention to hold that gold only as a transition to other foreign assets. Those opposed to sizable gold holdings always held the fact that it does not generate any income against it. Nevertheless, the old stock of gold was retained.[19]

Curiously, adoption of the euro led the Central Bank to move its remaining investments almost entirely into euro-denominated instruments, eschewing "foreign" currency assets. This policy would insulate the Bank's balance sheet from measured capital losses resulting from exchange rate movements, but it also reduced diversification. In the past decade the Bank has reverted to a more diversified portfolio both in terms of currency composition and in terms of credit and market risk.

over-indebtedness, and damaged careers. Ensuring that this lesson is learnt and remembered and that the needed financial and fiscal discipline is maintained in the third decade is self-evidently vital.

* * *

The debate on the economic decision to join the euro was, for Ireland, relatively finely balanced. The country's economic performance in the five years before membership was of unparalleled success.

---

[19] I recall, as a young economist in the Central Bank, preparing a well-timed memo in 1980 arguing for the sale of the gold at the very high price it had reached (a peak so high that it was not reached again for a quarter of a century). My recommendation was not acted upon, and the Central Bank still owns the old gold bought at the outbreak of World War II. Long stored in the Central Bank's old offices in Foster Place, Dublin, it now sits for convenience and cost in the vaults of the Bank of England in London.

But the political imperative was to membership. Had fiscal and prudential policies been more effective and adapted to the new regime, Ireland's
performance could have continued on a strong but sustainable path with
a setback on the scale that occurred.

It was not Ireland's decision to join the euro that should be faulted.
Instead it was the poor implementation of macroeconomic and prudential
policies at national level (as well as weak – though not altogether absent –
surveillance of these from the centre) that really created the vulnerabilities
that have proved so costly to Ireland: most other member states avoided
excesses on such a scale.

This, at least, is how I have seen matters for the past decade. I do
acknowledge, however, the legitimacy of a wider political economy perspective which is more critical of the euro as a construct. Designing
a system that so sharply punishes weak macroeconomic and prudential
policy may have been a bad strategy for the European Union given the
track record of weak policy-making that has dogged many of the euro
area's early members. From this perspective, seriously imperfect policy-
making by one or more of the member states was inevitable, and the nature
of the system's resilience – robust to modest shocks, brittle in the face of
major errors – was thus likely to result in severe problems sooner or later.
This perspective does not exonerate Irish policymakers. What it does
suggest is that much stronger fiscal and prudential policy institutions
needed to be built if the euro was to remain safe. Some of this has now
been put in place.

3

The Euro Area Crisis

Was there more that the new monetary authorities of Europe, including Ireland, could have done to prevent or mitigate the effects of the global financial crisis (GFC) as it affected the euro area and Europe as a whole? If there was, why was it not done? These questions have resonated in real time over the past decade and will be raked over for years to come. As a member of the European Central Bank (ECB)'s Governing Council for some of the crisis, these are also questions which exercised me while I prioritized the more acute task of dealing directly with the Irish component of the crisis.

WHAT IS THE EURO AREA CRISIS?

The euro area crisis is best seen as a strand of the GFC which broke into public consciousness in August 2007, had its peak in the autumn of 2008, and was gradually resolved over the following years. Each strand can be traced back to the growing scale and complexity of finance in the previous couple of decades and the inadequacy of risk management that accompanied it. The crisis emerged when investors realized that they had underestimated both the scale of the risks embedded in the system and the difficulty of predicting how each instance of over-indebtedness would be resolved: who would bear the losses?

The initial central strand of the GFC was the part that related to the securitization of US mortgages and which has been so exhaustively discussed that it does not require an elaborate description here. Several large euro area banks were severely affected by this strand, and government-funded rescues were put in place in Germany, France, the Netherlands and Belgium, to mention only the largest affected countries. The sums involved were large, but these governments had the fiscal headroom to be able to meet the cost of recapitalizing the affected banks without destabilizing the rest of the economy.

Neither in Ireland nor in the other most severely affected parts of the euro area banking and financial system was entanglement in the problems of the US securities with their 'slicing and dicing' a major contributing factor to what happened next.

The euro area strand separated from the rest of the crisis in May 2010. This was the moment when investor confidence in the prospects for an over-indebted Greek government vaporized. From then on, the euro crisis was a saga of recurrent waves of investor scepticism about policymaking for Greece and for other stressed countries in the euro area.

When they engulf the entire economy, these kinds of episodes are generally referred to as macro-financial crises. The defining feature of most macro-financial crises is what is known as a 'sudden stop': a sharp drop in the access of government or of large parts of the financial sector to finance. Typically the sudden stop reflects a general reassessment by lenders and investors of the recoverability of their claims on the country in question, whether relating to government debt, or to the debt of its chief financial and non-financial firms.

There are numerous historical examples of macro-financial crises (Caprio and Honohan 2015). These include countless currency crises, usually ending in a devaluation. The largest recent macro-financial crisis before the GFC was the one that swept through East Asian countries in 1997–8. But the GFC was much deeper, being surpassed in modern times only by the Great Depression of the 1930s.

The sudden stops in the GFC came in waves as the fears of lenders and investors grew and widened. In August 2007, investors began to worry about the recoverability of their claims – direct or indirect – on funds invested in those notorious securitized mortgages. In the following month, there was a run on a British bank, Northern Rock (which too had used borrowed resources to acquire mortgage-backed securities) as investors and depositors worried about recovering their money. A much larger US firm, Bear Stearns, suffered the same fate in March of 2008.

Policymakers did react in a number of ways during the early months of the GFC in order to contain the widening waves of lender concern. This phase of their protective actions culminated with the US federal government's takeover of the already semi-public mortgage security wholesalers Fannie Mae and Freddie Mac in September 2008. But these policy reactions were insufficient and the number of firms coming under suspicion continued to grow.

Seemingly underestimating the scale and depth of the underlying problems and the speed with which they would accumulate, the US authorities allowed the next big investment bank that faced a sudden stop, namely Lehman Brothers, to collapse into a rather disorderly bankruptcy. The date was 15 September 2008. At that point investor panic became general on an unprecedented scale.

Sudden stops do not come out of the blue. The seeds would have already been sown in any of a number of ways. Three distinct channels are particularly prominent in the list of causal mechanisms that have been observed in such crises: first, exuberant private sector borrowing (and lending), often reflecting low interest rates; for a small economy this implies borrowing from abroad either directly or indirectly through the banking system; second, excessive public sector borrowing; and third, a loss of competitiveness through price and wage increases that have not been matched by exchange rate depreciation.

While developments along these channels can be tracked in advance, the threat any of them poses is often masked by a narrative which suggests that fundamentally new considerations have shifted the acceptable or safe level of borrowing or of cost competitiveness.[1] For example, overconfidence by bank management in the ability of their newly developed financial risk management technology to cope safely with larger levels of credit goes some way to explaining why so many large and well-resourced banks allowed themselves to assume the huge risks which materialized in 2008.

The consequences of a sudden stop affecting large parts of an economy include the downward spending adjustments that follow, both by firms and households that can no longer access the funding that they were relying on, and from others reacting in a precautionary manner and hoarding their resources in preference to spending. There is a flight to safe assets and a reluctance to grant credit. Reduced levels of spending result in a build-up of unsold stocks and in layoffs of workers who are not needed to meet a now reduced demand. The prices of risky assets fall. Hitherto unaffected firms find themselves in financial difficulties; payments defaults grow. In short, there are losses of actual and potential output, involuntary unemployment increases and the distribution of income and wealth can be strongly affected. All of this amplifies the deterioration of confidence, thereby generating a feedback loop.

---

[1] We have already described this phenomenon for Ireland during the boom.

Even if government borrowing has not played a significant role in the build-up of a particular crisis, the fiscal situation usually deteriorates after the crisis breaks. Shrinking tax revenues and growing pressures for spending (for example on unemployment payments) are valuable automatic stabilizers that kick-in to dampen the downturn by protecting the spending power of households; but they add to the government deficit and debt. If large banks are failing, governments will often step in to socialize the private indebtedness of the banks, further increasing the government's indebtedness. Depending on the starting position and the depth of the crisis, investors may infer a threat to the sustainability of the public finances, which will raise the government's borrowing spreads, worsening its finances once more. This too can tend to amplify the deterioration of confidence.

Historians of financial crises have tracked downward spirals of this type unleashed by the initial loss of confidence and sudden stop in countless cases. Each case has its distinctive features, though, and it is this that has often misled observers into taking comfort from the thought that 'this time is different'.

Much of the early discussion of the problems of 2007–8 focused on the novel aspects of the structured finance market and in particular those over-priced mortgage-backed securities constructed in a manner that embodied distorted incentives (and created ample opportunities for fraud) for the loan originators, for those that packaged the loans to create the securities, and for those who provided trusted credit ratings for the various tranches of the securities. But behind this was a larger story of excess in the huge build-up of credit across the world.

The euro area crisis was characterized by sudden stops in Greece, Ireland and Portugal in 2010; Italy and Spain came under pressure the following year, and the crisis spread to Cyprus and Slovenia in 2012–13. Each of the three causal channels that we have mentioned was in evidence: Ireland epitomized euphoric private borrowing; Greece was a case of government over-borrowing; and Italy can be taken as an example where the underlying problem was one of a loss of export competitiveness in a shifting world economy with resultant anaemic economic growth.[2]

---

[2] As is often the case, each country also displayed some elements of the other channels. For example, Ireland also had an incipient fiscal deficit inasmuch as it had been relying on transitory boom-related tax receipts; Greece had a chronic lack of export competitiveness and Italy a chronically high level of government debt.

WHY WAS THE EURO AREA CRISIS SO SEVERE?

There are three competing views as to what made the euro crisis special.

First View: Bad Luck

The first view emphasizes the contrasting experiences of the most affected euro area countries and concludes that it just so happens that the euro area is unlucky enough to harbour more than its fair share of severely affected countries. Sure enough, many non-euro area countries in Europe had parallel experiences, for example Iceland, Latvia (which did not join the euro until 2014, well after its crisis had peaked) and even the UK. But although these outside cases were very severe, the subsequent recoveries were faster. And there do seem to have been spillover effects in the euro area that slowed and weakened the recovery in a way which non-euro countries did not experience.

Second View: Systemic Design Flaws

The second view (already mentioned in Chapter 2) is that the construction of the euro gave it design flaws which should receive the blame for the depth and slow recovery from the crisis. Various flaws are identified including the fact that adoption of the single currency made it too easy *pre-crisis* for both banks and governments to borrow internationally. No exchange rate risk was involved in cross-border borrowing in euro yet the borrowing bank was dealing in local currency. Part of this is undoubtedly true: membership of the euro brought wholesale interest rates in all euro area countries close together up to 2008 (Figure 3.1). There was no exchange risk premium and apparently no perceived credit risk either for euro area governments. Yet the ease with which large cross-border borrowings occurred in the early 2000s regardless of exchange rate risk has to be recalled. The scale of over-borrowing by Latvia and Iceland (both then outside the euro area) suggests that the additional borrowing advantage of having the euro cannot have been decisive in resulting in the scale of borrowing that occurred.

While a more conservative approach to bank supervision would also have helped, and perhaps a single euro area supervisor (such as the Single Supervisory Mechanism which was eventually created in 2014) might have done a more clear-eyed job in restraining the excesses of Irish and Spanish banks, it is hard to consider this lack of banking union a decisive design

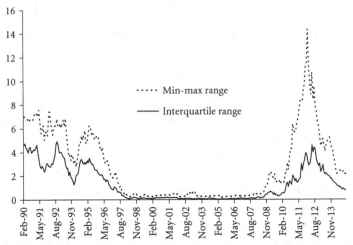

Figure 3.1 Yield spread roughly equals exchange rate risk plus credit risk, 1990–2013.
Sovereign 10-year yields in euro area.
Source: ECB Financial Integration Statistics.

flaw. National supervisors had the responsibility and the powers to exercise that restraint anyway.

One supposed design flaw *post-crisis* is the members' inability to use the devaluation tool to help speed correction of the imbalances that had emerged. Undoubtedly devaluation is one convenient way for policy-makers to quickly achieve a stabilizing adjustment of an important array of relative prices. For example, the sharp devaluation of the Icelandic krona helped speed the correction of Iceland's imbalances at a lower cost in involuntary unemployment than in Ireland, for example (as the consequent reduction in real wages was just what was needed to achieve that end). But of course the inability to devalue is a *feature* of the euro, not a bug. All-too-ready recourse to devaluation in many European countries in the 1970s and 1980s had resulted in high inflation, high nominal interest rates and no sustained trend in competitiveness or growth. This corrosive experience had been one of the main factors driving those countries towards euro membership.

Countries choosing to adopt the single currency as a type of commitment device were thus reacting to the inflationary bias that had crept into policy-making in the 1970s. Although policymakers desired to maintain low inflation, when immediate pressures reflecting the emergence of a generalized loss of competitiveness arose (showing up in the balance of payments or in unemployment) they frequently did devalue in those years. Very often the pressures had been home grown – the result of excessive spending to curry short-term political favour. While devaluation eased the immediate problem, it ensured that expectations of continued inflation driven by recurrent devaluations got built into wage settlements, perennially weakening competitiveness and ensuring that inflation did not actually come under control. This is an example of time-inconsistency in policy: the measures adopted to fix each immediate problem had the effect of indefinitely postponing achievement of lasting stability. Joining the euro was expected to break that trap. As currency manipulation was now out of the question, investors, employers and trade unions could reasonably expect that government policy would be disciplined in such a way that the recurrent need for devaluation – or something equivalent to it – would no longer be baked into the system. The bias towards excessive deficits would be eliminated. After all, adjusting to losses of competitiveness would now be too costly for governments to lightly adopt policies that, while seemingly beneficial in the short run, would lead to the need for greater adjustment later.

This was the macroeconomic logic of the euro, a logic which was understood at the time the euro was agreed on. It was at least as important to the policymakers of the time in the inflation-prone countries as the microeconomic benefits (which lay in reduced foreign exchange transactions costs and reduced price uncertainty: these would help boost trade within the euro area).

While it is a plausible way of dealing with moderate shocks, the problem with any commitment device is that it does impose severe pain if the shocks are too large. Ulysses tied himself to the mast in order to resist the blandishments of the sirens; but if the ship had developed a leak he would have drowned. Even if government is disciplined, there may be a need for overall price and wage adjustment (in order to restore full employment and a balance in payments). Adjustment might be needed in an economy hit by a shock coming, for example, from a surge in the price of oil or some other vital import good, or in a drop in international demand for some product on which the country has a heavy reliance. (The fall in Nokia output in Finland in the last few years would be an example.)

Moderate needs for adjustment can be accommodated over time, especially if the government and the banking system have sufficient access to borrowing to tide over the problem and if the path of adjustment is clear and credible. But if the size of the shock is very large and coincides with a sudden stop of funding, the adjustment will be severe indeed and hard to engineer politically and economically.

If there is a design flaw built into the euro, it is that it was not designed to provide a ready solution to such a severe shock. And that is what happened for a few countries – Greece and Cyprus certainly, and to an extent Ireland – even if the shock was to a large extent home-grown.

Although the scale of the shock was too large for individual countries to absorb comfortably, it could in theory have been absorbed by the euro area as a whole, had it not been for the Treaty prohibition on transfers of resources to bailout an over-indebted member state, including the prohibition on the financing of governments by the central banks.[3] Those prohibitions had been introduced for good reasons. Structurally disciplined and high saving countries like Germany feared the moral hazard of a system that opened the door to such transfers, that is to say the temptation for borrowing countries to indulge in further profligate behaviour in the expectation of repeated bailouts.[4] The more disciplined countries would not have accepted the euro without the protection of those prohibitions.

Had those prohibitions not existed, though, then Europe as a whole could have financed the shocks in a manner that resulted in much less unemployment and loss of output throughout the euro area and especially in the stressed countries. In the end, a considerable amount of financing was provided but, as we will see, too little and too late.

Third View: Policy Errors

This brings us to the third view on what made the euro crisis so severe. This view sets aside the question of regime design and emphasizes instead the errors of policy that were made by governments and by the European financial authorities both in the pre-crisis period and in the management of the crisis itself. Before the crisis, the focus of the ECB had been on building understanding and awareness of the functioning of the euro area as a whole. Statistical (econometric) models of the area were constructed in

---

[3] These prohibitions are found in the Treaty of the Functioning of the European Union (TFEU), which, together with the other primary legal texts of the EU, the Treaty on the European Union and the Charter of Fundamental Rights, consolidates all of the various Treaties agreed over the past sixty years. In this book, 'Treaty', where unqualified, generally refers to the TFEU.

[4] The term 'moral hazard' has long been used in the insurance industry to describe the risk that insurance might encourage reckless behaviour. Its use in political economy came into full flower during the financial crisis.

order to enable the appropriate policy measures to be adopted to ensure that inflation tracked the stated policy of keeping average inflation in the euro area 'below but close to 2 per cent in the medium term'. The specific macroeconomic performance of individual countries was downplayed: differences as between the member states were not seen as an important focus of ECB policy. This should not be overstated: staff did dutifully prepare regular papers on each member state's economy. The Treaty is explicit that national macroeconomic policies are matters of legitimate interest to the EU as a whole, and there was some discussion of emerging imbalances, especially when it came to assessing compliance with the Stability and Growth Pact (SGP) on fiscal policy.[5] However, the fact that France and Germany violated the SGP in the early years without incurring sanctions was symptomatic of the fact that national macroeconomic policy was of secondary concern.

National policymakers in turn seem to have become relaxed about macroeconomic imbalances. In particular, there was much less emphasis on national balance of payments data. Why should one worry about the national balance of payments deficit if there was no danger of the central bank running out of reserves, or overall inflation getting too far out of line? In essence national policymakers acted as if these issues were for the ECB to deal with, and as if the ECB had the power and mandate to do so.

In fact inadequate national fiscal policy and extensive failures of the prudential supervision of banks generated severe imbalances which were temporarily masked pre-crisis by the fact that deficit countries and banking systems had ready access to plentiful flows of international borrowing. But the imbalances were dramatically exposed when those flows suddenly stopped.

Better pre-crisis policy was within the reach of each national jurisdiction. The United States failures and the collapse in international trade and economic activity across the advanced economies in 2008–9 would not have been avoided, but recovery would have been much faster in the countries of the euro area if so many of them had not managed their own affairs so poorly in the preceding years.

After the crisis broke, could management and policy have been better? And if so why were better options not taken? An overarching interpretation

---

[5] The SGP was a rule limiting the scale of government borrowing and debt for euro area countries. Introduced in 1997 chiefly as a way of ensuring that the fiscal discipline criteria for euro area membership would be maintained over time, it has since been expanded and deepened, especially post crisis following the Fiscal Treaty of 2011.

here is that the euro area lacked governance institutions to resolve political differences effectively and to agree quickly on policy responses on the scale needed. The repeated ministerial and summit crisis meetings, often extending long into the night, are sufficient evidence of this.

But were there better available policy options once the crisis broke? I believe the answer to this question is that there were. Indeed, either of two diametrically opposed policy strategies could have resulted in much better overall economic performance had they been adopted soon enough and pursued consistently.

There would have had to be earlier recognition of the scale of the problem and a more decisive course of action. And this action could have been either towards collective socialization and mutual assistance, or in the diametrically opposed direction towards a strict approach to bail-in.

That neither of these courses of action was adopted owes a great deal to an uncritical adherence to an over-interpretation of the agreement that there must not be a 'transfer union' and of the Treaty's prohibition on monetary financing, as well as to an exaggerated and undiscriminating fear of the consequences of bail-in.

The former (no transfer union) could be considered well-justified by residents of the creditor countries given such evidence as the disclosure that the Greek public finances had been misstated and the alarming scale of emerging bank capital shortfalls in Ireland.

The latter (fear of bail-in) is quite understandable given the aftermath of the Lehman Brothers bankruptcy, generally (though not universally) understood to have contributed significantly to the sharp global economic downturn of 2008–9.

This proposition deserves closer examination to which we now turn.

WHAT ELSE COULD HAVE BEEN DONE AND WHY WAS IT NOT TRIED?

The euro area was not alone in displaying ambivalence and indecisiveness. The behaviour of US and British authorities to the early symptoms of the crisis can also be characterized in this way. Still, it is striking that the same features were present even eighteen months after the Lehman Brothers bankruptcy when the distinct euro area strand of the GFC emerged more clearly in May 2010. Even at this stage the European reaction failed to recognize both the scale of the problem and more generally the need to act on a sufficiently large canvas to cover the risk of the problem being much larger. There was also a continued ambivalence about deciding who was to bear the ultimate costs of the hole that was emerging.

In mid-2010, debt restructuring by a euro area sovereign was seen by many in official circles as unthinkable. Such action was deprecated as implying that the creditworthiness of a euro area government had been dragged down to the level of a Venezuela or a Zimbabwe – countries whose chaotic monetary and financial arrangements were often evoked. Yet Europe's political leaders were not prepared to deal comprehensively with the implications of this view. Instead they temporized by providing loan finance that transferred the heavy government debts, even the unpay-able Greek ones, from private to public ownership, prolonging a debt overhang that would discourage investment and leaving required levels of fiscal adjustment which proved to be manageable for some of the debtor countries, but not for others.

Turning the clock back to 2008–9, it is possible to identify earlier points at which more sweeping and decisive action by EU authorities could have been envisaged and where any of a number of comprehensive lines of approach could have been chosen, each of which, it has been suggested, would have resulted in a much less severe euro area crisis. But would they have succeeded? And would they have had adverse longer term side effects? Certainly, these alternative approaches would have differed in their dis-tributional impact, and in their potential to influence longer-term moral hazard.

The two alternative approaches contrast sharply. One would be for Europe to have adopted a liberal and accommodating official approach to debt: this would have entailed a systematic bias in the direction of using collective European public resources to bail out creditors. The other would have adopted a strict approach enforcing creditor losses where bank insolvency or an unsustainable public debt had emerged. We consider them in turn.

(1) An early decision to accommodate in Europe: Would it have worked?
First, consider the stated view of Chancellor Merkel – expressed privately perhaps as early as late September 2008, and more openly by early October – that each country should take care of the failures in its own banks. There would be no pan-European solution, even though it was to be understood that no major European banks should be allowed to follow Lehman Brothers into bankruptcy. This decision seems to amount to two operational rules, each questionable, for deciding on whom the bank losses would fall: first, no bail-in of bank creditors; second, losses to be

absorbed by national Treasuries. Both rules are problematic. The first can be criticized because of the large moral hazard it opens up. Why should investors in bank debt bother to assess the competence and risk appetite of the management of the banks they are investing in if they are certain to be bailed out? (Indeed quite the opposite approach was eventually taken later with the 2014 Bank Recovery and Resolution Directive [BRRD] on resolving bank failures.) Depending on the scale of the problem, the second rule could threaten the sustainability of the government's debt.[6]

Indeed the sustainability of government debt became the centrepiece of the euro area crisis (though mostly not because of bank losses). This brings us to another accommodating mechanism which might have been used sooner and more energetically, namely central bank purchases of government debt. Already in November 2008 the US Federal Reserve had started their first 'QE' program (as such actions are colloquially known, the initials standing for 'quantitative easing'), extending it to cover government bonds early the following year. This would have been a natural thing for the ECB to have considered. Why did they not follow suit?

One reason is that the ECB felt they were doing enough to meet their mandate. From October 2008 they had provided open-ended liquidity support to the banks, thereby substantially relieving the money market blockage that then seemed to be at the heart of the financial crisis. QE would be needed only if interest rates reached a floor, and perhaps not even then.[7]

But lurking in the background was a central preoccupation of ECB staff and many of the national central bank governors. This was their fear that actions that made it too easy for stressed governments to financing their deficits could be seen as a circumvention of the outright prohibition set out clearly in the Treaty, that central banks must not lend to governments nor purchase government securities from the issuer. The reason for the Treaty prohibition is clear: to lend to governments extensively and on a systematic basis would turn the euro from a mechanism delivering low inflation and stability into the opposite. Such concerns are not without substance: history is full of examples where central bank financing of excessive

---

[6] It also fits poorly with the idea of a single European market in banking. If national treasuries are to bail out creditors, only banks headquartered in the largest countries can hope to compete at scale: the value of the treasury backstop depends on the resources of each country!

[7] This was in line with the 'separation principle' assigning different tools to price stability and financial market disruption which was being pursued by the ECB at the time as discussed below.

government deficits led directly to inflation. In a multi-country currency regime, deficits of an over-spending government financed in this way would effectively be paid by holders of cash and other monetary assets throughout the zone: Germans picking up the cost of Greek deficits, as it would be portrayed.

There was certainly a fear in the ECB that outright purchases of government bonds – even in the secondary market – might fall foul of criticism that it was too close for comfort to the prohibited forms of monetary financing of government, even though the explicit prohibition in the Treaty refers specifically only to purchase of government bonds in the *primary* market, whereas that part of QE involving the purchase of government bonds, both as conducted in the United States and as eventually conducted by the euro area central banks in 2015–8, was conducted entirely in the *secondary* market.[8]

Still, such fears would not have been very pronounced in early 2009, when Ireland and Spain still had an AAA rating; with Italy and Portugal at AA. Even Greece was A-rated until December 2009. If QE had seemed necessary to achieve the central objective for which the ECB was established, namely price stability, it could have been introduced then – after all, it was eventually introduced in 2015. But, even though euro area inflation dipped to a record *minus* 0.7 per cent in July 2009, no QE was forthcoming. By May 2009, the ECB had lowered its main policy interest rate to 1 per cent and money market rates hovered just above zero: these actions were seen (rightly as it turned out) as being sufficient to ensure that inflation returned towards 2 per cent before too long. So QE was not embarked on at that point.

But if it had been, it would have helped insulate the bonds of at least some governments from the turmoil that ensued when the depth of the Greek fiscal problem emerged. As we have seen since government bonds were included in the ECB's QE programme in 2015, it is not only the risk-free long-term rate which falls. Clearly, when there is credit risk or a liquidity premium on an asset being purchased in a QE programme, the premia are likely to contract as a result of the purchases. This has been the experience of peripheral euro area countries, whose spreads against the securities issued by Germany's federal government (bunds) has narrowed sharply since 2014 (when the likelihood of their inclusion in a QE programme increased). This is an incidental side effect of a programme being

---

[8] The distinction is fine, but certainly not meaningless. Purchases of government bonds in the primary market could easily occur at off-market prices. Indeed, there are countless historical examples, not only in developing countries, of central banks helping out by acquisition of low-interest bonds that would not be marketable.

undertaken for monetary policy purposes, but it is valuable for speeding a return to conditions of financial stability.

It is fascinating to speculate what might have been the consequences – apart from a boost in overall aggregate demand in the euro area – if QE had been introduced on a large scale in early 2009.[9] Would the Eurosystem being in the market as a big buyer (in particular of Greek debt) have been sufficient to remove the sensitivity of bond investors even to the shocking news of the falsified Greek deficit numbers later that year? Could an orderly adjustment of Greek public finances have been achieved in an environment less pressurized by a rapidly increasing cost of funds? Perhaps not, but the more orderly bond market conditions could likely have meant no need for Ireland or Portugal to have recourse to programmes. And the Italian and Spanish yield spreads might not have widened as much as they did (cf. Figure 3.1).[10]

By May 2010 the ECB did act quickly, though with insufficient force, in the face of the sudden market loss of confidence in some peripheral government bonds, especially that of Greece. It introduced what it called the Securities Market Programme (SMP), and started buying the bonds of Greece, Ireland and Portugal in the secondary market.

But some were concerned that the ECB had overstepped its mandate and was, in effect, supporting the stressed governments of Greece, Ireland and Portugal. How valid were these concerns? Once it had been decided by the EU governments to provide loans to Greece to enable it to service its private debt (however questionable that decision), the SMP was justified as a tool for ensuring a sufficiently effective transmission mechanism, pending the construction by the member states of the agreed lending facility.[11]

Certainly the transmission of monetary policy had been impaired. Interest rates to customers in stressed countries had fallen less than elsewhere. The imperfect transmission of the ECB's low interest rate to weaker economies was particularly unfortunate given that inflation and economic conditions in those stressed countries would, if anything, have justified even lower interest rates.

---

[9] Simulations of a plausible quantitative model by Martin and Philippon (2017) suggest that such a measure could have had a significant effect, even for Greece.

[10] Several scholars have discussed the possibility, also evoked here, of the euro area being prone to multiple equilibria and the possibility of central bank policy to move the area from one equilibrium to a better one (e.g. De Grauwe and Ji 2013).

[11] Since large-scale cross-border support of stressed governments by other governments could not readily be part of the EU structures because of the Treaty prohibition, the lending facilities required innovative legal constructions resulting eventually in the creation of the European Stability Mechanism (ESM), which was set up under a separate treaty.

For me, these disturbed market conditions fully justified energetic action by the ECB to stabilize matters. Yes, it was for governments to find the longer-term solutions for the issue of Greek debt, but meanwhile the ECB should not relinquish its responsibility for ensuring market conditions that would allow the impact of expansionary monetary policy to reach all parts of the euro area.

In the end, even though it was extended to Italy and Spain in 2011 as those countries came under pressure, the SMP was implemented in a half-hearted way throughout and it had generally weak and transient effects on yields. The underlying reason for this half-heartedness was the same hesitation as all along. To intervene more heavily in what, by 2010–11, was the debt of evidently stressed countries would have been to court further accusations of circumventing the Treaty prohibition on monetary financing of governments. Such accusations were already being made, including legal challenges to the Bundesbank's participation in the SMP brought before the German Constitutional Court. Thus, in a manner that would not apply to the central bank of a single country, the ECB found itself hemmed-in by the distributional consequences (as between different member states) of policies adopted in the general interest of the euro area as a whole.

Clearly the moral hazard of such an aggressively accommodating stance vis-à-vis government bond yields could have been severe. How quickly would the deficit governments move to restore balance in their budgets? But then too, the double-dip recession of 2008–13 and the slow recovery therefrom were costly to the whole area.

(2) A strict approach to bail-in: the current mantra, but is it viable?

For those who would advocate a systematically liberal approach to financing in a crisis, there are thus many examples of missed opportunities in the period 2008–11. Yet those who advocate strict policies are not satisfied either: for them the SMP was an unacceptable intervention.[12] In short there was ambivalence here too – and indeed indecisiveness.[13]

---

[12] It is well known that Bundesbank President Axel Weber and ECB Chief Economist Jürgen Stark both opposed the SMP and both were to leave the Governing Council in 2011 before the expiry of their terms, surely to some extent reflecting this opposition (though other considerations were surely also present). Axel Weber's position was interesting: ever the intellectual, he was intrigued by the economic possibilities of innovations such as the SMP, but these thoughts were trumped by the legal and political minefield of monetary financing. Jürgen Stark's concerns were deep-seated: his involvement in and advocacy for the creation of the Monetary Union had been predicated on the assurance that it would not become a 'transfer union' through the back door. For him, the SMP was a step too far in that direction.

[13] Financial market participants had begun to expect an asset purchase programme from the ECB, and market prices reacted badly when that expectation was dashed at the press

The indecisiveness is perhaps best illustrated by Europe's *volte-face* on bailing-in bank debt-holders. The case of the Irish bank debt is discussed in more detail later; but it is by no means the only example. Indeed, no senior euro area bank debt was bailed-in in the euro area before 2013. But, as early as late 2010, some European governments, notably that of Germany (despite it having been one of the earliest to ensure that the debt-holders of the several failing German banks were indeed bailed out in 2007–8), began to advocate a regime in which even senior debt-holders of failing banks would be bailed-in.[14] By 2012 this concept was being formalized in the draft Bank Recovery and Resolution Directive (BRRD – which was enacted in 2014 and became operational from the beginning of 2016). The general notion behind this law (discussed more fully in Chapter 11) is that professional investors such as insurance companies and pension and other investment funds would be the buyers of bailable bonds and would be well-equipped to assess the risks.

Bail-in of private debt-holders of an unsustainable sovereign debt had also by then become accepted, and had already been implemented for Greece. How would the evolution of the euro crisis have looked if, instead of waiting until 2012, bail-in of the holders of sovereign debt had been on the cards from 2008?

For the sovereign borrower whose debt had become unsupportable, namely Greece, the position seems clear. Relative to what actually occurred, it would have been far better for Greece to have undertaken a deep restructuring of its debt as soon as the difficulties became evident

conference of 6 May 2010 in Lisbon following the Governing Council's meeting (one of the rotating meetings outside Frankfurt). Indeed some national central banks had been considering coordinated use of their investment portfolios to help stabilize the bond markets. But more was needed: ideally collective action and urgently. After all, an asset purchase programme could be backed by the collective – and in theory unlimited – resources of the Eurosystem. Adding to the sense of market panic on that day was a sudden dramatic sharp fall in stock prices in the USA; it later turned out that this, the famous so-called 'flash crash', had little to do with the European developments, but it helped concentrate the mind of decision-makers! The Portuguese hosts had arranged a pleasant dinner after the Governing Council meeting at a vineyard just outside Lisbon. Reflecting the felt need to ramp up the ECB's response to the deteriorating market conditions, there were informal, impromptu, discussions after dinner in the somewhat incongruous antique surroundings of the winery building. As wives waited impatiently in another room in the winery wondering just how long the talks would last (so that they could get back to their hotel in Central Lisbon), governors pondered whether an asset purchase programme should, after all, be started up.

[14] Though not before much of the holdings of stressed bank and government debt by German financial institutions had been disposed of. In the opinion of some, calculation rather than dithering better characterizes the change of stance by the German authorities.

in May 2010. That way it would have ended up less indebted to the IMF and the official European lenders (and less indebted overall, having avoided high interest rates for some time 2010–12). There is no doubt that the Greek people would have benefited significantly from early recognition that the level of debt that had been accumulated was unpayable and from early action to correct this situation through a debt restructuring. Yes, the restructuring would have limited Greece's access to future financing and increased its cost. And the whole business would have had a damaging effect on the credibility of Greek governments and on business confidence. There would also have been a confidence impact on other stressed sovereigns (for evidence on this see Cole et al. 2016). But all of these adverse effects happened anyway less than two years later with the difference that Greece now owed more of its debt to other European governments. This official part of Greece's debt has not been reduced (though it carries a low interest rate). Instead it will be rolled over only under circumstances of a resumed degree of external control of the public finances of Greece (cf. Gourinchas et al. 2016).

As to banks, while much more could have been done to hold senior managers accountable for self-serving recklessness, there must also be some doubt as to whether a strict bail-in regime for creditors would in practice have been implemented in a completely coherent and rigorous manner. Even though the fears of contagion across European banking markets (seared into policymakers after the Lehman Brothers bankruptcy) had subsided, there were other obstacles. In several countries subordinated debt had been sold even to middle-income individuals. Bailing-in would mean imposing losses on these customers who had unwittingly invested in high-risk assets. National authorities hesitated to do this.

After the fiasco surrounding the Cypriot bank restructuring, the controversies about the treatment of different sets of bonds in the resolution of the Portuguese Espiritu Santo bank, and the lengthy debates over the use of Italian government resources to protect bondholders in the resolution of several banks in that country during 2015–17, as well as litigation surrounding the 2017 resolution of the Spanish bank Popular, it is clear that bank bail-in is always fraught (a point which we take up in more detail in Chapter 11).

These then are the two sharply contrasting approaches, either one of which could have been pursued systematically – but only one of them. Many confused discussions of the euro area crisis complain that both approaches should have been used; to a large extent the problem was deepened and prolonged by dithering between a half-hearted attempt to do just that.

Flip-flopping over bail-in or bail-out certainly prolonged the agony. It is harder to decide which decisive course of action would have given the best results, but I believe that decisiveness and consistency from the outset would have seen a quicker return to growth and would have avoided the slide during 2012 into a generalized loss of confidence in the survival of the euro.

STEP-BY-STEP TO LARGER SOLUTIONS

It is ultimately a matter for governments to decide on policy issues of bail-in and bail-out, though central banks offered advice and sometimes pressure. Other matters were squarely in the bailiwick of the ECB. Evidently this included getting a positive momentum behind price inflation again in 2009–10. But it also included restoring financial market stability and moving the economy back towards a sustainable growth path, both as ancillary steps to achieving the inflation target and as part of the ECB's secondary mandate to support the economic policy of the Union.

In these matters, the ECB, under the focussed and resolute leadership of President Jean-Claude Trichet, a cultured Breton, had not been inactive from the outset of the crisis. The first task was to try to limit the interruption of credit flows that was emerging as a result of the scramble to hold safe assets amid a generalized loss of confidence. The second task, which emerged only with the downturn of September 2008, was to boost overall economic demand in order to bring the falling price level back towards its objective.

To meet these two objectives the ECB adopted a twin tool approach known as the 'separation principle'.[15] Interest rates would be used for the price stability and macroeconomic goal and 'non-standard measures' to restore the smooth functioning of the interbank and other financial markets. These non-standard measures included temporary relaxation of the rules surrounding the collateral that had to be presented by any borrowing bank and the length of time for which the ECB would lend cash.

The collapse in aggregate demand from late 2008 saw a sharp decline in euro area inflation, which went below zero for a time during 2009. In accordance with the separation principle, the policy interest rate was

[15] The separation principle and its consequences are discussed in greater detail in Honohan (2018b).

lowered from October 2008, ensuring that short-term money market rates (available to the most creditworthy large banks) hovered close to zero from early 2009.

Banks not considered strong enough to secure funds in the private financial markets could get funding from the ECB at its policy rate – down to 1 per cent from May 2009 – in amounts limited only by the collateral they could present as security. And the ECB eased the collateral requirements quite considerably during 2008. Longer-term lending operations were launched by the ECB in order to provide further assurance to banks that there would not be a liquidity squeeze and that they could therefore enter into banking relationships that would entail longer-term lending commitments.

Other innovations included the creation of government-guaranteed own-use bonds whereby a bank without sufficient eligible collateral on its books could, if its government would provide a guarantee, issue a bond to be held by itself, and as necessary presented to the ECB as collateral in order to raise cash.[16]

This separation principle was little more than a heuristic device to help thinking about the myriad of instruments and policy issues that presented themselves (cf. Buiter 2009). But it was not innocuous. It may in particular have led to a serious misstep by the ECB in early 2011. A surge in energy prices at that time threatened to bring average inflation in the euro area above 3 per cent by the end of the year. Should the ECB react to this overshoot of its target by increasing interest rates? Many observers, myself included, felt that energy prices were too volatile for this surge to require an early adjustment of interest rates, especially with uncertainty about wider economic prospects in many European economies. A tentative aggregate economic recovery was only getting under way, and had not started in several parts of the euro area. However, to my surprise, ECB Chief Economist Jürgen Stark did propose a 25 basis point (¼ percentage point) interest rate increase in the ECB's policy rates in March 2011.

I suppose that, for Stark, it was especially important to avoid giving the impression that the ECB was indifferent to inflation, at a time when the

---

[16] I myself was uneasy about the contrived nature of this particular 'own-use' bank bond device to generate eligible collateral (which I understand was a German invention). I agreed to go along with it for Irish banks only when pressed to do so by ECB colleagues who were reluctant to allow an even larger amount of ELA going to those banks in the early months of 2011. As reliance on this device narrowed progressively to banks from the stressed economies, support for use of it waned among members of the Governing Council and a phasing out was decided upon in March 2013.

ECB was operating a programme (the SMP) that he would have seen as lax, risky and legally questionable. Trichet agreed to his proposal, likely in part to help maintain a middle course between the diverse views of members of the ECB Governing Council. A degree of deference to the views of the president is inevitable in such matters, and – although I don't think that I was alone in my surprise at this turn of events – no strong opposition could be detected. Those who actively supported the increase could, after all, argue that, according to the separation principle, the non-standard measures were still available to deal with financial market uncertainty. Even though financial markets were still jumpy, interest rates could (on that view) safely be used target inflation.

But, while a reasonable case could be made for a small rate increase presented as a warning shot against any re-emergence of an inflationary psychology, the more obvious policy would have been to wait.[17] (Besides, no attempt was made to communicate that this would be a one-shot increase.)

Inflation did eventually briefly exceed 3 per cent that year. Nevertheless, a second 25 basis point interest rate increase, made effective in July 2011, was even less justifiable. In 2011 the euro area was suffering from a deficiency of demand which should have been met with continued fiscal expansion; but that had come to a premature end the previous year. Now, higher interest rates would dampen demand further (Eichengreen 2015; Mody 2018).

Soon it became more evident that these interest rate increases had been a mistake. Already in September there was talk of a reduction. It was not quite possible to convince a majority of colleagues on the Governing Council to reduce rates at their Berlin meeting in October, but by the end of the year the policy rate was back to 1 per cent.

---

[17] I was not well-placed to argue effectively for this position, having just succeeded single-handedly in forestalling a proposed technical change in ECB bank lending rules which would have seriously damaged the interests of Ireland. While the interest rate increase was not opposed (there being little point in formally objecting – and some loss of leverage on other issues likely if one did object), I was a bit taken aback to see the decision recorded as unanimous. As scholars had already noted before the crisis emerged, the ECB is among the central banks most anxious to present a united front on important monetary policy decisions (cf. Blinder 2009). This reflects in part its multi-country nature. Most other leading central banks acknowledge diversity of decision-makers' opinions, conducting formal votes monetary policy matters as a matter of routine and publishing minutes that identify individual positions. More recently, especially with the publication of an account of each monetary policy, there has been more acknowledgement of the range of opinions held within the ECB Governing Council.

This mistake was not to be repeated, but it may have contributed to further losses in market confidence in the ability and determination of European policymakers to decisively restore smooth functioning of the system. By late 2011 market fears were extending to Italian government debt and to Spanish and even French banks. A sequence of emergency finance minister meetings and summits of the heads of government failed to reassure.

Markets began to feel that nobody was in charge. Some painted scenarios in which Greece might exit the euro by creating its own currency and defaulting on euro-denominated debt. By making exit conceivable, such a step might lead to irresistible speculative pressure on Portugal. If Portugal too were to abandon the euro, another and another might follow.[18] Ultimately the whole system could be unzipped. Market participants and policymakers began to make contingency plans for the worst.

This was the background to Mario Draghi's historic July 2012 promise to do 'whatever it takes' to save the euro, and his unscripted promise 'believe me, it will be enough'.[19] Presented in London to an audience of financial sector grandees in the presence of Bank of England Governor Mervyn King – a well-known euro-sceptic – the full effectiveness of this statement also depended on there being no demurral from creditor countries; and there was none. This piece of theatre convinced markets that Mario, and the ECB, meant business.[20] It was well understood by specialists that the ECB had the technical capacity to avoid break-up. It also had the legal authority – despite niggling doubts in some quarters that the necessary

[18] The euphemism used was 'redenomination risk'.

[19] By insisting that the tools he was referring to were 'within our mandate', Draghi clearly signalled that the promise was not a casual and personal forecast, but a carefully considered policy intention underpinned by analysis of the legal framework needed to authorize the policy measures that would be needed. www.youtube.com/watch?v=hMBI50FXDps.

[20] Mario Draghi, who succeeded to the presidency of the ECB in November 2011, certainly deserves credit for the manner in which he launched the OMT, thereby shifting the euro area from a 'bad equilibrium' to a good one. Far from being a knee-jerk expansionist, he nevertheless had the breadth of vision to recognize that the euro area economy was at stall-speed and risked collapse if sweeping measures were not adopted. He had carefully prepared the ground and knew the degree to which he could command support. His professional background made him open to innovative financial engineering solutions, and the prolonged period of stagnation had swung the balance of opinion more decisively in favour of expansive action. He was also fortunate in the supportive teamwork led by Executive Board members Benoît Coueré and Peter Praet who were appointed to their positions within a few months of the start of Mario's term. From that point, the Executive Board proved to be more results oriented and less caught up in the ideological disputes that had been evident among members of the Executive Board in 2009–11.

actions could amount to an illegal circumvention of the Treaty prohibition on monetary financing. Carefully choosing from the technical options, the ECB Governing Council soon formally approved the Outright Monetary Transactions (OMT) programme, which gave substance to the London promise. It replaced the ineffective SMP with something that both aimed at, and had a strong legal underpinning for, enabling any country that wanted to stay in the euro (and was compliant with an agreed adjustment programme) to do so. Of course there was a legal challenge to the OMT programme, but the legal construction was sound and the relevant courts approved the ECB's authority to introduce it.

Still, despite OMT, economic recovery in the euro area was slow; forecasts in 2013 envisaged that the euro area could re-enter recession for the third time. What more could be done? All dimensions needed to be explored. Could short-term interest rates be lowered even into negative territory? (Yes, given enough prior notice to allow for adjustment of computer programmes where necessary.) Could use be made of forward guidance on what interest rate policy over coming months would be, departing from the traditional ECB stance of no pre-commitment on rates? (Yes, and this was used with some success to differentiate the ECB's intentions from those of the US Federal Reserve when it started to normalize its interest rate policy in mid-2013.) Could more be done to buy private bonds, stimulating that market and lowering the cost of borrowing for such segments? (Yes; though the scale of the relevant markets is small, so the effectiveness here was limited.) Could banks be incentivised to use ECB borrowings to increase bank credit to the private sector, rather than hoarding it or simply investing in securities? (Yes, one could try; though with limited effect especially when, despite my best efforts, the relevant scheme excluded mortgage lending.)[21] Step by step, the ECB tried almost all possible channels to boost spending and help the recovery.

Despite all that was being done, both inflation and – more importantly – expectations about future inflation drifted lower and it became evident that more was needed. As almost everything else had been tried, recourse to large-scale purchases of long-term government securities could not now be criticized as simply a disguised form of support for stressed governments. Large-scale QE would lower long-term interest rates, flattening the so-called yield curve. It would also shrink credit risk premia on stressed

---

[21] These were the Targeted Long-term Refinancing Operations (TLTROs), first announced in June 2014. They had similarities to the Funding for Lending scheme introduced earlier by the UK authorities.

government debt, a beneficial side effect which would tilt the benefits more in the direction of stressed economies.

Had those euro area governments with sufficient borrowing headroom continued to provide fiscal support to the recovery after 2010, the ECB would not have had to be as expansionary as it has subsequently become.

By 2015 the ECB was deploying a range of expansionary policies on a scale which could not by any means be considered timid or constrained by exaggerated scruples about monetary financing.[22] Gradually inflation edged up and the recovery continued.[23]

* * *

The euro area has not coped well with the Global Financial Crisis, which has tested the brittle nature of the commitment device that it embodies. While it is easy to point to design flaws, and to say that a more comprehensive union, embodying fiscal federalism, would have done better, the designers of the 1990s were determined to get a practical scheme up and running. To go further than they did would have required greater political solidarity between member governments. Had such solidarity been present, management of the crisis within the existing design could have been much better even under the existing architecture.

The system's reaction to the crisis was at first more tentative and ambivalent than the situation required. The ECB started well, but underestimated the scale of the macroeconomic downturn, and was hidebound by an overly constraining interpretation of the Treaty prohibition on monetary financing of governments.

Running repairs on the system have improved its functioning. Monetary policy is less hamstrung by an overly narrow perspective on the appropriate toolbox. The single supervisor and the single resolution authority are helping to raise the level of supervisory challenge to banks.

---

[22] That did not preclude highly critical German media commentary not only on legalistic grounds, but also because the low interest rate environment was especially unpopular in that high-saving country and also because of some fears that growing inter-central bank indebtedness (the so-called TARGET balances) – a side effect of the asset purchase programmes – could begin to present a default risk to creditor countries.

[23] Though not in Greece, which has not been able to benefit as much from the easy ECB monetary policy. For example, the delicate compromises forged over the years enabling QE to go ahead in 2015 could not accommodate the purchase of Greek government debt while its credit rating was so far below investment grade. Emergency central bank lending (ELA) to Greek banks was capped by the ECB Governing Council in June 2015 (as described in Chapter 11).

It is not at all clear, though, that there is the political will for the needed intensification of shared sovereignty. The lack of collegiality that marked decision-making in the early years of the crisis is not entirely dispelled. Solidarity has not yet grown to the point where there is assurance of economic success of the system's third decade.

PART II

CREDIT

4

Safe and Sound Banking

The unsustainable boom that flattered the Irish public finances in the early years of the new millennium had its origin in the gross lending excesses of the banks in Ireland. Accordingly, when the bust came, not only did it expose the underlying weakness of the public finances, but it also resulted in heavy banking losses, some of which were assumed by the Irish government, adding directly and substantially to government debt.

The cautious and conservative banks which had dominated the Irish financial sector for well over a century had been swept into reckless over-lending and proved wholly unable to weather the collapse. In terms of risk-taking, this was far from their performance in previous decades, when, reluctant to lend into the Irish economy, the banks had consigned a large fraction of their assets to the safety of the London money market.

In the 2000s, though, the banks were, without exception, caught up in a frenzy of lending, each determined not to lose its share of what seemed to be a highly successful property financing business. Two UK-owned banks were among the leading players in narrowing margins and growing market share, but the most aggressive market participant was the locally controlled Anglo Irish Bank, for which the government eventually incurred net costs approaching 30 per cent of the bank's total assets in meeting the senior creditors' claims.

Why did Ireland escape bank failures for more than a hundred years and then succumb to one of the most costly systemic banking crises ever experienced in world history? Despite several inquiries, it is hard to understand fully in the cold light of day the influences and behavioural traits that resulted in these banks deviating so far from their hitherto prudent behaviour. Part of the story seems clear enough. Risk management techniques were rudimentary in not focusing on the potential downside of a bubble. Given the collective blindness about the risks they were incurring, the incentives for senior and middle management were all in the one direction: for growth. Some of the executives were buccaneering in their approach. Non-executive directors were insufficiently probing.

All of these remarks could be applied to a number of banks around the world, but the degree was greater in Ireland. Only the Icelandic banking system displayed hubris on a comparable scale. (And the Iceland case involved abuses and excesses along several dimensions that were not much evident in Ireland.)

THE INHERENT FRAGILITY OF BANKING

What is it that makes bank failures such dramatic and costly events? Why has society not found ways of insulating economic activity more effectively from bank failures? If banks are inevitably fragile, will they be displaced in time by some other forms of financial service provider? There are a few home truths, applicable generally and in all countries, that need to be thought through if we are to understand the Irish banking debacle and how it played out.

Why Banks?

There is a certain perceived mystery to the persistence and centrality of money and banking at the heart of commercial activity not just in market economies, but for the past several hundred years. Most historical accounts have the flavour of the 'just-so story'. But today it is less obvious that modern economies need to depend on a single type of institution for carrying out not one but three quite different vital functions: transmitting payments, storing liquid assets and providing credit.

Admittedly, there are forces that could further entrench banks' dominance in this distinctive multi-product role. An earlier trend towards further consolidation of other financial services into multi-purpose financial supermarkets could resume. Such supermarkets, each with a bank at its centre, can embrace fund management, insurance and private equity as well as other services. Indeed the growth, during the decades before the crisis of 2007, of giant universal banks, such as J. P. Morgan Chase, Deutsche Bank, Barclays and BNP Paribas, headquartered in Europe and the USA, seemed to point in that direction. The crisis raised regulatory concerns and doubts about this model, not least because the scale of such banking groups – some of which had several trillion US dollars or their equivalent in liabilities on their balance sheets – represented a concentration of financial risk which was both hard to manage and a threat to overall economic stability. Although renewed regulatory pressures post-crisis have so far had only a limited impact on the average scale and scope of many of the world's largest banks, Irish banks, like others that failed in the crisis, have all experienced substantial downsizing.

All in all, though, it seems equally likely that the distinctive role of banks could be eroded by competition from various forms of technology and social media companies in the years ahead. Futuristic discussion of the potential for distributed ledger or 'blockchain' technology to create an opportunity for new technology entrants to capture significant market share in parts of the financial services business now dominated by banks could foreshadow reality faster than many now suppose (Philippon 2016). If so, households and firms will turn to diverse providers of the different financial services for which at present we look to banks to provide.

But for the present and the foreseeable future, society will require well-functioning banks that do not fail with catastrophic consequences for the rest of the economy. Avoiding systemic bank failure is not something that can be guaranteed without any cost: the prevailing model of how banking services are provided entails each bank having a structure of assets and liabilities that leaves it fragile and vulnerable to shocks.

Insolvency and Illiquidity

In order to mobilize the resources it uses to fund advances to borrowing customers, a bank offers payment services and assurances of depositor access to their funds. This presents two distinct types of risk to the operations of a bank; economists generally refer to these as insolvency and illiquidity. The task of distinguishing these two risks is both essential and the source of much confusion and miscommunication.

Insolvency refers here to the risk that the bank's loans and other assets will not perform as intended and that losses will occur. Insolvency in this sense is sometimes referred to as 'balance sheet insolvency'.

Illiquidity refers to the risk that withdrawals by creditors will bunch together so much that the bank cannot honour its obligations as they fall due. Illiquidity can occur even if the bank has enough assets on its balance sheet to repay what is owed to the creditors given sufficient time to realize the cash value of these assets. Confusingly, the term insolvency is sometimes also attached to this condition, but if so it should be qualified as 'cash flow insolvency'.

This scope for semantic confusion around the word 'insolvency' is especially acute for banks and, as we will see, has been the source of much misunderstanding about the condition of Irish banks in 2008.

The liquidity and solvency risks are not unrelated. If depositors start to suspect that the bank will make large loan losses, they will want to withdraw their funds before others exhaust the bank's resources. Furthermore, a bank that is balance sheet solvent should normally have little difficulty in raising funds in the money market; once again, therefore, a state of illiquidity suggests some doubt in the money market about solvency.

But these two risks are inherent in the services that are provided by banks (Rajan 2018). After all, many depositors want to have access to their funds but don't know exactly when the need will arise. They value the ability to withdraw at short notice: this is a service the bank can provide because it is pooling the funds of many depositors. Provided the creditors' demands are not too strongly correlated, the bank can readily meet them with a small cash reserve and, if necessary (and at additional cost), its own access to the short-term money markets in which other large financial and non-financial firms participate. Furthermore, if a bank confines its lending to borrowers considered 100 per cent safe, then it is limiting its contribution to overall risk-taking in the economy, thereby limiting the economic advances that can be achieved only if some risk is taken.[1]

More generally, by making loans and investments that are less liquid than its liabilities, the bank is providing a valuable economic service. Slavish insistence on matching the maturity of its assets and liabilities would limit the service provided, and accordingly limit the profit opportunity for the bank. Good bank management balances these risks to ensure that the flow of profits is not eroded by frequent recourse to costly emergency funding. Indeed, some scholars argue that the vulnerability to illiquidity is key to keeping bank management on its toes (cf. Calomiris and Kahn 1991). The fact that retaining the confidence of large depositors on a continuous basis is essential to the bank continuing in operation means that management cannot slide into excessively risky investments or ventures.

The most obvious mitigants for these two banking risks are the holding of liquid asset reserves and capital reserves. The greater the bank's holdings of cash, deposits with the central bank or other liquid assets, the less likely

---

[1] Some scholars have suggested that banks providing payment services should be restricted in their choice of assets to risk-free investments such as government bills (see, for example, Chamley et al. 2012).

is illiquidity. But liquid assets are less remunerative than loans and other investments; accordingly the bank needs to trade off risk and return. The lower its liquid asset reserves, the more likely it is to have recourse to costly short-term borrowing from the money market or even from the central bank (whose lending facilities are generally priced to be more costly than market finance).[2]

Whereas liquid asset reserves are part of the bank's assets, capital reserves are on the other side of its balance sheet. Actually, capital is best measured as a residual: subtract the fixed contractual liabilities of the bank from the total value of its assets and what is left is capital. It represents that part of the bank's assets that is financed by the shareholders (and other risk-taking providers of funds). Its importance lies in the fact that the bank can absorb losses up to the value of its capital and still be able to meet, eventually, the claims of other creditors.[3]

Capital Adequacy Requirements

Capital adequacy requirements are the foundation of today's prudential regulatory policy. If a bank has enough capital, it will be able to withstand even large shocks without loss to its creditors: the shareholders and other providers of risk capital will absorb the loss instead. Ensuring that banks actually have enough capital (and that requires a reliable estimate of the true recoverable value of their assets) is the most essential part of bank supervision.

In the old days, even before there were regulatory requirements, bankers all over the world maintained capital reserves. That is because bankers wanted to be able to stay in operation in bad times as well as good. Over the decades though, as bankers' confidence and their ambitions for profit both grew, capital reserves fell sharply. Starting in the 1980s, trying to restrain this fall in capital reserves, regulators negotiated international agreements on bank capital, especially on how much capital would be regarded as

---

[2] A peculiarity of the USA is that the interest cost of borrowing from the Federal Reserve's discount window is usually lower than market rates, but banks borrowing there have traditionally been seen as incurring an implicit reputational damage.

[3] When a bank starts up, the equity shareholders will invest a capital sum in the assets of the bank, but are not promised any particular return. As profits are made and retained, the capital of the bank grows. If losses are incurred, the capital shrinks, thereby providing a buffer protecting the creditors of the bank from losses. Only if the losses are so big as to wipe out the capital does (balance sheet) insolvency occur.

adequate in a bank's balance sheet and what kinds of risk-taking claim on the bank should count towards this requirement.

The Basel I accord, agreed in 1988, set a capital standard for internationally active banks at 8 per cent of the bank's risk-weighted assets. The Basel I risk-weights were rather crude rules-of-thumb: a claim on the government of an advanced economy was assigned a risk-weight of zero, a residential mortgage had a risk weight of 50 per cent and so on. And not all of the capital requirement had to be in the form of equity: certain subordinated or 'junior' forms of debt liability could also be counted towards part of the capital requirement (essentially because too they could absorb losses in the event of a liquidation before the depositors and other 'senior' creditors would suffer).[4]

The Basel II accord was negotiated in the early 2000s and was intended – among other things – to add sophistication to the risk-weighting of assets. Banks could use their own internal statistical models to estimate the relative riskiness of different elements of their asset portfolio and, subject to the approval of their national supervisors, use the resulting risk-weights in lieu of the standard weights. The Basel II framework added considerable complexity to the whole process of determining capital adequacy and offered banks a way of reducing the amount of capital they would have to hold. While it was being brought into operation in the early 2000s, risk-management resources of the banks and the supervisors were arguably diverted from their main function towards constructing and policing statistical models that were being designed by banks chiefly to reduce risk buffers.

Thus, even when seemingly tighter requirements were imposed by the regulatory authorities, the complex rules defining them were cleverly exploited – especially by the larger banks – to shave down the real impact of the requirements. By the time of the crisis in 2007, the cushion of capital was far too thin.

The Global Financial Crisis broke just as Basel II was becoming operational. It accelerated the dawning realization that Basel II was easier for banks to manipulate than Basel I had been, and that the introduction of

---

[4] Interestingly, the business model of one of the first Irish financial firms to fail in the recent crisis was said to involve borrowing in order to invest in such subordinated liabilities of banks, eligible as regulatory capital. This unregulated firm was called International Securities Trading Corporation (ISTC) and it was run by Tiarnan O'Mahoney, who had previously been chief operations officer of Anglo Irish Bank. In November 2007, having lost the best part of €1 billion, it entered an examinership which left investors recovering only a few cents per euro invested.

these complexities had resulted in inadequate capital buffers. The fact that subordinated debt was, in most legal systems, useful as a buffer only in the event that a bank was liquidated also led to the realization that higher requirements should be set for going-concern capital, mainly in the form of equity, but also in the form of new types of 'bail-in-able debt', so that banks could continue to trade through a severe downturn. These and other reforms were introduced in Basel III after the crisis.

Choosing a level of capital adequacy and defining which liabilities will count towards the capital requirement are not the only problem posed for a regulator wishing to ensure that a bank has sufficient buffers to absorb losses while being able to meet the claims of its depositors and other senior creditors. Unfortunately, relying on accounting measures of capital does not provide a reliable indication of how much loss absorption capacity a bank – or a banking system – really has. The main problem lies in valuing the assets. International standards define how this is done, but current standards do not take full account of the impact of expected future losses in an uncertain environment. (New accounting rules to do so are coming into effect progressively between 2018 and 2021.) This is one of the reasons that banks (and their official supervisors) could claim that banks had plenty of capital just before they collapsed into insolvency (Jordà et al. 2017).

Decades ago, liquid asset reserves were also subject to regulatory requirements. Indeed, there was more policy emphasis on liquid asset reserves in the 1960s and 1970s than on capital reserves. In those days liquid asset reserves were used not just for prudential purposes but also for the monetary policy purpose of limiting credit growth to prevent inflation and other forms of macroeconomic overheating of the economy. (Liquidity requirements were also used as a covert way of easing governments' borrowing costs inasmuch as the government was the main issuer of securities eligible to be treated as liquidity reserves.) But over the years, the apparent efficiency of the interbank markets made prudential liquidity requirements seem redundant. A bank that ran short of cash could readily obtain whatever it needed at short notice from the interbank market. In addition, new techniques of monetary policy, based on steering whole-sale interest rates, meant that central banks could maintain price stability without requiring banks to hold sizable liquid asset reserves. Thus in the years before the crisis, prudential regulators and central banks had allowed the liquidity requirements to shrink or lapse.[5]

---

[5] Basel III has also greatly strengthened liquidity requirements since the crisis, indeed to an extent which may be misplaced.

Banking Collapses through History

The virtual collapse of the world's interbank markets in September 2008 was the epicentre of the crisis. Access of banks to money market funding was sharply reduced as a result of the sudden and widespread increase in perceived bank solvency risk in Europe and America. Banks feared that their counterparties might be insolvent. They woke up to how opaque were the risks in the famous sliced-and-diced derivative securities built on the US housing market. And they realized with shock from the Lehman bankruptcy that central banks and governments might not always bail out creditors of even a large failing bank. Any bank that did have surplus cash began to hoard it for fear that it too might find it difficult to borrow when needed. For those that were able to secure it, the cost of interbank borrowing increased sharply. Lenders required increasing quantities of collateral against such borrowing. Several banks were unable to secure the liquidity they needed.

In Ireland at that moment, Anglo Irish Bank was already in a liquidity squeeze, and it was on the verge of not being able to meet repayment obligations, leading (as discussed in Chapter 7) to the call for a government guarantee of bank liabilities.

Market concerns about bank solvency proved to be well-founded, especially for European banks. Sizable prospective loan and investment losses threatening to bring capital below the regulated minimum, and in some cases below zero, were eventually uncovered not only in Lehman Brothers but also in a range of other banks from Hypo RE in Germany to RBS in Britain, and from Anglo, INBS and AIB in Ireland to all of the Icelandic banks. The US subprime mortgages were not the ultimate main source of these problems. For this we must look to the wider exuberance of bank lending and investment policies in the early years of the new millennium.

Nothing like the severity of the peak weeks of the global crisis in 2008 had been experienced for at least eighty years. A smoothly functioning money market had been taken for granted in most advanced economies for decades. Emergency liquidity assistance (ELA) from the 'lender of last resort', i.e. the central bank, had become rare indeed.

But bank balance sheet insolvency was far from unknown in advanced and emerging market economies even in the last quarter of the twentieth century. The US savings and loan industry in the 1980s, Nordic banks in the early 1990s, Japanese banks in the 1990s and banks in several East and South East Asian emerging market economies in 1997–8 had all encountered relatively severe problems. Even the UK had seen problems, albeit minor, in the so-called secondary banking crisis of the mid-1970s.

More widespread, extensive and severe banking problems were encountered in a large fraction of developing countries. Indeed, according to one count more than 120 systemic banking crises around the world were recorded between 1970 and 2006 (Laeven and Valencia 2012). Some of the most spectacular of these arose when an unsustainable macroeconomic and asset price boom burst. Often this happened following a liberalization of previously repressed banking systems. Famous examples come from Argentina, Chile, Korea, Indonesia and Thailand. In less developed countries government directed lending and other forms of government intervention were the main drivers of bank insolvency. Cameroon, Côte d'Ivoire and the Philippines provide examples of this. And in a few cases banker corruption or self-dealing seems to have been at the heart of the problem (Dominican Republic, Venezuela).[6]

But the problems of 2008 were more widespread and affected larger banks in more countries than any previous crisis. In Chapter 11 we take up the story of how other European countries dealt with these problems; but first let us look at the Irish story.

Irish Banking before the Bubble

As in many other countries, the early history of banking in Ireland in the eighteenth and early nineteenth century is replete with recurrent small bank failures, often seemingly of the banker corruption or self-dealing variety, as well as cases in which poorly managed banks were unable to weather macroeconomic downturns. The 1856 case of the Tipperary Bank and its notorious boss John Sadleir, MP, who was expelled from parliament when it turned out that he had been helping himself to the resources of the bank, is the classic example of the first type, i.e. corruption. Although insider fraud was also involved in the Munster Bank's failure in 1885, that case chiefly illustrates the second variety: poor management. Munster Bank was resolved without eventual losses to depositors and

---

[6] I was fortunate enough to be working on these issues at the World Bank during the late 1980s and again around the turn of the century, allowing me to get an insider perspective of these problems, the costs they imposed and some ideas about how to reduce their frequency and deal with the clean-up when they occurred (Caprio and Honohan 1999, 2015; Honohan 1997; Honohan and Klingebiel 2003; Honohan and Stiglitz 2001; World Bank 2001).

effectively relaunched as the successful Munster and Leinster Bank, later folded into Allied Irish Banks (cf. Hall 1949; Ó Gráda 2002; Ollerenshaw 1987).

As in Britain, the smaller early Irish banks, which had been established as partnerships, gradually disappeared in the mid-to-late nineteenth century as a result of competition from the new joint stock banks with their ability to mobilize resources more effectively on a large scale.[7] The Bank of Ireland, which received its royal charter in 1783, was the first of these joint stock banks, and remained the leading bank, serving almost as a central bank for close on 150 years. It was followed by several other joint stock banks in the course of the early nineteenth century, providing competition for the Bank of Ireland and each focused on catering to a distinct geographic or social group.

The Munster Bank failure was the last significant banking failure in Ireland for a century and a quarter. How can this long period of stability be explained, when we have seen that so many other countries experienced banking crises in the twentieth century? And why did the period of stability come to an end so dramatically?

After all, there was much economic turbulence in Ireland in that period, including the turmoil of two world wars, the troubles embodying the War of Independence, the Civil War, the Great Depression, and severe recessions in the mid-1950s, the mid-1970s and the early 1980s. Through this period, only a couple of small banks went under (Ken Bates' Irish Trust Bank in March 1976; Patrick Gallagher's Merchant Banking Ltd in April 1982).

The conservatism of Irish banks in that period mirrors the behaviour of British banks in their reliance on short-term lending and their maintenance of a high proportion of liquid assets with negligible credit risk (Collins 1991). Finding few limited lending opportunities that suited their risk appetite, the Irish banks placed very large surplus funds in the London money market. Before 1950 the net foreign assets of Irish-licensed banks fluctuated between 32 and 55 per cent of Irish gross national product (GNP). As late as 1967 the figure was higher than 10 per cent.

Largely in broad-based private ownership, most of the banks continued to be associated mainly with the social or geographical groups to which

---

[7] Among the partnership banks, even the family bank of the animator of the Bank of Ireland, David La Touche, had faded away by 1870; the victim, it was suggested, of too much forbearance to its borrowers, or perhaps an excess of religiosity in the family (McGinley 2004).

they had catered from their establishment in the nineteenth century or before, and they continued to make their profits from provision of a limited range of short-term banking services to which – following the British model – they had largely confined themselves. As such they were less exposed to the kind of credit risk that might have been triggered by economic turbulence. (The government did create two development banks, the Agricultural Credit Corporation for agriculture and the Industrial Credit Company for industry, in the 1920s and 1930s but these were relatively small.)

Cartelized throughout much of the twentieth century, banking in Ireland operated with high interest spreads and other charges. It was sufficiently profitable to enable top bankers to satisfy their personal income ambitions, while still delivering the stable flow of dividends expected by their equally conservative dispersed shareholder base (Ó Gráda 1993).

Bank profitability was further underpinned by a wave of consolidation that got under way in the late 1950s. Already the two Belfast-centred banks were subsidiaries of larger London-based concerns. Then Bank of Ireland acquired two of the other five main banks. This triggered in turn a merger of the remaining three to form Allied Irish Banks (AIB). This consolidation seems to have been encouraged by the public authorities, perhaps fearing growing competition from American and other foreign banks, and also in the hope that economies of scale would be achieved. When external competition failed to materialize on any noteworthy scale, the two groups that emerged from this initiative dominated the market with a combined share of 60 per cent or more, depending on how the market is defined. It was not until the 1980s that the cartel formed by this generally profitable oligopoly was substantially disbanded.

Conservatism and market power probably helped the Irish banks survive the deep recession of the 1980s. They were not excessively exposed to some of the major corporate collapses of those years (Irish Shipping, Irish Steel and the slightly later GPA and Goodman Group), as those firms had sourced most of their funding abroad.

Gradually some of these traditional behaviours evolved in ways that reduced the buffers and increased the risks. But the long period of banking stability had likely lulled bank directors and the official supervisors into a false sense of security.

There were some straws in the wind. The most spectacular example was the sudden failure (discussed in Chapter 5) of AIB's insurance subsidiary Insurance Corporation of Ireland (ICI) in March 1985, shortly after its acquisition by AIB. That AIB had not detected the scale of risks that had been assumed by the re-insurance activities of ICI's London branch should have raised concerns about the quality of the diligence exercised before the acquisition.

A few years later (1990) the same bank was hit again when, in one of the largest such frauds recorded anywhere up to that time, John Rusnak, a currency trader in its US subsidiary AllFirst Bank, ran up losses of US$691 million (Creaton and O'Clery 2002). And during the early 1990s Bank of Ireland experienced sizable losses in its recently acquired US banking subsidiary First New Hampshire.

Although not large enough to threaten the solvency of AIB or Bank of Ireland, these events should have revealed that Irish banking as it had evolved by the late twentieth century was no longer the risk-free business it had been. Instead, in line with trends in Britain and elsewhere, bank managements were placing increasing focus on market share and new profit opportunities. But neither they nor the official supervisors had adjusted their mindset to the risks entailed by their new approach. Probably both considered that these specific events, occurring as they did in foreign subsidiaries, were exotic exceptions that need not generate a fundamental reassessment of their approach to risk.

Up until the 1980s it was specialized 'building societies' rather than the main banks that provided most residential mortgage credit in Ireland. They did so based on their ability to mobilize retail deposits thanks to a favourable income tax arrangement that operated with respect to build- ing societies.[8] From 1986, though, the tax treatment of bank and building society deposit interest was harmonized. That tax change, together with other legislative changes – especially those designed to improve govern- ance of building societies – led to a rationalization of the mortgage credit system with banks and (a diminishing number of) building societies providing mortgage credit on what was described as a 'level playing field'.[9] In subsequent policy action some years later, controls over building

---

[8] The societies paid interest net of a standard tax charge which released the depositor from any income tax liability on the interest received. Not only was the standard tax charge (called the 'composite rate') seen as advantageous by many depositors, but the lack of any individual reporting was sometimes seen as allowing untaxed income of depositors to be hidden.

[9] These changes arose from the April 1986 recommendations of an interdepartmental committee set up by the government and chaired by myself, then Economic Advisor to Taoiseach Garret Fitz Gerald. The committee's recommendations also addressed the self- perpetuating nature of building society boards of directors which, despite the nominally mutual institutional structure, were not effectively controlled by the members, and which had presided over a variety of commercial practices not evidently in the interest of the members.

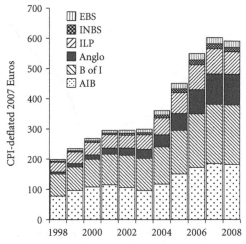

Figure 4.1 Total assets of six Irish banks, 1998–2008.
Source: Banks' Annual Reports.

societies were further relaxed, allowing the remaining two societies to enter also into property development finance (with fatal consequences). (In what follows I will generally refer simply to banks, distinguishing the two remaining building societies only where that legal status is relevant.)

THE GREAT IRISH PROPERTY BOOM

The Credit Build-up

The great Irish property boom was an instance of the international financialization excesses of the turn of the millennium. It got under way from about 1995. There was one brief interruption in 2001 and an acceleration in the period 2004–6. As in the USA, UK and Spain at the same time, Irish banks sharply expanded their lending to property developers and to residential mortgages in a rising market. Relative to the size of the economy, the scale of this lending in Ireland was much larger than in those other countries, reflecting the ease with which banks could now tap the extraordinarily liquid international financial markets (cf. Figure 4.1 which shows the growth in the assets of the Irish-controlled banks).[10]

---

[10] Though this relative scale was greatly exceeded by Iceland – a much smaller economy less than one-tenth of the size of Ireland. See Ó Riain (2014) for a sociological account of the Irish financialization in its international context.

Figure 4.2 Dublin real house prices, 1971–2018.
Source: Pre-1996: Department of the Environment new house prices (Ireland) (quarterly entries interpolated from annual series); 1996–2004 ESRI series (Dublin); 2005–18: Central Statistics Office (Dublin).

The sharp fall in Irish interest rates as membership in the euro area neared during 1998 represented one impulse contributing to tolerance of higher property prices. The fact that there need be no exchange rate risk involved, as the banks' international borrowing and the lending to households could both be in euros, likely also played a role.[11]

This borrowing not only allowed the financial of transactions in the existing housing stock at rapidly appreciating prices, but also financed a huge increase in housing construction. Credit pushed up prices and the price rises encouraged a greater demand for credit as more and more people sought to get into housing before further rises put home ownership beyond reach. By lending to homeowners, the two big banks felt they would easily recover what they had advanced to the builders and developers. At first this may have seemed to be working well. The substantially increasing supply of housing seemed to have no effect in dampening the price rise until the winter of 2006–7, by which time Dublin house prices in real terms (adjusted for the general cost of living) had risen by 400 per cent since 1995, an increase for which it is not easy to find many international rivals (Figure 4.2).

[11] Even when they borrowed in US dollars or sterling, the banks could turn these into euro liabilities through the swap market.

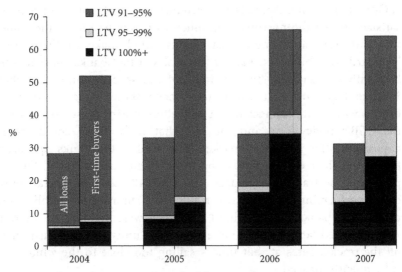

Figure 4.3 Share of new mortgages at high loan-to-value ratios, 2004–7.
Source: Department of the Environment Housing Statistics.

Loan-to-value ratios were high and showed a strong tendency to increase as the bubble persisted and as the banks reached further down the income scale in mortgage lending to households. The higher the prices went, the greater the risk that they would fall back. But instead of insisting on a larger buffer against such a price fall, they lowered their requirements with regard to how much of the property's value the purchaser should have saved themselves. Indeed, the fraction of loans where the value of the property was more than 10 per cent above the loan value shrank year after year. In other words, the banks increased the proportion of their lending that went to very high loan-to-value (LTV) ratios of greater than 90 and even 100 per cent. By 2006 more than a third of mortgages granted to first-time buyers were at 100 per cent (or more) (Figure 4.3).

This innovation in lending technology was not home grown. It was Ulster Bank, a subsidiary of the UK bank RBS, that introduced the 100 per cent LTV residential mortgage to Ireland in 2003. Interestingly, though, this counterintuitive pattern of increasing LTV ratios was not observed in the contemporaneous US housing boom (Adelino et al. 2016).

A more forgivable mistake was the decision of the banks (beginning with Bank of Scotland's Irish subsidiary) to offer tracker interest rates which specified a fixed spread over the European Central Bank

(ECB)'s policy rate. Actually this product was, in theory, much more satisfactory for the borrower inasmuch as it was free from the somewhat arbitrary adjustments that banks could make to their other 'standard' variable rates. Part of the problem that banks subsequently had with trackers was the tightness of the spreads, often less than 1 percentage point, at which they made these loans. Even more critical was the disconnect which opened up during the crisis between the ECB's policy rate and the rate that Irish banks could secure deposits in the wholesale market. The weaker the banks appeared, the higher their cost of funds; the higher their cost of funds, the less profitable the tracker mortgages. During 2010–12 in particular, most of the performing tracker loans in the banks' mortgage portfolio were costing the banks more to fund than they were yielding in interest. As mentioned later, banks took every opportunity to move customers off the tracker rates at that time – sailing too close to the wind, as it subsequently proved.

Ireland was not the only location of the properties that were being funded by the Irish banks. With their sizable footprint in Northern Ireland and Britain, it is not surprising that the banks did sizable lending secured on properties there. And in addition, developer finance was provided for many ventures further afield: the USA, China, Eastern Europe and beyond.

This kind of behaviour was seen in many other banking systems during the boom years. But the Irish boom was distinguished by its outsize scale. The vulnerability to a property downturn was existential for the Irish banking system to an extent not matched elsewhere.

Government policy in Ireland also fomented the bubble, with extensive tax incentives for construction introduced and prolonged pro-cyclically. At the height of the boom, tax concession schemes existed for a long list of categories including the promotion of urban renewal, rural renewal, multi-storey car parks, student accommodation, buildings used for their level educational purposes, hotels and holiday camps, holiday cottages, park and ride facilities, 'living over the shop', nursing homes, private hospitals and convalescent facilities, sports injury clinics and childcare facilities (Honohan 2010).

More generally, fiscal policy in the 2000s was considerably more expansionary than it appeared at first sight because of the transitory surge in tax revenues coming directly from the property boom. This also helped support demand for housing.

The End of the Boom

The Irish property price and construction bubble came to an end in early 2007. As is often the case in property markets, the fall in prices in the few transactions that occurred was slow but sure, and it continued for the following five years. Construction activity stalled more abruptly, with employment in the sector halving in two years. Irish property prices overshot what might be thought of as their steady-state path. After falling by 54 per cent from peak to trough, there was a strong recovery from mid-2012. Nevertheless, after ten years, average residential property prices in the Republic were still more than 30 per cent below the peak. In Northern Ireland (where the same banks also dominated the market) property prices fell as far peak to trough, and recovered more slowly.

With property-related lending having grown to account by 2007 for more than two-thirds of the average Irish bank's lending, these price declines devastated the recoverable value of their loan assets. Inasmuch as they had planned on selling on the property for which they borrowed, the capacity of developers, builders and buy-to-let purchasers to repay the loans they had taken out was severely undermined. Numerous small enterprises had also encumbered themselves with loans used to buy or build properties part of which they envisaged selling or renting; the unprofitability of such ventures was also becoming evident. The general economic decline, partly a knock-on effect of the collapse of construction, partly a reflection of reduced demand from the global downturn, also had its effect on the recoverability of business and residential loans. Owner-occupier households facing negative equity and suffering income losses or unemployment added to the growing stock of non-performing loans.

By 2009 it was evident that Ireland had been hit by what, in relative terms, was going to be one of the costliest banking collapses in world history. The costs of the boom and bust went far beyond the financial losses of the banks and the knock-on effect on the public finances. There was also a devastating effect on the finances of numerous households that had become over-indebted. The normal activities of numerous small businesses that had got diverted into a side-business of property development were also disrupted. The sudden collapse in construction activity triggered a massive increase in unemployment that would take a decade to be eliminated.

The main protection that a society has against its banks failing is the responsibility which the management and the directors of the bank have to operate the bank in a safe and sound manner. (This is supplemented by official regulation and supervision, discussed in the text that follows.) In considering what went wrong we should first and foremost ask why the bankers failed in this respect.

Why Did Bank Management Let It Happen?

It is worth bearing in mind that the boards of the main banks included some of the most highly regarded business leaders in the country. The senior managers were well remunerated: aggregate cumulative remuneration of the CEOs of the six local-controlled banks 2002–8 came to more than €70 million.[12] Accordingly their interest was in maintaining their banks in business: these flows on that scale would not continue for them when the banks failed. The large errors that were made must have reflected a fundamentally flawed awareness on the part of these people about the nature and scale of banking risks and a wholly inadequate approach to risk management.

Six locally controlled banks accounted for almost four-fifths of the total stock of domestic bank lending in 2007; the subsidiaries of two large UK banks accounted for almost one-sixth, and most of the remainder related to Belgian-, Danish- and Dutch-owned concerns.[13] Not one of these banks escaped severe loan losses sufficient to wipe out most or all of its capital. It is hard to explain this pattern without assuming that all of the banks were hit by a shock against which they had built insufficient protection.

Clearly every one of the Irish banks got into trouble in part because its management and directors were caught up in the mass psychology of an unprecedented property bubble – the steepest and longest of the several national property bubbles of the late 1990s and early 2000s around the world. They were influenced by similar though not quite so vigorous property price booms in the UK and the USA, their usual reference points for good banking practice. Because of their shared

---

[12] Anglo comes top of the list with €19 million, followed by Bank of Ireland, AIB and INBS with €17 million, €12 million and €10 million, respectively. The vivid account by Ross (2010) provides much colour on such matters.

[13] In order of size these were AIB (Allied Irish Bank), Bank of Ireland, Anglo Irish Bank, ILP (Irish Life and Permanent) and the two much smaller building societies INBS and EBS.

and common optimism, they lowered their guard and did not consider the consequences that would ensue if and when the bubble burst. Instead, they lent more and more, and in particular to property developers.

This indeed was the conclusion of the 2011 Report of the Nyberg Commission of Investigation into the Banking Sector which spoke about groupthink. But that inquiry was held behind closed doors and the report did not flesh out that conclusion in a way which would allow a satisfyingly deep understanding of why risk management at the banks failed to prevent disaster. The inadequacies of the risk culture inside the two worst banks (Anglo and INBS), each with its buccaneering style and business, models centred on relationship lending mostly to property developers, are well described in Carswell (2011) and Lyons and Curran (2013). The two larger banks, AIB and Bank of Ireland, await comparable treatment. It continues to puzzle outsiders how the governance and systems of the two big banks could have failed to prevent resulted in losses on what was (as we will see) – especially for AIB – an astonishing scale.[14]

If the questioning at the public hearings of the 2014–6 Oireachtas Banking Inquiry, extending over hundreds of hours and covering some 136 witnesses, had been conducted in a more systematically probing manner, they might have thrown more light on why those in charge at the two largest banks – some of the most experienced and respected businessmen in the country – allowed their banks to be managed into failure. As it was, the Inquiry provided only glimpses of what must have gone wrong (see Box 4.1).

It is possible to raise questions about operational mechanisms such as the role of explicit or implicit incentives for staff to expand property-backed loans; the pressure on senior management in the less proactive banks to respond to the more aggressive and buccaneering banks, such as Anglo and INBS, in order not to lose market share; or the cost of having contracted for floating rate loans at fixed tracker spreads above the ECB policy rate. But all of these aspects, valid though they are, are clearly secondary in their relevance to the

---

[14] Lunn (2013) has drawn from recent psychological research in behavioural economics to identify seven common behavioural biases that were likely at play in the behaviour of bankers (and others) in the boom. Casey (2018) catalogues the universal failure to foresee the scale of the banking and macroeconomic risks that were being taken in Ireland.

BOX 4.1 **Glimpses of the Banks' Risk Culture from the Banking Inquiry**

Evidence to the Oireachtas Banking Inquiry (archived at https://inqui ries.oireachtas.ie/banking/) throws some additional light on how things went wrong inside AIB and the other banks. For instance, the hearings illustrate ways in which bank staff incentives were not aligned with prudence.

One AIB managing director (Donal Forde) recalled (to the Inquiry) his expressed concerns in 2006 that 'many of the people involved in credit management in AIB had never seen bad times. That was an anxiety.' But he acknowledged that 'we had come to accept that large exposures to individuals who were long-established in the property and construction business were acceptable' and that accordingly not much action was taken to remediate the routine approval of exceptions to the bank's large-exposure limits. Some senior managers of the bank were themselves involved in property speculation, and that was seen as providing AIB with helpful market knowledge. Branch managers were not rewarded for increased volumes of lending (as they did not have the authority to make large loans), but they were rewarded for increased profit generation, which incentivised them to originate loan proposals.

As to the bank directors, testimony of the 2005–9 Chief Executive Officer of AIB (Eugene Sheehy) suggested that the extent to which the bank's board of directors focused on property-related lending in Ireland reflected the limited contribution (less than 15 per cent) of that business segment to the bank's profits; this emphasis on profit flow rather than risk exposure may help explain the failure.

Non-executive bank directors testified that the risk of a major property collapse was not presented to them for consideration. Implicit in such statements seems to have been an unwarranted degree of confidence in the risk-management practices of their banks. Non-executive directors must not have considered their own knowledge and understanding of banking and general economic conditions sufficient to probe such a risk unprompted.

---

dominant fact that bank decision-makers believed in the strength of the property market.

Perhaps there is no better evidence of this fixed belief in the robustness of the property lending business than the banks' apparent ignorance and unconcern about the degree to which their borrowing customers were indebted to other banks. According to supervisory investigations made just around the peak of lending (and discussed again in Chapter 7), none of the banks had persuaded several of the biggest property developer borrowers to provide a certified net worth statement. One of the big banks underestimated the indebtedness to another bank of one of its biggest borrowing customers by €1 billion: the borrower's total loans were in reality about 75 per cent larger than the bank thought. Clearly, this type of information was not a major factor in that bank's lending decisions.

Stress tests had been carried out, but the stresses imposed were too modest. More generally, banks' risk management practice did not make sufficient allowance for the fact that the risks associated with collateralized lending increase dramatically when a property bubble is in progress: a bursting of the bubble can result in unexpectedly sudden and sharp erosions of bank capital. (See Box 4.2 for two mechanisms that can accelerate and amplify the losses in a downturn.)

The success of the Irish economy for the previous decade and more presumably lulled the international investors also: why should they factor in a sudden collapse? Indeed, in 2005 and 2006 even subordinated debt of the main Irish banks was issued at a fraction of a percentage point above that of senior debt, reflecting lender confidence that default risk on the subordinated debt was negligible.[15]

Recalling the taxonomy of other historic financial crises, the role of government interference and fraud or management self-dealing also needs to be considered. Certainly the pro-construction elements of taxation policy mentioned earlier will have been a factor increasing the demand for construction finance. But at least the Irish government did not directly involve itself in steering bank lending decisions.

As to banking fraud and criminal self-dealing in the run-up to the crisis, sizable issues of this type were only uncovered in respect of the last pre-guarantee months in 2008 as some bankers cut corners in a gamble for resurrection. These were on a relatively much smaller scale than occurred, for example, contemporaneously in Iceland. There have been criminal

---

[15] The two last subordinated debt issues made by Anglo Irish Bank, in 2005 and 2006, carried risk premia of 0.25 per cent and 0.30 per cent (25 and 30 basis points); holders of these instruments eventually suffered heavy losses.

BOX 4.2 Two Costly Risk Management Failures: Neglecting Bubble Risk and Cross-Collateralization

Two risks that were underestimated by banks lending into the Irish property bubble related to the consequences of a fall in property values and the cliff-edge risk associated with cross-collateralization.

Bubble Risk

Lending secured on property can become very risky if a bubble takes hold. Given the growing uncertainty as to how long the bubble would last, and how steep a price decline would follow, banks overestimated the protection that collateral was giving them. The relatively typical profit margin on a performing bank loan could not justify the risk the bank was assuming. This is illustrated by the following numerical example (which first appeared in Honohan 2010).

Suppose the future can be either good (boom conditions, property worth €120 million with probability 0.75) or bad (bust conditions, property worth only €50 million with probability 0.25). In other words, the odds are 3 to 1 against the boom ending in the coming year. Such a scenario would rationalize a current property market price of around €100 million – indeed, the expected value of the property in the following year is €102.5 million.

Even if the bank lends only €70 million at 9 per cent interest, its *expected* rate of return can readily be calculated as –0.4 per cent, as the risk of losing €20 million outweighs the profit earned if the boom continues. Indeed, the needed capital cushion for such a loan would be of the order of 30 per cent.

The numerical example is chosen to match roughly what was happening in Ireland 2004–6. The banks were not holding that much capital!

Cross-collateralization

One remarkable feature of the Irish banks' boom-time lending practice was the extent of cross-collateralization. In lending to property developers the banks did not generally insist that the borrower was putting up additional cash for the new venture. Instead, they were

BOX 4.2 (cont.)

often happy to lend as long as the LTV ratio on the total exposure that would follow the new loan remained below 0.7.

As prices increased, all of the estimated increase in the value of the initial investment was credited as additional collateral – even if the capital gain was unrealized. The borrower could then leverage up using the additional collateral. This mechanism can generate surprisingly rapid accumulation of debt in a rising market. A simple calculation reveals that, used to its maximum (and ignoring interest), this practice could allow an initial €8 million of net wealth put up by the borrowing developer to snowball to more than €1 *billion* of total assets after six years of property price inflation at 25 per cent per annum, even if the bank retained a seemingly prudent 70 per cent loan-to-value (LTV) ratio throughout.

A subsequent 50 per cent peak-to-trough fall in property prices would then result in the developer's net wealth collapsing to a (negative) equity of less than *minus* €0.2 billion.

This kind of calculation helps to explain how the banks' lending to developers could grow so large so quickly, and how they could lose so much on developer loans.

(The key formula is $W(t) = (1 + \alpha\pi)W(t - 1)$, where W is the net wealth of the borrower; t is the date; α is the leverage factor: $\alpha = 1/(1 - \theta)$, where θ is the LTV ratio $\theta = 0.7$ in the example; and π is the rate of property price inflation $\pi = 0.25$ in the example.)

convictions in respect of two major cases of market manipulation, both of them involving Anglo. One of these related to an illegal share support scheme violating the prohibition on a company's lending for the purpose of financing the purchase of its own shares.[16] The other case related to a back-

---

[16] This was the so-called Maple 10 case where, apparently in order to eliminate the exposure of Anglo's share price to the loss-making speculative contract for difference (CFD) holdings of Mr Sean Quinn, ten of Anglo's main borrowers were persuaded to accept loans (totalling approximately €0.5 billion) for the purpose of buying Anglo shares totalling 10 per cent of the bank's equity. Quinn family members borrowed enough to buy a further 15 per cent. These transactions closed off the CFD position. The lengthy 2014 court case largely confirmed the graphic account of this affair in Carswell (2011). Even though it was in reality by far the weakest of the Irish banks, the ratio of Anglo's share price to that of the two larger banks rose during 2007–8, quite probably a consequence of the CFD business.

to-back loan arrangement between Anglo and ILP designed for the purpose of illegal window-dressing the accounts of Anglo, giving an exaggerated impression of Anglo's ability to source customer deposits.[17,18]

THE FAILURE OF PRUDENTIAL SUPERVISION

While the first lines of defence against imprudent behaviour are located in each bank – with its risk management function, its auditors and its board of directors – the spillovers of bank failures are so potentially large that public prudential regulation is nowadays everywhere imposed.[19]

But, in the boom of the early 2000s, the Financial Regulatory Authority, located within the Central Bank, took little action to restrain the banks right up to crash. Part of the reason for the failure of pre-crisis bank supervision was the wholesale adoption of a model of supervision made fashionable by the Britain's Financial Services Authority. This approach was based on the assumption that a bank that had sufficient capital, a sound governance structure and good

Quinn controlled a large conglomerate with interests ranging from the manufacture of cement and of radiators to wind power, insurance and property. Quinn connections emerge in several other aspects of the Irish crisis: the build-up of Quinn indebtedness into billions, especially to Anglo, and especially associated with on-account payments for the CFDs on Anglo shares during 2007–8; the large Quinn shareholding held in Anglo at the time of the guarantee in September 2008; and the misuse of funds in Quinn Insurance, followed by the dramatic collapse of that company in March 2010, discussed in Chapter 5 (and which, had the banking crisis not been raging at the time, would have counted as the financial *cause celebre* of a generation). (An intriguing account is provided in Daly and Kehoe 2013.)

[17] In this scheme Anglo lent ILP the sum of €7.2 billion which was lent back to Anglo and booked as a deposit made by ILP's insurance subsidiary, thereby appearing to boost the level of *customer* deposits (as distinct from bankers' deposits) at Anglo. Provocatively, defence lawyers sought to establish that such transactions were in line with a Central Bank recommendation made to the banks during 2008 that they should help each other in the liquidity crisis. Those eventually convicted in this case included David Drumm, Chief Executive of Anglo during the period 2004–8 (a period during which the bank's loans to customers tripled to €72 billion, losses on which account for most of the ultimate costs to the government from the bank guarantee).

[18] A third high-profile criminal charge related to the failure of Sean FitzPatrick, Chairman of Anglo during 2004–8, to disclose to the bank's auditors the large loans he had been granted by the bank. Two lengthy trials on this charge in 2015 and 2016–17 collapsed on technical grounds.

[19] The utter failure of the banks' auditors to restrain the Irish banking excesses is another sorry part of the story. Those concerned offer what I consider to be rather feeble excuses, including their reliance on the international shift in the early 2000s to focusing on incurred loan losses (rather than expected losses) in preparing a bank's balance sheet. At best, it can be said that this experience is mirrored in several other countries.

internal rules for decision-making would be very unlikely to fail. Since the career prospects and in many cases the income and wealth of the directors and senior management of the banks normally depend on a good flow of bank profitability, these decision-makers would not (it was supposed) knowingly take decisions that undermined the survival of the bank. Prime responsibility for verifying that the bank's cushion of risk-taking capital was as large as regulation required was assigned to bank's auditors.

This model of supervision had the advantage of being cheap to operate: if taken to the limit, it meant that relatively little had to be checked by supervisors on-site or off-site. There was no need to examine the business model of the banks in any depth or to apply rigorous and adequately quantified stress tests.[20] Close scrutiny or probing of the financial analysis of the bank's accounts was not really necessary. After all, these were already being audited in line with international standards.

This approach not only left the door open to reckless banker behaviour, but also meant that the supervisors did not have a good grasp of the scale of losses that might result from a property market crash. There was not enough focus on quantitative indicators of bank performance and bank risk. It is true that some stress tests were carried out as part of the parallel financial stability exercise. But these stress tests did not consider scenarios with sufficiently large macroeconomic shocks. In addition, they relied largely on the banks' own assessments of how such shocks would impact loan losses.

With the Irish boom well-advanced, the regulator did tighten capital requirements in respect of speculative property loans, but the tightening was too slight to have any impact. A misplaced concern that further tightening might have disadvantaged local banks relative to those that were foreign-controlled was part of the thinking that delayed even the measures that were adopted.

---

[20] My 2010 report (prepared with the assistance of a team led by Donal Donovan, Paul Gorecki and Rafique Mottiar) covers the regulatory failures in much greater detail. The pre-crisis regulatory approach to the large banks is encapsulated in a remark made by Michael Buckley (Chief Executive Officer of AIB between 2001 and 2005), in his 2015 evidence to the Oireachtas Inquiry, that the 'prudential side of the Central Bank ... weren't very demanding, they weren't very probing.' For other firms, even when the Regulator identified evidence of serious bank governance deficiencies (as in the case of INBS, about which an Administrative Sanctions Procedure Inquiry was initiated in July 2015 following a detailed investigation conducted by the Central Bank), it was not sufficiently forceful pre-crisis in ensuring prompt corrective action.

In the face of a property bubble which entailed a significant risk of price collapse, capital requirements would have had to be very much higher. If the value of the property collateral could fall by 50 or 60 per cent (as it did on average peak-to-trough), then the potential capital hole that would result was far higher than the few percentage points implied by regulation and the LTV ratios being allowed to property developers. This was not fully appreciated by the regulatory structure, which relied on measured capital ratios which would have been comfortable in more normal times when the risk of a large price collapse need not be provided for.

Deferential to the managers of the major banks, and lenient whenever they detected a pattern of abuse, the regulator unwittingly allowed excesses to cumulate to the point where they could threaten the solvency of the Irish state. When the international financial markets started to lose confidence in the banks' business model, with resultant sharp falls in their stock prices, the Irish authorities reacted by criticizing destabilizing speculation and short-selling.

* * *

The macroeconomic vulnerabilities created by such a heavy dependence on a construction and property price boom financed through inflows of capital were underestimated by banks and the public authorities alike: if they had fully realized the scale of the downturn to which the economy was vulnerable if and when the capital inflow stopped suddenly and/or price rise expectations went into reverse, they would surely have been more cautious.

The bankers took risks on an unprecedented scale, but show no indication of having realized this. Regulators in other countries can also be faulted for having been slow to restrict lending excesses in the run-up to the crisis, and these deficiencies surely had some effect in lowering risk awareness all around. But the Irish regulators watched growth in risky exposures cumulating to the point where they could threaten the solvency of the state.

Although international regulations have greatly increased the detail and expanded the rule book around prudential regulation, it is arguably not so much the quantity of information as the attitude of prudential supervision that needed to change. Today's Ireland prudential bank supervisors, now embedded in the multi-country Single Supervisory Mechanism, have committed to employing a more sceptical and less deferential approach to the regulated entities; to probing the vulnerabilities of the banks' business models including through quantitative stress tests; and to insisting on higher levels of capital.[21]

If, as it appears, bankers cannot be relied on to operate effective risk management systems when these interfere with the ambitions created by senior management over-confidence, then additional macro-prudential measures, albeit relatively crude, such as the loan-to-value and loan-to-income limits now in effect in Ireland (since early 2015) will continue to be needed.

But there is no perfect methodology of bank supervision and the prudential authorities will need to be constantly alert to the emergence of new risks, and especially new waves of enthusiasm. At least the new steps to empower resolution authorities to step in and financial restructure failing banks in an orderly manner will help if supervision does not deliver.

---

[21] Directors of the failing Irish banks were replaced as the scale of the problems deepened. In most cases it was the shareholder that acted on this; indeed, the power of the Central Bank to remove unsuitable directors was very limited before new legislation was enacted in 2010. Relying on this new legislation, the Central Bank in 2011 informed all of the remaining bank directors who had been in office before September 2008 that they would be liable to a formal fitness and probity reassessment. Soon only two of some 70 original directors remained.

5

Faults in Financial Services

Having experienced at close quarters a near-death experience of the bank-ing sector, people in Ireland are more aware than most of what can go wrong in a country's financial sector. But avoiding bank failure is a low bar for any assessment of a country's financial services sector. Despite the large sums invested in putting the banks back on their feet and more intrusive regulation than in the past, there remains considerable scepticism about whether the Irish financial system is delivering the optimal quality of financial services fairly and at a reasonable price.

Every country needs a banking system to effect payments, to facilitate maintenance of working liquid balances demanded by normal commercial activity. An effective banking system also makes creditworthiness judge-ments, monitors debtor performance and enforces credit and other contracts. Its liabilities are generally more liquid than its assets: thus it transforms maturity in a socially valuable manner. Scholars have identified the existence of a well-functioning financial system and in particular a sufficiently deep banking system as one of the key drivers of economic growth and prosperity.

Yet over the years Irish banks have not stood out as important con-tributors to Irish economic growth. They did little maturity transforma-tion. Far from recycling all of the funds they mobilized back into the Irish economy, they held an unusually large portion of their assets abroad. This behaviour reflected long-standing links dating back to pre-independence time, as well, probably, as a long-standing banker scepticism about the creditworthiness of many Irish enterprises and other would-be borrowers. Much of the external financing of Irish firms in the period of economic expansion of the past half-century has been based on foreign direct invest-ment and government grants.

The most essential services provided by banking to any economy are in the nature of a utility. Ensuring that the banks that operate this utility are focused on success through the high quality and low cost of their services has proved challenging especially when bankers are distracted from this core business by the glamour of involvement in wholesale markets.

Openness to foreign entry – a hallmark of Irish banking policy – may have protected Irish banking from abuses that occurred in other countries in the past, but it has clearly not always guaranteed either sound or efficient service provision.

This chapter looks at several distinct aspects of the economic contribution and performance of the Irish financial system asking how well it has performed.

Focusing first on the banking system we look at issues of cost, efficiency and fairness, and on its success in dealing with loan restructuring and recovery. Should banking services be provided more cheaply, and with greater attention to the interests of consumers? When things went wrong were there better ways of dealing with over-indebtedness? Here we digress, going beyond what banks could do themselves, to consider whether a government-subsidized programme of debt relief might have made sense by speeding the resolution of the over-indebtedness problem at a reasonable cost to the rest of the public finances; the answer appears to be no.

Of the non-banking parts of regulated finance providing services to the domestic economy, the insurance and credit union sectors are the most important? We consider the challenges both have faced in recent years.

Turning finally to cross-border aspects, we offer some remarks on the extent to which the offshore, foreign-facing, financial services sector make a net contribution to the Irish economy, and on the arrival of foreign-based investment firms specializing in the purchase of distressed debt and other assets at bottom-of-the-cycle prices.

COST AND EFFICIENCY OF BANKING

Comparing bank intermediation spreads relative to some concept of best practice is an undeveloped and disputed practice. In the good years, profitability of banks suggested that spreads might be wider than would occur in an efficient economy. If the banks were reporting such unduly high profits, surely narrower spreads would be better for the economy as a whole? But the emergence of large prospective loan losses in 2009–11 suggested the opposite. Indeed, what appeared to be profits in the good years proved to have been based on over-optimistic assessments of the recoverability of loans. Clearly, spreads would have had to be much higher for the profits on the performing loans to cover the losses on those that became non-performing.

We already saw in Chapter 4 how a large fraction of the residential mortgages granted by Irish banks in the boom were at interest rates which track the European Central Bank (ECB) policy rate plus a very low spread. Not only was the spread too low to cover loan losses on the scale that subsequently occurred, but for quite some time during the crisis the Irish banks were also unable to source funds in the market at anything like as close to the policy rate as they had assumed when pricing the loans. Not surprisingly, the banks sought to compensate as much as they could by adjusting the rates that they could change, especially the so-called 'standard variable rate' (SVR), a floating rate at which most earlier loans had been made before the boom.[1] There is no tight contractual constraint on a bank making a change in its SVR. The only real constraint in practice on such changes was that traditionally the SVR would typically also apply to new loans: so setting the rate very high on existing loans could shut banks out of the market for new lending. That was not much of a constraint in the crisis years while banks had little appetite or opportunity to make more than a very few loans. Besides, they had begun to design contracts that could allow them to make new loans that were not 'standard'.

SVR rates did fall somewhat at first in the crisis but, observing the practice of UK banks, from early in 2009 Irish banks gradually increased the spreads of their SVRs relative to the ECB policy rate. Part of the increase can be seen as reflecting the fact that the banks' average cost of funds was at first rising (relative to the ECB policy rate). But, despite improving funding conditions for the Irish banks from 2011 on, the rates they charged on non-tracker mortgages showed no downward trend, and these rates did not respond to the lowering of the ECB policy rate from 1.5 per cent in mid-2011 to 0.25 per cent two years later (and subsequently lowered to zero). In other words, spreads continued to widen. By end-2013 the gap between the rate on tracker and non-tracker variable rate mortgages in Ireland stood at about 3 percentage points (Figure 5.1).[2]

---

[1] The banks' legal entitlement to increase these SVR rates was considerable, as evidenced in a case (the Millar case) in which the decision of the Financial Services Ombudsman was appealed to the High Court and then to the Appeals Court with the final conclusion (June 2015) that the bank in question (Danske Bank) was not in violation of its contract even though it had sharply increased its SVR rates relative to euro area rates in general.

[2] For analysis of the trends in mortgage rates in those years, see Goggin et al. (2012) and Holton et al. (2013). This is not quite visible from the usual ECB statistical data series on aggregate mortgage lending rates for those years because some tracker rates – mostly on restructured mortgages – are included in the standard definition for that series. From 2014

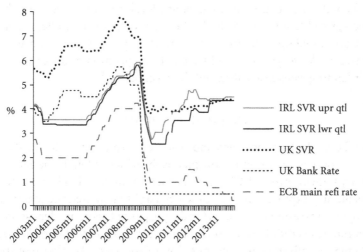

Figure 5.1 Variable mortgage interest rates Ireland and the UK, 2003–13. Shown are lower and upper quartile of the standard variable rate charged by six main banks providing residential mortgages.
Source: Central Bank.

At first, the same pattern was seen in other peripheral countries under stress, but from about 2014 those other countries saw a faster narrowing of spreads than in Ireland, where the tracker-SVR spread was still around 2¾ percentage points in 2017. Perhaps banks in Italy and Spain were now being over-optimistic about their likely future loan losses; and to some extent the comparison may not take adequate account of loan-related non-interest fees charged by banks in other countries. In addition, though, insufficient competition in the Irish market was likely allowing the banks to maintain wider margins helping them rebuild their capital. Operating costs of the Irish banks were also high by international standards, something that dates back many decades, and which implies a need for higher spreads to cover those costs.[3]

It is true that, given the level of their costs and the slow progress in dealing with distressed loans, the banks needed wider spreads to restore

---

the Central Bank has been publishing more disaggregated data on a regular basis, allowing separate analysis of tracker and other rates and rates on new and outstanding mortgages.

[3] Data from Organisation for Economic Co-operation and Development (OECD) statistical reports in the late 1980s suggest that staff costs in the main Irish banks were larger than those in the eighteen other advanced countries for which the data was available by enough to add more than 1 percentage point to the required interest spread on their total balance sheet. Figure 1.23 in the IMF's spring 2017 Global Financial Stability Report shows the persistence of relatively high costs in Irish banks by international standards.

profitability and ensure that their capital levels remained high. But, having under-priced lending so badly in the early years of the millennium, they arguably ended up over-pricing it thereafter. A well-performing and competitive banking system would have got to a position of lower spreads on their lending rates faster than did the Irish banks.[4]

FAIR BUSINESS PRACTICE

And the banks have not been above some sharp practice, to say the least. This is not new, as was most conspicuously evidenced in the parliamentary inquiry known as the DIRT Inquiry, which commenced in December 1998. This inquiry explored the way in which banks facilitated the maintenance of bogus non-resident accounts for the purpose of avoiding deposit interest retention tax (DIRT). As a result of the inquiry, banks had to make sizeable settlements with the Irish Revenue Commissioners.[5] Another high-profile violation reported in the early 2000s related to overcharging on a large scale with respect to foreign exchange charges.

The more recent abuse of mis-selling to vulnerable customers of payment protection insurance (PPI) of little or no practical value to them was first uncovered in the UK and investigated by the British financial regulator starting in 2005; it proved to have been practised by most of the banks in Ireland as well. In 2012, the Central Bank insisted that customers who had been mis-sold PPI should have their premiums refunded, and it imposed penalties, though these were proportionately lower than those in the UK because of the lower ceilings for such penalties set by the Irish legislation then in force.

The largest systematic shortcoming uncovered in regard to consumer protection relates to the tracker mortgages we have already mentioned. Keen to staunch the losses they were making on these products early in the crisis, banks stopped granting new trackers and were reluctant to restore trackers to borrowers who had chosen (before the crisis) to move off a tracker mortgage and onto a fixed rate for a few years. With post-crisis policy rates so low, borrowers were keen to get back to the very low tracker rates. But were the banks entitled to refuse them? That depended on each case. Because of vague or ambiguous contracts and poor loan documentation, the

---

[4] The oft-canvassed idea of legislation to place binding caps on mortgage interest rates is discussed in Chapter 6.

[5] www.audgen.gov.ie/viewdoc.asp?DocID=223. One of the banks involved, National Irish Bank, was found to have been not only facilitating tax evasion by some customers but also arbitrarily overcharging others (cf. Blayney and Grace 2004).

answer to that question was not always obvious. All too often, it turned out, banks adopted a high-handed and self-serving approach to these ambiguities.[6] Even where a careful and strict reading of the relevant contractual material would have shown that they might be entitled to return to the tracker rate when the period of fixity expired, banks often bundled the customers into the much higher SVR rate. This behaviour might not have violated the loan contracts, but it fell short of the banks' duty of care to customers.[7] Specifically they acted in a manner which was inconsistent with the Central Bank's Consumer Protection Code. The lender's obligation under the Code was to give the benefit of doubt to the borrower; all too often they had failed to do so.

Both the Central Bank and the Financial Services Ombudsman had been pressing banks with some success on such points from as early as 2010. But banks continued to resist, citing legal opinions, and challenging cases right up to the High Court – which had the practical effect of impeding more decisive action by the Central Bank. Eventually, in early 2015, brushing aside one bank's intention to appeal one case to the Supreme Court, the Central Bank resolved to ramp up its efforts steeply to clarify and correct the tracker mortgage situation. A pattern was emerging of widespread failure throughout the banking system to deal accurately, fairly and 'in the best interest of the customer' as required by the Consumer Protection Code.

The problem was turning out to be on a much larger scale than had previously been suspected. Only a time-consuming and costly case-by-case look-back examination of hundreds of thousands of cases could confirm who was truly entitled to the tracker rate and exactly what rate they were entitled to.

In October 2015 (shortly before I retired) the Central Bank announced that fifteen banks and other lenders were obliged to conduct just such a review.

---

[6] The borrowers affected by these abuses were not necessarily the largest borrowers, or the worst hit by the downturn. The contrasting demographics and other characteristics of loans with tracker, fixed and standard variable rates at end-2013 are documented in Kelly et al. (2015).

[7] Criticizing PTSB's interpretation of a contractual provision in one key High Court case (the Thomas case, August 2012), Mr Justice Hogan remarked: "This, undoubtedly, is a sophisticated and clever argument which, for example, had it been advanced in an undergraduate law examination would have attracted high praise from the examiners as an original demonstration of legal craft and skill. But this type of argument should really have no place in the construction of financial documents involving retail customers" (www.courts.ie/Judgments.nsf/ 09859e7a3f34669680256ef3004a27de/a61b07984bcc3d8680257a6f004b05da? OpenDocument).

While some bankers likely continue to feel hard done by, believing that they had acted within their contractual rights, eventually the banks accepted the arguments of the Central Bank that led to tens of thousands of cases being given redress and compensation, triggering total payments by the banks of close to €1 billion. A number of borrowers lost their homes in part as a consequence of the higher-than-contracted interest rates they were being charged.[8]

Although the process of reassessing each case was inevitably slow, the lengthy delays, stretching into 2018, in determining entitlements properly and making correct restitution also provide discouraging evidence on the ineffectiveness of the banks' systems.[9] Indeed, many of the corrections related not to the borrower's contractual right to a tracker, but to the incorrect application of the agreed tracker mark-up, allegedly attributable to administrative errors (not all of which were in favour of the lender).

Like the position with the SVR interest rates, and the previous scandals, these and other practices seem to have reflected a culture of entitlement on the part of the banks to play fast and loose with charges – sometimes seemingly arbitrary – being imposed on customers. This high-handed approach has deep roots. In past decades banks in Ireland were rarely forthcoming about their pricing, sometimes seeming entitled to charge whatever was needed to meet profit targets.

The culture of the Irish banks was surely also infected by the deterioration in banking culture in their main reference countries, the UK and USA, where recent reports have exposed significant abuses.[10] Even if the

---

[8] Most of the tracker cases did not relate to loans in arrears: a separate Code of Conduct on Mortgage Arrears had been the main focus of the Central Bank's efforts to ensure fair and proportionate dealings of the banks with their mortgage customers in the period 2011–14.

[9] Technical shortcomings were also displayed very clearly in the lengthy interruption in the payments system of Ulster Bank during June 2012; this was attributed to a software error in its parent RBS.

[10] Examples could be multiplied. The Promontory (2016) report on the Royal Bank of Scotland's 'Global Restructuring Group' provides evidence of 'widespread inappropriate treatment of customers' by the bank which 'failed to take adequate account of the interests of the customers it handled.' More specifically, corruption and fraud in the impaired-assets division of another large British bank HBOS between 2003 and 2007 led to small companies in financial distress having their assets in effect stolen; five bankers were jailed for this in 2017. In the UK, the Salz (2013) Review documents in detail corporate culture defects in Barclays Bank.

A major US case involving a large and formerly respected firm is documented in action taken in 2017 by the US Consumer Financial Protection Bureau against Navient, a firm formerly known as the student loan management firm Sallie Mae. According to the charge, Navient 'systematically deterred numerous borrowers from obtaining access to some or all of the benefits and protections associated with [the US student loan] plans.

Irish abuses may not have been any worse than those detected in other countries – and may perhaps have been less egregious than some – and although the banks have not been credibly accused of predatory lending, their record in this whole area is disappointing. It suggests the need for deeper reforms in banking culture, an intractable issue on which the Central Bank continues to work.

The Central Bank's consumer protection efforts in smoking out the unpalatable facts of the tracker abuses and ensuring compensation took quite some time, in part reflecting the fact that priority was being given to dealing with those struggling with mortgage over-indebtedness.

WHEN THINGS GO WRONG: LOAN RECOVERY

When borrowers are servicing their loans and have the capacity to continue to do so, monitoring and managing the existing loan port-folio is not a very challenging part of a bank's activities. But matters are quite different when a large number of outstanding loans have fallen into arrears. Although the number and value of non-performing loans (NPLs) continued to rise at accelerating rates as the recession deepened during 2009–10, the banks seemed unable to take effective action to stem the deterioration. This was partly due to their lack of experience in distressed loan recovery. (It likely also reflected top bank management's limited bandwidth given the existential problems they began to face in retaining deposits and raising the needed additional capital.)

With almost one in every hundred owner-occupier mortgage loans newly slipping into the 'more-than-90-days' arrears category each quarter (despite low interest rates), the problem of NPLs both reflected wider economic distress and heightened the risk of non-recovery of loans. Indeed, the scale of NPLs was one of the key drivers of the increase in

Despite assuring borrowers that it would help them find the right repayment option for their circumstances, Navient steered these borrowers . . . into costly [short-term] payment relief . . . instead of affordable long-term repayment options that were more beneficial to them' (http://files.consumerfinance.gov/f/documents/201701_cfpb_Navient-Pioneer-Credit-Recovery-complaint.pdf).

And, at the time of writing, the 2017–9 Australian Royal Commission into Misconduct in the Banking, Superannuation and Financial Services Industry was taking evidence uncovering a further catalogues of misdeeds in that country, including alleged systematic overcharging in that country's pension fund industry.

projected loan losses that led to the additional capital requirements that became necessary in 2011.[11]

As the months passed with an uninterrupted growth in the percentage of NPLs, the Central Bank became increasingly concerned that the banks were not taking the necessary actions to stem the rise, including triage between 'can't pay' and 'won't pay' customers, nor were they putting in place sustainable long-term restructuring of debts that could not be repaid in the short term. To the extent that banks were dealing with distressed borrowers that approached them for relief, it was mainly in the form of temporary deferrals of amortization payments: 'kicking the can down the road'. And many non-performing borrowers chose not to engage with the lenders.

Some of the borrowers who have not serviced their loans for years are likely still hoping for some great amnesty or relief to come from the government, however unlikely that may be. This is not strategic default in the US sense of the borrowers walking away from the loan and the property because the bank cannot pursue them further: it is more a wait-and-see attitude, being reluctant to reduce their other spending if some relief seems possible. For others, of course, it is a question of inability to pay, whether because they became over-indebted with a view to selling on a buy-to-let property, or because their income and circumstances deteriorated in the bust.

Very few individuals had been made bankrupt in Ireland over the years. The relevant legislation dated to the nineteenth century and was hopelessly costly and oppressive to the debtor. Long overdue legislative reform to make personal insolvency law workable was introduced. This included pro-debtor provisions that were strongly supported by the Central Bank (even though the banks complained that in important respects the new legislation impaired their ability to recover collateral).[12]

Indeed, the banks gave (other) deficiencies in the legal framework for repossessing the collateral or defaulted property as an excuse for their

---

[11] One possibility for incentivizing speedier debt relief measures on the part of the banks would have been to make the injection by the government of bank capital that was needed by the banks in 2011 conditional on debt relief being applied where needed. As the capital was intended to cover for likely and potential loan losses, speeding the needed reliefs need not have resulted in additional costs to the government. However, the possibility of making recapitalization injections conditional on write-downs was not on: the Troika had established a strict timetable for the capital to be put in and would not have waited.

[12] These included sweeping legal changes in personal insolvency law as well as successive versions in 2011 and 2013 of a detailed Central Bank Code of Conduct on Mortgage Arrears, designed to ensure that lenders worked 'sympathetically and positively ... in assisting the borrower to meet ... mortgage obligations'.

inability to get control of the NPL situation.[13] In addition, lenders frequently complain about procedural delays, a finicky and legalistic approach from courts; in reality, though, lenders cannot expect flawed documentation to be accepted as the basis for home repossession, and due process does need to be carefully respected in matters of such importance to distressed borrowers. Likely of equal importance in postponing repossessions has been an understandable reluctance on the part of many bankers to attract the likely public opprobrium of too aggressive a stance when the main folk memory of home repossessions relates to the history of nineteenth-century Ireland, with absentee landlords appealing to the colonial power to effect evictions.

But if they were slow to repossess (even in the case of investment properties), the banks were equally slow to deliver other potentially better solutions. In all cases, they were slow to offer write-downs to borrowers who could not realistically make full payment for fear that such offers would create a clamour for like treatment from others who could.

In mid-2012, having examined how the banks were going about loan recovery (including for non-mortgage loans – which indeed accounted for more non-performing debt than mortgages) and comparing it with best international practice, the Central Bank concluded that the banks' capacity in this area was not improving at anything like the needed rate. Taking a more forceful line (perhaps somewhat belatedly), the Central Bank mandated an accelerated and time-bound process of NPL treatment designed to place each loan on a long-term sustainable basis, if that could be done. For mortgages, in what was labelled the Mortgage Arrears Resolution Process (MARP), a variety of treatments was used from interest reductions and term extensions through split-mortgages (where part of the mortgage was temporarily parked, to be serviced in the future only if conditions for the borrower improved sufficiently). Repossession of the collateral might also be considered a sustainable solution if no viable restructure could be designed; this could include a write-off of some or all of the residual debt.

Residential mortgage NPLs peaked in the summer of 2013 at 27 per cent (13 per cent for owner-occupier homes; much higher for buy-to-let properties) and have been falling steadily since then – though by 2018 the

---

[13] There was much focus on a legislative flaw which for a time blocked the most natural route for banks to pursue repossession. O'Malley (2018) provides evidence that this flaw did contribute to moral hazard, increasing debt default.

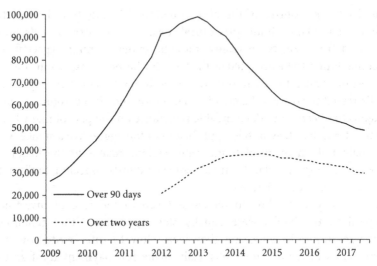

Figure 5.2 Number of owner-occupier mortgages in arrears, 2009–18.
Source: Central Bank of Ireland.

percentage for owner-occupiers was still over 6 per cent, and two-thirds of these had been in arrears for more than two years (Figure 5.2).[14]

A growing number of owner-occupied properties have been surrendered or repossessed through court proceedings (Figure 5.3), though by 2018 these still came to only about 1 per cent of the stock of 800,000 mortgaged owner-occupied properties, far less than in (for example) the United States.

The system's failure to grasp this problem more energetically does not offer easy lessons. Over-optimistic expectations, weak operational systems and a societal reluctance to enforce hard choices may all have played a part in the slow resolution of the legacy indebtedness of households and small businesses.

Although bringing the problem of NPLs under control took much longer than hoped for, it remains unclear what additional policy measures could have been taken by the Central Bank that would have been effective in speeding things up, while still protecting stressed borrowers from the disruption of unnecessary loss of their homes.

[14] These figures refer to arrears of more than 90 days; they include loans already sold by the banks to other firms. McCann (2017a, b) provides extensive statistical material describing the progress during 2012–17 in bringing the residential mortgage arrears under control. Donnery et al. (2018) provide a detailed account of MARP and other policy measures employed.

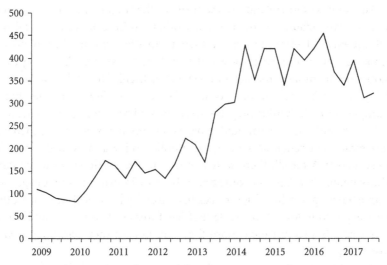

Figure 5.3 Repossessions and surrenders of owner-occupied properties, 2009–18. Quarterly data.
Source: Central Bank of Ireland.

COULD THERE HAVE BEEN GOVERNMENT-SUBSIDIZED DEBT RELIEF?

I believe that debt relief should have been a larger component of Irish banks' approach to customer over-indebtedness, both from a narrow profitability perspective and as part of their ongoing responsibility to have regard to the interests of their customers.

The initial fear of the government and the Central Bank was that, as was happening in the USA, banks would move too quickly to repossessing mortgaged properties where the borrower had fallen into arrears.[15] To prevent this, a moratorium on repossessions was declared.

But the pendulum can swing to the opposite extreme. Over-optimistic bankers may defer action if they think that they will be able to recover from an over-indebted household, especially if and when property prices recover or the household's employment situation improves. Furthermore, lengthy delays in the process of negotiation and, where necessary, legal action mean that needed loan restructuring is often long delayed, leaving over-indebted borrowers in a corrosive limbo of uncertainty.

---

[15] Mian and Sufi (2014) describe the disappointing efforts of the United States authorities to deal with over-indebted households. Foreclosures of US mortgages ran at far higher rates in the US than in Ireland, despite the greater severity of Ireland's crisis.

And so it was in Ireland. As mentioned, the Irish banks, unaccustomed to extensive defaults, were, like many others in Europe, slow to deal with delinquent debt, either to write it down to an affordable level or to move to repossession where write-down did not make sense. The progressive reduction in money market interest rates, thanks to ECB policy, made delay in debt resolution seem relatively costless for the banks. Complications in bankruptcy law were blamed for adding to the delays.

But should the government have taken further steps to deepen and accelerate debt relief, as a matter of public policy and even if it implied a fiscal cost? After all, there were significant distributional issues at stake. Many people had been encouraged to borrow in order to buy property at a time when, given how high prices had risen by historical standards, they were exposed to losses on a scale that few foresaw. The boom and bust left many people owing much more than the houses they had bought were worth.

Should more have been done by the government to undo some of the damage done by the fall in property prices to people who had borrowed heavily shortly before the collapse? Perhaps so, but arguments from considerations of fairness also need to take account of other categories of household who lost out.[16] The distributional effects of the boom and bust (further discussed in Chapter 12) were multidimensional. Given how strained the public finances were in the crisis years, resources assigned to debt relief for heavily indebted households would entail squeezes elsewhere. It is for politicians to make these judgement calls.

Example of Iceland

The European country with the most extensive blanket debt relief measures for household mortgages after the crisis broke was Iceland. Iceland exploited three approaches for delivering such relief: regulatory cramming down of indebtedness; judicial assessment that the loans were in some way wrongly priced or unjustly made; and government-financed debt relief.

As we have seen, the key distinguishing features of the Icelandic crash along with the decline in house prices – sharp, though less so than in Ireland – were the sharp fall in the exchange rate and a surge in inflation

---

[16] After all, the lengthy delays in resolving the mortgage arrears problem presumably also allowed some households who could easily have serviced their mortgages to live effectively rent-free, by simply deciding not to service their mortgage debt, through to a time when others, who had not borrowed, were struggling to pay the high rentals that now prevailed.

not matched by wage increases, and the fact that the value and repayment schedule of most mortgage loans in Iceland had been linked either to a foreign currency or to the general consumer price level. With the exchange rate and inflation movements, not only did many people lose their jobs, but the local currency value of their debt also jumped. This exchange-rate jump seems to have been the proximate trigger for the debt relief measures that followed.

The main measures employed in Iceland happened in several stages and involved much detail which we need not go into here (cf. Jonsson and Sigurgeirsson 2016). In addition to a moratorium on foreclosures (such as was also introduced in Ireland), a key feature of the first stage, effectively mandated by the government in 2009, was that all mortgage debt in excess of 110 per cent of the property value was to be written off. Second, Icelandic courts found mortgage debts linked to foreign currencies to be unconstitutional, and mandated a substantial reset of repayment schedules. Third, a new government in 2014 delivered further debt relief, paid for with budgetary outlays, in effect removing index-linking above a certain retrospective cap (4 per cent inflation). There were certain ceilings on the use of these and other reliefs introduced, but they did benefit a majority of households in Iceland.

While one can debate the equity of such reliefs, they appear to have commanded general public approval in Iceland despite the evident cost to the Icelandic public finances.[17]

A route not chosen in Iceland was an incentive scheme to induce the banks to accelerate debt relief, like the Home Affordable Modification Program (HAMP) and its cousins introduced by the Obama administration in the USA. These programmes incentivised the banks to offer restructurings on smaller unpayable mortgage loans such that servicing on the restructured loan would be below 31 per cent of the borrower's gross income. The scheme had mixed success: a worthwhile number of loans were restructured, but many fell into delinquency again.

Exploring the Possibility of Blanket Debt Relief in Ireland

Could something similar have been done in Ireland in order to speed the resolution of over-indebtedness? One obstacle could have been political: extensive debt relief that went to rich and poor alike would likely have been

---

[17] As explained later, Iceland had the fiscal headroom to absorb these costs because of the measures taken to ensure that the bank losses were borne by foreign creditors.

politically contentious. In fact, the Central Bank was never asked to explore possibilities along these lines. But we decided to try, asking ourselves whether some practical across the board or blanket mandatory scheme for speedy debt relief could be designed that would be seen by the government as offering a better social outcome.

Armed with extensive loan-by-loan data on the distribution of Irish mortgage loans including information on the borrower's income at loan origination (and sufficient information about the property to allow a fair estimate of the trend in loan-to-value ratios), the Central Bank was in a reasonable position to estimate the fiscal cost and potential effectiveness of a debt relief scheme. This was nowhere near enough to make a case-by-case evaluation of ability to pay, but it could be used to estimate the cost of a blanket or across-the-board debt relief scheme. It seemed important to explore whether a government-sponsored scheme for applying some simplified mechanism for ensuring speedier and deeper loan restructurings or debt relief could be designed to remove the overhang of unpayable debt. Research staff enthusiastically analysed the data and, among other things, modelled a range of potential across-the-board debt relief schemes.

Circumstances in Ireland were different from those of Iceland. House prices had fallen further than in Iceland and loan-to-value ratios were much higher. There was almost no use of foreign currency or price index-linked loans, and no surge in inflation (rather the contrary). Clearly most of the severely affected households were those with high loan-to-income ratios, and especially those whose income was now low.

We examined in particular whether some simple scheme analogous to the US schemes could help speed the resolution of over-indebtedness on mortgages taken out in the boom years by removing the need for in-depth analysis and negotiation and at a cost to the state that might prove acceptable. Evidently, with the depth of the Irish problem, a small incentive on the scale that was offered to the US banks would be insufficient to induce much activity. Most of the debt relief would fall on the government's finances (mainly through its ownership stake in the banks). And another difference with the USA was the fact that most of the Irish restructured loans allowed the lender no recourse to the borrower for a shortfall in the value of the collateral property.

Any such blanket scheme for Ireland linked to simple indicators such as borrower income would inevitably result in unnecessary subsidies to borrowers who could have many other ways of servicing their debts.[18] If not too large, though, perhaps such deadweight costs to the state could be justified by the speed with which such a scheme could resolve a large part of the mortgage delinquency.

Unfortunately, despite considerable attempts at ingenuity in scheme design, our calculations revealed that the cost to the government's finances of any such scheme, even if limited to smaller loans, seemed to be well out of proportion to the benefits: no sensible scheme could be devised that would command approval. Essentially, even if we restricted the scheme to small loans, too many debtors who could afford to pay would receive unneeded but costly relief and the fiscal cost would have been high, eating into other government spending priorities.[19] This initiative proved to be a disappointing dead-end. No blanket scheme could be recommended; debt restructuring would have to be case-by-case, and that would prove to be a very slow process.

THE SERVICES PROVIDED BY NONBANK FINANCE

Though banking is the dominant financial sector catering to the Irish economy, there is more to finance than banking.

For the general public, credit unions and insurance companies are the most familiar nonbank entities. Neither subsector has been trouble free. The credit union sector survived the crisis better than the banks, but its longer-term structural shortcomings mean that this sector underperforms in the community banking services it should be able to provide. The history of insurance in Ireland over the past few decades is littered with significant failures.

Credit Unions

Ireland's extensive network of credit unions complements the mainstream banks, and offers basic savings and credit services to their wide membership. This can be called Ireland's community banking network, in that most of the credit unions are based on a town or other local community, others (including the largest) having, as the defining common bond, an

---

[18] The bigger the sums at stake, the more likely defaulting borrower could use legal devices to put assets beyond the reach of the lender (cf. Keena 2018 for just one apparent example that was discussed in the media).

[19] After all, as discussed in Chapter 12, the over-indebted are only one of the badly affected groups.

occupation or employer (though these categories are becoming blurred following recent mergers). To the extent that local and personal knowledge is a valuable element in the assessment of creditworthiness, and local and occupational solidarity can help sustain a credit union through times of stress, community banking can be a very valuable segment of finance for households, clubs, small businesses and the like, especially now that credit decisions of mainstream banks are increasingly automated.

Although facing severe pressures, the finances of most Irish credit unions survived the crisis relatively well.[20] They retained the confidence and the loyalty of their members, and did not shrink in total assets during the crisis. Despite being warned that mortgage arrears could lead to the loss of a home, credit union borrowers seem to have prioritised servicing of credit union debt even at the cost of putting the mortgage servicing on the long finger.

The Central Bank had already imposed lending restrictions (of varying severity) on a large number of stressed credit unions by the time I arrived there. This limited the scope for further deterioration of loan losses though it also prevented some credit unions from expanding their lending.[21]

Overall, the outcome was less severe than feared. A number of stressed credit unions merged with stronger ones before their situation became too serious, sometimes supported by the fund maintained for this purpose by the Irish League of Credit Unions. A handful of credit unions did have to be closed, though this was managed without loss to depositors.[22]

Anxious to protect and strengthen the functioning of community banking, the Central Bank devoted a lot of effort in the case of the largest failing credit union, the Newbridge, to try to find a solution that would provide continuity of these services within the credit union sector. Given the parlous state of this credit union, which had been closely monitored by the Central Bank for several years before intervention, it had proved

---

[20] With the sharp rise in unemployment, higher taxes and the effects of the downturn more generally, the ability of credit unions to recover loans to members seemed at risk. If the loss experience of banks was going to be replicated in credit unions, up to €1 billion of additional capital would have had to be injected. Furthermore, most credit union loans were uncollateralized, likely making it more difficult to recover anything from the defaulted loans of a failed credit union. The Troika worried about this and pressed the government in 2011 to set aside a sizable pot of money to facilitate restructuring and to supplement the cash available from the Deposit Guarantee Fund to make good on depositor losses arising from credit union liquidations.

[21] By 2016, 85 credit unions were still operating under lending restrictions.

[22] The Deposit Guarantee Fund managed to pay out promptly to depositors in the case of liquidations. A handful of credit union members had deposits of more than the €1,00,000 guaranteed by the Fund, but none in credit unions that were liquidated.

necessary to replace the existing management with an outside manager and in early 2013 the High Court acceded to our request that this be done. The manager confirmed that extremely heavy losses were inevitable, and the Central Bank devised a sensible risk-sharing contract attractive to an acquiring credit union while protecting the investment of the government money that would have to be injected. Over a period of months we tried to find a suitable buyer and almost succeeded with a nearby credit union, but in the end they pulled out (partly, I suspect, because the potential acquirers feared being outvoted by Newbridge members in the general members' assembly of the merged entity). PTSB, by then a Government-owned bank, stepped in: the members of Newbridge continued to be served, but not immediately by the credit union sector. (Eventually neighbouring Naas Credit Union opened a branch in Newbridge town in 2016.)

I would have liked to see the opportunity of the crisis being used to adopt structural reforms in the sector that would improve the capacity of the unions to serve their members more effectively, including an expansion of their lending, and to grow into a more vibrant community banking sector. As I saw it, this would mean consolidating the network of credit unions much more systematically. I envisaged a sector composed mainly of larger credit unions achieving scale without losing the community dimension. There could, I envisaged, be about 50 or 60 unions – say one per county plus the larger occupational unions – rather than the 270 or so with which we ended up by 2017 (down from more than 400 at the start of the crisis). Each of those consolidated unions would be able to afford much more professional management than many of the smaller unions have had, and their risk would be diversified. They would also have been better equipped to deal with the essential requirements of prudential supervision.

However, parochial-level interests won the day politically and the Central Bank was given no mandate to drive such a consolidation, nor could I persuade the leaders of the credit union movement of the merits of consolidation on such a scale. Nevertheless, more limited consolidation has since been occurring including under the auspices of a temporary Credit Union Restructuring Board (established on the recommendation of a special Credit Union Commission established by the government in 2011). By 2015, 42 per cent of the credit union's assets were in the 37 largest unions – each of these operating on a reasonable scale with asset size of more than €100 million; and the number of unions with assets of less than €20 million had fallen from 223 in 2007 to 130. Still, there is a long way to go before the credit union movement can be said to be providing as vigorous a contribution to society as might be.

Insurance

The insurance sector is particularly large in Ireland. As in the UK, there has been a long tradition of tax concessions which have enabled the sector to become the major provider of vehicles for long-term investment by households, especially for retirement income. Ireland has also become a prominent export hub for insurance services.

Insurance firms pool risk and provide services related to long-term portfolio investment. The quality and cost of these services is a constant source of debate, as is the measurement of the risks being assumed by the firms.

Indeed, pricing of insurance policies in the domestic market, especially in the largest sectors of health and motor, have been perennially controversial in Ireland.[23] As in other countries there tends to be a cyclical pattern in premium rates. Competition drives them down until realization that losses will be made sets in, resulting in price hikes and the withdrawal of some firms. Covert collusion, if it exists as has been suggested and is being investigated, is unlikely to have removed this pattern completely; it certainly has not been effective in sustaining high profits in the sector in recent times. Legal costs and judgements are also factors that are widely discussed in this context. Complaints that premiums are too high need to be taken in context where profitability of the insurance sector has been very weak. With profits low, or non-existent, then if prices are too high it must be costs that are driving them. Innovations such as the legislative introduction of some form of no-fault insurance might help.

If dealing with over-charging is challenging, under-pricing is also a fraught area. This has been a regulatory preoccupation in both the domestic and off-shore or foreign-facing parts of the Irish insurance sector.

In terms of premium income, the foreign-facing insurance business in Ireland is a multiple of the local business. Some of the foreign insurers offer quite complex lines which are challenging to supervise. I was quite concerned to learn that Ireland was a leading global centre for a product known as variable annuities, as I wondered whether this reflected a kind of regulatory arbitrage, implying that were too tolerant of this line of business and might well be underestimating its riskiness. Central Bank staff were already looking closely at this product and I encouraged further analysis and exploration. In the end we decided that capital reserves against

---

[23] One of my father W. A. Honohan's tasks, after he retired from the Department of Social Welfare in the mid-1970s, was to chair a government-appointed advisory group examining allegations of over-charging in motor insurance!

the risk of this type of business had to be appreciably higher, thereby helping ensure that this would not become a ticking time bomb.

A complex and elaborate structure of insurance regulation known as 'Solvency II' has been introduced in Europe as a tool for more reliable prudential regulation of insurance firms and in particular of the minimum solvency (or capital) reserves they are obliged to hold. Sometimes, though, complexity is the enemy of clarity and decisiveness. Like Basel II (for banks), the new regime has an elaborate and sometimes hard-to-track structure; and like Basel II it is far from being perfect. Besides, Ireland's insurance failures over the years have been along simpler dimensions.

For insurance is also a field which is prone to mismanagement and ownership abuse. The interval between the payment of the insurance premium and the payout on claims offers temptations. The history of insurance is full of examples of insurance companies using these funds to build ownership stakes in banks, or to take highly speculative investment decisions structured to give advantage to the promoter in the case of success and failure for the policyholder otherwise. Foolish or aggressive insurance business promoters undercharge the early policyholders in the short-termist hope of building the business fast enough so that payouts on the early policies can be partly covered by the cash-flow of later-arriving customers.

Insurance in Ireland has had more than its fair share of solvency mishaps over the years.

The motor insurer PMPA failed in 1983 as a result of over-ambitious expansion driven by unrealistically low premia; it had built up an impressive 32 per cent of the private car insurance market in Ireland. The PMPA failure meant that the Government's Insurance Compensation Fund, funded by levies on the sector, had to pay for the deficiency.

And the 1985 failure of another general insurer, Insurance Corporation of Ireland (ICI), already mentioned in Chapter 4, was even more spectacular. ICI had been acquired by Ireland's largest bank AIB from the state-owned shipping company Irish Shipping Ltd as a vehicle for expanding the bank's activities into a new sector. Unfortunately, the firm's origins as a marine insurer (it had been created in the 1940s as an in-house insurer for the fledgling Irish Shipping) had resulted in its London office having expanded in an uncontrolled manner into exotic lines of reinsurance. When it realized the extent of the losses already crystallizing and the potential tail risk of additional losses on this London business, the bank decided to cut its losses by liquidating the subsidiary unless the Irish government was willing to take it over. In the event, mainly because of the disruption that liquidation would cause to ICI's Irish policyholders (though there was also some concern about the impact on the bank's access to money market funding), the government did step in; the costs of the liquidation were ultimately recovered by levies on AIB and (to a lesser extent) on the rest of the banking system – much of which can be assumed to have ultimately fallen on bank customers through their impact on interest rates and charges (Honohan and Kelly 1997).

It is generally during economic downturns that mismanagement of financial intermediaries is brutally exposed. The failures of PMPA and ICI in the 1980s were the main Irish examples before the recent downturn, which saw an even more dramatic case, Quinn Insurance.[24]

Quinn Insurance was a major firm prominent in health and motor insurance and operating on both sides of the Irish border and in Britain. Since 2008 it was under close scrutiny since the abuses of that year which had led to the Central Bank imposing financial penalties on both the firm and its chairman, Mr Sean Quinn, who then stood down from that position as part of the settlement.[25] Here again, as with PMPA, there was a history of aggressive expansion in motor insurance, relying on cash flow from the growth in premium income from under-priced policies, used in this case to finance diverse activities.

By early 2010 the Central Bank was exerting pressure on Quinn Insurance, insisting that it bring its solvency margin up to the required level. In this process the Central Bank became aware that Quinn Insurance had guaranteed, through its subsidiaries, some €1.2 billion of debt of the remainder of the Quinn Group, a diversified conglomerate controlled by Mr Quinn, which was also in financial difficulties. Given the large hole that now promised to open up in the accounts of Quinn Insurance bringing it to the point of collapse, it was clear that the Central Bank as financial regulator must move decisively, despite the prominence of the firm (and despite the timing clash with the jumbo stress test announcement,

---

[24] It was one of a handful of troubled financial firms catering to the Irish market which were mentioned to me as being under special scrutiny and control when I started at the Central Bank in late 2009. The others included a couple of credit unions (as mentioned earlier), and Custom House Capital (CHC), a brokerage and investment advisory concern controlling a number of funds. Despite Central Bank staff's over-optimistic hope that CHC could be turned around, and their assumption that the firm's principals could be relied upon, it collapsed in early 2011 as a result of 'deeply dishonest' behaviour of the principals who indulged in 'systemic and deliberate misuse' of clients' funds (language used in the High Court findings). Losses to creditors ran into tens of millions.

[25] These related to the use of Quinn Insurance funds in the Anglo Irish Bank CFD affair mentioned in Chapter 4.

described later, of bank recapitalization, which risked being overshadowed – as indeed it was).

This was a test of the Central Bank's determination to follow its statutory mandate despite the inevitable political fall-out. The Central Bank's new head of financial regulation Matthew Elderfield and I informed the Minister for Finance, Brian Lenihan, of the situation in a tense late-night meeting. There was little the Minister could do to alleviate the situation that had emerged. Central Bank staff worked through the night to prepare for a High Court hearing the following morning at which the Bank successfully petitioned for the appointment of Administrators to the firm. The Administrators moved quickly to secure control of the firm. It turned out that its financial condition was even worse than suspected, with loss-making operations that needed to be restructured. Once again the Insurance Compensation Fund was drawn upon; this time to the extent of more than €1.1 billion. This insurance debacle was just one strand in the unravelling of a major Irish industrial-financial group which had taken a disastrous wrong turn.

The Irish subsidiary of another large firm, UK-based RSA Insurance, got into trouble three years later when the Central Bank detected once more a pattern of under-pricing of insurance policies relative to loss experience. Its UK parent company had to inject a couple of hundred million euros to restore its solvency. This time Central Bank action was taken in time to prevent any losses to customers or to the Insurance Compensation Fund.

And insurance woes did not end there. Two foreign-registered insurance firms (Setanta and Enterprise) selling motor insurance into Ireland also failed during the recent downturn. Even if these were foreign firms, supervised by regulatory authorities in Malta and Gibraltar, some of their policies had been sold by Irish brokers. The Central Bank had been pressing those regulators to do more to rein in what seemed to be weak companies gaining market share by under-pricing, and it would have been great if the foreign response had been more energetic. It is not easy to see what more the Central Bank could have done in this situation. Indeed, some legal purists say what was done already exceeded the Bank's legal powers. For example, to have issued public warnings against these companies would certainly have been an abuse of the Central Bank's mandate. Strictly speaking, prudential supervision of foreign-based companies selling under the authority of a foreign license was none of the Central Bank's business. For some commentators, this raises questions about the merits for Ireland of the EU-wide passport for financial services. But given that

Ireland is one of the chief users of this passport to export financial services to the rest of Europe, such commentary is at best one-sided.

Insurance has certainly provided some roller-coaster experience in Ireland over the decades. Perhaps now it has been placed on a sounder basis with insurance company management aware that risk or recklessness will be dealt with firmly and decisively.[26]

FINANCE AS AN EXPORT SECTOR

Almost disconnected from that part of the financial sector that provides for the financial services needs of the Irish economy is a wholly export-oriented part which for a couple of decades has employed up to half of the people working in the financial sector in Ireland and also draws on specialist legal and other services. For Ireland is a major international centre for the export of financial services, including aspects of banking and insurance, and also extending to aspects of investment fund management and other products. Indeed, the scale of these operations has contributed to Ireland being ranked 15th among global financial centres in a recent IMF review.

Not contributing as much to employment as its public profile would suggest, the booked profitability of some (though by no means all) of the firms in this international financial services sector ensure that it is nevertheless a significant contributor to Irish tax revenue (cf. Everett et al. 2013). A large number of financial institutions have established sizable operations in Dublin (and continue to do so, not least as a result of Brexit). EU and euro area membership are draws, as is the tax system, as well as the other features of the economic environment which make Ireland an attractive destination for footloose multinational company investment. If there was a perception at one stage that, as a light touch supervisor, Ireland would be the beneficiary of regulatory arbitrage, this has now vanished. Ireland recognizes that the reputational and potentially financial costs of inadequate regulation

---

[26] Other nonbank sectors have been less active contributors to the Irish economy. The equity market is very small and inactive, partly because of the ease of access to the London market and others. There is no active domestic bond market apart from that in Irish government debt. There is also a large number of investment advisors and other ancillary firms, most of them very small, which are also supervised by the Central Bank. Licensed money lenders offer short-term loans at very high interest rates; tolerating their activities seems justified when the likely alternative is that uncreditworthy people in temporary money troubles would have to turn to loan sharks charging far higher rates, perhaps accompanied by much more aggressive and predatory behaviour.

and supervision far outweigh any short-term benefits from inward investment.

As is discussed later, some banks and other financial firms in this sector went under in the crisis, one of the first being the German regional government bank Sachsen, another being Depfa (the name a contraction of Deutsche Pfandbriefbank), once the bank with the largest balance sheet in Ireland. But for the most part the sector survived the crisis and has continued to grow, most recently as a side effect of Brexit.

Ireland is one of the main global hubs for investment funds, with a specialization in US dollar denominated funds. These funds are listed on the Irish stock exchange giving them a valued status with customers as listed funds. While the funds themselves do not provide much employment directly, their reliance on Irish law firms has generated a spin-off into the national economy.

Some other international financial firms likely provide less added value to the Irish economy than the reputational and financial risks they represent. Most of the activities of some firms are conducted elsewhere, even though business is booked in Ireland. Some complex firms of this type entail sizable supervisory costs and until 2017 only half these costs was charged back to industry.[27] It is not altogether clear that the investment promotion efforts of the government are well directed towards such firms.

A number of other types of financial entity exist in Ireland, benefit from the tax regime and have sizable balance sheets but, because they do not sell financial services on a retail basis, are not covered by international or Irish law relating to regulation. Sometimes grouped with other firms as 'shadow banks' (though that term has specific and narrow definitions which do not always apply to unregulated financial firms), they are the subject of increased interest on the part of the Central Bank, which tries to find out what they are doing, and in particular to make sure that, given what they are doing, they are indeed legally entitled to be exempt from regulation. The Central Bank has enthusiastically contributed to international attempts to build information about unregulated finance (Murphy 2015).

---

[27] Following several years during which the Central Bank has advocated a move to 100 per cent chargeback to regulated financial firms of the regulatory cost, and after a consultation process initiated in July 2015, the Minister for Finance agreed to a phased increase, and the percentage chargeback in 2017 was 65 per cent.

THE 'VULTURES' ARRIVE

Inward investment has for decades been a defining characteristic of Ireland's economic performance. Forming a new category of foreign-based financial intermediary active in Ireland, investment funds of various types became prominent purchasers of real estate and distressed bank loans as the recovery took hold. The supply was ample. The Government's asset management body National Asset Management Agency (NAMA, described later) was keen to recover cash from the loans it had acquired in 2010–11. Furthermore, rather than dealing with the problems of loan recovery themselves, and under renewed supervisory pressure to reduce the share of non-performing assets in their books, banks were increasingly turning to sales of loans, and have in particular been selling large blocks of mainly non-performing residential mortgage loans at prices that reflect deep average discounts on the face value of the loans.

The arrival of these firms has been greeted with a distinct lack of public enthusiasm. Their use of tax loopholes has been criticized, though competition between foreign bidders for Irish assets likely drove up the price they had to pay for those assets to the point where most or all of the benefit of the tax concession effectively passed to the seller. There has also been concern that funds will have less inhibition, than the banks seem to have displayed, towards repossession of housing collateral. It is indeed likely that funds whose exclusive focus in Ireland is on recovering their investment in a discounted package of mortgage loans will be less influenced by two countervailing factors that have likely made the banks hesitate in resolving cases of over-indebtedness namely, on the one hand, the bankers' wish to avoid the public opprobrium associated with repossession and, on the other, their reluctance to concede a write-off of debt to one borrower lest it spill over into a deliberate increase in arrears by others.

To the extent that such funds have bought, and are tackling the problems of, defaulted mortgage debt, it is hard to tell yet whether their performance in terms of fair and reasonable dealing with distressed borrowers is better or worse than that of the banks from which they bought the loans.[28] Anecdotal evidence is consistent with the traditional view that such funds are keen to make a realistic deal with the borrower quickly, whereas banks have been slow to fully recognize when a loan cannot be fully repaid.

---

[28] The quality of some of the blocks of loans purchased from the banks by funds was low. For example, the average duration of arrears of the owner-occupier loans that made up half of the €1.4 billion face value of the block sold in mid-2018 by Ulster Bank to Cerberus Capital Management was 83 months.

If so, some over-indebted borrowers may be able to make a fresh unencumbered start more easily if their loan has been taken over by a fund, whether or not it deserves to be classified as a 'vulture'.

Conscious, however, of the risk that some of the firms coming from abroad to buy NPLs and turn them into cash quickly and profitably might be inclined to cut corners in their dealings with borrowers by treating them unfairly, the Central Bank pressed very hard and ultimately successfully for legislation to be introduced that would ensure that the existing consumer protections for mortgage holders would continue to apply even after the loans were sold by banks. The resulting Consumer Protection (Regulation of Credit Servicing Firms) Act was enacted in July 2015.

North American private equity firms famously invested more than €1.1 billion in Bank of Ireland equity at the turning point of confidence in the economic recovery in July 2011, taking just under 35 per cent of the equity and allowing the government's equity stake to fall to just over 15 per cent. Vultures or not, these firms were well rewarded for good timing, as the share prices rose well in the subsequent years. Their decision to take this risk may also have helped build the momentum of confidence in Ireland's finances at a crucial moment in the recovery.

MEDIOCRE FINANCE IN A PHOENIX RECOVERY

Finance has been a powerful driver of modernization and productivity growth around the world. In Ireland, though, a mediocre financial system has contributed relatively little to prosperity.[29] For years the small contribution resulted from conservatism and stagnant management. More recently, insouciant buccaneering bankers surfed a tidal wave of global liquidity that resulted in bankruptcies on a scale exceeded only in Iceland and in the near-collapse of the public finances. While the scale of banking grew rapidly pre-crisis, nonbank finance has remained rather undeveloped.

And in the post-crisis phase, banks were slow to resolve over-indebtedness situations leaving them with a large block of NPLs. The dreaded 'vulture funds' who have bought some of these loans may be more effective in resolving them, and not necessarily to the long-term disadvantage of the borrower (relative to what the banks have been doing).

---

[29] As I reported in Honohan (2006), little of Ireland's above average economic growth over the decades from the mid-1980s seemed, from econometric analysis, to be attributable to the depth of its financial sector.

Perhaps it is not all that surprising that the recovery of the economy after 2012 got well under way without any aggregate expansion of credit, a phenomenon mirroring, as pointed out by Central Bank chief economist Gabriel Fagan, what had been called 'phoenix recoveries' in several Latin American and other Emerging Market countries after systemic crises.

All in all, finance has disappointed Ireland. What are the prospects for improvement in the culture of customer loyalty and prudence? Apart from acknowledging the substantial increase in vigilance on the adequacy of capital and other prudential aspects, one can construct some arguments to support optimism in regard to the quality and cost of service to household and small business customers.

For example, the crisis may have made some financiers recognize the limitations of purely transactional finance. Bankers have certainly lost the trust of their customers over the past number of years. They must surely realize that the quality of service and some reversion to paying attention to the individual concerns of retail customers can, despite costs, contribute to sustained profits.

The gradual re-emergence of competition could also help, as new entrants (including non-banks) gain the courage to enter the Irish market despite it being so heavily dominated by large incumbents.

Public policy has a role to play: the continuous refinement of codes of conduct is important, even though these inevitably focus on the kinds of procedural matters which can be enforced, and carry their own cost burden which will tend to be passed on the customer. The sharp increase in enforcement, discussed in Chapter 6, certainly provides both a signal and an incentive for better behaviour. The Central Bank, which is increasingly looked-to as society's main animator of good practice in the financial sector, will continue to search for effective ways of improving things, including – but not limited to – seeking additional statutory powers. Its recently launched programme requiring, among other things, banks to enhance diversity in their governance and staffing might help.

Ultimately, though, the complexity of finance means that the effective-ness of the tools at the disposal of public authorities to achieve decisive reforms of culture in financial services firms may be inherently limited.

6

The Role of the Central Bank

THE 'CONSTANT AND PREDOMINANT AIM'

The Central Bank of Ireland is not mentioned in the Irish Constitution, which predated its establishment. But Article 45 of the Constitution sets the tone, stating that: 'in what pertains to the control of credit, the constant and predominant aim shall be the welfare of the people as a whole'. This is stated as one of the directive principles of social policy in the Constitution intended to guide the Oireachtas – the Irish parliament – in the making of laws, and was indeed carried into the first Central Bank Act establishing the Bank in 1942. It is vague but clearly prescriptive in regard to the approach to be taken to central banking inasmuch as the Central Bank is the chief institution of the state charged with 'the control of credit' and all that is conveyed by that phrase.

But how large should the ambition of a central bank be in aiming for the welfare of the people as a whole, and what limitations, if any, should be placed on these ambitions? Indeed, who is to judge the success of the central bank's efforts?

In 1930, as the Great Depression began to deepen, J. M. Keynes wrote of the financial sector, 'to-day we have involved ourselves in a colossal muddle, having blundered in the control of a delicate machine, the working of which we do not understand'. For some conservatives, the message to be taken from such a sentiment is to retreat from activism. I think instead that the correct response to the failures of the early 2000s is twofold: first, having made blunders, central banks need to be more active in order to set things to right; at the same time, there are limitations. The 'delicate machine' of finance needs to be understood if the adverse indirect effects of plausible interventions are to be correctly assessed: not all intervention achieves its ostensible overall aim.

By the 1990s, the creation of the euro, with its multinational European Central Bank (ECB) tightly focused on price stability as the primary objective, seemed to narrow the scope and ambition of central banking in Europe. Yet when the global financial crisis (GFC) broke out, central banks would have had a hard time both in dodging responsibility for the conditions that had resulted in crisis and in defending their performance in stabilizing the situation that had emerged.

Seeming sometimes to be almighty and yet at other times making excuses based on restrictions of mandates and legal powers, the central banks in recent years have been more controversial in their performance than at any time in their history. This is no less true of Ireland than of anywhere else.

It has to be said that the crisis has greatly increased contestation of the proper role of central banks. For more stable times, an adequate toolkit, orderly and mechanical, had been developed that could and did deliver price stability, thereby establishing a platform for the financial sector to contribute to economic growth with few setbacks. Once the crisis created problems of a scale and complexity that had not previously been observed, central banks found that this toolkit was wholly inadequate. Instead they had to fall back on a larger, but less well-defined, collection of tools, drawing on institutional memory and on academic expertise based on the historical experience and lore from previous crises and also on theoretical understanding of economic and financial processes developed by insightful experts.[1]

In general, governments relied on the central bankers in place to advise on the best responses to the crisis. The result was an international explosion of extraordinary innovations in institutions,[2] regulatory legislation[3] and policy.[4]

---

[1] The role of central banks in crisis management is discussed more fully in Honohan, Lombardi and St Amand (2019); the topic is also taken up by Tucker (2018).

[2] To take just a few notable examples abroad, the Financial Stability Board, a committee representative of central banks and finance ministers of twenty-four countries, along with several international agencies and charged with monitoring the global financial system, was established in April 2009; the reintegration of prudential bank regulation into the Bank of England took place in April 2013; November 2014 saw the creation at the ECB of the Single Supervisory Mechanism (SSM) for banks.

[3] This included rules for maintenance of bank liquidity, frequent and aggressive asset quality reviews and stress tests of banks and large increases in bank capital requirements.

[4] This included negative interest rates in several jurisdictions (though not in the USA or the UK), a vast expansion in the liabilities of central banks and in their purchase of

Already in 2009 developments abroad had begun to have an effect in Ireland, whether through the adoption of new regulations in line with international and European accords, through the indirect influence on Ireland and Irish banks of market links with the UK and the rest of the world, or directly through the fact of Ireland's membership in the euro area. In addition, other foreign steps were paralleled at home, for example with the fuller integration of the Irish Financial Services Regulatory Authority in the Central Bank, first on a non-statutory basis, and subsequently when new legislation was brought into force in September 2010.

Its absorption since 1998 within the Eurosystem (as foreseen in the Maastricht Treaty), with maintenance of price stability as the primary objective, is sometimes wrongly thought to have narrowed the goals of the Central Bank of Ireland and even to have compromised its loyalty to Ireland. Under the Irish legislation implementing this Treaty, sole authority for the Central Bank's performance of the price stability mandate was vested in an independent governor, instead of in the Board of Directors as a whole.[5] But this did not remove the governor's responsibility to take account of the impact on Ireland of ECB decisions. Furthermore, the very exclusion of its Board from the monetary policy role provides a clear hint of the importance of the other functions, powers and objectives that are expected of the Central Bank. Indeed a very great part of the Central Bank's work is not closely related to the price stability mandate.[6]

The scope of the Central Bank of Ireland's explicit mandate has been extremely wide compared with that of other central banks around the world. In addition to supervision and regulation of banks, building societies and credit unions, the Central Bank has long had responsibility for consumer protection, for the regulation and supervision of insurance firms, for licensing of certain financial market intermediaries and for the regulation of market conduct. There are specific tasks such as management of the Deposit Guarantee Scheme and the assembly and processing of financial statistics. It prints banknotes and manufactures coin. And

---

government and other securities, and bank closures in several countries with and without bailout of creditors.

[5] This was an unique arrangement motivated by the desire to keep a seat on the Board for a representative of the Department of Finance. That would not have been permissible if the Board had retained responsibility for the Treaty obligations because it would have compromised the Bank's independence of the government in this respect.

[6] Indeed, the legislation clearly states that for the Central Bank maintenance of price stability is the primary objective only 'in discharging its functions and exercising its powers as part of the ESCB' (Central Bank Act, 1942 as amended, Sec 6A(1)).

provision of economic policy advice has long been an accepted practice of the Central Bank.

All of these activities can in principle be conducted with different degrees of energy and intrusiveness. What defines the correct level of engagement? There is really no adequate summary statement.

The failure of Irish prudential regulation in the early years of the new century prompted new Central Bank legislation in 2010, a considerable expansion of staffing and new institutional and policy approaches to the tasks of central banking and above all to prudential regulation of banks.[7]

The list of functions, objectives and powers set out for the Central Bank of Ireland was updated in the 2010 legislation, but remains rather vague. Naturally, the goals include price stability and they also include financial stability and 'the proper and effective regulation of financial service providers and markets, while ensuring that the best interests of consumers of financial services are protected.'[8] The broad unconstrained character in legislation of the functions and objectives may be a good thing inasmuch as it leaves the Central Bank sufficient flexibility to respond to unforeseeable disturbances such as we have experienced in recent years. But it does place the onus on the Central Bank to keep informing the Oireachtas and the general public about what it is doing and why it is doing it.

In this chapter we review four dimensions of central banking, asking what boundaries should be placed on the role of a national central bank within the euro area, such as that of Ireland. How much autonomy does the national central bank have and how should it use that autonomy? Has there been too little or too much activism? Should national central banks be still more innovative and aggressive in the tools that are used and the extent to which they employed?

The first dimension is that of the *classical* central bank, chiefly charged with price stability and protection of the currency regime that is in place.

---

[7] The previous complex structure in which a separate regulatory authority with its own board was embedded within the Central Bank was abandoned in favour of a unitary structure. For some unknown reason, the board of directors of the newly constituted 2010 Central Bank was titled the 'Commission'. Sweeping changes in top management were implemented between 2009 and 2011; comparison of the Annual Reports for 2008 and 2011 shows no overlap between the lists of top managers in the two years.

[8] Until 2010, the list of functions included promoting the development of the Irish financial services industry. Persuading the government to remove this potentially severe source of conflict with the requirements of financial stability (the latter had been given explicit priority in the legislation) was a source of personal satisfaction to me. (Minister Lenihan mischievously teased me that, if I insisted on this, I would have to drop my opposition to the revised legislation being formally titled the Central Bank *Reform* Act, as it ultimately was.)

This is the core activity of the ECB (though it should not be forgotten that the ECB is also required, without prejudice to the objective of price stability, to support the general economic policies in the EU). Achieving price stability has proved challenging since the crisis began, not because inflation has been too high, but because it has been too low.

Though it does not provide banking services to households or non-financial firms, the central bank is the *state's chief bank*. How does this relationship sit with the perceived need to maintain independence of monetary policy from short-termist political forces? In the euro area, lacking a single fiscal counterpart, how should the ECB engage with the national governments, and where does that leave national central banks such as the Central Bank of Ireland in their financial relations with their national governments?

The *assertive* central bank places itself firmly in a regulatory role vis-à-vis the banks and other financial institutions. Here too the crisis revealed failures; reforms were put in place, ultimately including transfer of final authority over the supervision of large banks to the central supranational Single Supervisory Mechanism (SSM) within the ECB. Rightly more intrusive, the internationally agreed structure of financial regulation has also become much more complex in an attempt to plug gaps in an increasingly complex financial world. Yet central banks cannot – and do not hope to – micromanage financial institutions. Some of the regulatory complexity is likely counterproductive, distracting supervisors from a more holistic approach to improving the safety and social efficiency of finance.

Finally we look at some suggestions that have been made to take policy innovation further and would characterize a more *expansive* central bank. To what extent should such ideas be entertained, or are they likely to present problems of democratic legitimacy or to engender unintended systemic side effects that damage economic efficiency?

THE CLASSICAL CENTRAL BANK

Suddenly, in the summer of 2007, a long period of economic prosperity, seemingly underpinned by financial stability, was disrupted by bank failures leading to a collapse in business and consumer confidence. Where had the central banks been; why had they not foreseen the risks of such failures and taken steps to prevent them?

While some commentators have criticized central banks for doing too much since the crisis broke, the more important fact is that they had done too little beforehand. Even after the first shocks the reaction of most central banks still underestimated the gathering storm. Here I will focus on their monetary policy actions (leaving aside for the moment the issues of bank failure and fiscal crises).

True, the US Federal Reserve started lowering its target for money market interest rates in September 2007 from a relatively high 5¼ per cent and had brought it to 2 per cent by the following April. As for the ECB and the Bank of England though, they interpreted the liquidity pressures facing some European banks as mainly a limited spillover from problems in the USA. While easing these liquidity pressures by making larger sums available for overnight borrowing by banks, the ECB kept its main policy rate at 4 per cent and then even made a small increase in July 2008. The Bank of England kept its bank rate at 5¾ per cent until the end of 2007 and it still stood at 5 per cent when the crisis reached its peak at the end of September 2008. Only during and after the extreme events of those weeks, when the global financial system faced imminent catastrophic failure, did central banks really move into the aggressive crisis management mode which characterized the following several years.

The delay in recognizing the scale of the emerging problems can be interpreted as reflecting the quarter century of highly successful central bank policy that preceded the crisis. This period of 'great moderation' with low and stable inflation and a steady economic growth in most advanced economies, interrupted only by a couple of shallow recessions, led central bankers to believe that the problem of business cycles and inflation had been definitively solved. A quasi-mechanical approach to monetary policy gained many adherents. Having been made independent of short-termist political pressures, central banks could concentrate on establishing a platform of monetary stability by steering short-term interest rates: raising these rates sufficiently above their normal level if inflation expectations were increasing and lowering them in case prices and economic activity were dipping below the desired growth rates. But mechanical policy rules that are appropriate in normal times to maintain price stability are not always sufficient either to prevent the emergence of risky financial excesses, or to restore financial stability after a crash.

Being a small peripheral country in the euro area – accounting for less than 2 per cent of its total activity and conducting an unusually large part of its international trading and financial relations with countries outside the euro area – Ireland's pre-crisis consumer price inflation for the ten years running up to the crisis was more volatile than in other euro area countries and averaged 3.9 per cent – twice the ECB's objective for the area as a whole. With nominal interest rates low thanks to the removal of exchange rate risk, these high inflation rates in Ireland depressed real interest rates, further fuelling the glut of borrowing in the early 2000s.

In contrast, since 2008 the deep recession in Ireland has resulted in generally static prices: the consumer price index fell sharply during 2008–9 (partly reflecting the fall in mortgage interest rates, and partly also the fall in sterling lowering import prices) and remained for the following decade below the peak.[9]

It might be thought that zero measured inflation for a decade was a good result, but that is not the case, for two reasons. First, current statistical measures of inflation overstate the true change in average prices in times of rapid introduction of new and improved products. This bias is hard to calculate, but could be of the order of 1 per cent per annum. This alone would have been sufficient reason for the ECB not to have chosen zero measured inflation as its operational objective, instead going for the formula 'below but close to two per cent per annum in the medium term'.[10] The second reason is that, having convinced markets that it would succeed in keeping inflation close to that objective, the ECB created an expectation that underlay price, wage and interest rate contracts. When price inflation turned out to be lower than expected for an extended period, this meant that contracted wages were more uncompetitive and that the real burden of debt was heavier than had been expected. In short, lower than expected inflation implied a slower recovery for a country like Ireland hit by over-indebtedness and high unemployment in the recession. Should we have done more about this?

Actually, until about 2014, the ECB had quite a degree of success in stabilizing overall euro area inflation close to its objective. As mentioned, Ireland's inflation volatility was an outlier in the system. And it is the euro area price level as a whole that the ECB aims at stabilizing: it does not have tools to affect prices differentially in different member states. It is chiefly in this respect (choosing instruments to target inflation for the area as a whole) that members of the ECB Governing Council have to largely disregard national deviations from euro area averages. If euro area inflation

---

[9] The other main index, the so-called Harmonised Index of Consumer Prices (HICP), behaved in a broadly similar albeit less volatile manner.

[10] This operational definition, adopted by the ECB in 2003, is sometimes debated. Some scholars, including former ECB Chief Economist Otmar Issing, have argued that one per cent would be a better target. Many others take the opposite view, arguing for the removal of the asymmetric 'below but' words. A few have discussed the merits of increasing the target to 4 per cent (cf. Ball et al. 2016).

is on track, then there is no justification for adjusting monetary policy to bring the inflation of a particular country closer to target; to do so would only push other countries away from the target. Like other member states, Ireland has opted for a currency regime which delivers price stability in the euro area as a whole. By contributing to the design of monetary policy to ensure that euro area inflation remains close to objective, each member of the Governing Council is in fact loyal to the policy endorsed by their own country in adhering to the Maastricht Treaty.

In practice, during my time as governor, no occasion arose where I saw a conflict between the direction for monetary policy appropriate for the euro area as a whole and that which might have been appropriate for Ireland taken in isolation; such a conflict could exist, but it happened not to during my time. And I would, of course, have been legally obliged to ignore any suggestion from any Irish government official as to the stance that I should take in ECB monetary policy discussions.

That is not to say that every policy move actually adopted was, in my view, optimal or timely for the euro area as a whole – that is a different question. It is easy to find fault with certain elements, such as the two interest rate increases in 2011 already discussed in Chapter 3. Furthermore, I now think we were too slow to see and exploit the powerful effects of quantitative easing (QE) – i.e. the outright purchase of securities – especially on long-term interest rates. But by 2015 the ECB had, despite much hostility from conservative voices, deployed an unmatched suite of expansionary tools.

One by one, potential legal, technical and policy objections were overcome to such measures as negative policy interest rates and large-scale purchases of bonds. The ECB was even purchasing bonds at the lower limit of the investment grade.[11] Getting to that point required careful analysis and it was rewarding to be part of this effort and contributing to the building of a consensus around it.

By 2018, the ECB's bond holdings were in excess of €2½ trillion (including more than €28 billion of Irish government bonds bought in the QE programme), and long-term interest rates had been pushed down right across the euro area (with Irish 10-year bond yields averaging about 1 per cent during the period of QE purchases 2015–18).

---

[11] The Government of Portugal was given only speculative-grade ratings by all of the three main rating agencies during 2015–7. Orphanides (2017) has argued that the ECB should have accepted all national government securities, and not just those considered as 'investment grade' by the rating agencies.

In short, in its performance of the classical price stability function, the ECB in my time was right to move to the adoption of extremely expansive monetary policies. It should have been prepared to do so earlier to help accelerate the recovery of aggregate demand and avoid an undershoot of the inflation objective.

THE STATE'S CHIEF BANK

Though organically part of the Eurosystem, the Central Bank of Ireland is still the State's chief bank. It is not, of course, a normal bank and does not provide banking services to the general public, or to non-financial firms.[12] And it is not (any more) the provider of general banking services to the government. But the Central Bank's profits – very substantial in these recent years – are largely remitted to the government.[13]

Advising the Government

An important role for most central banks is the provision of economic advice, drawing on their expert staff resources. The extent to which such advice should focus on fiscal matters is a matter of some debate. Some central banks, considering the independence they have been granted to deliver on a specific mandate of price and financial stability, refrain from such commentary and get on with their main task. Others seem to relish every opportunity to pontificate on fiscal matters, frequently straying into issues of the size and efficiency of government which are rather distant from the topics of macroeconomic balance for which the central bank may be expected to have some special expertise.

Conflict between central bankers and finance ministers on fiscal issues is a recurring feature in financial history. Ireland's first Central Bank governor, Joseph Brennan, eventually relinquished his office in 1953 in some degree of annoyance at his inability to convince the government of the errors of its ways, and at the tactic of public criticism of the Central Bank which the government had then embarked on.

---

[12] And its balance sheet is not normally the largest among Ireland's banks (though with a peak balance sheet of €204 billion on the cusp of the bailout in 2010 it was briefly the largest).

[13] And the Central Bank of Ireland was the conduit of the financial assistance flows coming from the EU and International Monetary Fund (IMF) sources (as witness the fact that, as governor, I was required to co-sign the memoranda of understanding setting out what was agreed to by Ireland as conditionality for the loans).

In the Irish legislation, the Central Bank is given 'the provision of analysis and comment to support national economic policy development' as one of its objectives. So it would be hard to avoid offering some advice on fiscal issues. An annual pre-budget letter has traditionally been sent to the Minister for Finance setting out the Bank's views. I decided to continue this practice, with the significant difference that my letters were sent on my own authority, without trying to arrive at a compromise that would, at the almost inevitable cost of focus and impact, satisfy the entire Central Bank Board or Commission.

It was impossible during the crisis to avoid discussion of fiscal issues, and I mention later a number of points at which it seemed important for the Central Bank to make its views on fiscal matters clear, usually in private, sometimes in public. In more normal times, I think that the need for confidential advice has diminished. The expansion of freedom of information legislation now makes it likely that most such advice will become public quite quickly. And the creation of the Irish Fiscal Advisory Council (IFAC) makes much of what the Central Bank might otherwise do in this field largely redundant.

Role of the National Central Bank in the Eurosystem

But national central banks also retain considerable autonomy from national governments as the representative of a member state participating in the euro. According to the distributed architecture of the Eurosystem, each national central bank has responsibility for operationalizing in its own country key central banking functions such as the provision of notes and coin and the wholesale electronic payments system.

Each national central bank also participates fully in the decision-making processes of the Eurosystem.[14] (Doing this well both demands considerable expertise and interpersonal skills on the part of the national central bank specialists participating in these committees, and gives those staff members valuable work experience. Given the opportunities and job mobility of such experts, the important task of ensuring that the Central Bank of Ireland is able to send experienced and engaged participants in these committees is challenging.)

---

[14] Most Eurosystem decisions are ultimately decided by the Governing Council, based on preparatory work conducted in committees formed of officials from each national central bank together with ECB staff. National conditions can be relevant to the overall design of euro area policies and it is the national central bank that must represent those interests in the committees.

Supporting the Irish presidency of the EU Council in 2013 entailed a very substantial and highly technical contribution from Central Bank of Ireland staff, not least because the legislative agenda of that presidency was concentrated on post-crisis financial sector reform. It was a boost to morale at the Central Bank to realize how much our staff had contributed to what was seen as one of the most successful recent EU presidency semesters.

The suggestion has sometimes been made in connection with the so-called Troika EU–IMF programmes of assistance that the governor of a national central bank might have to divide his or her loyalty; but this misunderstands the position in practice. Actually most of the ECB's engagement with these programmes ('in liaison' with the European Commission and the IMF) was not formally considered or approved by the Governing Council but decided by the six-person full-time Executive Board of the ECB. Thus, while the members of the Governing Council were kept generally informed about the programmes, the Governing Council never had to approve a programme.[15] The logic here is that the ECB was not a provider of funds to these programmes, and its participation was more a technical than a policy matter.

Nevertheless, there were a number of crucial points at which Troika programmes intersected with matters the Governing Council did have to decide on; notably the provision of emergency liquidity assistance (ELA). And the Governing Council did make public statements endorsing programmes that had been agreed on.

When it came to the Irish programme, it was clear to me, and to every other member of the Governing Council, that my primary role in any such discussions, formal or informal, must be to explain and represent the interests of Ireland. If I did not do that, who else would? And if the Governing Council was not fully informed about the detailed interests of Ireland in relation to a programme designed to support the Irish recovery, how could it make decisions that were in the best interest of the euro area of which Ireland was the most directly affected member?

During the crisis, as detailed in Chapter 8, it was necessary for the Central Bank of Ireland to make ELA loans to Irish banks to enable them to meet the outflow of deposits as confidence in the government's guarantee ebbed. As implied by its name ELA lending is unusual, and it is intended to be short term. For some time Ireland was the only user. At first the sums required were relatively modest, and related only to

---

[15] Another example, discussed more fully in the text that follows, was the Governing Council's statement of approval of Ireland's 2011 bank stress tests in March 2011.

Anglo Irish Bank. As we will see, though, from September 2010 the need for ELA grew. If ELA had been withdrawn or capped, the Irish government would not have had the capacity to honour its guarantee to bank creditors promptly, and the result would have been instant administrative restrictions on deposit withdrawals and a decline into the kind of financial chaos that the guarantee had been designed to avoid. Indeed, the chaos would now have entailed not only a bank default but also default of the government on its guarantee. As discussed in Chapter 8, for Ireland this was clearly a more than unpalatable scenario.

The growing scale of ELA borrowing, which I had to pre-clear with the Governing Council on a twice-monthly basis, began to cause other members of the Governing Council great concern in the second half of 2010. Allowing such a scale of borrowing could create a precedent that, if repeated in other countries, could result in so much credit expansion as to undermine overall inflation control in the euro area. Besides, the governors too were beginning to be concerned about credit risk: much of the ELA was being collateralized by Irish government promises. In this environment, my primary role at the Governing Council was clearly to explain and justify the continuation of this ELA. No divided loyalty: the members of the Governing Council needed to know the Irish situation and Irish needs. No one else in the room was in a position to conduct this advocacy.

When it came to the negotiations between Troika and Irish officials, the Central Bank was unambiguously on the Irish side of the table. Furthermore, I made a point of never making any policy recommendation to the Irish government on the basis that it was the desire of the ECB. I felt that my advice would be worthless if I was reduced to being an ambassador for views held in Frankfurt. When there were messages that I was asked by Frankfurt to transmit, I did so, but qualified it by adding my own, sometimes differing, advice (for example in the case of Jean-Claude Trichet's letter of 19 November 2010 to Brian Lenihan, discussed in Chapter 9).

Nor, however, did this imply a lack of loyalty to the ECB on my part. In particular, confident that the government was committed to honouring the promissory notes that were now being used as collateral for ELA, I did not believe that the ECB's financial condition was being placed at risk in this matter of ELA.

As far as I was concerned, the Central Bank is an arm of the state. Of course that does not mean that the national Central Bank is bound to make any loan or advance to the government; on the contrary, it is precluded from doing that by the Treaty (TFEU).[16] The assessment of the ECB of the value of its claims – or indeed the claims of a commercial bank – on a member government might well be that they are not absolutely safe. But my own view, perhaps controversial, is that a guarantee to the Central Bank of Ireland from the Irish government must be treated by the Central Bank as absolutely certain (unless there is some evidence of bad faith, which there was not).

Wider Role in Financial Diplomacy

Outside the euro area the national central bank still exists as an autonomous participant in international central banking discussions. For example, it has a seat at the European Systemic Risk Board (ESRB), which covers the EU as a whole, not just the euro area. Admittedly, though, Ireland does not have a direct seat at the most important international central banking meetings beyond Europe.

Despite efforts (which I remember working on in the late 1970s as a young central banker), Ireland does not have a seat on the Board of the Bank for International Settlements (BIS); but the governor can attend the Global Economy meeting and some other sessions during the bi-monthly meetings of central banks at the BIS in Basel: this provides the opportunity to track wider international economic and financial developments as seen from the world's principal central banks and to build diplomatic relationships with central bankers from beyond the European Union. In earlier positions I had occasion to interact with some of these central bankers before.[17] It was useful to obtain perspectives from outside Europe on what Ireland's best approach might be to its deepening financial crisis in 2010 and to take the pulse of the wider international central banking community as we built the recovery within the EU–IMF programme.

At the IMF, Ireland joins with Canada and several Caribbean countries to elect an executive director and a member of the ministerial IMF Committee; an alternate executive director (usually a Central Bank or Department of Finance staff member) directly represents Ireland at the IMF – an entity whose remit extends well beyond money and banking.

---

[16] Nor should it take on any unremunerated tasks that don't fall within the ambit of central banking. This rule would apply regardless of the Treaty: democratic governments should not seek to evade in such a way the need for parliamentary approval of their spending.

[17] Counting up, I estimate that I have had some kind of interaction – whether from policy meetings during my stints at the World Bank, or conferences and bilateral discussions before and since then – with more than seventy national central banks around the world.

Except through its membership of the EU, Ireland is not part of the Financial Stability Board or the G20 or the Basel Committee of Bank Supervisors; our economy and financial system are not quite big enough to secure us a place in those important groupings – whose governance structures are not well adapted to protecting the interests of smaller countries. That has limited the influence Ireland could have in designing the international reforms of bank regulation, though, as mentioned, we did play a significant role in ensuring the implementation of these reforms in Europe thanks to Ireland having the EU presidency in early 2013 at a crucial time for the enactment of financial legislation.

THE ASSERTIVE CENTRAL BANK

For the first half century of its existence the Central Bank of Ireland scarcely concerned itself with the prudential supervision of financial institutions, and certainly not with the main banks.

Fifty years ago there was no formal arrangement for prudential supervision of banks in Ireland. Even twenty-five years ago, as reported in the Bank's Golden Jubilee report, the total number of financial sector supervision staff was fifty-nine, only some of whom were dealing with banks.

The lack of success it had in dealing with Ken Bates and his failing Irish Trust Bank in the mid-1970s likely contributed to the Bank's reluctance to devote attention and resources to this area in practice.[18]

Although staffing and focus on regulation and supervision were nevertheless built up progressively, adoption of a complacent principles-based approach along the lines developed by the British Financial Services Authority (as described in Chapter 4) implied that staffing would not be very great. Only 48 of the 344 staff dealing with financial regulation in 2007 were assigned to prudential regulation of banks; the team assigned to deal specifically with Bank of Ireland and Anglo Irish Bank was three persons strong; that for AIB and Irish Life and Permanent had just two persons; another three-person team dealt with no fewer than eight smaller institutions, two of which, INBS and EBS, failed (Honohan 2010).

It was a false economy. This complacent supervisory approach was not justified by the actual vulnerabilities of banks or by the information and incentives facing senior decision-makers in the banks. After the banks' deficiencies were uncovered it was shockingly clear that the very light

---

[18] There is an accessible account of the saga of this small bank at www.independent.ie/unsorted/features/escape-artist-supreme-26310371.html.

staffing of bank supervision could not be defended. Much more information on the activity, financial performance and risk of the banks must be assessed and in an intrusive way especially in order to measure more reliably the adequacy of the banks' capital reserves and in order to assess the robustness of each bank's business model.

The system clearly needed an overhaul, and the search for a new Chief Executive of the Financial Regulator within the Central Bank was well underway when I was appointed governor. Matthew Elderfield was a front runner and he arranged to meet me at Knock Airport in September 2009 for a one-on-one interview which we conducted in a somewhat unorthodox manner, rambling through medieval ecclesiastical ruins and along the byways of Mayo. Matthew had been heading up the Bermuda Monetary Authority and had previous bank supervision experience from his time at the Financial Services Authority in London. He had gained an understanding of the strengths and weaknesses of the British supervisory system which was now in the process of rapid adaptation in response to the deficiencies exposed by the crisis. Decisive, tough and gregarious, he was the right choice to reorganize and build a much more extensive supervisory apparatus for Ireland.

Supervisory staff numbers had to increase; even though staffing in other public services was being constrained by budgetary policy, after the crash the general public would not have tolerated a penny-pinching approach to reform of the bank supervisory structure. And all the more so given that we were in crisis management mode at that moment and for some years later. Assessing recapitalization needs; innovating in response to the huge and growing problem of non-performing loans; trying to ensure that, while they dealt with legacy issues, the banks were taking the necessary steps to improve the quality of their ongoing business decisions – all of these dimensions meant that a sizable increase in staffing would be needed.

And it was not just bank supervision that had been understaffed. As mentioned in Chapter 5, problems in insurance and other non-bank firms were bubbling away in the background. Although the first-ever fine for regulatory violations had been imposed on a bank in late 2008, there was no stand-alone department in the Central Bank for dealing with enforcement.

All of these shortcomings were addressed by the reorganization and expansion energetically spearheaded by Matthew. Staff numbers increased by 327, or 31 per cent, in two years (compared with a total of 53, or 5½ per cent, in the four years before the crisis).[19] We pushed ahead on this while being conscious of the risks. Engaging so many new people could present serious risks in itself: careful selection, management and training would be needed and these functions also needed be greatly strengthened. And if the international financial services sector were to shrink post-crisis, as many analysts forecast, how easy would it be to downsize again? In the end the effort was largely successful. Many of those who came to the Central Bank even for just two or three years – many of them from abroad – made outsize contributions by bringing fresh ideas, an outside perspective and enthusiasm to what was a massive programme of change being carried out in the middle of a national economic crisis.

Still, questions must remain. While it is unlikely that banking blunders on the egregious scale of the past crisis would go undetected, it is less clear how effective supervision of banks would be in weeding out problems that are on a smaller scale or that relate to financial transactions involving more complicated risks than the simple forms of loan finance that were involved in our failures. Is there really a fully effective way of supervising the performance of banks? This must be considered an open question. While no one can dispute that the Central Bank is much more intrusive in its prudential engagement with the banks, some of the additional interactions focus on minutiae of what is an increasingly complex set of international rules. (After all, recall that much of the efforts of the most skilled Irish supervisors in the years running up to the crisis had been absorbed with the distracting task of implementing the internationally agreed Basel II system of capital regulation – a system now seen as over-complicated and, in the end, counterproductive.)

On the other hand, the international prudential rules omit some areas that have proved to be important. For example, the instructions given by the Central Bank of Ireland in 2012 and 2013 to banks – and certainly regarded by them as costly and intrusive – insisting on more effective and speedy action to find sustainable solutions for distressed mortgage and small and medium enterprise (SME) debt have no counterpart in the international rules and had to be invented locally to ensure a sufficient response.

Central banks cannot and should not aspire to micromanagement of financial institutions. Setting clear parameters and penalizing failures to comply is normally the only practical way to proceed.

---

[19] Employment in the Irish financial services and real estate sector had jumped by 22 per cent in those four pre-crisis years, while total credit more than doubled.

As far as prudential regulation is concerned, international standards about how big the reserve of risk-absorbing capital must be relative to the risks assumed have been greatly tightened since the crisis both quantitatively and in terms of the prescription of risk weights. Although some of the calculations on which these standards are based can (paradoxically) be questioned as both overly complex and in certain respects crude and clunky, change was badly needed. But the final choice of which risks to assume should remain for the banks themselves to make.

Sometimes this presumption has to be overridden. Deficiencies in financial firm conduct, especially regarding consumer protection, have provided many examples where, left alone, bank behaviour has fallen well short of what would be expected from a well-adapted corporate culture. As a result, the regulatory response has had to be much more prescriptive. The pattern of sharp practice and operational deficiencies uncovered in Ireland with respect to tracker mortgages is a key example (already discussed in Chapter 5). Unwinding these widespread deficiencies took more than two years of detailed interaction with the banks from October 2015 before the Central Bank was able to declare itself satisfied that the situation had been brought under control. In this case the Central Bank had to behave very intrusively to hold a firm line on the interpretation of its code of conduct.

Uncertainty as to effectiveness applies also to the rules about market conduct of regulated non-bank financial institutions. A sizable fraction of Central Bank supervisory staff deals with this segment, reflecting Dublin's scale in such segments as the global investment fund industry. The main goal of the international rules for this segment is to ensure that investment funds state clearly to investors what they are getting into and are not subverted in the interests of the promoters at the expense of investors – but their application is far from simple. Indeed, many observers begin to worry that the new legislation has become too complex to achieve its goals or even to be fully digested by regulator or regulated.[20] Nevertheless, as long as nonbank financial regulation remains at national level within Europe, compliance with these rules needs to be checked regardless of their intrinsic value: otherwise the standing and credibility of Ireland in

---

[20] I too fear that this complexity (which drives further increases in staffing) may hamper effective supervision, and ironically weaken the hand of enforcement. An alert supervisor with broad discretionary powers to restrain the behaviour of an errant market participant could be better able to head off risks than the current international tendency to rely on detailed regulatory prescriptions that in practice offer a safe haven to the regulated firm.

international financial transactions would be undermined, with knock-on effects on broad economic prosperity.

When he succeeded Matthew as Deputy Governor for Financial Regulation in 2013 (the new title arising out of the new institutional structure for the Central Bank defined by the 2010 Act), Banque de France alumnus Cyril Roux brought a meticulous analytical mind to the job. It became clear to him that the wave of new post-crisis international financial legislation that has been transposed into Irish law meant that further staffing increases were going to be needed already in 2015. Even the centralization of euro area bank supervision in the SSM based at the ECB in Frankfurt entailed more staff in Dublin, as much of the detailed supervisory work, including a considerable increase on-site inspections of banks, is still carried out by Central Bank of Ireland staff who also need to brief and coordinate with the headquarters of the SSM. This has meant a renewed sharp increase in staffing from 2015, after three years in which we paused to absorb the large increase of 2010–11.[21]

The Central Bank is now a big organization, making large demands on senior management skills in order to ensure that communication between different parts of the organization are as smooth as necessary.[22] Never again must gaps be allowed to emerge such as that which led the banking supervisors to say, of the crisis, "If we had only known how vulnerable the macroeconomic situation was, we would have taken a different view of the soundness of the banks" while the macroeconomists said, "If we had only known how exposed the banks were to property-backed loans, we would have taken a more pessimistic view of the macroeconomic risks."

Enforcement of central bank regulations does require that penalties are imposed when violations occur not least so that the credibility of the regulatory framework is maintained. In 2010 a separate enforcement directorate was established at the Central Bank in order to ensure both that such work was given sufficient priority and that it was separate from ongoing supervision. This is an area that calls for painstaking and ultra-careful work to build cases that stand up to challenge. Some administrative cases took years to prepare. The legal environment in Ireland is such that

---

[21] Adapting to the SSM also involved a further re-engineering of the Central Bank's working methods for the prudential regulation of banks, a task undertaken by Sharon Donnery, who was soon to succeed Stefan Gerlach as deputy governor.

[22] Reflecting the increased organizational complexity of the Central Bank, the position of Chief Operations Officer was created in early 2011 (two years before the Bank of England realized they too needed one). It was a considerable relief when Gerry Quinn took on this challenging responsibility.

a burden of rigorous proof is very much on the Central Bank, and its enforcement judgements may be quite vulnerable to judicial and quasi-judicial review.[23]

Often the violator accepts guilt and an out-of-court settlement is negotiated.[24] Sometimes, though, guilt is not acknowledged. This applies especially to individuals because, in the nature of things, they have more at stake than firms. Yet the disincentive effect of an individual penalty is surely much more effective. That means that the Central Bank cannot shirk and has not shirked the responsibility of continuing to prosecute regulatory breaches attributable to individuals even if it means going through what seems to me to be an extremely onerous quasi-judicial procedure (known as Inquiry). And the Central Bank must be no respecter of personalities: managers and directors of financial firms are generally prominent figures in the community. That cannot be allowed to insulate them from the rigours of regulation.

It was also made clear to enforcement staff that the Central Bank had moved decisively away from a policy approach which accepted no legal risks. The Bank's legal powers to enforce against clear breaches of regulation have to be tested, even if there is risk: should these powers prove inadequate the legislature will want to know so that tighter legislation can be enacted.

As evidenced also in the various criminal cases that have followed the crisis, these processes are astonishingly slow and cumbersome apparently reflecting what is mandated by Irish legal practice (cf. Daly 2019). This does raise questions about the adequacy of the law and of legal procedures in respect of white-collar crime generally, as Matthew Elderfield observed in 2013.[25] He suggested that the criminal justice system was not as effective as it should be in dealing with individual accountability when it came to financial fraud or failure, and proposed that the whole question deserved a special review by relevant experts. The idea of criminalizing an offence of reckless mismanagement of a financial firm was aired by myself, among others. Though an offence of this type was introduced in the UK in 2014,

---

[23] Investigation and prosecution of most criminal offences are the responsibility of the Garda Síochána (National Police), to whom the Central Bank passes relevant information, and the Director of Public Prosecutions.

[24] The maximum financial penalties specified in law were also too low, though there have been increases in respect of more recent violations.

[25] In the period 2012–8 about a dozen persons were jailed in Ireland in relation to matters surrounding Anglo Irish Bank – though this includes those convicted for tax matters and for contempt of court.

the idea has not received much parliamentary attention in Ireland, perhaps because it is thought that achieving a conviction for such a hard-to-define but serious crime would be too difficult in practice. And sharp practice disadvantaging consumers, even if in violation of Central Bank codes of conduct, is not per se a criminal offence.

THE EXPANSIVE CENTRAL BANK

The Central Bank of Ireland has tested the boundaries of its mandate during these years. It was vital to take decisive and intrusive corrective policy action; democratic legitimacy not only permitted, but demanded, such action. But it was equally important not to overstep the mark.[26]

One particularly high-profile example of intrusive policy relates to the introduction in early 2015 of relatively tight macro-prudential rules relating to loan-to-value (LTV) and loan-to-income (LTI) thresholds for mortgage lending, designed to prevent the re-emergence of bubble-like developments in the property market.

The speed at which Irish housing prices bounced back from their trough in early 2013 risked triggering the return of a bubble psychology in the market. If enough people believed that prices would spiral up, a price-credit-price spiral could get under way. To be sure, the total volume of new bank credit being extended was small – most of the house purchases were now cash sales – but this was the time to put in protections. Given the poor recent record of bank risk management, there could be no assurance that the banks would be sufficiently prudent in their lending, and at the Central Bank we were sceptical that the higher capital buffers being held by the banks would be sufficient protection for society as a whole. Accordingly we decided to introduce macro-prudential rules to make it clear that high-risk credit would not be allowed to fuel a bubble.

In October 2014, we proposed limits on the proportion of bank lending for house purchase that could exceed a threshold for the LTV and for the LTI. The proposal was supported by a quantity of supporting analytical material published by the Central Bank. It was not to be an outright prohibition on high-LTV and -LTI loans, but the thresholds being proposed for these ratios were much lower than were becoming common again in bank lending.

---

[26] The challenges for a central bank in both achieving policy efficiency and retaining political legitimacy are well discussed in Tucker (2018).

Public consultation on the macro-prudential proposals generated much comment, about half of it favourable. But, although the government had assigned responsibility for macro-prudential policy in Ireland to the Bank, it was in the face of considerable controversy – and the public opposition of the Department of Finance – that these rules were introduced in early 2015.[27]

There was an immediate effect in stemming the risk of a bubble emerging. During the eighteen-month period ending in October 2014, Dublin residential property prices rose by 46 per cent. The following eighteen months saw the price rise stemmed to less than 4 per cent.[28]

Other examples of a relatively expansive use of the powers of the Central Bank in recent times, discussed in detail in this and other chapters, include its use of liquidity tools and the handling of the complex legacy issues of financial engineering related to bank failure; its intrusive supervisory engagement with individual regulated entities; its advice to and support of the government in public and in private for example in negotiations with the international lenders and in many other ways.[29]

Despite this testing of the boundaries (and although it received the gratifying accolade of 'Central Bank of the Year 2015' from an international panel assembled by CentralBanking.com), there will still be some observers who imagine an even more expansive role for the Central Bank.

The ideas that are canvassed include that of a binding cap on mortgage interest rates; of helicopter money; of specific directions to commercial banks with regard to debt relief. Such ideas deserve careful consideration. But on the whole such consideration fails to find such measures convincing in present circumstances.

The downside of each of these three ideas illustrates a distinct type of boundary.

Control of retail interest rates by the Central Bank is not provided for in legislation, and, despite legislative proposals in this direction, I believe it should remain so. Capping interest rates typically falls foul of the law of unintended systemic consequences. Because of the likely medium-term effect on bank entry and competition, a binding cap is likely to end up

---

[27] Actually, the Central Bank's power to introduce such macro-prudential rules is not unconstrained; there is a parliamentary control in the form of a twenty-one-day period following their introduction during which such rules can be rejected by a vote of the Dáil.

[28] Kinghan et al. (2016) document the impact of the restrictions on the structure of lending. Property price increases at a faster rate did resume later in 2016.

[29] For example, there has been significant strategic and tactical innovation in the investment of the Central Bank's financial asset portfolio.

reducing availability of credit to the less evidently creditworthy, while increasing the cost of credit to those who get it. Competition and entry would be chilled: aggressive official interest rate spread control would be the clearest warning signal to would-be entrants that they might not be permitted to earn sufficient profits to justify the costs of entering.

Although capping is not the solution, there are problems with the contract design of the standard variable rate mortgage as it has been operated in Ireland. Improved compulsory disclosure of the way in which these rates will be adjusted (as has now been mandated) is one limited way of helping this.

Helicopter money is not necessarily a daft idea. Distributing cash to households could be more effective, euro for euro, as a means of increasing aggregate demand than QE, which exchanges cash for government bonds. The distributional effects would be different, likely overall more progressive than under QE; interest rates would be higher. Such a measure would be economically equivalent to the government selling bonds to the central bank and distributing the proceeds. But distributed to whom and in what quantities? Could the central bank be thought to have legitimate authority for such action without reference to the government? This equivalence makes the essential role of government in such action clear. Cooperation with government is not necessarily inconsistent with independence. Still, this also suggests the legal obstacles that might be in its way in the euro area.

Another activist form of central banking sometimes advocated (and used extensively in the past in many developing countries) is the making of detailed directions to banks regarding to whom they should lend or whose loans they should restructure and in what way. Such directions override the lending bank's commercial judgement and substitute that of the central bank. The objection to this is not ideological, but practical and political. How detailed can such instruction become before it is clear that it goes beyond the expertise and organizational capacity of the central bank? It amounts to steering hidden subsidies through credit to selected sectors: an opaque quasi-fiscal role lacking democratic accountability (and potentially opening a door to corruption). It is unlikely that this is the best way to improve the behaviour of banks from society's point of view.[30]

This is not to say that there are no possibilities for improvement. More could be done to improve consumer protection, building on the codes of

---

[30] Kay (2015) provides a very convincing presentation of the challenges in moving to a more effective approach to regulation and supervision of finance.

conduct that are already in place and have been strengthened over the years. The challenge is to define rules that are workable, do not have excessive adverse side effects, and provide a worthwhile advance for the consumer.

For some, all such ideas risk moving the central bank further away from the necessary focus on its core mandate of price stability and from tried and tested policies. But monetary and financial stability are multidimensional; reluctance to intervene must be weighed against the danger that what seems peripheral now may become central later. One senior colleague from a successful country counselled me to stay away from such intrusive policies as our 2015 macro-prudential rules for mortgage lending; but a couple of years later he too was warning that urban house price increases in his county were unsustainable.

Effective measures to improve the performance of the financial system are often unpopular. It takes time for their protective function to manifest itself and, inasmuch as they prevent crises, their success is often invisible. That means that they will be even more difficult to adopt if left to elected politicians instead of being pushed forward – always subject to democratic control – by expert agencies appointed to safeguard, in matters of credit, the welfare of the people.

* * *

If one wished to pinpoint a persistent weakness in the approach of the Central Bank of Ireland, not just in the years immediately preceding the crisis, but over the previous decades since its establishment, it would be the tendency to passivity. For a long time it did not seek to use the full additional statutory powers it had obtained when it was created out of the previous currency board arrangement. The interest rate blunder of 1955 was not opposed with sufficient energy; and it failed to take the advisory initiative when a devaluation was needed in 1986; later (at the 1990s DIRT [deposit interest retention tax] Inquiry) it reasoned that bank facilitation of tax avoidance by their customers was not a matter requiring action. And of course it exercised grossly insufficient restraint on the bank lending surge of the period 2004–7.

Ireland's Central Bank has also displayed important persistent strengths. A key dimension is institutional integrity. I do not refer here to the honesty of individuals, which should be taken for granted, but to the fact that the monetary system in Ireland has not been actively abused by the Central Bank for political advantage, as it has in many other countries, whether through grossly subsidized lending through, or at the direction of, the central bank, or by multiple exchange rates opaquely taxing some and subsidizing others, or more generally by what the old writers called 'debauching the currency', i.e. high engineered inflation. Most new states created in the twentieth century did not avoid such hazards.

A recurrent question since the start of the euro has been what the proper role of national central banks is in this construct. It would, after all, have been possible to construct a fully centralized Eurosystem into which all of the national central banks would have been dissolved. That they were not so dissolved may be seen as the result of the composition of the Delors Committee which, in the late 1980s, hammered out the main elements of the design of the euro area. After all, the governors of the national central banks formed the majority in that Committee. Indeed the Treaty allows national central banks to perform tasks other than those specified for the ECB provided this is not opposed by a two-thirds majority of the Governing Council. Clearly this is a relatively high threshold for an objection, so it seems that the original design anticipated that NCBs would continue to perform a variety of national tasks. Ireland is far from being alone in performing additional functions such as the regulation and supervision of nonbanks, consumer protection and policy advice to the national government. Although most of the prudential regulation and supervision of banks is now a European responsibility with the national central banks operating under a kind of delegation from the SSM, there are still forms of regulation, such as the macro-prudential tools introduced in Ireland in 2015, for which no European legislative framework exists and which therefore fall to national central banks to be carried out. In general, performance of these national functions has not generated much controversy.[31]

As constructed, the ECB can seem a purely technocratic centralized monetary authority whose decision-making bodies are free of any national loyalties. And that is how ECB monetary policy has been analysed in the professional literature. But by leaving the national central banks in place, the Delors Committee may have unwittingly retained structures that proved essential in coping with the strongly contrasting stresses which the crisis placed on different national economies. National central banks were thrust into roles not clearly foreseen by the architects of the system. All in all, I find it hard to imagine that the member states would have fared as well without the presence of a national central bank.

---

[31] Though from time to time the question of whether it is consistent with Article 123 of the Treaty for any cost of these functions (not recouped from regulated firms) to be borne by the national central bank. If they are thought of as government functions, should the government not pay for them?

PART III

CRISIS

7

The Guarantee

The bank guarantee of 2008 is the most talked about event in Irish financial history.[1] 'Unconditional and irrevocable' was the confident commitment made by the government, following a rushed overnight decision on the morning of 30 September, in guaranteeing essentially all of the liabilities of the Irish-controlled banks. The decision was triggered by an emerging panic that the banks would be unable to retain their funding in the days ahead and that this would lead to a full-fledged run and collapse of the banking system.

Although the market concerns had been building up for more than a year, and despite many meetings, wargames and policy notes during that time, Irish policymakers had not fully engaged with the scale and immediacy of the risks they faced and ultimately were unprepared for the end-game.

Was it a mistake? If so, what should have been done and how much difference would it have made?

WARNING SIGNS

While first-line responsibility for bank failure lies squarely with the management and directors of the banks, Irish society's interests were to be protected by the Financial Services Regulatory Authority (call it the FR for short), which was a part of the Central Bank although with its own governance structure. But, even though the fall in property prices was well under way by mid-2007, eroding the value of collateral backing so

---

[1] Earlier extended treatments are in Honohan (2010), Cooper (2012), Donovan and Murphy (2012) and Oireachtas (2016).

much of the banks' assets, the FR remained relatively complacent right up until the crisis broke.[2]

At least five danger signals should have heightened regulatory concern about the Irish banks. But the FR failed to react. Indeed, the FR seems to have drawn the wrong lesson from each of what might otherwise have proved to be wake-up calls to the fact that the banks were facing widespread insolvency.

The Liffey Quays Conduits

The first sharp shock of the financial crisis to hit Dublin related to some obscure entities known as conduits. Conduits were firms that had been created as subsidiaries by many banks worldwide as a way of indirectly investing in the securities that were being sold by the mushrooming US mortgage industry. Although conduits were financial firms, indeed bank-like entities, they were not subject to the same regulation as banks. Their legal form and business model had been structured in a way that left them outside the regulatory perimeter. They were not carrying out any of the kinds of business that would have required them to hold licenses or be subject to restrictions beyond those generally applying even to non-financial firms.

Conduits established in Dublin by the Irish banking subsidiary of a German regional bank, Sachsen Landesbank, got into difficulties in mid-2007, being caught up in the general collapse of confidence in US mortgage-backed securities. Investing in US assets and sourcing their funding in the international financial market, their choice of Dublin as a location for Sachsen's conduits was presumably in part for tax reasons. Cheekily, the largest of these entities was called Ormond Quay, the name of the stretch of the river Liffey which the Central Bank's headquarters building overlooked.

The inability of these conduits to continue to roll over their short-term funding caused the failure of their German parent. This was bailed out by the German authorities in late August 2007.

Ironically, the early failure of Sachsen, so conspicuously linked as it was to the collapsing US subprime market, may have lulled Dublin officials into

---

[2] This echoed the reaction of many regulatory authorities elsewhere. While losses from the US subprime market were inevitable by mid-2007, the overall scale of the losses was expected to be small. The main problem perceived was the uncertainty as to where the losses might fall given the complexity of the structured finance products that had been constructed from the original loans.

a false sense of security based on the assumption that the financial turbulence was all about these exotic US instruments in which the locally controlled Irish banks had little involvement.

A much larger entity, Depfa, German-owned but operating in Ireland, was also dependent (in the same way as Sachsen's conduits) on maintaining access to the international money market at very keen interest rates. If the spread of the interest rate they had to pay were to rise too high, it would make the whole operation unprofitable. The failure of Sachsen could have awakened doubts about the solidity of Depfa – which had grown to become the largest bank in Ireland – but that hint seems to have passed largely unnoticed in Dame Street.[3]

The Run on the Rock

The run on the British mortgage bank Northern Rock (NR) in September 2007 was closely watched by the Irish authorities, not least because NR had sourced relatively sizable deposits from middle-class savers in Ireland keen to avail of the higher interest rates it was offering. Anxious to limit moral hazard, the Bank of England at first resisted the idea of granting NR emergency 'lender of last resort' liquidity assistance (ELA) to NR, but it soon relented.[4] Nevertheless, the poorly handled announcements in London surrounding the rescue of NR resulted in disturbing images of panicking depositor queues. Once members of the general public became aware that the bank was in such difficulties as to need ELA, many wanted to withdraw their deposits.[5]

The NR experience showed how quickly a loss of market confidence could be transmitted to retail depositors. The lesson to be learned was the need for quick and decisive action to deal with the causes of such a loss of confidence.

As a result, British officials determined that legislation was needed to give their regulatory authorities the power to resolve a failing bank quickly

---

[3] As subsidiaries of German banks, the chief responsibility for prudential supervision of these entities when they failed lay with the German authorities; however, Depfa had been supervised by the Irish Financial Regulator up until its acquisition by Hypo RE in 2007.

[4] In this context, moral hazard referred to the risk that, if they understood their bank deposits to be de facto fully protected by the Bank of England, depositors would be insouciant in choosing where to place their money.

[5] Even relatively small deposits were only partly covered by the British deposit protection scheme at the time.

and effectively, with a minimum of disruption to necessary financial services.[6]

Unfortunately, the main operational conclusion drawn by the Irish financial authorities from the NR event was that ELA could erode depositor confidence rather than building it. Irish resolution legislation was not brought in until much later.

The St. Patrick's Day Massacre

The collapse and rescue of US investment bank Bear Stearns in mid-March 2008 was a major event which inevitably affected stock market prices of other banks in the following days. But the price of Irish bank shares, especially those of Anglo, fell much more sharply than those of others. This suggested that market participants had begun to form particularly adverse opinions on the ability of the Irish banks to survive banking turbulence (as indeed was also beginning to be suggested by analyst and media reports). Investors were, in short, becoming doubtful about the viability of Irish banks, recognizing that, although not exposed to the US subprime-related assets, these banks were heavily invested in other property-related loans, and were very dependent on the short-term money market for their funding. The downturn in the evidently overpriced Irish property markets was undoubtedly an underlying factor in market concerns.

Already the geographic scope and maturities of funding available to the Irish banks had shrunk: they had to renew their borrowings more and more frequently, and an increasing proportion was being sourced from London rather than from further afield, as more remote investors began to doubt their ability to track the emerging problems. The market price of subordinated debt of the banks, already down since the middle of the previous year, moved sharply lower, reflecting investors' increasing fear of default.[7]

---

[6] This was a lesson already well understood in international circles: in the World Bank team (of which I had been part) advising developing and emerging market governments on financial sector issues, such legislation had long been part of a standard package of recommendations. One assumes that it had not been considered necessary to implement in as mature a financial centre as London, where adequate official supervision should enable preventative action to be taken well before any question of resolution or liquidation arose.

[7] Yield spreads in the secondary market on the subordinate debt of Anglo Irish Bank briefly topped 700 basis points in March–April 2008; the figure for other banks was almost half that (Lane 2015). Recall that, when issued a few years before, the initial yield on some of these bonds had been as low as 25 to 30 basis points above risk-free equivalents.

But rather than asking themselves whether these concerns of market participants were justified by facts, the Irish authorities responded by speaking out against speculators, and imposing a ban on the short-selling of Irish bank equities.

The Quinn Contracts for Difference

A fourth wake-up call came through the contracts-for-difference (CFD) saga with Anglo Irish Bank (alluded to in Chapter 4). The speculative position built up from late 2007 by Sean Quinn in the equity of Anglo made its share price vulnerable.

Although it is often suggested that Quinn controlled a quarter of Anglo through his CFD positions, this is not actually the case. By buying CFDs he did not in fact acquire any of the shares, but had paid for the option to buy the shares at a certain price. This right was contingent on his putting up cash margin payments in case the share price fell below the exercise price, as it continued to do. As we know from the subsequent court case, Anglo lent Quinn very substantial sums during 2007–8 (almost €1 billion – about doubling Anglo's total Quinn exposure), enabling him to make the margin payments.

If, instead of borrowing money to meet the margin calls, Quinn had let the option expire, there would more than likely have been a further sharp fall in the share price of Anglo. This is because the firms that had originally sold the CFD options to Quinn would presumably have then sold any Anglo shares they had acquired to hedge or protect their positions.

The perceived fragility of Anglo Irish Bank, whose access to funding had been further impaired by a sudden fall in the market price of their equity, was a matter of acute concern to the FR. Here again the FR's analysis was superficial: the focus was on whether the CFD overhang threatening the value of the bank's shares could be eliminated (which it was in July 2008 through the so-called Maple 10 affair mentioned in Chapter 4). But removing the overhang would not remove the underlying weaknesses of Anglo's business model – which was the basic reason for the vulnerability of its share price.

And the approach of Anglo's management in dealing with the problem they faced (for which executives were subsequently convicted of criminal offences) should have triggered alarm and action from the FR. Instead comfort was taken from the fact that Anglo's share price bounced back relative to that of other Irish banks after its sharp dip in the 'St. Patrick's Day massacre', returning to the relative position it had held since mid-2007 – thanks in part to the Maple transactions.

Look Behind You!

In early September 2008, market rumours suggested an emerging insolvency in the relatively small building society INBS. Weak governance in this firm had been identified by the FR several years before, and it had hoped to see the problem resolved through a sale to (ironically) one of the Icelandic banks.

Now market commentary suggested that INBS was about to fail. At last the Irish public authorities began to prepare for decisive action, preparing emergency legislation to nationalize INBS if necessary within days. As always the fear foremost in the authorities' mind was one of liquidity: that INBS could run out of cash. If so, taking it into state ownership would restore confidence and enable it to retain funding in the market.

But, even if liquidity was the immediate problem, the Irish financial authorities were now focusing on the wrong bank. In fact, none of INBS's bonds were about to fall due. So, unless the small depositors panicked en masse, it would be able to meet its cash requirements for some time to come. That was not going to be true for Anglo.

PREPARATIONS

The trigger events failed to point the Irish authorities in the right directions: in each case, the lesson drawn was wrong. Still, it would be unfair to imply that no contingency planning was undertaken: there were preparations. But the authorities should have been better prepared, in terms of (a) a better understanding of the portfolio of the banks and the potential scale of losses in a worst-case scenario; (b) a more articulated plan, including for the detailed design of a guarantee (for example distinguishing between depositors, other senior creditors and subordinated creditors); (c) better liaison with other financial authorities abroad; and (d) having a broader group of experienced senior banking system experts equipped to improvise with better understanding of likely consequences.

How Deep Might the Hole Become?

Because, as explained in Chapter 4, the design of Irish banking supervision paid relatively little attention to the overall business model of each bank, the structure and quality of its portfolio and the risks to which it was exposed, there was very little relevant information for decision-makers to form an impression of how extensive the loan losses might become.

Against this background, it was inconceivable to the Irish financial authorities that the main Irish banks could get into such deep trouble that they might fail, suffering losses in excess of their capital. After all, they had for generations been by far the largest firms in the country and were led by boards consisting of the elite of Irish business. Admittedly, each of the two big banks had had the missteps already mentioned in Chapter 4: the ICI and Rusnak affairs in the case of AIB, and the heavy losses from First New Hampshire in the case of Bank of Ireland. But the banks' ability to ride out these high-profile setbacks, combined with the legendary conservatism over decades of the banks' domestic and UK lending, meant that a scenario of loan losses exceeding bank capital was not really on the supervisors' radar.

The drastic increase in the scale and risk profile of the banks' loan portfolio in the previous few years, with the increasing share of high loan-to-value ratios in residential mortgage lending, and especially with lavish lending to property developers, had moved them into uncharted waters. Whereas loan losses had in previous decades been almost negligibly small, it should have been clear that the potential for large losses on this new type of loan portfolio could be large in the event of a sharp downturn. Such lending required close supervisory examination.

After the first tremors in autumn of 2007, the FR decided for the first time to quantify the exposure of the banks to the largest property developers. The findings should have shocked the supervisors.[8] Between them, the largest five property developer groups had total bank borrowings from the five banks well in excess of €8 billion. Clearly a general property downturn would affect them all, so these were highly correlated exposures. But there was worse: when each bank was asked how much it believed each borrower had obtained from the other banks, the estimates were far lower than reality. Presumably each bank might have been slower to lend had it known how much was owed to its competitors. A personal guarantee by the borrowing property developer was worth much less if it had been made to several other lenders also. Besides, the personal wealth of the providers of those guarantees was not always verified. (One wonders whether the net wealth of the biggest players was ever verified by some banks.) Alarming

---

[8] More graphic detail on this special supervision exercise, which covered lending by the five largest banks to the five largest property groups, is provided in Honohan (2010: 70–71).

though this information should have been, I have seen no evidence that it caused the top decision-makers at the FR serious concerns or that it triggered commensurate action.

For example, it would have been prudent at that point to require each of the banks to raise more capital to meet the heightened risks identified in the exercise, including if necessary by suspending dividends. Such a measure would have had an adverse impact on their share prices in the short run, and would likely have been too little and too late, but it would have reduced the risk to the depositors and the government. Furthermore, with more capital, at least some of the banks might not have had such difficulties in funding themselves in the debt markets the following year.[9]

By September 2008, increasingly dissatisfied with the quantity and quality of the information coming to them from the Central Bank and FR, the Department of Finance was seeking independent sources of information by drawing on financial sector experts at the National Treasury Management Agency (NTMA) and engaging consultants from the accountancy firm PWC and the investment bank Merrill Lynch. These provided more pessimistic forecasts of the cash position and – to a lesser extent – the potential for future loan losses at Anglo, INBS and ILP, the banks giving rise to the most concern.

War-Gaming a Bank Failure

There had been contingency planning during 2008 for a possible Northern Rock-type event in Ireland. A few policy papers were prepared, under the auspices of the so-called Domestic Standing Group (DSG) on Financial Stability, an interagency group set up as part of a pan-European initiative and representing the Central Bank, FR, Department of Finance and the NTMA.

The policy papers discussed the issue at a relatively high level of abstraction. It seems that no one drew up an actual term sheet or draft legislation for a bank guarantee. If that had been done at leisure, it would have become evident that a number of detailed questions about the scope and duration of any such guarantee needed to be answered.

One telling incident happened during a 'wargame' exercise during the policy response to a liquidity crisis at a bank was explored. I'm told

---

[9] Capital requirements were increased in 2006, for example in relation to that part of property loans that exceeded 80 per cent of appraised security value. However, the measured excess capital of each bank was sufficient to absorb this modest increased requirement without any need for the banks to actually raise additional capital.

that the Central Bank participants took it for granted that the government would bail out the bank irrespective of circumstances. At one point in the wargame the provision of emergency liquidity assistance (ELA) was proposed, but the Central Bank participants insisted that such an ELA loan would have to be guaranteed by the government. The Department of Finance wargame participants refused to entertain such a guarantee. Apparently the deadlock in the wargame was not resolved. If it had been, participants might have realized the importance of deciding what part of the state's institutions was to take responsibility for assuming those losses.

None of the planning exercises envisaged more than isolated bank failure. The idea that confidence would become so eroded that the entire system might be in need of a guarantee does not seem to have arisen. Perhaps that is not surprising, as the loss of confidence in banks that occurred in late September 2008 was without precedent on such a global scale.

What Was Wrong with the Guarantee?

Having had nothing at all to do with the guarantee, I am often asked about it and specifically whether it was the best course of action available to the government at the time. Ultimately, by September 2008 it was too late to avoid a severe banking crisis in Ireland. It is clear that, by the night of the guarantee, most of the damage had already been done by reckless banking and inadequate official supervision.

Still, I believe that they could have done a bit better. A better-prepared and careful application of decision theory would have warned the decision-makers to take better account of the known fact that they lacked information. They expected and hoped that the banks losses would not prove so large as to imply a heavy cost for the guarantee. That was the baseline expectation. But they should have designed their policy to fail-safe: to give a good outcome not just on the baseline but in the event that bank losses were much worse.

The following four points summarize an approach that would have generated a better outcome.

1. Some form of extensive guarantee was surely inevitable. Just doing nothing and watching the banks close their doors one by one would not have been a good alternative for Ireland. Indeed, the action taken on the night of the guarantee was impressively quick and in some respects decisive.

2. But costs could have been somewhat contained by judiciously limiting the guarantee to exclude some categories of debt.
3. ELA should have been employed to buy time during which some form of risk-sharing with Europe could have been explored more forcefully.
4. Finally, although the scale of likely loan losses was not known with any precision, the clear failure of their business model should have led to both Anglo Irish Bank and INBS being taken into government control.

Let us consider these four elements one by one before asking why they were not chosen on the night of the guarantee.

(i) No guarantee option

What about the libertarian option of stepping back from any attempt at guarantee or rescue of any of the banks and just relying on normal bankruptcy proceedings, as has been suggested by some commentators? This option would have simply meant that Anglo would close their doors on the following day and be put into bankruptcy proceedings without any guarantees beyond the normal deposit insurance. The shock of such an event would undoubtedly have accelerated the outflow of funds from the remaining Irish banks as alarm about the safety of Ireland as a place to keep your money escalated. The banks would have failed one-by-one as they ran out of cash.

It is hard to see this as a plausible policy option. Not only would it have totally disrupted normal payments in the economy, but it would also have deprived households and most businesses of access to their liquid assets for a prolonged period implying massive disruption to economic activity, employment lay-offs, loss of export contracts and enormous reputational damage. Even the amounts guaranteed by deposit insurance (which had recently been increased to €1,00,000) could surely not have been made available in cash to the depositors for many weeks – if at all.[10] As the banks slid into failure, it is sure that foreign wholesale depositors would have been faster than small local businesses and households to get their money out safely. In the end, although the government might not have been saddled with direct bailout payments, Irish society at large would have

---

[10] The speedy deposit insurance payouts achieved in the liquidation of IBRC in 2013 and in the case of two small credit union liquidations followed intensified preparation in the intervening years, and related to a small number of depositors.

experienced enormous economic losses.[11] In addition, other European partners would have seen it as the European Lehman moment which they feared: the Irish government would have been treated as a pariah, with consequences for general Irish welfare.

(ii) A more limited guarantee

The decision-makers were not presented with a sufficiently articulated and worked-out range of guarantee options.[12] One option that was considered on the night of the guarantee was some form of restriction of the guarantee. It was surprising that even some subordinated debt was covered, as this debt is intended to be loss-absorbing in the event of bank failure. The government would have been in more conventional territory if it had excluded all subordinated debt from the guarantee. A more limited guarantee could also have excluded old long- and medium-term debt: since old debt did not represent funds that could be withdrawn, excluding it would not affect the banks' liquidity directly.

At first sight it might seem almost pointless, when €375 billion is being guaranteed, to exclude only a few billion. However, such a view would be flawed. After all (all else being equal), each euro of subordinated debt excluded from the guarantee could have reduced the government's outlay by a euro.[13]

Exclusions (which would be mandatory today as a result of the adoption of the European banking resolution legislation of 2014) could thus have saved some billions of euros – though the issue of creditor *pari passu* discussed in the text that follows could have reduced this amount; and we now know that there would have been vigorous opposition of European partners to a bail-in. Anyway, the old debt and subordinated debt was much less than the total losses that ultimately occurred at Anglo and INBS;

---

[11] With less than €0.7 billion in hand, the deposit guarantee fund would not have had the cash available to pay covered depositors promptly if any large bank failed. Any shortfall in the fund should be made up by the remaining banks, but in the scenario being painted, none of them would have had cash available for this purpose. Financing the shortfall would have brought the authorities into uncharted territory.

[12] A short paper hastily prepared by consultants from Merrill Lynch was the best effort, but it was telegraphic and not fully argued.

[13] At the end of September 2008 Anglo had €2.1 billion of dated subordinated debt and €10.6 billion of medium-term notes outstanding. (€5.9 billion of this was due to mature within the following year); INBS had €5.1 billion of term notes outstanding (of which €1.5 billion was due to mature within the following year). Some of this debt was actually reduced through liability management exercises during 2009–10.

excluding them from the guarantee would still have left most of the budgetary cost of the actual guarantee.

It was argued at the time in Ireland that the sweeping coverage of the guarantee would help its credibility: no need for investors to fear that some fine print in the legislation is going to leave them vulnerable. That view was not taken by other countries that subsequently announced more carefully crafted guarantees; the Irish guarantee looked somewhat ham-fisted in contrast.[14]

(iii) Help from Europe

As Europe was so determined at that point to avoid a bank failure any-where in the Union, and despite the indication that no shared or common approach was being contemplated, one possibility would have been to try more aggressively to put a European loss-sharing arrangement of some sort into effect right away. Ireland could have put it to European counterparts that assuming the large risks involved in the troubled balance sheet of Anglo (and indeed INBS) was beyond the capacity of the Irish government. If the other European countries wanted to avoid a bank failure, they would have to agree a burden-sharing arrangement. Even if such a *démarche* could have involved an element of bluff on Ireland's part, the European partners needed to be made aware of the acute situation facing Ireland's financial authorities. Admittedly, there was already strong political resis-tance to a collective European solution to the banking turmoil, and the gambit might well not have worked. But there was little to be lost from trying. (It would also have required recourse to ELA to bridge the days during which this was being negotiated.)[15]

---

[14] For example, it would also have been desirable to exclude from the blanket guarantee liabilities deriving from transactions with parties related to the bank directors and top management, as had been done elsewhere. Apparently no such exclusion was considered in the Irish case.

[15] As defined in the Eurosystem, ELA is a loan provided by the national central bank (in this case the Central Bank of Ireland) to tide over a bank's temporary cash shortage. Intended to be short term in nature and provided only to a solvent albeit illiquid bank, ELA can be granted at the initiative of the national central bank provided the ECB does not object, which it would not have done, given what was already being done at that time and would be done for German, Dutch, Belgian and French banks. ELA is provided only against collateral but, although Anglo did not have any remaining unused collateral satisfying the relatively strict and specific requirements of the ECB for its normal operations, it had sufficient other collateral to cover ELA for immediate needs. One possible difficulty would have been solvency; ELA should not knowingly be given to an insolvent bank – not least because that would simply be providing cash to allow short-term and well-informed creditors to exit, leaving more of the capital deficiency to fall on those less well informed

The exact extent and nature of interaction between the Irish authorities and other financial authorities in Europe in the days before the guarantee remain somewhat clouded, given the degree of confidentiality which has been attached to these interactions. A number of points are clear. There was no consultation with the European Central Bank (ECB), the European Commission or other governments to share with them what the government was planning to do in advance of the decision being taken to guarantee the banks.[16] The ECB had communicated the position that no collective European solution would be available to deal with the bank panic: it would be up to each government to take the steps needed to protect the operation of their banking systems. But it was left quite unclear as to what steps would be deemed appropriate by the ECB, and as we have seen, different countries adopted different solutions.

The failure of the German bank Hypo RE over the weekend before the guarantee did generate considerable consultation, but in the other direction. German officials asked what steps the Irish authorities might take to ensure that liquidity was available to Hypo's large Dublin subsidiary Depfa, which had now run out of cash, triggering the whole group's collapse. Might there be an Irish contribution to a guarantee for this bank? Sensibly, the Irish authorities declined to contribute. But one wonders to what extent that refusal might then have contributed to a reticence in approaching the ECB for help when the spotlight in Dublin shifted to the onshore Irish banks the following day.

The events of the night of the guarantee have been extensively recounted: the request by the chairmen and CEOs of the two main banks to meet the Taoiseach to request immediate action, preferably to take Anglo and INBS out of the market and provide a guarantee for the other banks; the Central Bank's confirmation that a general guarantee seemed to be the only viable way forward, given that Anglo would not be able to repay maturing obligations on the following day, and its caution against intervening mid-week in Anglo for fear of a 'fumble'; and the decision by the Taoiseach and the Minister for Finance to go ahead with a sweeping guarantee adapted from the proposal of the two banks, which in turn

---

or who had lent on a longer-term basis. But this would not have presented an obstacle to the Central Bank providing ELA to Anglo at end-September, as it did not believe that Anglo was insolvent (though events proved otherwise). Indeed, a small amount of ELA was approved for Anglo on the day of the guarantee discussions.

[16] At most, Ireland sought a temporary relaxation of the ECB's general collateral rules (which was subsequently done in mid-October).

agreed to provide bridging finance to Anglo until the weekend, guaranteed by the government.[17]

It seems that Brian Lenihan probably did not speak directly to J. C. Trichet in the days before the guarantee. He certainly never claimed to me that he spoke directly with Trichet at that point, instead remarking only that 'it was made clear' to him that Trichet wanted the banks to be saved. And his own words suggest that he received Trichet's views only through an intermediary: in a 2011 BBC radio interview with Dan O'Brien the wording he used was, 'I caught up on Mr. Trichet's message, which was that you must save your banks at all costs' (https://www.youtube.com/watch?v=WDN7NiEdNJ0). The interview left it unclear who communicated this message and in what detail. For his part, Trichet agrees that his message to all countries that weekend was to avoid bank failures, and stresses that this was not specifically a message for Ireland, but was being given generally (including to Germany). The idea, which later became popular in some circles, that the ECB somehow instigated the guarantee lacks any evidential support.[18]

It was a surprised and dismayed Trichet who learnt, on the morning of the announcement, of the decision to provide a blanket guarantee.[19] Such

---

[17] Those funds were not needed in the event; and Anglo was not intervened until more than three months later following scandalous revelations.

[18] Referring to his contacts with the ECB between 26 and 28 September, John Hurley, governor of the Central Bank of Ireland at the time of the guarantee, told the Oireachtas Banking Inquiry in 2015 that 'as a result of these contacts three key messages emerged: a Lehmans-type situation was to be avoided in Europe; countries were expected to stand behind their banks; a European initiative, of which Ireland might be part, was not being countenanced and decisions in relation to Irish banks were a matter for the Irish authorities.' He clarified that the 'governments to stand behind their banks' message was not expressed in a specifically Irish context. He declined to elaborate specifically on any conversation with Trichet in the days before the guarantee, but stated that 'the question of a guarantee, or a broad guarantee, was not put in any of the ECB meetings.'

Nor is there any indication in the evidence provided to the Banking Inquiry by Kevin Cardiff, the best-placed civil servant in this matter, of ECB pressure on the Irish Government to introduce a guarantee. All he has to say on this is that, a day or so before the guarantee, Hurley had reported to the Department of Finance that he had told Trichet that Ireland would face 'significant troubles in . . . the next few days', and the message back was 'Well, look at what we've just been discussing. The Belgians are looking after Fortis; the Germans are looking after HRE; Ireland has to look after its problems.'

The Irish authorities' failure to consult their EU partners in advance of introducing the guarantee was explicitly criticized by the ECB Governing Council in its formal opinion on the draft legislation, published on 3 October 2008 (CON/2008/44).

[19] It was a different story two years later, though, when, despite the guarantee having expired for some of those bank liabilities, the ECB was insistent that the government should nevertheless provide funds to make the creditors whole.

a step would naturally put pressure on other governments to follow suit and indeed (as we saw) several did, albeit with more limited scope and mostly without the legally binding conditions that hamstrung the Irish government for the following two years. Even if other governments and central banks were taken back and inconvenienced by the sudden Irish action and would have preferred to have been consulted, officials from several countries have told me that they did not, at first, see the action as foolhardy.

Not only did the Irish government miss any opportunity there might have been to get some risk-sharing agreement, but by not consulting with other European countries before introducing its guarantee the Irish government also placed the others on the back foot – or at least gave them an excuse to blame Ireland for some of their own problems. UK Chancellor of the Exchequer Alistair Darling (already facing massive – albeit concealed – problems at several large UK banks) told Lenihan on the morning of the guarantee that the British government 'had been put in an impossible position and would take action if it became clear funds were flowing from British to Irish banks' (Darling 2011). In the words of James (2017): "With that one unilateral decision, Ireland destabilized the rest of Europe. Suddenly, other governments had to fear that their own banks' depositors would flee *en masse* to the backstopped Irish banks." In the febrile atmosphere of the time, this pressure was felt more than it should have been.

By the end of the week the German government, which had also been critical of the Irish move (and also faced depositor nervousness as a result of the collapse of Hypo RE/Depfa), promised German savers that their deposits would be fully protected (though no additional legislation was enacted). Denmark's largest bank, Danske, had a large branch in Ireland, and (like Depfa) this was not going to be covered by the Irish guarantee, placing heavy pressure on the Danish authorities to introduce their own bank guarantee (Bank Package I), formalized on 10 October. And others were equally discommoded: by mid-October Austria, Slovakia and Slovenia had introduced blanket deposit guarantees and others had raised the ceiling on their existing deposit guarantees. Though none of these was as sweeping as that in Ireland, many officials cited the relevance of knock-on effects from the Irish scheme in creating pressure for their schemes. No wonder there was a certain amount of *Schadenfreude* in other European capitals when the full cost of the Irish guarantee eventually became clear.

(iv) The nationalization option

In fairness to the political decision-makers, they were hampered on the night of the guarantee by inadequate information. Had the government known how large the losses would be, and had they been presented with a more articulated set of options, they might well have come up with a different approach.

In late September 2008, the Irish banks were far from being the only ones suffering from a loss of confidence from the investors on whom they had been relying for funding. But was this loss of confidence justified by the underlying condition of the banks, or was it merely a reflection of the inflamed global financial atmosphere? The political decision-makers were told by their financial advisers in the Central Bank (and specifically the FR) that it was a general market phenomenon, a shortage of liquidity world-wide, and not a reflection of serious problems of potential balance sheet insolvency in Ireland.

But there were clear indications that at least two of the banks were fatally wounded. Based on a necessarily abbreviated assessment of the books of Anglo, the advisers from Merrill Lynch, which had been engaged by the Department of Finance, communicated a gloomier prospect.[20]

Merrill Lynch's team signalled quite clearly their view that Anglo's business model was irretrievably broken. The consultants could see the possibility that, in a worst case scenario, loan losses at Anglo might become so large as to erode essentially all of its capital. The combination of these prospects and the fact that it had run out both of cash and out of collateral eligible for normal borrowing at the ECB should have been enough to trigger the need for decisive public intervention into the bank, as was recommended by the Merrill Lynch team. Merrill Lynch specifically advocated taking both Anglo and INBS into 'state protective custody' and proceeding to run them down to an eventual liquidation.[21]

The nationalization legislation that had been prepared could have been used, and this was considered on the night, and for good reason. A failing

---

[20] Ironically Merrill Lynch itself was in so much trouble that month that it was taken over by the much larger Bank of America.

[21] They noted that such intervention would heavily dilute or wipe out the equity of existing shareholders including, as they mentioned, the sizable Quinn family shareholding. Note, however, that Merrill's envisaged the government guaranteeing dated subordinated debt in the intervened banks. [See Banking Inquiry Volume 3 BIDOFCoreBook18: 170–174. Also more complete correspondence sent to 30th Dáil, Public Accounts Committee.] On the night of the guarantee, Bank of Ireland and AIB also recommended that Anglo and INBS be taken into some form of state control.

bank should not be left in the hands of its controlling insiders.[22] A distinction needs to be made, though, between nationalizing the bank and guaranteeing its liabilities.

What Might Have Been Done with a Nationalized Anglo and INBS?

In November 2010, Brian Lenihan, Ireland's energetic and determined Minister for Finance since May 2008, told me that he had argued strongly on the night of the guarantee in favour of the nationalization of Anglo and INBS, but he didn't say what he would have done with the nationalized entity.[23] Presumably the shareholders would have received little or no compensation (as indeed was the case subsequently) – devastating for many, including Quinn family interests and the others who had participated in the unwinding of the Quinn CDS position just a few weeks earlier. Taoiseach Brian Cowen makes no secret of the fact that he did not favour nationalization at that point but he insists that Brian Lenihan was not overruled on this point. He was there; I was not.

What might have been done with Anglo if control of it had been seized at the end of September 2008? It does not follow that creditors must have been made whole. After all, the Irish government had not covered the debts of Irish Shipping Ltd when it collapsed in the 1980s.[24] And indeed when IBRC, the successor bank to Anglo, was eventually liquidated in 2013, the government then made no suggestion that it would ensure that all of the creditors would be paid; had there been insufficient funds (as was then conceivable, given the uncertainties of asset valuation), they would not have been paid.

However, the indications are that participants in the discussion on the night of the guarantee did not contemplate such a distinction. If they had nationalized Anglo, they would probably have provided a guarantee also.

---

[22] One of the risks in leaving a failing bank in private hands is that insiders could use their powers wrongfully to loot the remaining assets of the bank while they still could. This of course would be a criminal offence, and there is no evidence of large-scale self-dealing of this type in the case at hand. But it was a risk that should not have been taken.

[23] In 2015, Dermot Gleeson, former chair of AIB, told the Oireachtas Inquiry that Lenihan had said the same thing to him. Senior Department of Finance official Kevin Cardiff, who was present at the meeting, also urged nationalization (Cardiff 2016).

[24] Irish Shipping Ltd, a sizable state-owned company, was put into liquidation in November 1984 with significant losses to creditors including current employees and pensioners (though the latter received some official compensation a decade later).

Indeed, I don't think that, when contemplating nationalization at that time, Lenihan had in mind to bail-in senior bondholders. His whole thinking was rather to extend the protective arm of the state to the economy by ensuring that the functioning of the banking system would not be disrupted by a loss of confidence. Nationalization, although removing the shareholders, and presumably the top management, would provide continuity of function.

Besides, he was very much aware of a serious legal obstacle to distinguishing between depositors and bondholders, namely that these senior creditors ranked *pari passu* in Irish law, as in most other European countries at the time (though not in the USA). Thus to prefer depositors over bondholders in the resolution of this failing bank would certainly require legislation and, as it would in effect be applying retrospectively, such legislation might very well be declared unconstitutional; this was certainly the view of many Irish lawyers at that time.

Still, although Anglo had lost about a quarter of its bond funding from nonbanks in the previous twelve months and was now heavily reliant on secured borrowings from other banks, there was still about €17 billion of Anglo bonds held by nonbanks in September 2008. It would be interesting to know who owned these bonds at that point, not least because such holders would have been strongly motivated to lobby for bailout. Because of the way in which beneficial ownership of such assets is often managed through foreign intermediaries, the Central Bank found no way of obtaining a complete picture of who the current owners of these bonds were.[25] Some were Irish, but most were probably not.

The 2014 European legislation on bank resolution (the Bank Recovery and Resolution Directive [BRRD]) imposes a new approach to situations such as this. Were the emergence of a deep insolvency, like that of Anglo, to emerge today, the strong presumption – indeed the intention of BRRD – is that bondholders would not escape loss. It would be consistent with the

---

[25] An almost complete list of the *initial* holders of subordinated debt and other non-equity capital instruments provided to the Central Bank by Anglo in October 2009 showed that about half were issued to UK-based institutional investors (mostly insurance companies and investment or hedge funds), followed by French firms with about 7 per cent. Irish institutional investors accounted for about 2½ per cent. Of course, these instruments were marketable, so the initial holders might have sold them on. Asset management firms also form the largest group in the unquantified list, published by blogger 'Guido Fawkes' (Paul Staines), of the holders of some of Anglo's senior bonds in October 2010; however, this list is thought to be very far from complete. https://order-order.com/2010/10/15/anglo-irish-bondholders-should-take-the-lossesis-the-ecb-forcing-ireland-to-protect-german-investments/

BRRD approach for the government to have taken control of Anglo and, under special legislation, to transfer Anglo's deposits into a new entity while leaving most of its other liabilities behind to share in the proceeds of a liquidation. The same could have been done with INBS, which had more than €5 billion of bonds outstanding. Handling these two banks in that manner would have shifted much of the cost to non-deposit creditors of the banks and greatly reduced the net fiscal cost of the bank guarantee. There is much to be said for that approach. (Of course the knock-on effect on confidence in the remaining banks would have been severe: a guarantee would have been needed for them.)

Anyway, there is no evidence that any such drastic steps were being considered at end-September 2008. After all, there was no expectation of devastating losses that would need to be shared. (Yet burden-sharing with bank creditors is the route that was chosen by the Icelandic government with its banks the following week.)

Consequences of the Guarantee

The guarantee could have been improved on, even given the limited information available on the night of the guarantee. An alternative package could have provided some insulation against the worst case scenario – a scenario that actually materialized – but it would have represented a bigger short-term shock to the market and to holders of Irish financial assets. Ultimately, the decision to go with a blanket guarantee probably reflected a view that this sweeping gesture would do the trick. The long run of national economic success, the low debt ratio and the AAA credit rating of the Irish government probably suggested to the decision-makers that the overall financial position of Ireland was strong enough to absorb any hidden risks of the guarantee. If so, they were wrong.

Even if alternative courses of action on the night of the guarantee would not have altered the net position of Ireland by much, they could have had rather different distributional effects. It was assumed that a sizable proportion of the protected bondholders were foreign: I doubt if concern for their welfare was an important consideration in Dublin. The government's action protected the savings of small and large depositors alike – but the rich have larger bank deposits than the poor.[26] It was incumbent on the government to have regard to that aspect when it came to designing the tax

---

[26] The guarantee could also have helped the shareholders – as the senior AIB and Bank of Ireland directors who attended some of the discussions on the night of the guarantee will

and spending adjustments that would prove necessary to pay the bill: these measures needed to be progressive, probably more so than they were.

Despite the guarantee, after an initial respite there were outflows, especially from Anglo, in the following months. A revised guarantee scheme was put in place in December 2009 covering new deposits and new bond issues for maturities of up to 5 years, but this scheme was increasingly ineffective in retaining the banks' access to private funding as the government's credit rating declined during 2010. As the end of the initial two-year period approached, maturing deposits and bonds were not renewed, leading (as discussed in Chapter 8) to the banks having increased recourse to funding from the Central Bank.

The two-year guarantee bought Ireland some time to prove that the banks were safe and sound. But they were not sound, and making them so would take more time and more cash than the government had at its disposal.

The Bill

A decade after the guarantee it is possible to arrive at a rough estimate of how much the Irish government had to pay over the following years in net terms to meet the promise made to bank creditors in September 2008. Ultimately only about €1 billion was actually paid out under the terms of the guarantee (this was under the IBRC liquidation described in Chapter 10); instead much larger capital injections by the government substituted for further guarantee payments. Table 7.1 shows the main banks in Ireland, together with the total government outlays in respect of each.

A gross total of almost €68 billion was provided to the six guaranteed banks in capital injections and guarantee payouts during 2009–11, of which about half is now likely to be recovered from guarantee fees, dividends and the sale of the capital instruments acquired by the government.

But these receipts are being realized only after several years during which elevated interest rates have had to be paid to service the debts incurred by the government to fund the capital injections. There are different approaches to calculating these. Using the approach of the Comptroller

have clearly understood. However, the loan losses ultimately proved so great that in the end the shareholders were virtually wiped out.

Table 7.1 Main banks in Ireland in 2008[a]

	Total assets 2008 € billion	Ownership[b] in 2008	Received ELA?	How Resolved?	Government cost € billion		
					Gross[c]	Net(I)[d]	Net(II)[e]
Bank of Ireland	197.4	Widely held	Yes	Recapitalized	6	–3	–2
AIB	182.1	Widely held	Yes	Nationalized	22	0	5
Anglo	101.3	Widely held	Yes	Liquidated	31	28	28
ILP	80.1	Widely held	Yes	Nationalized	4	0	1
Ulster	64.2	Sub (RBS, UK)	No	Recapitalized			
BOSI	39.3	Sub (HBOS, UK)	No	Exited			
KBC	24.1	Sub (KBC, BE)	No	Recapitalized			
ACC	21.7	Sub (Rabo, NE)	No	Exited			
EBS	21.4	Mutual	Yes	Nationalized[f]			
INBS	14.4	Mutual	Yes	Liquidated	5	5	5
Danske	12.0	Branch (DK)	No	Recapitalized			

[a] The list includes the largest banks catering to the domestic market.

[b] 'Widely held' banks had listed equity and no dominant shareholder. 'sub' means subsidiary of the foreign bank identified in parentheses.

[c] Total capital injection by the Irish government.

[d] Net(I) is capital injection plus guarantee payments to IBRC creditors net of guarantee fees, dividends, repayments and sales of capital instruments to end-2016 (C&AG 2016) plus the estimated value of residual capital instruments owned by the government, higher expected dividends from the National Asset Management Agency (NAMA – €3.5 billion apportioned) and from IBRC liquidation.

[e] Net(II) equals Net(I) plus estimated net cost of servicing of associated debt to end 2016 per C&AG (2017).

[f] Data merged with AIB by which it was acquired in 2011.

Source: Author's calculations drawing on C&AG (2017) and annual reports of the banks and NAMA.

and Auditor General (2017) to include net servicing costs to end-2016 gives a net aggregate expected cost of about €37 billion.[27]

The main contributors to the total are Anglo (about €28 billion), INBS (about €5 billion) and AIB (also about €5 billion – even though it was a much larger bank).[28] Adjusted back to 2010 or 2011, this amounts to about 24% to 25% of one year's gross national income (GNI) at its crisis trough, and to between one-fifth and one-sixth of general government debt post-crisis.

While this €37 billion is the direct cost of the bank bailouts, I don't want to call it 'the cost of the bank guarantee', because, as mentioned, alternatives to the guarantee would also have entailed costs. I also don't want that number to be seen as the total cost to the government or to Ireland of the banking mess: the damages to the tax revenue, to demands on public spending (including on other interest payments), and to the economy more widely were much larger.

Losses were also suffered by the equity shareholders of the six guaranteed banks (about €29 billion when measured at book value) and by their subordinated creditors (about €14 billion).[29] In addition, parents of the foreign-owned banks had to inject about €28 billion in replacement capital. Adding these (not precisely comparable) figures suggests that the total net losses for these banks in Ireland come to well over €100 billion, of which the Irish government absorbed a bit over one-third (cf. Figure 7.1).

Although the guarantee was thus flawed both in its design and in the failure to discuss the alternative possibilities in advance with other

---

[27] I would prefer a slightly different approach from that adopted by the C&AG, but the differences would not materially alter the net figure presented. C&AG assumed that the servicing cost of each capital injection equalled the rate at which the NTMA was borrowing at that time. This might be an underestimate of the opportunity cost of these funds to the extent that they were actually drawn from the state's sovereign wealth fund whose benchmark portfolio (substantially invested in international equities) yielded more in the relevant years. Given the early repayment of IMF and other high-interest borrowings, and thanks to the IBRC financing arrangements, net financing costs beyond 2016 can be neglected. The net figure of €37 billion is intended to update the figure of €40 billion in C&AG (2017) to take account of higher expected dividends from NAMA and IBRC and residual value of remaining bank shares.

[28] For Anglo and INBS, the net financing costs of the associated debt during 2010–16 was very small because of the special financing arrangements that applied to IBRC as described in Chapter 10; without these arrangements, the net cost figure would have been very much higher. Note that the capital investment in Bank of Ireland is reckoned to have yielded a net profit.

[29] Banks can satisfy part of their regulatory capital requirements by issuing various forms of subordinated debt, that is, debt that will not be repaid in the event of the bank's liquidation until all other debt has been repaid.

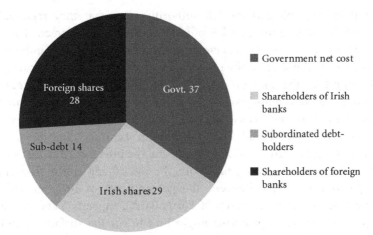

Figure 7.1 Ireland: Allocation of banking losses (€ billion).
Source: Author's calculations based on published information.

European authorities, the best alternative course of action that I can envisage (failing the removal of legal and constitutional obstacles to providing depositor preference over other general creditors) would likely have saved at best a moderate portion of the €37 billion actually incurred by the government in making good on the guarantee.[30]

WHAT DID OTHER COUNTRIES DO?

Ireland's reluctance to allow a bank to fail was widely shared at end-September 2008. Shaken by the extraordinary financial market turbulence unleashed by the bankruptcy of Lehman Brothers on 15 September, central banks and governments across the world began to shift to the view that exposing creditors of any significant bank to loss in a bankruptcy must henceforth be avoided.[31] The shift was at first sharpest in Europe, where

---

[30] It is not sufficiently recognized that (as spelled out further in Chapter 10) this direct cash cost of the bank failures represents only a fraction of the budgetary savings that were needed (and achieved through 'austerity' measures) in the process of restoring balance to the public finances. In a wider sense, though, the imbalances that led to all of this adjustment being needed can be blamed on the unsustainable bank-credit-driven boom of 2003–7.

[31] This was publicly stated most explicitly in respect of 'systemically important financial institutions' in the Communique of the G7 Finance Ministers and Governors in respect of at their meeting in Washington on 10 October, but, according to Bastasin (2012, p. 16), the gist of it had already been agreed by the G7 on September 22.

central bankers blamed the US authorities for what they regarded as a policy blunder. Although US officials subsequently claimed that they would have saved the Lehman creditors had they had the legal authority to do so, they had not yet shifted to a policy of avoiding all creditor bail-ins.

Interpreting the loss of market access by a number of significant European banks as *mainly* a liquidity shock, not fairly reflecting the underlying strength of the banks' balance sheets, policymakers quickly determined that there should be no European Lehman. Yet the lack of enthusiasm for a Europe-wide solution, and the intergovernmental squabbling over who was going to absorb the underlying credit risks (most conspicuous in a spat between the governments of Belgium and the Netherlands over the carve-up of Fortis Bank), suggests fears that more deep-seated solvency problems might lurk below the surface, as indeed proved to be the case in several countries.[32]

The scale of panic in international financial circles in those weeks should not be forgotten. Thus, the governments of many other European countries also took steps in September and October of 2008, following the Lehman bankruptcy, to ensure that no senior creditors of their banks suffered losses in the face of a collapse in the banks' access to cash. The list includes Belgium, Denmark, France, Germany, Luxembourg, the Netherlands and the UK. The most seriously affected banks in these weeks had all drawn heavily on the international money markets. (Balance sheet weaknesses of banks in Italy, Spain, Portugal, Greece, Cyprus and Slovenia, for example, that emerged in later years were not yet so evident. This was because those banks were not so dependent on the international wholesale money markets which had been disabled by panic. As such, those banks were not yet as vulnerable to the suspicions and doubts of international investors.)

The rescues were on an unprecedented scale. Some of the action took place a few days before the Irish guarantee, some of it a few days afterwards.[33] Most took place in an atmosphere of high political and financial tension, with governments reluctant to assume the losses caused by bankers, but persuaded by financial experts that the alternative of doing nothing would be economically and politically catastrophic.

---

[32] Nevertheless, French President Sarkozy was still pressing Chancellor Merkel for some cooperative European approach on 4 October, albeit unsuccessfully (cf. Bastasin 2012).

[33] Over the following years several other countries saw substantial government funds used to bail out the creditors of failing banks. An IMF study lists fourteen European countries in which *gross* outlays for this purpose exceeded 5 per cent of GDP (Bova et al. 2016 – *net* outlays, i.e. after subtracting subsequent recoveries, would be considerably lower).

In each of these cases, the ultimate cost to the governments proved to be much smaller (in relative terms) than that which fell on the Irish government (Honohan 2017). This is the case even for tiny Iceland, despite the scale of its banking collapse (Box 7.1).

BOX 7.1 Iceland

The most interesting case, because diametrically opposed to the route followed by Ireland, is that of Iceland. It deserves a closer look.

On the weekend after the Irish bank guarantee, the three largest Icelandic banks were in similar trouble. The Icelandic authorities' initial reaction was to try to keep the banks afloat. Already over previous months the Icelandic central bank had buttressed them with extensive liquidity loans secured only on bonds issued by the banks themselves. Now the Icelandic authorities proposed to make further loans and to nationalize the weakest of the three, Glitnir. But Iceland did not really have the ability to protect the creditors of their banks fully. This was because the Icelandic banks had spiralled out of control over the previous few years. Their business model was to borrow in international markets to finance vigorous acquisition of foreign firms by Icelandic conglomerates controlled by a handful of ambitious entrepreneurs. Buccaneering though some of the Irish bankers may have been, they were outclassed in this respect by the Icelanders. Admittedly, the Icelandic banks did not stand out as being particularly large in a European league table. But they were out of scale relative to their home country. Although together the aggregate assets of the three main Icelandic banks were only about the same as those of Anglo, the population of Iceland is only about one-fifteenth that of Ireland.

At this point, the Icelandic authorities got some very good advice from consultants from the London office of the investment bank J. P. Morgan who warned against drawing the government any further into a banking mess that they could not pay for. Isolate the depositors of the on-shore branches of the banks, they advised, and let the rest be worked out over time.

The subsequent working-out of the Icelandic bank failures is a complicated story. Emergency legislation was introduced to give priority to depositors over other claims (including bonds), and to transfer the deposits and most of the assets booked in onshore branches of the banks into new banks that became the nucleus of a new, much

BOX 7.1 (cont.)

smaller, banking system. Capital controls were introduced to prevent international movements of funds (other than those needed for current imports). And, to provide the financing needed to protect the economy from shrinking even further than it did, Iceland had immediate recourse to the International Monetary Fund (IMF), which, along with four Nordic governments, provided substantial financing. When the banking and financial situation was eventually resolved in 2017, things had worked out relatively well for depositors with Icelandic banks (at home and abroad), and for the Icelandic government's finances, which managed in the end to recover all of the heavy outlays it had to make initially to stabilize the situation.

Admittedly, Iceland suffered reputational damage from what were in some cases arbitrary and retrospective actions against the creditors of the failed banks.[34] In addition, the Icelandic government had to inject funds amounting to about 44 per cent of Iceland's GDP into the new banks to keep them afloat (Laeven and Valencia 2012). But there were recoveries, which substantially repaid these fiscal outlays.

All in all, the ultimate net losses to creditors of the failed banks amounted to €33.9 billion (Jónsson and Sigurgeirsson 2016: 185; see also Baldursson et al. 2016 and Benediktsdottir et al. 2017), or about 200 per cent of Iceland's GDP in 2010. In addition to these creditor losses, a 'stability contribution' (in effect an exit tax) of €2.6 billion (or almost a fifth of GDP) was paid in 2015–6 by the creditors of the failed banks as part of a deal that freed them from the capital controls that had prevented them from repatriating the amounts recovered. By the time it was negotiated, the original holders of these claims had long since sold out to hedge funds at a steep discount. Prevailing attitudes at home and abroad had shifted decisively in the direction of imposing loss sharing on such creditors in order to protect the public finances. It was this stability contribution that more than offset the net outlays that had been

---

[34] Iceland famously resisted paying for the claims of foreign depositors, mainly in the UK and Netherlands, leading to the use of anti-terrorist legislation by Britain to ensure that Iceland would not repatriate relevant assets from the UK. In the end the relevant international court (the EFTA court) found that Iceland's refusal to pay even the funds needed to meet deposits covered under the Icelandic deposit protection scheme was not unreasonable. In the end, there were enough recoveries in the assets of the banks to meet all depositor claims (but not other claims).

BOX 7.1 (cont.)

made by the Icelandic authorities to cover the deposits of the protected local depositors in the bank failures.

Of course, once the Irish guarantee, with all of its absolutist features, had been enacted, none of these Icelandic burden-sharing expedients could be applied to the losses of the Irish banks.

(Apart from this direct fiscal cost, the macroeconomic adjustment of the Icelandic economy to the shock followed quite a different path to that of Ireland, partly reflecting the sharp devaluation of the Icelandic krona which had the effect of lowering Icelandic real wages, as shown in Figure 2.4. Although other factors also contributed to the tourism boom which got under way, the sharp improvement in price and wage competitiveness speeded Iceland's return to full employment.)

A variety of routes were adopted. Some government guarantees were provided, but – although the Irish example was seen as a factor aggravating pressure on other countries to follow suit – nothing with the scale and unambiguous commitment of the Irish guarantee. Several of what looked like guarantees amounted only to political commitments, lacking the force of law or contract; I do not know that any of them guaranteed already outstanding bonds, or subordinated debt.

For example, the Danish bank guarantee, provided in the week following the Irish guarantee, covered all deposits and some interbank claims, but it did not go beyond that. At the same time a fund was created in Denmark to be used to recapitalize banks where needed (the banks were required to make financial contributions to the fund).

Other European examples, as shown in the following list, involved central bank emergency loans (ELA) along with injections of capital into several banks – including some of the world's largest. ELA was repaid relatively promptly in each of these cases, generally within a few months.

- The weekend before the Irish guarantee, the German authorities were already in the process of arranging for a suite of special financing arrangements for Hypo RE bank, whose Dublin subsidiary Depfa had, as mentioned, run out of cash (and which was also facing heavy albeit unacknowledged loan losses in the parent).[35]

---

[35] At the time of the rescue, media commentary attached most of the blame for the Hypo collapse to Depfa, which was the part of the Hypo RE group most exposed to the

- ELA and a complex restructuring involving recapitalization was also being arranged in the weekends before and after the Irish guarantee for the large Belgium-based universal bank Fortis by the three Benelux governments in whose countries it was mainly active.
- Belgium and France intervened with ELA, as well as an injection of capital and guarantees on new borrowings of the specialized public sector financing bank Dexia.[36]
- The UK, which had already nationalized the building society Bradford and Bingley in previous weeks, covertly provided ELA to two very large banks, HBOS (whose merger with Lloyds had just been agreed on) from 1 October and RBS from 7 October; the UK government also injected capital, acquiring majority stakes of the equity in both of these banks. A credit guarantee scheme was offered to the UK banks (i.e. guaranteeing that loans the banks had made to customers would be repaid), and the other main UK banks were pressed to increase their capital also by sales of shares.
- The Swiss state's rescue of its very large bank UBS, announced on 16 October, also involved a recapitalization by the Swiss federal government; in this case there was no ELA as such, but a large block of UBS's problematic assets was transferred to a special fund largely financed by the Swiss National Bank.

Each of these interventions involved sizable injections of funds, some matching or exceeding that of Ireland in absolute terms, but not relative to national financial resources.

The United States responded to the seizing up of its wholesale financial markets in the weeks after the Lehman bankruptcy with a range of liquidity instruments, guarantees and a bolstering of capital into all of the major banks, whether the banks thought they needed it or not. Washington Mutual Savings Bank (WaMu), formerly a savings and loan institution which had grown to become the sixth largest bank in the country, had been intervened by the US authorities on the Thursday before the Irish guarantee; its deposits and assets were sold to J. P. Morgan Chase bank, but its unsecured bonds were not covered and their holders suffered heavy

---

international money markets for its funding. Eventually though, it was the rest of the group that proved to have the most severe loan losses. The German government-controlled asset management company which took over the assets of Hypo RE (and paid the full book price) indicated it did not expect to have disposed of all of them within half a century.

[36] Dexia's losses continued to grow and it needed further assistance in 2011 and 2012.

losses.[37] Fragility in the US banking system continued for some months, but the sector recovered well from mid-2009, thanks to the rescue and support measures adopted by the US authorities. Furthermore, although ex ante these measures presented risks to the US public finances, they were structured in such a way that they did not in the end result in net fiscal losses.

Some of the European countries involved in these September–October 2008 crisis bailouts will also eventually have recovered all or most of the funds initially committed; but this will not be true of others, including (along with Ireland) Belgium, Germany and the UK.

* * *

All experts agree that quick and decisive action is needed to stem a banking panic. In this respect the Irish government should receive high marks for some elements of its action on the night of 29/30 September 2008. The action was certainly quick, and it was so sweeping that, until the scale of the embedded loan losses became clear, it seemed likely to be decisive. But the government acted on the basis of inadequate information provided to them: even the 'stress case' scenarios implied no long-term cost to the public finances.

Would it have been better for Ireland if more of the banking losses could have been absorbed by the holders of bank bonds? I believe so. But on the night of the guarantee, no legislative framework (such as has since been created with the BRRD) was in place or could readily have been put in place to achieve this. And the meetings' participants had no concept of the scale on which losses would crystallize. Although I have suggested that there were better courses of action available to the government on the night of the guarantee and sufficient information to justify adopting them (i.e. engaging with European partners, excluding subordinated and old debt from the guarantee, nationalizing Anglo Irish Bank) I am reluctant to attach too much blame to the decisions of the night of the guarantee. The failings that had led to these legislative and informational deficiencies were not faults of one night.

---

[37] The €6 billion of senior unsecured debt will only be partly repaid. A recent estimate suggested that less than $3 billion will be available from the bankruptcy assets to pay the $6 billion of senior unsecured debt of WaMu. But it is noteworthy that subsequent US bank failures, which were numerous but much smaller than that of WaMu, have been managed without losses to senior debt holders.

The main point remains that the economic damage of the Irish banking boom was largely done long before that fateful night. Of course – as soon became increasingly evident – the losses latent in the balance sheets of the banks were far greater than anyone imagined at that moment. Market confidence in Ireland eroded in the months after the guarantee, as mis-behaviour of Anglo staff and directors became known, leading to that bank's nationalization in January 2009. While some two-thirds of the losses fell on the shareholders and eventually on subordinated debt holders of the banks, a large burden had been assumed by the state. In effect, the financial instability, created by the banks, and which the central banking system had failed to prevent, was met by decisive but ultimately unwise action by the government (encouraged by the Central Bank).

For me later, that history implied that the central banking system had to ensure that it avoided any unnecessary roadblocks being placed in the path of the government as it struggled to deal with its own financial pressures in the following years.

Every crisis has its decisive turning point when the gravity of the situation is disclosed. For Ireland the night of the guarantee is that turning point. The guarantee did constrain the nature and timing of the resolution of a wider situation of economic and financial imbalance that had emerged, created by a costly series of errors in both private and public sector actors in Ireland. On the night of the guarantee, the decision-makers faced a difficult and urgent problem armed with insufficient information. They could have done a bit better for Ireland, even with the information they had, but nothing they could have done at that point would have avoided a severe economic and financial crisis on a scale comparable to that which was about to unfold.

The Race to Stabilize the Banks

The first half of 2009 was a period of deepening concern as Ireland's economic and financial position continued to slide.

Employment continued to fall month after month (as had been happening since mid-2007), with the worst of the job losses concentrated in the first twelve months of the guarantee, during which employment declined by about 200,000 – or half of the total peak-to-trough decline in job numbers (see Figure I.1 in the Introduction). This was the sharpest recession since independence. Meanwhile, declining tax revenues and the additional public spending costs of the recession began to undermine the government's financial capacity to meet the impending costs of bailing out the bank creditors.

The Irish banking situation darkened further, highlighted by the nationalization of Anglo Irish Bank in January. Media reports about market manipulation by Anglo (in the Maple 10 share support scheme and the back-to-back Irish Life and Permanent (ILP)–Anglo loan arrangement) began to circulate, further contaminating Ireland's international financial standing. As the government injected capital into the main banks, Standard and Poor's rating agency removed Ireland's AAA rating at the end of March, predicting gross banking costs to the government in the region €15 to 20 billion (still much lower than subsequently transpired).

Suggestions were even beginning to be voiced that Ireland might default. As early as January, influential contrarian commentator David McWilliams was advocating withdrawal from the euro. But in February, European Central Bank (ECB) president Jean-Claude Trichet flew to Dublin to address a meeting of business leaders, government officials and academics at the Institute for International and European Affairs, signalling the ECB's backing for Ireland's efforts to stem the economic and financial decline.

Stemming the economic decline and rebuilding confidence would take some time. Ireland was entering on a period of intensive crisis management and resolution.

From the point of view of Irish financial sector policy, the two years following the guarantee were a race to try to underpin the solvency and viability of the banks. The full extent of the banks' exposure, especially to property development loans, but also to the residential mortgage loan book, was beginning to become clear. If the banks were to be able to stand on their own by the time the initial government guarantee ran out, they would need to be able to show a healthier asset portfolio. They would also need sufficient capital, replenished by the government to the extent necessary.[1]

Property prices had already been falling for about eighteen months before the guarantee decision of end-September 2008. As they continued to fall, concerns grew as to the potential scale of loan losses. The government realized that it would have to inject capital into the main banks if they were to be able to get back into normal functioning post-guarantee, but nobody knew how much capital was needed. The extravagance of the banks' lending policies, the scale of the price decline and the overall weakness of economic activity in the downturn all brought the assessment of the recoverability of loans into wholly uncharted territory.

With the government's finances greatly weakened by the collapse of the bubble, its capacity to inject funds to recapitalize banks was limited. In the end, the amount of capital needed to restore market confidence in the banks proved to be more than the government could provide without official external assistance.

TOWARDS NAMA

Hearing in December 2008 of the government's intention to recapitalize the main banks, I took it on myself to write to Minister Lenihan to caution about the consequences of casual injections of capital. Injecting capital would underpin the functioning of the banks, but it would also boost the value of preference shares and any subordinated debt which remained or would subsequently become unguaranteed. Perhaps now, I suggested, was the time instead to start winding up Anglo,

---

[1] The domestic politics of the years 2008–12 are well covered in Leahy (2013) and Lee and McConnell (2016).

transferring deposits and other good business to continuing banks (and imposing losses on the unguaranteed subordinated debt holders). Thus began my involvement in providing advice to the government on management of the crisis, at first very much at a remove, from my position as a university professor in Trinity College Dublin, responding to occasional phone calls with the minister and meeting him from time to time.

The NAMA Design

I was far from being the only person from whom he sought advice. Lenihan was a gregarious, ideas man and liked to discuss options and alternatives freely. Peter Bacon, a shrewd and imaginative economic consultant with whom I had worked occasionally over the years, was asked by Lenihan in early 2009 to come up with a practical proposal for dealing with the looming non-performing loans problem, and specifically to look at the approach that had been adopted in the Swedish crisis of two decades earlier, involving the creation of asset management companies to acquire, and dispose of, the banks' non-performing loans. Over the years, Bacon had prepared several studies for the government on tax and other policies affecting the price of housing, and he had recently been working for one of the biggest property development companies. Thus he was well equipped to design the outlines of a practical scheme, and this he did in cooperation with the National Treasury Management Agency (NTMA). I exchanged some ideas with him early in that process, drawing on the experience of my years at the World Bank working on, and studying the history of, banking crises in developing countries. I was not surprised at the general idea of what Bacon was proposing when (at Lenihan's request) he showed me the draft plan just after he had presented it to the minister in March 2009. Nevertheless, the scale on which his asset purchase plan was conceived did rather take the breath away – even though, as I pointed out to him, he had left out one important distressed segment of the bank's loan book, namely residential property mortgages. That segment, though not yet showing sizable arrears, would clearly present problems too, but to have included them would have created an unmanageably large entity.

The National Asset Management Agency (NAMA) plan would substitute government guaranteed bonds for the large property-related loans (distressed or not) in the banks' books. The loans would be bought by

NAMA at a realistic price, thereby crystallizing losses for the banks. The banks would therefore have to replenish their risk-bearing capital with new issues of equity, diluting the existing owners' stakes. However, by reducing the riskiness of the banks' portfolio, the operation could speed their return to financial soundness and hence their ability to provide essential banking services to the economy.

The banks' ability to retain access to loanable funds would be enhanced by receiving NAMA's bonds because, backed by the portfolio of assets that it was acquiring, as well as by government guarantee, these bonds would easily qualify as eligible collateral for normal borrowing at the ECB, even if they were not accepted in the market.

If NAMA was to be a success for Ireland, it would be important to pitch the purchase price of the loans at a realistically low level; NAMA should not be used as a vehicle to recapitalize the banks at the expense of the public finances by overpaying for the loans. The rise in bank share prices as the NAMA proposal was being aired in the spring and summer of 2009 suggested that many investors thought this would happen. But it did not happen. The risk of overpaying was also guarded against by the adoption of my suggestion of paying a portion of the purchase price of the loans in the form of unguaranteed subordinated debt of NAMA.[2] Fairness also demanded that, when NAMA disposed of the assets, it would not bail out non-performing property development borrowers by selling back the mortgaged properties to the developers at knock-down prices.

The NAMA scheme was ambitious: it would create another large contingent liability for the state (albeit to a large extent substituting the same liability as had been incurred in the guarantee decision) and could threaten confidence in the public finances. The operational challenges would be significant, especially ensuring the integrity of its sales processes, and making the best judgment calls on when recovery was sufficiently established to justify sales of the assets it had acquired.

Still, built as it was on some of the best-practice lessons from asset management schemes that had been employed to deal with other banking crises around the world, it seemed a viable way forward; perhaps (as

---

[2] This left some of the risk with the bank shareholders. In the event, the banks' losses were so large that virtually no original shareholder value was left.

I already wrote to Lenihan at the end of March 2009) it was the best option.[3] I still cannot see that there was a better option.[4]

Alternatives to NAMA

Other ideas were being canvassed by observers at the time. One alternative would have been to leave it to the banks, under new top management, to work through the non-performing loans. This was being done in Britain; but their problems were proportionately much smaller. In practice, the Irish banks would have their work cut out for them dealing with the distressed parts of what was left in their portfolios. Indeed, it took them long enough to get things under control, and they made many mistakes along the way. They were also very slow to re-launch their lending capacity. Management bandwidth would not have been sufficient to take on the big developer loans as well.

A more radical idea that was floated was to create one or more de novo banks, unencumbered by the legacy of the property boom, to which the deposits and good lending business of the existing banks would be transferred while the latter were wound down. Attractive though such an approach still seems in the abstract, and suitable for applying to a situation in which there was just a handful of failing banks, it would have encountered fatal difficulties if employed for the entire system (and by mid-2009 it was increasingly clear that serious problems affected all of the banks without exception). For one thing, a remarkably high fraction of Irish households and businesses were financially distressed at the time. The lending business of the new bank or banks would ultimately have to relate to these distressed borrowers, whose financial affairs would need attention and possibly restructuring. If the economy was to recover, these entities could not

---

[3] Though I did warn him that, depending on how it was implemented, the asset purchase plan might limit the options for bailing-in bondholders eventually if necessary. I thought at the time that bondholders of some more US banks might well be bailed-in by the new Obama administration. That did not happen (White House discussions at around that time are described in Tooze 2018, chapter 13), but if it had, Ireland might have been able to follow suit.

[4] I would have preferred a greater degree of transparency in NAMA's operations. Even now, the full list of 800 borrowers whose loans were acquired has not been made public, reflecting the secrecy built into NAMA's legislative authority. This could have helped to avoid some subsequent problems of perception relating to fairness and value for money. The fact that performing developer loans as well as non-performing were being acquired by NAMA was, I understand, one of the considerations underlying the decision to maintain traditional banking secrecy around the loans acquired by NAMA.

all be left simply to languish in the gone-concern banks. Second, staffing and accommodating the new banks would require a huge exercise involving tens of thousands of workers; in practice the new banks would inevitably end up largely staffed by former employees of the failed banks.

Though in the following years I sometimes hankered after the undoubted advantages that would have been brought by starting over with a clean sheet, there was no such realistic option. Replacing top management of the existing banks and relying on the new management to reform working methods and ensure a workout of the distressed loans (apart from the large property loans that had gone to NAMA) was the only practical way forward.

Choreography of Bank Recapitalization with Insufficient Information

When I became governor of the Central Bank of Ireland in September 2009 the question of how a functioning and sufficiently capitalized banking system could be ensured was no longer just an interesting academic question but had become a central part of my new professional responsibilities.

Since the banks' property-backed loans were going to be bought by NAMA at prices well below what they had been valued at in the banks' accounts, the purchases were going to erode the banks' capital. This meant that the banks would need a capital replenishment. It was not likely that much equity funding would be immediately forthcoming from a sceptical market. The government would likely have to step in (it was already whole owner of Anglo).

The asset purchases from, and recapitalizations of, the banks would require some careful choreography if it was to be pulled off successfully. If the banks were to be convincingly recapitalized and able to fund themselves in the market by the time the initial guarantee ran out, there was no time to waste. We needed to know what price each bank would get for loans being transferred to NAMA – in other words, what discount or 'haircut' would be applied. We also needed to ensure that the banks had sufficient capital to absorb the losses that would occur over the coming few years on the rest of their portfolio. Given the economic downturn, significant losses were, in a sense, already baked into these loans even though the banks' accounts did not reflect that reality.

It was quite conceivable that the required recapitalization would mean that one or both of the two main banks would end up majority owned by the government at the end of that process.[5]

Under these circumstances, we had to try to avoid a prolonged period of uncertainty as to how much additional capital the banks needed. We set a firm date of 30 March 2010 for a 'jumbo' announcement. Not only would NAMA announce the price of the first tranche of loans on that day. In addition, the Central Bank would specify what additional capital the banks must raise, given a projection of the remaining NAMA loan prices and our estimates of what was needed to cover the prospective loan losses in the remainder of the banks' portfolio.[6] Taking a leaf from the US Federal Reserve's Comprehensive Capital Analysis and Review (CCAR) playbook of the previous year, we called this exercise the prudential capital adequacy review of 2010 (or PCAR2010).

The key unknown was how much NAMA was going to pay for the property-backed loans that it was to purchase over the following year. What haircut, or discount on the face value of the loans would NAMA pay? This would remain unknown for many months, and indeed there was scarcely any indication until days before the big announcement was to be made. Only the first tranche of purchases would be priced by the time of the end-March announcement, yet a public decision on the scale of the additional capital needs of the banks had to be based on a guess as to what the prices of the remaining tranches would be. It would not have been sufficient to state that no estimate was being made of the level of subsequent haircuts: that would have undermined any hope of restoring confidence promptly.

In the event, the choreography did not work out as well as planned. Alert to the danger of illegal state aid being provided to failing banks through NAMA, the Directorate General for Competition (DGCOMP) of the European Commission closely scrutinized the pricing methodology. The Commission was right to do so, but by insisting on over-elaborate procedures, it slowed and complicated the process. As the end-March date

---

[5] This is exactly what I told an Oireachtas (Parliamentary) Committee in late 2009.

[6] As NAMA was understood to be buying at realistically low prices, it may seem odd that the banks' own accounts did not already reflect those realistic valuations, or something close to them. That they did not partly reflects banker over-optimism and partly international accounting practice which was slow to recognize likely future loan losses happening in a general downturn. At the Central Bank, we took the view that, as international regulatory capital requirements are based on accounting rules, it was defensible to await the first tranche of NAMA prices before requiring banks to raise more capital to meet any shortfalls thereby crystallized.

for the first asset purchases approached, it became clear that only a handful of the largest loan connections for each bank would be priced in time. This was not enough to provide a robust estimate of the remaining prices. But it was all we would have to go on. NAMA advised us that there was no reason to expect the haircut on the first tranche to be any lighter than that on subsequent tranches. Accordingly, Financial Regulator Matthew Elderfield and I decided (over the complaints of bankers) that we would not wait for further loan valuations to come in before insisting on the additional capital. Instead, we would calculate the new capital requirements on the assumption that whatever haircut percentage was announced for the first tranche could be extrapolated across the remaining NAMA-bound loans.

Given that the first loans were the largest and, one might have assumed, likely a priori to be the most overvalued in the banks' books, this might have seemed prudent and cautious, potentially demanding more capital than would ultimately be needed if the later haircuts were to prove less severe. But what if NAMA later tranches were to suffer higher haircuts? We well knew that this was the Achilles heel of the approach we adopted. We could only hope that any additional amount could be absorbed within the capital buffers we were building in. In fact we had decided, in the face of some bitter bank objections, that each bank would have to meet higher capital standards (ratio of risk-weighted assets) than the current international minima even after application of the higher loan loss estimates.

Meanwhile, for the end-March 'jumbo' announcement of capital requirements, we also needed to take account of the rest of the banks' portfolio: the part that was not being bought by NAMA. Given what seemed to us to be over-optimism on the part of bank management in relation to these loans also, we decided to base the capital requirements on more pessimistic loan recovery estimates. Therefore Central Bank staff embarked on the task of estimating a more credible figure for the recoverable value of the remainder of the banks' portfolio. The banks' portfolio was subdivided into a dozen or so categories: by location (Ireland, the UK and the Rest of the World); borrower type (such as retail, small business and large commercial); and purpose of loan (such as residential or commercial mortgage, development finance, non-property). To each category we assigned a percentage loss rate, typically much higher than was expected by the banks. The percentages were based on the judgement and experience of what was already a considerably strengthened team of experienced credit specialists at the Central Bank; it also made reference to the generally gloomy projections that had been made by rating agencies and other outside commentators.

Two cases, a base case and a stress case, were drawn up. We decided that banks would be required to hold sufficient capital to absorb the base case losses over the coming three years with a sufficient margin to still have an internationally comfortable 8 per cent capital (using the relatively demanding 'core capital' measure); banks would also have to have enough capital to absorb the stress case losses albeit with a tighter margin of just 4 per cent capital.[7]

To complete the calculations, the Central Bank team also needed to make projections of net earnings over the coming three years, taking into account, for example, the erosion of bank earnings from the fact that many mortgage loans were priced at interest rates that tracked the ECB's main policy rate with just a small margin at a time when the banks were no longer able to attract wholesale deposits at anything close to the policy rate.

It was the NAMA haircuts that were mainly responsible for the big numbers determining the additional capital requirements that were announced at end-March 2010. At 35 per cent for Bank of Ireland, 42 per cent for Allied Irish Banks (AIB) and 55 per cent on average for the other banks, these haircuts proved to be higher than had been foreseen or signalled by NAMA until just before they were announced. It is worth pausing to reflect on the astonishing level of estimated losses embedded in these haircuts. These showed how little was going to be recoverable from the debts of the largest property developers to the Irish banks – banks which had been feted so recently in at least some international commentary.

Combined with the additional capital requirements imposed by the Central Bank, reflecting not only the higher capital standards but also the additional provision for future loan losses on those parts of the portfolio not going to NAMA, these actual and projected losses meant that the main banks would have to raise sizable amounts of additional capital.

---

[7] The loan-loss assumptions in the stress test were well beyond all previous experience. But they were not pessimistic enough. For example, a 5 per cent loan loss ratio was assumed for Irish residential mortgages at the two largest banks; 15–16 per cent loan loss on other retail loans; 11–12 per cent on other non-NAMA Irish commercial loans; and 60 per cent on such Irish development property loans as were not going to be purchased by NAMA. In the event, actual non-NAMA loan loss provisions made by Bank of Ireland during 2009–17 come to about €10 billion – roughly equal to what was projected in the stress. But for AIB, for which projected loan losses were also about €10 billion, the outturn was much worse, with losses several billion higher. Although the comparison is complicated by several factors (mentioned later) that subsequently intervened, it remains something of a mystery not only why AIB's loan losses ended up so much worse than those of Bank of Ireland, but why this was still not evident by early 2010.

The future capital needs of Anglo remained unclear pending decisions about its future, but both it and Irish Nationwide Building Society (INBS) needed immediate capital injections if they were to continue in operation satisfying international rules.[8] This capital was supplied by the government in the form of promissory notes (PNs), carrying the government's promise to make instalment payments over a long period of time chosen to ensure that the total discounted value of the instalments was sufficient to fill the capital deficiency. These PNs would become emblematic of the social cost of the bank failures, and their refinancing on favourable terms after 2013 was an important part of the recovery process.[9]

The other banks, still compliant with the international capital standards according to their accounts, were given until the end of the year to raise the additional capital.[10]

Irish public reaction was one of shock to the scale of the losses set out in the 'jumbo' announcement. The public were also mesmerized – and to some extent distracted – by the denouement of the Quinn Insurance affair (discussed in Chapter 5), with the dramatic High Court appointment of examiners to that company announced the very same day. Journalists referred to the day of the announcements as a 'black day'. Still, at the Central Bank we hoped that, moving quickly to acknowledge and deal with such a high level of banking losses, we could put the widespread but undefined market concerns over the stability of the banks to bed. It was not to be.

But at first, the strategy looked as if it might work. Curiously, given the large losses that they crystallized as well as the likely implications for the public finances, the markets took the first tranche NAMA announcements at end-March and the Central Bank's additional capital requirements in their stride.[11]

---

[8] Without an injection of capital, these two banks would have been technically insolvent and could not be allowed to continue in operation. Their closure would have triggered an immediate unpayable call on the guarantee.

[9] Inasmuch as the guarantee impeded the government's ability to take the banks out of operation without triggering a default on its guarantee, the promissory notes were a material expression of the promise embodied in the 2008 legislation.

[10] The US banks found to be short of capital in the Federal Reserve's 2009 CCAR stress tests had likewise been given several months to fill the hole.

[11] For example, on 12 April the yield spread on 10-year Irish government bonds over those of Germany closed at less than 130 basis points (1.3 per cent). In effect, by trading in the market at these prices you could buy insurance against the Irish government defaulting at a 1.5 per cent annual premium. Yields and credit default swap (CDS) spreads for Irish bank bonds were little higher, reflecting the Irish government's guarantee.

Markets have only a limited bandwidth for thinking about small economies. During April 2010 they were distracted by the rapidly deteriorating fiscal situation in Greece, and devoted little attention to absorbing the full implications of the Irish banking announcements.

The Choreography Fails

After March, NAMA continued the work of valuing the loans it was going to purchase. The elaborate valuation procedures mandated by DGCOMP made this a slow process. It was only in August that it became evident that the haircuts were becoming higher. This bad news dripped out gradually and progressively during August and September 2010, undermining the credibility of our end-March announcement. Doubts began to be raised about the effectiveness of the Irish bank resolution process.[12]

Why had we not overcapitalized the banks? Could that not have been done at sufficient scale to guard against the danger that later NAMA tranches would work out worse or indeed against any of the many other uncertainties that existed around the recoverability of the loans the banks had made so recklessly? Alas no: to have done so would simply have brought forward the melt-down that happened in the autumn. To have pressed the Irish government to come up directly with the resources to overcapitalize the banks would have been to push it over the edge and straight into an International Monetary Fund (IMF) programme. In early 2010 the Irish fiscal accounts were too close to the cliff edge; in these circumstances it would have been irresponsible to try to over-capitalize the banks at the cost of what might prove to have been an unnecessary collapse of the public finances.[13]

---

[12] DGCOMP subsequently realized that their insistence on an elaborate loan-by-loan evaluation of the haircuts was unduly cumbersome and had had a destabilizing effect. After persistent requests from the Irish officials, DGCOMP allowed NAMA to decide later tranche haircuts on a simplified portfolio basis.

[13] IMF staff recognized this fragility (Mody 2018: 270). In April 2009 they had already privately suggested that Ireland might do well to apply for a Flexible Credit Line arrangement, a precautionary facility created in 2008 and granted to countries 'with very strong policy frameworks and track records in economic performance' but faced with actual or potential payments pressures. (Only Colombia, Mexico and Poland have used this facility.) In May 2010 a Flexible Credit Line was no longer on offer, and IMF staff suggested it was already time for the Irish government to apply for a precautionary stand-by arrangement, one step short of actually borrowing. I agreed; but the Minister for Finance did not find this option attractive.

A Digression on the Performance of NAMA in Subsequent Years

Although a full analysis of NAMA is well beyond the scope of this study, let me digress briefly on the degree to which NAMA ultimately proved to be a success.[14]

In the end, the NAMA purchases, when completed in 2011, resulted in even higher haircuts, averaging 57 per cent, for a total in cash terms of €42.1 billion of which €26.1 billion for Anglo and INBS alone.[15] Although the banks made large losses on the rest of their portfolio also, these large numbers illustrate the extent to which the net costs of the banking losses can be attributed to the big developer loans.

To the surprise of many, as of 2018 NAMA was expecting to return a profit of more than 10 per cent on its total initial outlay at the end of its operations (even after fully paying off its subordinated debt). The fact that NAMA will have made a profit in the end suggests to some critics that it may have paid too little for the assets they acquired at the outset. But this is not necessarily the case. Pricing at acquisition was to be based on information and valuations available at the time and had to follow the strict rules set by DGCOMP and designed to avoid over-pricing. Indeed many commentators in 2010–11 were highly sceptical about NAMA's chances of breaking even.

On the other hand, the lower the price paid by NAMA for the loans, the lower would be the psychological threshold for NAMA in achieving sale prices. It is plausible that, when it came to selling the assets that they had acquired, NAMA would have held out for higher sale prices if it had paid more for the loans. That would have meant a slower completion of the job of disposing of its portfolio, as NAMA would have had to wait in hope for prices to rise further.

---

[14] I cannot throw any insider light on the recovery operations of NAMA; the Central Bank was not involved at all. This type of work is very far from normal central banking and indeed I was most concerned to ensure that, in the other major operation of this type, namely the liquidation of IBRC in 2013, the Central Bank would not end up holding and having to dispose of banking assets. That is why these assets were transferred to NAMA and new NAMA bonds received by the Central Bank in return. (At one point in 2012, some officials at the ECB expressed an interest in the ECB obtaining a position on the Board of Directors of NAMA given its important role in generating a cash flow for the government; I discouraged them for the same reason, and they desisted.)

[15] The average percentage haircut in the first tranche, at 50 per cent, was very rosy when compared with the average of 59 per cent for subsequent tranches. For AIB the gap was even bigger: 42 per cent in the first tranche, 59 per cent in the rest. Bank of Ireland, systematically the best performer with a first tranche haircut of 35 per cent, suffered 45 per cent in the remainder.

Overall timing of NAMA disposals was a constant subject of public debate. As property process continued to fall in 2010, before NAMA started selling on a large scale, a chorus of market participants called for rapid sales in order to get the property market working again; I recall many pundits arguing in 2010 and 2011 that faster sales by NAMA would help kickstart a market recovery, even at the cost of a sharper initial price fall. When NAMA subsequently accelerated its sales into a rising market after 2012, loud voices (some of them the same) now condemned its impatience. Government pressure in 2013 for NAMA to speed up its sales may indeed have reduced the ultimate profit. The continued rise in property prices in subsequent years does suggest that a somewhat slower sales path might well have yielded higher average prices. But we will never know for sure. Clearly, though, choosing the optimal timing strategy for asset disposal was never going to be easy. Certainly NAMA's portfolio was so large that the timing of its sales was likely to influence market psychology with regard to the pace and extent of the price decline and recovery.

Some market participants (several of them not disinterested) have pointed to particular loan or collateral sales alleging that they had achieved less than they could have given better positioning, structuring or timing. There were some allegations of favouritism or corruption (some still being investigated at the time of writing), albeit limited in scope and not made against top management.[16]

Dealing with the recovery of collateral on defaulted debt is never likely to be uncontentious. Even if some of the criticism has merit, on present evidence NAMA has certainly outperformed expectations held when it was first announced.

In early 2010 the question of NAMA asset sales was well in the future. The focus was still on acquisition prices and the large haircuts they implied, not least for Anglo Irish Bank, the specialist property lender.

---

[16] The large 'Project Eagle' block sale of loans in Northern Ireland was criticized by the Government Auditor (see C&AG 2016; NAMA 2016) and is the subject of an Irish Government Commission of Investigation established in May 2017 (https://merrion street.ie/en/News-Room/Releases/Statement_on_The_Establishment_of_ Commission_of_Investigation.html). In 2016 a former NAMA official, Enda Farrell, was convicted of disclosing confidential information to potential asset purchasers, a criminal offence (www.irishtimes.com/business/financial-services/suspended-sentence-for-leak ing-sensitive-nama-documents-1.2645457).

Winding Down Anglo

Increasing evidence of the disastrous state of Anglo's portfolio made me increasingly concerned about its future during the summer of 2010. I had never bought into Brian Lenihan's vision for that bank. He had hoped that a slimmed down and restructured Anglo, under wholly new management and with a cleaned-up balance sheet, could become an effective bank for funding small business and thereby contributing to Ireland's economic prosperity. It was on this basis that he had attracted an energetic team of experienced senior bankers from abroad to rebuild Anglo.

But, as I told him, Anglo brought little of value beyond a banking license to this party: its entire pre-crisis operation had been built around a misconceived and failed model, with a heavy concentration on large property-backed loans seemingly granted on the basis mainly of personal contacts with apparently successful developers. The average haircut on the second tranche of developer loans purchased by NAMA from Anglo was 62 per cent, much higher than that of the two main banks, and providing further evidence of the poor quality of loan underwriting at Anglo, suggesting recklessness and incompetence on a breath-taking scale.

Anglo had failed to recover the confidence of lenders and there was a steady drain of funding out of the bank. After the NAMA purchases and hiving off more than half of the remaining loan book into an asset recovery company (as was being recommended by the bank's new management), the rump of Anglo would have a very small customer base on either side of the balance sheet; its domestic branch network extended to just five cities. Its reputation could hardly have been lower. Building a profitable going concern on this foundation would be challenging indeed.

On the contrary, the continued existence of Anglo was toxic to Ireland's standing in financial markets. Keeping this tarnished bank alive was undermining Ireland's claim to be cleaning up its banking problems.

Nothing decisive could be done to Anglo until the original guarantee period ran out, because any liquidation or resolution would be treated as an event of default likely triggering a vast cash call on the government's guarantee from the bank's bondholders. But, as the end of the guarantee period approached, my expressed view that it was time to plan the Anglo end-game was increasingly shared by other senior officials – John Corrigan of the NTMA, Kevin Cardiff and Ann Nolan of the Department of Finance. It was not until early September that the minister finally accepted our approach and abandoned the plans that had been developed by Anglo's new management. The new plan, announced in early September, put an end to Anglo's ambitions. It would split the bank into an asset recovery firm, which would own and manage down essentially all of the loans and other risk assets, and a narrow funding bank holding no loans, with the Central Bank as by far the largest creditor of the latter entity.[17] Remaining unguaranteed bondholders would be creditors of the asset recovery firm, and would enjoy no increase in their security. Indeed, any decision to take more drastic steps against these bondholders would have been simplified by the new construction.[18] (In the end this solution was superseded by the EU–IMF programme, though the ultimate liquidation design of Anglo's successor institution Irish Bank Resolution Corporation (IBRC) went some way towards achieving desired results.)

The Cookie Crumbles

As had always been evident, the coming months would be decisive in whether the Irish banking system could recover market confidence sufficiently to be able to refinance the very heavy bond and deposit maturities that were scheduled for September 2010. This funding cliff reflected the terminal date of the initial government guarantee. (In the early weeks of the guarantee, the banks had found it easy to borrow for any term up to the end of the guarantee period; after all this was the guarantee of a sovereign state with what had – at the outset – been an AAA rating.)

Despite the scale of the capital needs identified by the end-March 2010 announcements, and despite the other fiscal pressures which had emerged in the downturn, financial markets were still prepared to lend to the government. In that sense, the scale of the problem still seemed at mid-year to be potentially manageable.

There was thus a chance that the flow of financing to both the government and banks could be sustained through the rest of the year and beyond, assuming that the European Commission approved a continuation of the bank guarantee on new borrowings allowing the banks to secure refinancing of their September funding cliff. This was Plan A. Its viability also depended on the valuations of the loans in the later NAMA tranches resulting in haircuts no larger than applied to the first tranche. And there was also the underlying assumption that the

---

[17] The assets of the funding bank, including the NAMA bonds and the promissory notes, would all be guaranteed, by the government, which would in turn receive a claim on the asset recovery firm.

[18] There can be little doubt that, by this stage, many of the minister's main advisors in Dublin were contemplating such drastic steps, even if such imaginings remained unspoken.

government's fiscal consolidation would continue to deliver the needed shrinkage in the deficit.

All three provisos began to unwind during July and August. First, the budgetary prospects were found to be trending worse than had been hoped. It should not be forgotten that much had already been done to stabilize the fiscal situation. Even before the bank guarantee arose, Minister Lenihan, recognizing the sharp deterioration that was happening in the public finances, had begun a multi-year programme of fiscal correction with expenditure cutting measures announced in July 2008, followed up with an early budget in October 2008. The trend in the budget deficit did begin to turn, helping Ireland retain international financial market confidence well into 2010. However, the multi-year fiscal plan which he had rolled out in January 2009, though on firm foundations at first, had assumed a quicker and stronger domestic and international recovery – and more inflation. By July 2010 it was looking quite over-optimistic.

In July, our macroeconomic forecasters at the Central Bank showed me their latest multi-year fiscal projections. These made it clear that the government's deficit targets would not be met in 2011 and 2012 on current policies: even more austerity measures, tax increases or spending cuts, would be needed to reach these deficit targets. This was happening regardless of the additional debt coming from bank recapitalization. But that extra burden would make the correction more urgent by triggering a sharp increase in Ireland's government debt ratio: by end-year 2010 it could easily reach 100 per cent of GDP, a classic warning level. And the debt ratio would continue to grow thereafter because of the rest of the budget deficit.

While Lenihan was not immediately convinced that the prospects for the public finances were that bad, his discussions in Brussels as well as at home (as I later learnt, his own departmental officials had also begun to press him to do more) led to a growing realization on his part that more drastic action was needed. But building the political case for more cutbacks or tax increases was inherently time consuming; from the financial market perspective, time would soon start to run out.

We had been waiting since March for further information from NAMA about the value of the loans they were buying. After all, the bulk of the loans had not yet been priced. In mid-August, as I checked in for a flight to Singapore (where I was to begin a series of speeches and meetings in the Far East) I got a phone call which removed any remaining optimism that we could get through this difficult patch without problems.[19] This was my first indication that loans in the second tranche of NAMA purchases were incurring even more severe haircuts than those in the first. I recognized that, if and when confirmed, such information would undermine and discredit our strategy and cause market participants to extrapolate a more severe deterioration. I would have to tone down what was already planned as a very cautious account of our situation in my public statements.

Plan B: Rely on ELA

Against these headwinds, Plan A now had little chance of success. The banks would not be able to refinance themselves given growing market scepticism. This scepticism was symbolized by rising CDS spreads and by a rating downgrade by Standard and Poor's on 24 August, accompanied by a very negative commentary. That the European Commission failed to approve before the August holidays the government's request for an extension of the guarantee on new bank borrowings beyond September was only a small additional hiccup: with the diminishing perceived creditworthiness of the government, a guarantee was no longer the silver bullet it had once seemed to be.

Plan B for the banks had to be emergency liquidity assistance (ELA) from the Central Bank. It will be recalled from the previous chapter how sensitive reliance on this exceptional type of central bank lending was seen to be, bearing in mind what happened with the run on Northern Rock in 2007. ELA was already a reality for Anglo (since February 2009) and its recourse to ELA would clearly grow. The likelihood was that other banks might soon also need recourse to ELA.

More Drastic Alternatives

I had to pause to consider more drastic alternatives. To the extent that a bank's repayments were covered with ELA, then the government would directly be on the hook to the Central Bank, and indirectly to the ECB, since there was a commitment from the Minister for Finance to make good

---

[19] I had decided that there could be some diplomatic advantage in traveling to visit some of the most influential of my counterparts in Asia, to explain our strategy for navigating through what was evidently a delicate Irish financial situation. I made speeches in each of the five cities – Beijing, Tokyo, Singapore, Hong Kong and Kuala Lumpur – which included the most important financial centres in the region.

on any ultimate shortfall. Might it be better for the government to repudiate the guarantee at this moment (and cancel the PNs which had been
injected into Anglo and INBS, and were now being used as collateral for the
ELA)? This was not a matter for the Central Bank to decide, but I should
not shy away from recommending it to the government if I thought it was
in the national interest. Not that anyone in government circles seemed to
be considering this option.

For the government to repudiate the guarantee would certainly be
a breach of contract and of faith. It would also have required legislation.
But the option had to be considered given that the situation was deteriorating sharply relative to what had been hoped for some months before.[20]

Nevertheless, I concluded that such a course of action would be clearly
unwise and bad for Ireland. For one thing it seemed likely to me that,
despite the deterioration, the government's finances would be placed on
a sustainable path. More to the point, if that proved not to be the case, it
would be safer and more orderly to renegotiate or restructure public
indebtedness than to have a sudden repudiation of the bank guarantee.[21]

---

[20] It was time to re-examine the literature on sovereign debt default, something that had not
arisen in Irish economic policy since the 1930s when the government decided to stop
sending to London the annuity payments that farmers had been making on the amounts
that had been borrowed for land purchase decades earlier (cf. Foley-Fisher and
McLaughlin 2016a, b). The international debt involved in the 1930s was eventually settled
on what were very favourable terms for Ireland, but not without a protracted and costly
dispute with the London government (the so-called 'economic war'; cf. O'Rourke 1991).
How best could the international indebtedness that resulted from the bank guarantee be
settled now? Would it be better for Ireland to try to force an open default on the
government's guarantee to the bank depositors and bondholders, or to allow the debt
to be settled later between governmental bodies? That this had been an important
decision point was noted in a critical newspaper article by imaginative University
College Dublin Economics Professor (and brilliant policy commentator) Morgan Kelly
some eight months later.

[21] In Chapter 3 the point was made that it would have been much better for Greece to
engineer a much deeper and earlier restructuring of its sovereign debt. That is because
Greece's debt had been allowed to grow to unsustainable levels. Now that official lenders
have substituted themselves for the private sector, they are refusing to admit to their
constituents that the Greek debt will not be fully paid. In order to maintain this fiction,
they continue to impose a fiscal regime so severe that there has been almost no macroeconomic recovery from a downturn much deeper than that of Ireland. I have sometimes
been asked whether there should be some read-across to Ireland. My most persuasive
answer is that, despite the bank bailout, Ireland's sovereign debt never got close to the
Greek level of unsustainability, especially when Ireland's post-crisis financing conditions
improved. Accordingly any aggressive attempt to restructure or default on the Irish
sovereign debt would have been seen as unacceptably opportunistic and met with damaging counter-measures by creditors and official partners alike.

Besides, any attempt by the government to repudiate would surely be fiercely contested by European governments and the ECB to the point where the Irish government would likely end up having to reinstate the guarantee, having destroyed its own creditworthiness in the process.

The Central Bank of Ireland had a responsibility to advise the government on such matters, and a specific mandate regarding financial stability. If I had considered that repudiation had any merit, I would have discussed it with the minister. I did not, nor did he raise the possibility. Subsequent developments eventually proved us both to have taken the correct course on this.[22]

But the expected increase in ELA would still be needed and this required an OK from the ECB, as it entailed the Central Bank of Ireland drawing funds from the rest of the Eurosystem.[23] The sums involved looked large even by ECB standards so the ground would need to be prepared. Already at the end of July I had alerted the ECB to the likelihood of a large increase in Anglo's ELA borrowings in September and to the possibility that ELA might also be needed for other Irish banks (as indeed was the case by the end of September). I followed up towards the end of August with further detail and greater pessimism: bank funding was now very tight, what with the higher spreads on government debt and the apparent increase in the haircuts on NAMA purchases.

THE CLIFF-EDGE APPROACHES

Focused up to then on Greece and Portugal, ECB staff only now began to realize fully the precarious state of Ireland's finances – and the likelihood that the ECB would find itself – one way or another – in the frontline of financing the emerging shortfalls for longer than they had anticipated (Figure 8.1). Probably the quite correct decision of Eurostat to classify

---

[22] And so the holders of deposits and bank bonds maturing in September were repaid as they had been promised by the guarantee. Interestingly, most of the funding cliff related to banks other than the failed Anglo. Of the €46 billion (net) of funding that evaporated from the Irish banks in September 2010, only about a quarter related to Anglo (much of whose funding had already gone since its nationalization 20 months earlier; €20 billion in 2009 alone). And most – perhaps all – of the more than €7 billion of Anglo bonds (and all but about €1 billion of INBS bonds) redeemed that September had been issued under guarantee.

[23] A loan from the Central Bank of Ireland to enable an Irish bank to make a payment has the quasi-automatic effect of increasing the Central Bank's indebtedness in the euro area's payment system known as TARGET. The interest rate on such indebtedness is the ECB's main policy rate, which was 1 per cent at the time. ELA loans carried a higher interest rate, typically 0.75 per cent above the main policy rate.

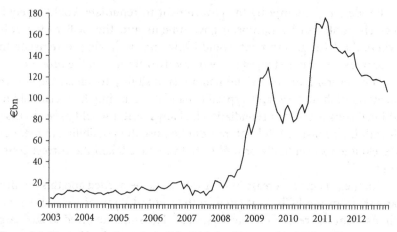

Figure 8.1 Central bank financing of the Irish banking system, 2003–12.
Source: Central Bank of Ireland.

the government's PN injections into Anglo as part of the government deficit, driving it to an unprecedented 32 per cent of GDP, was a turning point in making ECB staff and others who had not fully focused on the situation realize how serious it was.

Seeking to limit its own exposure, the ECB, with a knee-jerk reaction, suggested to me that the Irish government should obtain a loan from the European Financial Stability Facility (EFSF – which had been established as part of the Greek loan exercise) and lend the cash to the banks to enable them to meet the upcoming bank deposit withdrawals and bond repayments. I could certainly see recourse to an official loan as the core of a Plan C – and indeed had already mentioned to Brian Lenihan at the end of August that he might have to have recourse to an IMF loan in case it became difficult or impossible for the government to fund itself in the market. But I did not see it as a preferable (or for Ireland cost-effective) pre-emptive alternative to ELA for the banks. For me, provision of bank liquidity in a crisis was the responsibility of the central bank.

Still, the weakness of banks and government was interacting to create an overall deterioration in Ireland's finances, showing up in government bond yields (already destabilized by the Greek crisis of May), that would now quite likely lead to the need for recourse to an official support programme, presumably involving the IMF as well as European funds.

Concerns were escalating in the ECB about the prospective scale and duration of ELA, which is supposed to be a short-term emergency expedient. At this point Ireland stuck out like a sore thumb as the only user of ELA. ECB concerns went beyond ELA to the overall borrowing trend of the Irish banks. These concerns persisted despite the fact that the non-ELA borrowing was fully collateralized to the ECB's standards, and as such should actually present little or no credit risk. The concerns manifested themselves in a variety of ways. I made a note on 1 September of a remark made to me in Frankfurt to the effect that it would be 'only a matter of days before the Irish crisis blows up'. The following day, in response to a question about Anglo at his press conference, ECB President Jean-Claude Trichet remarked, 'it is the responsibility of the Irish government and of the Irish authorities in general to take the appropriate decisions', which was taken by market participants as casting doubt on whether the ECB would permit ELA to be used to repay the heavy debt maturities coming in the following few weeks.[24] There were other, less public, suggestions to me in early September that the prospective growth in ELA might be refused. I recall musing in response on how ironic it would be if, for example, Bank of Ireland, which had been, in effect, Ireland's central bank for a century and a half, were to be turned away by today's lender of last resort.

By mid-September the deteriorating financial market situation facing Ireland was being openly discussed as possibly leading to the need for an IMF programme. (One senior ECB colleague offered the somewhat ominous analogy that if Greece was Europe's Bear Stearns; Ireland was shaping up to be Europe's Lehman Brothers). Although stressful, I regarded this pressure as unlikely to materialize in a binding refusal to permit the needed expansion in ELA. My confidence on this point was based on the consideration that such a refusal would undoubtedly have triggered financial instability throughout the euro area. Besides, it would not have been easy for the ECB to find legal justification for a refusal: the ECB statute envisages a refusal only under restrictive circumstances. Nevertheless the possibility of refusal had to be taken seriously. I did take the precaution of some contingency planning: I would not have allowed such a refusal to go without legal challenge.

September came and went, as confidence in Ireland's finances seeped away with a relentless drumbeat of bad news. Particularly damaging to our

---

[24] I was not mollified by his addendum 'and I have confidence that they will manage this difficult issue as well as possible, as they did in the past', and felt I had to point out to him how destabilizing his observations had been. In fact the Governing Council had that very day acquiesced in my proposal to increase the provision of ELA to meet the demands on Anglo's resources from maturing claims.

reputation were the facts, emerging in the second half of the month, that AIB and Anglo would both need more capital than previously foreseen. The AIB news derived from the NAMA haircuts; Anglo from a sharp management reassessment of needed provisions, following the government's decision to wind the bank down.

Not only did these new pieces of information undermine our delicately constructed Plan A, but it also gave ammunition to pessimists inclined to project further deterioration.

AIB's news also undermined the results of the EU-wide Committee of European Bank Supervisors (CEBS) stress test of all the major European banks; these had been published as recently as the end of July. In fact the design of that stress test was much less testing than it should have been and the Central Bank of Ireland had insisted on over-riding several of the basic CEBS assumptions in order to make them *more* pessimistic and in line with the haircuts of the first NAMA tranche. But as the NAMA haircuts increased, even that conservatism proved to have been insufficient.

Some observers also got confused between AIB and Anglo. The latter had not been included in the CEBS stress test, and no overall loss estimates had hitherto been published for it by the Central Bank. In the circumstances, correcting such confusion was seen as only hair-splitting. Besides, suggestions (albeit vague and without much substance) that AIB's non-NAMA portfolio was in even worse shape than we had projected in March were coming in to me, and I was worried.

Day by day, as September wore on, the Irish banks had to pay out large sums as maturing funds were not being rolled over by depositors and other investors. Reliance on central bank funding, including ELA, to meet these outflows, grew substantially; and this led to further warnings from the ECB to the government (and to me) reminding us that recourse to ELA was limited in both size and duration. The collateral backing the ELA now included the government PNs which had been provided to Anglo and INBS to make up their capital shortfall.[25]

Could the surge in ELA have been slowed? Probably not. Admittedly, NAMA's subsequent profit means that the haircuts proved to be somewhat more severe than necessary for NAMA's solvency, suggesting that the valuation rules imposed by the European Commission were too limiting.

---

[25] In accordance with established procedures, the Minister for Finance was also kept informed of the actual and prospective developments in ELA and asked to confirm his intention to make good any shortfall in repayment of ELA: this practice ensured that there was a degree of political buy-in to the fiscal consequences of these measures. (Tucker 2018 discusses the democratic need for such engagement in what he calls a 'fiscal carve-out'.)

But lowering the haircuts by 2 or 3 percentage points would not have removed the loss of confidence. The drip-feed of bad news during August and September would have been avoided if the NAMA valuations and purchases had been concluded sooner, and this might have helped limit reputational damage to the Irish administrative system during 2010, but the sheer scale of the losses, if discovered already in March, would merely have brought forward the bank run by six months.

* * *

Given the sizable maturities falling during the second half of September, some market participants feared that the bank guarantee might not be honoured by the government. They were wrong to do so. The outflows were financed by additional bank borrowings from the Central Bank including ELA. Official creditors of the banks thus took the place of the private.

But the attempt to restore market confidence had failed. The government resources used to recapitalize the banks meant a record-breaking government borrowing requirement for the year 2010. Publication of this 32 per cent of GDP figure was a wake-up call to investors highlighting the risks to the government's debt sustainability, its ability to service and repay its large and still growing debt. As a result, those investors still prepared to buy Irish government debt would do so only on terms which were increasingly onerous. The ECB too was feeling exposed, given the growing scale on which banks were borrowing. September 2010 was the month when the chance of Ireland managing to recover financial stability without an IMF programme faded.

9

The Bailout

It was not only the bank losses and their impact on the mounting government debt that was undermining financial market confidence in Ireland.

For, long before the fateful events of September 2008, the end of the property price and construction bubble had begun to eat into the numbers at work, lowering aggregate economic activity and destabilizing the public finances. The situation was aggravated by the international downturn. Irish tax revenue fell by a quarter in real terms between 2007 and 2009. The downturn also triggered additional government expenditure on unemployment benefits and other automatic stabilizers. And, unlike the bank losses, the resulting deficits were not one-off but threatened to cumulate year by year.

As mentioned, steps had already been taken as far back as 2008 to make spending adjustments and tax increases. But by mid-2010 it was becoming clear that the adjustment was not going to be enough. Further steps would be needed to restore balance to the public finances.

In the end, market confidence in the creditworthiness of Ireland seeped away too quickly for these tasks to be successfully concluded without the need to have recourse to the help of international governmental partners in the form of the International Monetary Fund (IMF) and the European Union. By the time the Troika arrived at the end of 2010, total employment had already fallen by more than 350,000, or about 16 per cent from its late 2007 peak.

How could the economic decline be halted and reversed? The need to placate investors and retain market confidence is too often used as a convenient excuse by conservative voices wishing to block radical policy action. But a government that is running as large a deficit as was Ireland in 2010 soon feels the cost of losing the confidence of the international financial markets on which it is dependent for borrowing.

Since 1944 the world has had a mechanism for dealing with such losses of confidence. The IMF had already participated in the huge Greek loan earlier in the year. Turning to the IMF, and to the European facilities that had been drawn on for the Greek operation, was beginning to look like the most promising way of ensuring that the rate of borrowing could be managed down in an orderly and safe manner. Such official loans would be accompanied by strict conditionality on many aspects of government policy, conspicuously reducing the government's freedom of action, with inevitably damaging consequences for the politicians involved. But these conditions would in fact be less severe for the nation than the implicit constraints driven by financial market participants' reluctance to lend any more, or even indeed to roll over their existing loans.

While it was not until early November that the Irish authorities gave up hope of restoring market confidence and avoiding the need for an official bailout, the writing was on the wall from September. Government debt was so high and still rising, and the economy was so weak that the measures to rebuild bank capital had not fully convinced the markets. What was needed was a clear and convincing narrative, backed up with a credible action plan, to bring the economy back onto a growth path. Though its first months were not promising, in the end, the EU–IMF programme of assistance delivered. In the process it provided financing to allow the remaining fiscal adjustment to be more gradual and more orderly than would otherwise have been achievable.

EROSION OF CONFIDENCE IN THE PUBLIC FINANCES

The Irish government's ability to continue borrowing from abroad to maintain services, given the huge shortfall in tax revenue compared with spending commitments, depended on financial markets' assessment of the sustainability of Ireland's fiscal plans.

The best summary measure of that assessment is the gap between the yield to maturity on Irish government bonds in the market and that of risk-free euro-denominated bonds such as those of the German federal government (known in market slang as 'bunds').

In the years before the euro, this spread mainly indicated the remuneration required by investors to assume the risks of exchange rate fluctuations. There could have been some element of default risk also, especially during the fiscal crisis of the 1980s. But as soon as the euro began, simple exchange rate risk vanished, with the result that, for the first nine years of the euro, Irish government bonds traded at yields scarcely different from bunds (or indeed other euro area governments). The crisis of 2008–9 changed all that, as financial markets became increasingly sensitized to default risk. From then on yield spreads, and the closely related CDS spreads, provided a much-watched window on shifting market opinions on and confidence in the Irish public finances and those of the banks.[1] By 2012 the additional complication of market speculation regarding some form of break-up of the currency union would also influence yields, but during the 2010 run-up to Ireland's application for official international financial assistance, the yield spread measured credit or default risk.

Although it was not much more than 1 per cent in early April 2010, in the following months, despite fluctuations, the trend in this spread crept inexorably higher and higher. By early September it had reached 4½ per cent.

Correcting the Fiscal Deficit Drift

At last focusing in greater detail on the overall Irish economic and financial situation, foreign officials and market participants were beginning to catch up with what was already understood in Dublin, namely that Ireland's fiscal problems went well beyond the mere question of paying for the banking losses. The need for further tax and spending adjustments was becoming evident.

It was time for the Central Bank of Ireland to acknowledge publicly that more needed to be done. Because I have seen too many central bankers make kneejerk criticisms of fiscal deficits, it was with some reluctance that, on 20 September, I pointed out in public the need for a reprogramming of the multi-year fiscal projections. Such a statement by the Central Bank would make it a bit easier for the government to make unpalatable adjustments; it was also incontestably true.

Reluctant to pay the high yields now demanded by financial markets for its own funding, the government announced that it would not borrow for the rest of the year; it had enough in reserve to cover the government's deficit for some months. But any hope that this announcement would trigger an improvement was not fulfilled: market confidence did not return.

Minister Lenihan began to see the advantages of an IMF loan. Having an official backstop to protect the public finances from increasingly alarmist

---

[1] A financial market contract known as the credit default swap (CDS) offers holders of bonds a form of insurance against default. Movements in CDS spreads broadly mirror movements in the yield spread between Irish government bonds and bunds.

financial market sentiment would give him time to turn the finances around. At an October meeting in Washington with the officials who would soon lead the IMF's negotiating mission, he openly discussed the kind of arrangements and conditionality that might be involved.

A new four-year fiscal plan was being hastily developed by the Department of Finance. It would need to be tight if it was to receive the approval of official lenders.

This preparation was against the background of a sequence of knocks to market confidence in Ireland over a period of weeks. These included the public announcement at end-September of higher loss figures at Anglo and Allied Irish Bank; pessimistic analyst comments in Dublin; incautious remarks by senior euro area officials; and the badly worded and poorly judged Merkel–Sarkozy policy statement in mid-October (following their walk at the strand in Deauville) proposing that bail-in of private creditors should be a prerequisite to EU support operations for stressed euro area governments. After the Merkel–Sarkozy proposal was (in revised form) endorsed in a Summit meeting on 28 October, Irish spreads began to increase steadily, rising by 300 basis points in two weeks.[2] Portuguese bond spreads were also increasing, but not as quickly. One additional technical factor that unsettled markets on November 10 was the decision by London Clearing House (LCH), the clearing house for secured inter-bank loans, to increase the margin required for loans secured with Irish government securities, thereby reducing their value as collateral.

With each of these shocks Irish bond yields increased and bank deposit withdrawals accelerated. Thus in a spiralling feedback loop, rising spreads triggered defensive reactions by financial market participants, which in turn placed increased upward pressure on spreads.

Reflecting the increased concerns at both the European Commission and the European Central Bank (ECB), a sequence of technical missions to Dublin from Brussels and Frankfurt probed the government's plans and progress. In Brussels Finance Minister Lenihan and Taoiseach Brian Cowen were pressed for fiscal action.

Meanwhile, in the midst of market turmoil, the long-awaited new Central Bank legislation had been activated by the minister at the end of September. Among other things, this legislation introduced a new

---

[2] To emphasize the progressive influence of Deauville on asset price developments over the subsequent month as market participants gradually absorbed the implications is not to suggest that Deauville 'caused' the Irish bailout: but it did influence the timing (cf. Mody 2018: 277).

governance structure for the bank. Replacing the previous Board of Directors, from 30 September the new governing Commission included five non-executive members, all new to the Central Bank. In a series of briefing meetings, senior staff brought the new directors up to speed on the deteriorating situation. Even though they were all knowledgeable participants in Irish policy circles, it must have been a somewhat bewildering and alarming experience for them. They learnt for the first time the extent of the prospective scale of loan losses at the banks and the rapidly growing scale of emergency liquidity assistance (ELA). They were made aware that an IMF programme was becoming increasingly likely.

And the outflows of bank liquidity were enormous. Between the end of August and mid-October the six Irish-controlled (guaranteed) banks lost about €55 billion of funding; there was a short pause, and then the flows resumed: about €35 billion in November and December. This bank run, coming to 29 per cent of the banks' total funding, amounted to well over half of GDP in just four months. These funds were being replaced by borrowing from the Central Bank.[3]

In early November, I got a call from Brian Lenihan asking if I could make some announcement that would stem the outflow of deposits which was increasingly being talked about in political circles. Reports were coming into him from around the country of customer concerns about the safety of their bank deposits: could I not, he asked, make some statement of reassurance to people that their money was safe? But the time was not ripe. Why should anyone believe a promise like that if we in Ireland did not have the wherewithal to make good on it? On the contrary, such a statement would be more likely to accelerate the outflows and the panic. I told him that nothing I could say at that point would provide credible assurance, and an empty statement would be counterproductive.

With yield spreads approaching 700 basis points (7 per cent) in early November (implying that new long-term borrowing by the Irish government in the financial markets would entail interest rates in the region of 9 per cent per annum), the inevitability of an IMF programme

---

[3] Tighter rules being applied to Irish banks by the British authorities were an additional source of pressure in these months. The UK Financial Services Authority was insisting that Irish banks that had for years been doing business in the UK under the EU banking passport must now establish separate UK subsidiaries. Furthermore, those with surplus liquidity in the UK were not being allowed to lend it back to the Irish parent. It was not clear to us whether the UK authorities were fully compliant with EU law in making such requirements. This was not the only instance during the euro area crisis in which national regulatory authorities acted close to or beyond their legal rights to keep liquidity from draining out to weaker jurisdictions within the EU.

became undeniable. Only if the IMF were prepared to underwrite the government's policies with its own money was market confidence likely to be restored. ECB and European Commission staff were also beginning to circle around the same idea with increasingly pointed remarks. I thought it would be prudent to prepare the ground informally with our usual inter-locutors in Washington. Fortunately, I had known Ashoka Mody, who was in charge of the Irish desk at the IMF, as we had both worked at the World Bank years before. This made it easy for us to have a frank chat; so I called him on 4 November, letting him know that I personally felt the tipping point had arrived and that he could usefully prepare for a likely approach from Ireland. He was not surprised.

Of course I was simultaneously discussing our narrowing options with the senior officials in the Department of Finance. They were coming to the same view. On 6 November, Lenihan agreed, but he insisted that the initial meetings to discuss a loan should be discreet, with no visibility in Dublin.

A curious delay followed, as the Troika staff took quite a while to decide the architecture of the programme. We later learnt that they were in intensive discussion amount themselves. At issue in particular, I was sub-sequently told, were the issue of scale (ECB staff wanted to ensure that there would be enough money to be injected into the banks to reduce their dependence on ECB funding) and the question of bank bondholder bail-in (IMF staff wanted to explore the possibility of the private sector sharing in the costs of the bank failures).[4]

While these internal Troika discussions were proceeding without Ireland's involvement, I took the opportunity of the bi-monthly meetings of the Bank for International Settlements in Basel to sound out the views of ten of the most experienced central bank governors that I knew – European and non-European alike – to see if they agreed that an IMF programme was the best course of action for Ireland. Nine of ten agreed and the tenth said that for him it would be a last recourse. Under the circumstances I took that to be another yes. The wisest comment came from a very distinguished old friend who said: be clear on what you want from the programme, as the lenders will surely know what they want.

Even while we were waiting for the Troika to respond to the proposal for a preliminary meeting to explore the possibility of a programme of assis-tance, political pressures on the Irish government continued in a slightly

---

[4] Chopra (2015) and Donovan (2016) provide further insight into the contrasting approach of the IMF and the European teams to programme design. Chopra was the IMF mission chief for Ireland at the time of the bailout.

irritating manner. On 12 November here were telephone calls to us from Seoul, Korea, where the Group of Seven Industrial Countries' finance ministers and governors were meeting in the margins of the larger G20 meetings. They were anxious that Ireland should apply for assistance and communicated their anxiety to me and, I understand, to the minister. They did not seem to realize that in Dublin we were already waiting for the Troika to signal that they were prepared to start talks.

At last, with Dublin pressing for action, the Troika staff set a date for the start of talks: Sunday 14 November. The government still had several months of funding left in hand, but market yields on Irish government debt continued to jag upwards, and bank deposits were melting away. Brian Lenihan was not ready to make a formal application; he wanted to know from the initial discussions what he was letting Ireland in for. He may also have been stalling from reluctance to face all of his political colleagues with what could only be bad news for them.

For Ireland, though, early application for, and wholehearted participation in, an international official financing programme would be the key to correcting the financial and economic slide.

THE NEGOTIATIONS

Brussels

Having flown in to Brussels on the morning of Sunday, 14 November, on the government jet from the military aerodrome at Baldonnel, the team of Irish officials drove directly to the Commission Buildings in Beaulieu.[5] We got down quickly to what were, in all but name, negotiations. On the Irish side, the Secretary General of the Department of Finance, Kevin Cardiff, took the lead, supported by his senior colleagues and by Central Bank and National Treasury Management Agency (NTMA) staff, including myself. In all there were seventeen Irish officials in the Irish team at the Brussels meetings,[6] and there were at least that many on the other side, representing the Troika: the European Commission, the IMF and the ECB.

A top ('principals') group teased out the approximate scale and cost of the loan that might be arranged, as well as the likely nature of the

---

[5] Characteristically, Lenihan advised the team to have a good Irish breakfast on the plane in order to be well prepared for the discussions.

[6] Seven from the Central Bank, six from the Department of Finance and four from the NTMA.

conditions to be requested by the Troika. On the Irish side this Principals Group generally comprised the three most senior officials of the Department of Finance (the measured, careful and consistent Secretary General Kevin Cardiff, experienced financial diplomat Jim O'Brien and the tenacious and analytically shrewd Ann Nolan); John Corrigan, the head of the NTMA (whose responsibilities included financing the government's borrowing requirement); and myself. We had all come to know each other well over the previous year (and longer for some) and worked as a team.[7]

Figuratively rolling up his sleeves, Kevin Cardiff started to draft a kind of term sheet for what Ireland might envisage. For us to take the lead like this in the discussions seemed a good way of proceeding. It made it clear that we were scoping something to suit Ireland's policy approach, and not simply being dictated to – even though we knew that many elements of an ultimate agreement would be non-negotiable from the side of the Troika. Having listened to the Troika's opening remarks, and taking into account diverse discussions that had been held over the previous weeks, it was evident that the two main prongs of the accompanying policy programme would have to be fiscal adjustment and a new assessment of bank capital needs.

Although I had not been involved in negotiations of this type before, I did have the advantage of having worked at a comparable level of seniority to the Troika negotiators during my years at the World Bank. I had a feel for the motivations, methods of working, constraints and possibilities of our counterparts. They in turn needed to negotiate among themselves, not least because the Commission, the IMF and the ECB had, between them, substantially different objectives and mandates. Furthermore, the Troika had never worked together before the Greek operation of earlier that year: this meant long internal meetings into the evenings for them, giving the Irish side plenty of time to prepare our positions. The Troika negotiators were far from being plenipotentiary, and had to report back continuously to more senior officials in Brussels, Frankfurt and Washington.[8]

---

[7] The Irish and Troika 'principals' (in a somewhat larger composition, in particular including Matthew Elderfield from the Central Bank) would remain in regular telephone contact over the following three years. In addition to the quarterly missions which the Troika sent to assess progress, these teleconferences served to build and maintain trust. As well as allowing routine exchange of information, some of these teleconferences had their tense moments.

[8] It is worth mentioning that the Governing Council of the ECB was not involved in the negotiations, or in the context of the quarterly programme reviews of this or any of the other EU–IMF programmes. Only when some issue that specifically related to central

Other groups formed around details of banking and fiscal issues with my deputy Matthew Elderfield taking the lead on banking (where rebuilding market confidence in the Irish banks was the goal) and the Department's Michael McGrath on fiscal issues (where the lenders wanted assurance that there was going to be a detailed medium-term fiscal plan to reach a 3 per cent deficit target). Both of these officials were very well informed on all of the details of their sectors. They could foresee where technical, practical or political problems could arise, and skilfully steered the Troika into feasible waters.

For the IMF two banking system pillars would be key: first, an ambitious injection of capital into the banks, with the final amount to be based on new stress tests carried out by international consultants; and second, several steps of operational restructuring of the banking system, including an overall downsizing of the banking system and more work on Anglo.[9] The general approach seemed feasible to the Irish side, given that the programme would have the financial and moral backing of the lenders.

Based on the Irish government's revised fiscal plans, and making in addition what seemed to us on the Irish side to be an alarmingly generous provision of €36 billion for the banking recapitalization (more than twice what was eventually injected), the lenders calculated that a total sum of €85 billion (to include the government's existing cash balances as well as the Troika loan) was needed to ensure that Ireland would not have to access private financial markets for a couple of years.

These two days of meetings in Brussels confirmed that there was a workable basis for a loan and Minister Lenihan authorized that the Troika team could continue the discussions in Dublin on the following Thursday.[10]

As we concluded the discussions, one unpleasant incident occurred. The senior Troika people asked Kevin Cardiff and me to dinner at a restaurant near the Grand Place. Towards the end of the meal, just

---

banking, such as any objection to ELA being granted, was the Governing Council consulted; otherwise only informal briefings were provided to the Council on issues that had become salient.

[9] The Troika were also keen on an extension of National Asset Management Agency (NAMA)'s purchases (to segregate and dispose of further tranches of the weaker parts of the banks' loan portfolio). Various versions of this 'NAMA2' idea were discussed over the following months, but it never strongly appealed to the Irish side and in the end it did not happen.

[10] He had hoped that, instead of a straightforward loan, the arrangement could be a precautionary one: the IMF staff quickly put paid to that idea; conditions had deteriorated too far.

after Kevin excused himself from the table for a few minutes, Marco Buti, Director General of Economic and Financial Affairs of the European Commission, raised an entirely new point with me, the gist of which was as follows. Ireland must recognize that it could not maintain the 12½ per cent Corporation Tax regime as it stood; European partners would no longer put up with this. Although this matter would not be part of the negotiations, it would be well for the government to realize that this was the way the wind was blowing. Although I have personally never been an enthusiast for Ireland's approach to the Corporation Tax, I was astonished that such a senior Commission official would make this statement in such a pointed manner, given how central and settled the Corporation Tax regime has been for years in Irish tax policy. It was also extraordinary that it would be addressed in such a calculated way to me at the only point in the proceedings where Kevin, the senior representative of the Irish government, was not present.[11] Of course I gave Kevin a full account of it as we walked across the Grand Place towards our hotel. He remarked that this must be like what the Irish negotiators of the Anglo-Irish Treaty felt in London in 1921.[12]

Kevin briefed Brian Lenihan on the two days of negotiations in Brussels and he was sufficiently reassured by the progress and content of the discussions to agree that they should continue in Dublin on the Thursday. Despite this, the minister came under pressure, at the meeting of the Eurogroup in Brussels on Tuesday 16 October, to make an immediate formal application for official assistance.

Phone Call from Frankfurt

Like the finance ministers, senior officials and governors at the ECB were growing increasingly perturbed, fearful that Ireland would drag its feet in a manner that would only aggravate financial market tensions that could spill over into other countries. Besides, each day saw further outflows from the Irish banks which had to be replaced with additional borrowing from the ECB. The Governing Council had already sanctioned ELA up to

[11] Likely he wanted to communicate the message while being able to deny that he had spoken to the Department of Finance about it.

[12] The reference, I took it, being to the power imbalance between the Irish representatives negotiating the Treaty for what became an autonomous State in Ireland. As every Irish schoolchild is told, British premier David Lloyd George warned of 'immediate and terrible war' if the limited Treaty terms on offer were not accepted.

€42 billion – almost a quarter of Irish GDP – and this figure would rise to €50 billion the following week.

On Wednesday evening, 17 November, I was in Frankfurt to attend one of the fortnightly meetings of the ECB Governing Council, and was asked to let the Irish government know that the Governing Council too, anxious to steady financial markets, wanted Ireland to make a formal loan application. I duly passed on the message by phone, but got a cross response from Brian Lenihan, who rightly felt that all of the external actors were seeking to bounce him into formally making the application. He demurred, saying he had no government approval to do so – but did not at all suggest that he was having second thoughts about the course that he had embarked on. Instead, I assumed that he might want to exploit the fact that no formal application had been made as a lever in the negotiations, which were scheduled to begin very visibly in Dublin the following morning. There must also have been delicate domestic political calculations being made. That was how I understood the casuistical approach adopted by government ministers in public statements dancing around the question of whether negotiations had commenced.[13]

I had become increasingly concerned that the loss of confidence and home and abroad, which was leading to financial market pressures, including the huge outflows from the banks, would cause lasting damage to the Irish economy.[14] It was not just corporate and international depositors who were leaving: Irish retail customers were moving their money. On Wednesday alone, about €1 billion in *retail* deposits was withdrawn. Could the situation be stabilized by an appropriate statement?

Towards midnight that Wednesday, as the Governing Council dinner at the ECB broke up, I sounded out President Trichet on whether he would support a statement by me indicating that the ECB was standing behind the Irish banking system. The wording I suggested was along the lines of 'bank customers should be reassured by the knowledge that Irish banks will continue to receive all necessary liquidity support from the Eurosystem.' But I knew that it was unlikely that he would back such a categorical statement: the ECB was not as fully aware as I was that the Irish government would soon make the formal application for assistance from the IMF

---

[13] I wanted no part in such political games, for fear of undermining the credibility of the Central Bank. Established as an independent arm of the state precisely to remove the influence of short-termist politicians, it must not allow itself to be side-tracked from its financial stability mandate by the domestic tactical manoeuvring of government ministers.

[14] €7 billion had flowed out in the previous five days.

and EU funds. Given how much was already being borrowed by Irish banks from the Eurosystem (the equivalent of one year's GDP – an unprecedented amount) my request amounted to asking for a blank cheque.

Yet without assurance of continuing support from Frankfurt how could I convince the general public in Ireland that the situation was in hand? Already the website of the *Financial Times* was carrying an editorial for Thursday morning's print edition with the subtitle: "Prepare for bank failures – and not just in Ireland." If the Central Bank was to protect financial stability in Ireland, action was needed now. Things had got to the point where, had it remained silent on the state of play, the Central Bank would have not only failed in its responsibility to use timely communication to steady confidence, but would also have dashed a legitimate public expectation in Ireland that it could be trusted not to deceive through omission.

Overnight I decided that the fact – which had already been made public by the government – that intensive discussions on an assistance programme were beginning in Dublin would itself provide the basis and necessary backing for a message of stability from me. I could finesse the question of whether the ECB was committed to open-ended support.

Of course it was not for the Central Bank to make any formal application, and I knew from speaking with Brian Lenihan that evening that the government was not ready to take that formal step. I had to be careful not to commit Ireland while negotiations were still live, or to do anything that could undermine Ireland's position in those negotiations. But the fact that talks were taking place, and that the IMF and European officials were willing to help Ireland with a big loan, was exactly the kind of reassurance about Ireland that everyone needed.

In the telephone interview that I gave on national radio (RTE's Morning Ireland programme) the following morning I confirmed what was already widely surmised – and would within minutes become even more evident as the Troika team walked across the street from their hotel in Dublin's Upper Merrion Street to the Department of Finance to resume the face-to-face talks that had begun the previous weekend in the European Commission offices in Brussels. The IMF and the European lenders planned to offer a sizable loan of tens of billions of euros to be used if necessary to protect Ireland from the pressures of the international financial markets.[15]

---

[15] I explained in the interview that 'the purpose of this whole exercise [was] to provide reassurance ... that the policy stance that the government [was] adopting [would] be effective in getting us on a stable trajectory.' Asked about the deposit run I remarked that

The interview made much more of a splash than I had anticipated. After all, the arrival of the Troika team and the purpose of their mission had already been well flagged in the national media. Evidently, the general public in Ireland were tired of being given an over-optimistic spin on what had become a very sticky situation. I probably also underestimated the domestic political impact on the government's popularity, but if they had wanted to control the communications about what was inevitably a bad news story for them politically, they had left it far too late.[16]

For me, communicating what you are doing and why you are doing it is a fundamental modus operandi of the effective central bank. The value of such a strategy goes beyond the immediate impact on day-to-day developments. For me, the interview was a small part of an ongoing damage limitation effort that would continue for a further three years. It had some steadying effect on confidence and if anything improved the negotiating atmosphere somewhat to Ireland's advantage.[17]

The ECB remained unconvinced that Ireland would act promptly. Later that same day, Thursday 18 November, the ECB Governing Council

the Central Bank was in a position to provide 'exceptional liquidity', adding that 'I would have to make sure that the other members of the ECB, the Governing Council, don't object to making those loans, because that's always on a case by case basis. But of course if I ask them, they will not object.' I stressed that applying for the loan was not my call: "It's the government's decision." I concluded: "It's my expectation that that is what is definitely likely [sic] to happen, that is why the large technical teams are sitting down discussing these matters and I think this is the way forward. Market conditions have not allowed us to go ahead without seeking the support of our international collaborators so that is what's ahead. And I don't see it as something that is really worrisome or should lead to a huge change in direction, because as we know the fiscal discussions about €6 billion in cuts, all of that is part and parcel of what an IMF team would ask for, would suggest if they came in, in the absence of any such discussions. So I'm not saying that they'll rubber-stamp, but I think that they will not find all that much to disagree with." (The full transcript of the interview is reproduced in Donovan and Murphy 2012.)

[16] Brian Lenihan telephoned me shortly after the broadcast. He managed to suppress his annoyance, simply remarking that he could not disagree with anything I had said. (Indeed in his Parliamentary Statement he welcomed 'this morning's comments by the governor of the Central Bank'). However, it is clear that my interview had put the government on the back foot in domestic political terms, as Taoiseach Brian Cowen put it in his evidence to the Banking Inquiry half a decade later. I had not fully anticipated that party political impact, and I regretted it, not least because the central bank should generally avoid getting drawn into party political matters.

[17] In particular, my interview did not disclose anything that was not already publicly known. This is evident from the front page article of the *Irish Times* of the *previous* day. It quotes Lenihan as acknowledging that, while it was not inevitable that Ireland would enter an EU–IMF programme, urgent talks would begin in Dublin later that week. "When asked if he had any concerns about a possible erosion of Irish sovereignty, the Minister said: 'When you borrow, you lose a little bit of sovereignty, no matter who you borrow from.'"

authorized Trichet to write a tough letter to Lenihan calling for a prompt formal application if continued ELA was to be provided. I pointed out that there was no need for this, given that discussions were already well advanced. I also remarked that the letter would present the ECB in an unfavourable light if it were to be leaked. Why give the Irish government the excuse for blaming the ECB for everything it was doing in terms of cutting back public expenditure and increasing taxation? It surprised me that the letter was nevertheless sent. Its peremptory tone was received with some concern in the Department of Finance (Cardiff 2016).[18] My own view, which I shared with the Department, was that an element of bluff or bluster was involved on the part of the ECB. I could not see the ECB triggering bank closures at that time, as would have been the consequence.[19]

Was the ECB within its legal rights and its mandate to warn the government that availability of ELA was about to be cut off? Presumably so, but it would not have been within its mandate to dictate policy to the government. As drafted, the letter made no attempt to acknowledge the boundary between (on the one hand) the ECB's need to protect its own balance sheet and adhere to settled policy on emergency liquidity and (on the other hand) the government's sovereign responsibilities. It was unwise to allow such a letter to give the appearance of an overstepping of the mandate.

While in practice this rather gratuitous letter had little or no effect on the negotiations, the Trichet letter of 19 November did have consequences for the ECB when it was subsequently made public some years later. Its peremptory tone of ultimatum, and especially the threat that additional ELA would be blocked, did have the damaging effects I had foreseen on the ECB's reputation. It fuelled the exaggerated perceptions of a loss of sovereignty (cf. Hourigan 2017), which were also aggravated by the grovelling tone of the response sent by Lenihan – even though I am sure that response was drafted with clenched teeth.

---

[18] With the benefit of hindsight, the exact wording of the letter has been read as forbidding a bail-in of the unguaranteed bondholders, and indeed that may have been the intention of the staff who drafted it. The relevant phrase is: 'the plan for the restructuring of the Irish financial sector shall include the provision of the necessary capital to those Irish banks needing it.' But the drafting was too subtle, and Dublin did not recognize any such prohibition in the letter – the explicit prohibition came the following week.

[19] Though indeed that did subsequently happen in Cyprus (2013) and Greece (2015), albeit under different circumstances. On both occasions, the decisions to do so were taken in haste. I, for one, had misgivings about both of those decisions; but I could not at the time find the words to formulate convincing arguments against them.

Negotiations in Dublin

A most unexpected development took place on the evening of the first full day of negotiations in Dublin. I had returned from Frankfurt and joined the Principals' meeting just as they broke for a sandwich. Emphasizing that his remarks should not be taken as part of the negotiations, Ashoka Mody of the IMF raised the question of bailing-in unguaranteed creditors of the failing banks.

He asked for data on the volume of such debt and seemed to believe that the number was very high – my recollection is that he mentioned €70 billion. Actually most of the banks' senior non-deposit unguaranteed debt was in the form of covered bonds, that is to say, bonds that, if defaulted, would give the creditors the legal right to seize collateral in the form of the loans that 'covered' the bond. In practical terms, such bonds could not be bailed-in.[20] It was also hard to see how bail-in could be effected safely, or at all, for the remaining €16.0 billion of unguaranteed senior bonds outstanding from the four apparently solvent going-concern banks, even in a winding up.[21]

But there was a block of about €4.7 billion in unguaranteed and unsecured debt left in the gone-concern banks Anglo and Irish Nationwide Building Society (INBS). Irish officials had been cautiously exploring the possibility of finding ways of bailing-in these debts, but such ideas were being talked about only in the tightest of circles.[22] This could not have been done while the initial guarantee was in force; but that was now in the past. We were also conscious of the legal and contractual difficulties that would present themselves. We certainly had not expected the IMF to raise the matter. If the IMF were backing the idea, all doubts would have been removed on our side. Bailing-in bondholders under Troika pressure

---

[20] Even after compulsory bail-in subsequently became the law in Europe under the Bank Recovery and Resolution Directive (BRRD) legislation discussed later, secured bonds are exempt.

[21] Most of these bonds were issued under English law. A negotiated debt-equity swap might have been possible, though far from risk-free. This would have resulted in the bondholders rather than the government taking the needed equity stakes; in the end the bondholders would likely have recovered most of their investment in the going concern banks and some might well have turned a profit on the deal.

[22] It is worth recalling that bail-in of senior bondholders was not widely advocated in Ireland until late in 2010. Even the 46 Irish economists who signed a letter in August 2009 arguing that some bondholders should be required to accept reductions in value clarified that this related only to the subordinated debt holders remaining after the guarantee expired (cf. Whelan 2009). This category of bondholder was in fact subjected to substantial haircuts during 2009–11.

would remove much if not all of the stigma that might otherwise be associated with bail-in.

In the following days there were several other side meetings designed to tease out the possibilities of bailing-in unguaranteed bondholders. The interest of the IMF team in this idea was, however, evidently not shared by the other Troika negotiators. Indeed, I suspect that it was mainly disagreement within the Troika on this point that had caused the hiatus between Ireland's agreement to meet to discuss a programme and the actual meetings. Eventually the IMF staff had to retreat on this point.

It seems that the IMF's decision not to press the bail-in idea was taken as a result of a dramatic teleconference of the Group of Seven finance ministers on 26 November, where Trichet highlighted the dangers of bailing-in senior bondholders of Irish banks.[23] US Treasury Secretary Tim Geithner has confirmed his role in convincing the meeting that the expected cash benefits of a bail-in were not sufficient to offset the market turbulence and the overall increase in euro area bank funding costs that were likely to occur in the immediate aftermath (Geithner, 2014). Seemingly always reluctant to envisage bail-in, Geithner may nevertheless have been correct on this occasion from the point of view of the euro area as a whole, given what, in international terms, were the relatively small sums at stake. Not all participants agreed, but, with his most senior IMF colleagues seemingly split on the issue, IMF Managing Director Dominique Strauss-Kahn finally concurred with the Trichet–Geithner line. Perhaps, as is often suggested by critical commentators, some G7 ministers were also thinking of the direct losses that might be incurred by bailed-in bondholders in their countries, but I doubt if that was uppermost in their mind.[24]

The Troika met Minister Lenihan on Friday 26 November to tell him that there would be no programme if he insisted on bailing-in the bondholders. It was a dejected minister whom I met with Taoiseach Brian Cowen and their advisors that evening. It was not, after all, going to be possible to use this device to turn the negotiations into a dramatic political and economic success.[25]

---

[23] As is usually the case when the fate of a small country is in the hands of others, I did not participate in this meeting. My understanding of what happened (as already described in my 2014 paper) comes indirectly from several sources.

[24] It is somewhat ironic though, that, just two weeks previously at the G20 meeting in Seoul, the same ministers had endorsed new global principles for 'improving the authorities' ability to resolve [large banks] in an orderly manner, *without exposing tax-payers to loss*' (my emphasis).

[25] In the end, though (as explained later) the long-term financing solution for the central bank indebtedness of Anglo and INBS, the two banks whose bonds were chiefly at issue,

By the time the negotiations began, the government were just about ready to release their revised four-year fiscal plan, which now, consistent with domestic and international discussions over the previous couple of months, envisaged much more adjustment than had been envisaged in previous budget documents. It was published on 24 November, before the government made formal application for a programme. I think that ministers took some comfort from the home-grown nature of the fiscal plan. This was the start of a highly disciplined pattern of fiscal adjustment which proved invaluable in keeping the programme on course and building trust with the official lenders.

The negotiations proceeded surprisingly quickly. The lenders were convinced that a quick agreement of a programme would have a calming effect on the markets and were very eager to conclude. Multiple strands of discussion involving dozens of officials on the Irish side and probably also a couple of dozen on the Troika side took place in government buildings and at the Central Bank among other locations. Most of the discussions were among officials who then briefed their ministers on progress. There were a few meetings between the Troika and the Minister for Finance, but I did not attend these. (Meanwhile I attempted to ensure that the non-executive members of the Central Bank Commission were not left out of the loop – though they would probably have appreciated fuller and more prompt briefing. I also briefed the finance spokespersons of the chief opposition parties at their request over the following days.)

On the Irish side the negotiators had a few major concerns. One was the level of interest rate from the EU part of the loan. This was to be equivalent to the rate calculated in accordance with the IMF's standard rules, but as such it also embodied heavy surcharges over the IMF's base borrowing rate reflecting the large scale of the loan in relation to Ireland's 'quota' of borrowing entitlements. Second, we were disappointed that the lenders had rejected out of hand any idea of building-in some risk-sharing arrangement around future bank loan losses. (For example, they could have directly injected capital into the bank to absorb such losses, instead of lending to the government for it to inject into the banks, thereby potentially exposing itself to all of the

was ultimately relatively favourable to Ireland. This solution, arrived at only more than two years later, can be thought of as providing an offset to the cost of having to repay the remaining €5 billion of their bonds, especially as the Central Bank indebtedness was much larger – more than €40 billion.

unexpected losses.) Third was the scale of bank recapitalization that the lenders had in mind: we felt this €36 billion to be unaffordably high for the government; but at least it was to be finalized on the basis of an elaborate data collection and analytical stress test exercise. And we were very disappointed that the IMF staff representatives, having raised the possibility that some of the out-of-guarantee senior bank debt might be left unpaid, eventually withdrew this proposal and indeed told the government that such action would prevent a programme being agreed.

These concerns were communicated in writing to the government, but with a recommendation from the Central Bank that the loan should nevertheless be applied for. It seemed clear that there was little or no potential for give on the side of the lenders. For the government to refuse the loan would clearly threaten the government's ability to make the fiscal adjustment in an orderly manner: instead, as soon as cash ran out, much more drastic spending cutbacks would have been enforced by a lack of cash.

And so the loan was agreed. In cash terms (and as a multiple of its quota) Ireland's borrowing from the IMF was to exceed that of any previous borrower in history apart from Greece, and IMF staff calculated that Ireland's loan represented a higher percentage of the borrower's GDP than any recent IMF loan bar those to Iceland and Ukraine. Two-thirds of the total lending came from European facilities, including bilateral co-financing from Denmark, Sweden and the UK, whose governments wanted to help even though they were not part of the euro area.

I and other senior colleagues had our doubts as to whether the programme, as negotiated, would prove sustainable, especially considering the high interest rates that were being applied. Market participants had the same response when the agreement was made public. As mentioned, the interest rates charged were based on the IMF's standard formula for member borrowings; the bigger the loan (relative to the size of the member's IMF 'quota'), the higher the interest rate charged. This formula had been designed to discourage excessive use of the Fund's resources. Ireland's loan was exceptionally large, reflecting the depth of the crisis. It was understandable for the IMF to protect their resources in this way (otherwise they could run out of loanable funds), but the European lenders were not so constrained. They should have seen that the interest rates being charged (which would generate sizable profits to the lenders) were so high as to threaten the sustainability of the Irish public finances and put in doubt Ireland's ability to turn the financing crisis around.[26]

Nevertheless, it was clear to us that accepting the financing arrangement, and seeking to comply with it, would provide the best basis for securing any necessary revisions in the terms, or an accommodating approach to any debt restructuring that might subsequently prove necessary.

* * *

Indeed, it turned out that, without using up any diplomatic capital, the deep interest rate reductions and maturity extensions granted to Greece in July 2011 were applied also to Ireland, transforming debt sustainability. By that stage Ireland had already delivered on its programme undertakings for more than six months, making the read-across impossible to challenge.

On the back of this July 2011 improvement in financing conditions, market spreads on Irish government securities over bunds, which had spiked to unprecedented levels, narrowed sharply and permanently.[27] In parallel, the Bank of Ireland quickly managed to secure a sizable (€1 billion) equity investment from US and Canadian private equity funds. Although, given the many evident challenges, it was not clear at the time, for Irish financial stability and the public finances, the worst was over.

Ironically, rating agency Moody's failed to recognize the imminent turnaround in the creditworthiness of Ireland and took this moment to downgrade Ireland to Ba1 (just below investment grade) with a negative outlook (12 July 2011). Moody's was the only one of the rating agencies to put Ireland below investment grade, and it persisted in this surprising isolation until February 2014 – after Ireland's exit from the programme.

THE APPROACH OF OTHER COUNTRIES

I have often reflected on the stance and probable goals of the other side in the negotiations, and on the approach adopted by other countries as they accepted or resisted similar programmes. These reflections suggest to me that Ireland did as well as could be expected in the context of a surprising lack of innovation and especially of collegiality on the part of the lenders.

---

[26] This could be another example of a multiple equilibrium: high interest rates and a rapid repayment schedule might have driven Ireland into a debt restructuring; low interest rates and a long maturities were affordable.

[27] The yield on 10-year Irish government bonds touched 14.6 per cent on 18 July 2011, almost 12 percentage points (1200 basis points) above their German equivalents.

Among the lenders, the IMF negotiators, led by the urbane and affable Ajai Chopra and the subtle and far-sighted Ashoka Mody, were the most experienced and the most politically sensitive of our counterparts. Despite the fact that other EU member states had a large, indeed blocking, share in excess of 30 per cent of the votes in the IMF's governance structure, and despite the fact that the IMF was going to lend only one-third of the total amount, they did not simply row in behind the other lenders. The signal example was their attempt to keep the question of bond-burning on the table.

But in addition, for example, they pressed successfully for a more gradual reduction in the budgetary deficit, pushing back the target of getting below the 3 per cent ceiling by a whole year. (Whether that was in the long run a good thing or not can be debated; but it aligned with the preference of the government.)

On the other hand, the IMF had introduced a remarkable policy change earlier in 2010 according to which, deviating from previous policies, it was prepared, in order to prevent contagion to other countries, to lend to a government even if debt sustainability could not be expected with high probability. This 'systemic exception' rule was designed to permit the IMF's loan to Greece, at a time when a restructuring of Greece's debt to the private sector would have been a far better solution, but was being resisted on contagion grounds by Europe. The rule was also appealed to in the case of Ireland, given that the IMF staff had their doubts about Ireland's debt sustainability also.[28] The 'systemic exception' rule has since been discarded by the IMF (cf. Independent Evaluation Office 2017). Had it not existed, the European lenders would have had to improve the financial conditions of their lending to Ireland from the outset in order to ensure debt sustainability. In the end, of course, the conditions were improved in mid-2011.

The ECB negotiators seemed mainly focused on stopping and reversing the exorbitant level of Irish bank borrowing from the Eurosystem.[29] They tended to ignore or downplay the fact that Irish banks could not survive if the Irish sovereign remained under stress. Hoping, as it did, to reduce its exposure to Ireland by getting repaid while the others provided more

---

[28] The projections published by the IMF at the time the loan was made included a scenario in which the debt-to-GDP ratio after five years would reach 155 per cent and still be growing.

[29] Ironically, the loose statements, public and private, of some top ECB people in the run-up to the loan application certainly helped accelerate the run on the Irish banks, thereby increasing their borrowings from the Eurosystem!

finance, the ECB's position as a participant in the discussions was some-what anomalous. Thus, while the other two members of the Troika were arranging to provide additional financing and required assurance that government policy would not dissipate these funds, but would restore Ireland's creditworthiness, the main objective of the ECB participants seemed to be to reduce the ECB's net financing of the Irish banking system and as quickly as possible. Europe had decided to involve the ECB in such negotiations largely because of its organizational capacity and financial know-how, unmatched among the Union's institutions. But its involve-ment entailed conflicts of interest that had not been thought through. The ECB has since become less enthusiastic about this kind of role.

Actually, some of the Irish participants had expected a much more constructive financial contribution from the ECB, especially with regard to the long-term financing of the central bank indebtedness of Anglo. They pointed to such examples as the US Federal Reserve's preparedness to provide longer-term financing in the case of the failing investment bank Bear Stearns in March 2008, and the Swiss National Bank's support for UBS later that year. These hopes were probably illusory, not least because of the ECB's firm reluctance to accept any significant credit risk (which would rule out such actions as purchasing non-performing bank loans at close to face value), and more generally because of its aversion to any action that could be interpreted as leading to permanent transfers of resources across countries. It was not until more than two years later that the Anglo debt was finally put on an acceptable basis.

On the whole, the Irish side managed to bat away most of the ideas from ECB staff that were not clearly in Ireland's interest. If ECB staff had an expectation that Anglo's ELA would somehow be repaid promptly out of the proceeds of the loan, this was not realized.

The European Commission was nominally in charge of the negotiations, reflecting the fact that European entities would be advancing two-thirds of the funds, and the main decisions would be taken by European finance ministers. Their objective was to create and implement a fire-wall to prevent the heightened financial market doubts about euro-area sovereigns from spreading.

But instead of bringing the financial resources of the euro area as a whole to bear on the problem in innovative ways to absorb the risks of the crisis and accelerate the recovery, Europe approached the challenge in a heavy-handed manner seeing the stressed countries as blame-worthy and liable to moral hazard. For example, one confidence-boosting risk-sharing mechan-ism that could have been built into the loan would have been to link the loan repayment schedule to the recovery of economic performance, as I suggested in an opinion piece which appeared in the *Financial Times* in April 2011.[30] That would have built on European solidarity to a much greater extent than the provision of a conventional loan, and could have enhanced economic performance in both borrower and lender countries. (Greece could still benefit from such a scheme, which could now be calibrated in such a way that other borrowers would not feel hard-done-by relative to Greece; cf. Honohan 2018a.)

Wary of the political backlash that might result from appearing too accommodating to what were stigmatized as profligate countries, the Eurogroup Ministers had already decided at the time of the first loans to Greece that the interest rate on all such loans should match that charged by the IMF for loans of this size. Lower rates would be seen as encouraging laxity in other stressed countries. The European lenders therefore insisted on an automatic read-across to the rates to be charged on the lending to Ireland. But the IMF national quotas, to which loan size was referred, had not been sufficiently updated over the years, and implied heavy surcharges given the size of the needed loans.

High interest rates on the loans suited the lending ministers, who could report profitable lending to their national audience. Indeed, I had seen the political importance of that reasoning already back in April 2010 when Brian Lenihan had asked me for my opinion on whether Ireland should participate in the first loan to Greece. I had said we should, and he presumed that this was because of the sizable profit margin that seemed to be on offer. But I corrected him: the real reason for showing willingness to lend to Greece was the likelihood that we would be next in line for borrowing.

Brian Lenihan's response to me on that occasion was equally instructive. He denied that Ireland was at risk, saying that no such fear was being expressed among the Eurogroup ministers, who saw Portugal as the next main risk. Indeed, the degree to which the early steps of fiscal adjustment in Ireland had been hailed in early 2010 by creditor countries and European institutions (as an example to others who were prone to foot-dragging) likely intensified the shock and alarm of ministers as they saw Ireland, their exemplar, brought low.

---

[30] If this idea had received any traction, Irish negotiators would have had to make sure that the actual contract would not have been based exactly on GDP growth: it would have had to exclude the artificial elements of Ireland's GDP coming from the accounting activities of multinational corporations.

Analyzing the negotiating tactics of other borrowers in detail would take our story too far afield. Three dimensions seem important: speed, programme design and compliance. The latter two are best discussed in Chapter 10. The evidence suggests that speed is of the essence when it comes to applying for a programme to protect a country from the impact on its public finances of a loss of market confidence. Delay only worsens the situation as trust drains away. Iceland and Ireland moved quickly; Portugal and Spain were also bundled into comparable programmes in 2011 and 2012 when market confidence collapsed. In the case of Spain the concerns were essentially limited to the banking sector and the loan involved policy conditions focused mainly on that sector: still Spain did not, of course, escape the need for fiscal adjustment of much the same dimensions as that of Ireland. The counterexample is Cyprus, whose government stalled for the best part of a year during 2012 and 2013 before entering a programme as conditions deteriorated. While the Cyprus programme was ultimately successful, the delay led to the initial policy being more painful than would have been the case if application had been earlier.

* * *

The race to clean up the balance sheets of the Irish banks before the funding cliff of September 2010 proceeded in parallel with the government's attempt to stabilize the public finances. Because of both its scale and its complexity, the job proved too big to be completed without recourse to official financial assistance.

By moving the big property loans to the asset management company NAMA and insisting on a sufficient recapitalization of the banks to meet other projected losses, the bank restructuring laid essential foundations. NAMA's design avoided several pitfalls. Ultimately, though, the loan-loss projections of March 2010 (deep though they were) proved to be insufficiently conservative.

Yet if they had been sufficient, the implications for the already fragile public finances would merely have brought forward the need to look for international support. Being so close to the cliff edge made over-capitalization infeasible.

With the protection of the EU–IMF loans, the remainder of the needed adjustment, both to the public finances and to the banks, could be, and was, accomplished expeditiously. Without that assistance, the disruption to public services would have been much more severe. After all, the government had lost the confidence of the international financial markets. Without the EU–IMF lending, the state would not only have defaulted on its debt; more acutely, it would have been unable to quickly source the 7 per cent or so of GDP of borrowing needed (over and above tax revenue) to deliver the non-interest public services. The disruption to government services and payments would have been severe indeed, directly affecting beneficiaries of those services and spilling over into a wider economic crash. Indeed, prompt entry into a programme of assistance was the key to correcting the financial and economic slide.

The terms of the assistance at first left quite a bit to be desired, but the scope to redress these shortcomings, especially in regard to debt servicing costs, was soon to be fully and successfully exploited.

Nevertheless, the poor initial financial terms, and the widely leaked story about the prohibition of burden-sharing with unguaranteed bank bond-holders, fed a perception that the lenders were being mean-spirited and were driving an unnecessary degree of austerity. That the programme provided the resources to defer and stretch out the adjustment of the public finances (spending and tax) which had become necessary was not always appreciated by the general public.

On the bitterly cold Wednesday of 22 December I trudged across the snow-covered city centre streets to Minister Brian Lenihan's office to wish him a Happy Christmas. He did understand the policy dynamic and knew that the approach we had adopted was in the national interest. Gravely ill with cancer, though, he also knew that his days were numbered. He did not survive long enough to see the economy turn around.

The subsequent very substantial improvements in the financial arrangements also came too late to expunge the self-imposed reputational damage which some of the official lenders experienced among the Irish public.[31] From the lenders' perspective, conditions that were too easy would have generated moral hazard for the future and for other countries. For Greece a similar lack of collegiality was fatal; in Ireland we had adopted corrective action before it was too late.

---

[31] Brian Lenihan too was highly critical of some at the ECB – though not of Trichet; indeed he later stressed to me that he had been misrepresented on this front, recalling a lengthy and apparently helpful phone call he had had with Trichet on the day before the formal application to the Troika was made.

10

Cleaning Up

If the confidence of Ireland's political leadership was rattled by the need to appeal for international assistance, thereby placing much of their economic policy under the constraints of bureaucratic scrutiny, Ireland's administrative machine was energized to rise to the task of ensuring that the promised programme would be efficiently delivered and in a timely manner. For the Central Bank the first task, as the New Year 2011 began, was to complete the financial restructuring of the banking system in a more convincing way than had been managed so far.

No sooner was this accomplished than the government secured an important improvement in the financial terms of the European part of the loan package. By mid-year, then, the success of the adjustment seemed within reach. And while it would take about another year before the total numbers at work started to grow, and a further year before the level of nonperforming loans (NPLs) started to decline, the wind was now behind us.

Another task to be completed before programme exit related to the government's legacy banking debt. After all, the government had, back in 2008, been urged by the Central Bank (among others) to protect financial stability by guaranteeing the banking liabilities. Now it was clear that two of those banks had totally collapsed, leaving a largely unrecoverable bill of some €35 billion. The others were being propped up with government support that would reach an additional €30 billion or so, though most of this would later be recovered. The Central Bank had a moral responsibility to ensure that the servicing cost of this debt was no bigger than it had to be.

Other banking legacy issues would persist for years to come.[1] Still, the overall programme gradually achieved its core objective of stabilizing the

---

[1] The attempt to ensure that the NPLs would be dealt with in a manner that balanced efficiency with equity (already discussed in Chapter 6) would prove to be a multi-year task,

government's finances and the banks. And with this stabilization could soon come a turnaround in the opportunities and living standards of the people.

THE BANKING STRESS TESTS

Convincing the Market about Bank Capital

The market's perception that the Irish banks were still undercapitalized, despite the injections made during 2009 and 2010, underlay the Troika's insistence that more capital should be injected, on the basis of a new stress test.

Well before the Troika arrived, the Central Bank had announced that bank capital requirements would be reviewed again in March 2011, and that this exercise would involve a much more granular analysis of the banks' portfolio than had been possible in 2010.

Our experience with the reception of the March 2010 capital plan taught us that a new round needed external endorsement to restore credibility and to insulate the financial sector and the economy against waves of destabilizing speculation. Distracted by the Greek crisis (and locally the Quinn Insurance collapse), markets had not paid much attention to the March 2010 exercise. And we had to face up to the fact that the drip-drip of bad news from National Asset Management Agency (NAMA) valuations later that summer had undermined the credibility of home-grown loan-loss forecasts.

It was not that Ireland had eschewed the use of external consultants in the earlier stages. For example, Pricewaterhouse Coopers (PWC) had been engaged in 2008 in efforts leading to the early capital injections of 2009. But the methodology employed by PWC and others at that time had not hit the mark at all. The manifest inadequacy of their estimates had undermined Dublin confidence in the merits of such exercises. We were not convinced that accounting firms would necessarily do a better job than we could ourselves, now that that our staff had been augmented with fresh blood and wider experience. But Matthew Elderfield and I recognized that convincing the markets was now the immediate task: validation from a credible third

and one which was met with considerably less success. The overall proportion of bank NPLs peaked in 2013 at 27.1 per cent; by 2015 it had fallen but only to 16.1 per cent. The so-called Texas ratio, which basically expresses NPLs as a percentage of capital, fell below 100 for the first time in 2015.

party with a track record in projecting loan losses in a systemic banking crisis would be needed.

Like us, the Troika lenders were obsessed with the potential scale of still-opaque loan losses. They had not found deficiencies in our general approach to estimating capital needs. But, like us, they understood that loan-loss estimates were still subject to a wide margin of uncertainty given the evident inadequacies of the banks' credit appraisal functions in the boom and given the scale of the economic activity and asset price downturn.

One way or another, a new stress test, based on the loan-loss projections of outside consultants, was one of the conditions of the Troika loan. It was to be completed by the end of the first quarter of 2011 – a demanding schedule – and any additional capital deficiency detected would need to be filled with cash – not promissory notes (PNs).

Meanwhile the government agreed to provide in cash €10 billion of capital (to include the amount already mandated for Allied Irish Banks (AIB)'s 2010 capital increase but not yet achieved) as a sort of payment on account. This would serve, among other things, to repay part of the banks' indebtedness to the central banking system, the preoccupation of the European Central Bank (ECB) staff members on the Troika team.

This commitment to inject € 10 billion of capital into the banks (even before the stress test) led to an early hiccup when politics intervened. The collapse of the government and the calling of a General Election for 25 February 2011, made an immediate injection of capital highly problematic.[2] Brian Lenihan made the shrewd decision to postpone the action, leaving it to the incoming government to implement the needed capital injection in due course. While this may have been an act of party-political self-interest, it seemed to me to be a sensible and correct judgement on wider grounds and I indicated as much to the Department of Finance officials when they sounded me out on it. The political legitimacy of a capital injection on that scale by an outgoing lame duck government would subsequently have been challenged and it would have become a political football distracting from more consequential issues. Better to postpone this action until after the election, when it could be implemented by the incoming government (as it subsequently was).

The Troika team were, however, most upset. For them, this cash outlay represented the first important staging post in the programme and they were very uncomfortable that it should be deferred. The Troika assumed

---

[2] Leahy (2013) provides an excellent account of the change of government.

the worst, and there was even talk, behind closed doors, of the programme being 'off-track'. In the end, though, wiser heads prevailed and the lenders did not bring the matter to a head. As a sop to the Troika, it was agreed with Brian Lenihan that cash balances held by the National Treasury Management Agency (NTMA) would be lent to the main Irish banks for the interim period: that way the ECB would see the cash, even though it would not be in the risk-bearing form of capital.[3]

Direct Capital Injections

The more important question was about the wisdom of this whole approach. The Troika had pencilled-in a sum of €36 billion out of the total financing package to be applied if necessary to the recapitalization of the banks in cash. (Probably coincidentally, this was approximately the level of emergency liquidity that had been drawn down from the Eurosystem by the time the Troika arrived: injected cash was likely to be used by the banks to repay emergency loans.)

Along with other Irish officials, I felt that sustainability of the public finances would be doubtful if the recapitalization needs really went that high. We knew something that seemed to be less obvious to Troika staff: if the sovereign's debt was unsustainable, even well-capitalized banks could not recover their ability to function in the market. More capital for the banks paid for with money borrowed by the Irish government would strengthen the banks, but weaken the state's finances. If the state's finances were too weak, the solvency of Irish banks would inevitably be undermined in other ways (e.g. payments arrears by the government to its suppliers; arbitrary levies on the banks themselves; forced bank lending to government). By focusing on strengthening the finances of the banks at the expense of the state, the Troika risked exacerbating the bank-sovereign doom-loop which could engulf both.

A more comprehensive view of the situation would have acknowledged that precision about the banks' ultimate need of capital could not yet be attained. That being so, the best course of action would be to design a way of transferring this risk to a larger entity than the Irish state, one with the capacity to absorb larger losses. The obvious candidate here would have

---

[3] The cash was part of Ireland's sovereign wealth fund, the National Pension Reserve Fund (NPRF), managed by the NTMA. It had already been drawn upon for the first €3.5 billion of capital investment in each of AIB and Bank of Ireland in 2009, and €3.7 billion in AIB in late 2010.

been the European Financial Stability Facility (EFSF), through which the bulk of the European lending was being done.

Instead of lending money to the Irish government for it to take the risk of injecting more capital into the banks, the EFSF could have been empowered to sell the banks some credit risk insurance or even to buy newly issued bank shares directly (as had been done with the US Troubled Asset Relief Program [TARP] funds).[4]

Correctly priced, such a transaction need not in the end have yielded the European lenders any less than they have got from the government loans; indeed they might well have made a substantial additional profit – as indeed the private equity fund investors in Bank of Ireland subsequently did on their 2011 equity investment in that bank.

I raised this possibility in the negotiations, both with the Troika negotiators and directly with the top people at the most relevant agencies (the EFSF, the ECB and, for Germany, the Bundesbank). The elegance and appropriateness of the approach was acknowledged; but I was told it was wholly unrealistic from the political and institutional point of view. (I returned to promoting this idea some months later in an appropriate high-level forum, but only earned a sharp rebuke from German Federal Finance Minister Wolfgang Schäuble, who startled me by retorting that Ireland would do better to put its corporate tax affairs in order than to be proposing such ideas.)

The idea of direct injections of capital from a European fund into undercapitalized banks in stressed countries would not go away, though. It returned at the time of the pressure in 2012 on the Spanish banking system, and was (as explained in Chapter 11) eventually acknowledged by the European Council as a potential tool (to be employed by the European Stability Mechanism [ESM]), albeit hedged around with so many restrictions that it has never yet been used. Clearly, officials in creditor countries saw this idea, or any like it, as a device intended merely as cover for transferring to them the bank losses of stressed countries. That is an illustration of the poisonous lack of trust which had seeped into the divide between creditor and debtor countries in the euro area.

The real advantage of a well-designed scheme of that type would not have been a covert transfer to Ireland, but a sharp reduction in the risk facing Ireland. It would have ensured and speeded the success of the support programme. Along with the interest rate reductions on the loans (granted in July 2011), restoration of international confidence could have

---

[4] Though it was preference shares rather than equity that were acquired by the US Treasury.

helped Ireland to turn the corner before it did, putting the economy on a permanently higher path

The Stress Test of March 2011

We needed a convincing estimate of the capital to be injected into the banks. Only a highly reputable international consultancy could convince both the Troika and the markets that the depth of the hole had been bottomed out. The advisory arm of the large investment management firm BlackRock was the most credible and experienced firm for this work – its reputation having been forged in the Swedish banking crisis of two decades before. Time was of the essence and BlackRock were engaged to steer the data requirements and to provide estimates of likely loan losses given a base case and a stress case economic scenario.

Thus began the largest and most intensive analytical exercise ever conducted in such a short period on any aspect of the Irish economy. It was not just BlackRock; several other firms were also engaged in the collection and processing of the raw data, and yet others were charged with helping the Central Bank to control and assess the entire procedure with a view to arriving within four months at a new set of capital requirements for the Irish banks. In all, ten firms were engaged in the exercise; the aggregate bill for these consultancies came to an eye-watering €30 million. The money that was spent on the consultants would have paid for many hospital beds, remedial teachers and the like. But, given the height of the stakes in this strange world of high finance, it proved to be money well spent. The exercise quickly yielded abundant returns in lowering the cost of government borrowing and putting the economy back onto a growth path instead of sinking further into the mire of distrust and pessimism.

While the work done by BlackRock and the other consultants was very costly, it was also professional. It helped the Central Bank focus the data collection effectively to enable the granular analysis that had been promised. The data requirements were considerably more ambitious and demanding than the Central Bank had ever attempted to obtain from the banks, and more comprehensive than was customary in most central banks. Standard Central Bank data reporting requirements on banks regarding their lending had focused merely on totals for each of a dozen main sectoral categories (used for macroeconomic statistical analysis of credit trends), along with a small collection of the largest loans for supervisory purposes. Now the banks were being asked for loan-by-loan information on essentially their entire portfolio. Apparently information at this level of detail had never been assembled by banks for their own management information. Most of the underlying data existed in some form, but was not in readily accessible digital files. Assembling it now became a potentially existential requirement. Some banks were unable to comply with the data demand in the time available; the others were put to the pin of their collars.

The capital requirements exercise (which we named PCAR2011 to emphasize that we were deepening and updating the work of the previous year) was more than a test of how the banks would fare under a macroeconomic stress. It also involved a systematic and detailed reassessment of the quality of the banks' loan books: of their recoverable value if the economy performed as was now expected.[5]

The ultimate result was a rich trove of data which threw much needed light on the overall situation, though inevitably it did not answer all of the questions we had. The data templates proposed by BlackRock in 2011 have since been extended and refined; they continue in use today, with regular updates enabling the Central Bank to track developments in loan performance to an extent which makes it the envy of many other prudential authorities abroad.

The Central Bank's subsequent ability to build on the 2011 data reflects a decision made early on not just to supervise BlackRock's work intensively, but also to shadow closely the analytical calculations that they were carrying out. We were not about to abdicate our responsibility on a matter of such vital importance to the financial wellbeing of the nation by wholly outsourcing an exercise which would determine how much more cash was going to be injected by the government into the banks. We needed to understand fully and validate as reasonable the estimates that were being made of potential loan losses. After all, there was and is no fully accepted or reliable way of pinpointing prospective loan losses in such a systemic collapse. What if a few of the consultants had exaggerated or unrealistically one-sided views of the matter? The computer programmes used for BlackRock's actual methodology, though explained to us in detail, were proprietary. Accordingly, I made sure that Central Bank economists used the newly available comprehensive and granular data to – in effect – reverse-engineer BlackRock's approach, enabling us to verify and validate the BlackRock approach and consider whether it led to estimates that were defensible and realistic.

---

[5] As such it was a forerunner of the asset quality review introduced by the Single Supervisory Mechanism three years later.

BlackRock's methodology for converting the raw loan-by-loan information into the scale and time-path of future loan losses was plausible and coherent, though it was clear that it did not take account of many of the factors that would inevitably influence the eventual outcome and it could not provide tight bounds on the range of the possibilities.

The most intriguing part of the task related to losses on residential mortgages. This was and is the largest part of the banks' portfolios, though not the worst performing. As there had so far been almost no repossessions of mortgaged homes, the task of forecasting repossessions was especially challenging. What would be the main determinants: unemployment, income losses, negative equity? The BlackRock analysts seized on the fact, already well known, that loans in negative equity were more likely to be non-performing. From the data, they calculated what proportion of the performing loans in negative equity fell into arrears in each quarter. If this proportion remained constant, the growth in NPLs could be calculated for every quarter up to the maturity of the loan, given an assumption of the future path of house prices.

This mechanism, emphasizing negative equity, was at the heart of BlackRock's approach to predicting mortgage loan losses. It needed many additional assumptions if the analysts were to estimate the evolution of losses over time. How many NPLs would cure? How many would end in repossession? How much would be recovered by the bank on that part of the loan not repaid from the sale of the repossessed house?

At the Central Bank we thought (and could provide evidence) that employment status, income losses, family break-up and other factors were also important in influencing the degree to which homeowners kept current on their mortgages. We felt the US-based analysts relied more heavily than was warranted on experience derived from the US sub-prime market.

Although we didn't fully agree with their way of modelling each mortgage, on average the BlackRock approach did not seem to be systematically too pessimistic in its overall forecasts for the coming few years.[6] (Indeed, non-performing mortgage loans subsequently continued to rise up until late 2013, as was envisaged by the BlackRock projections, though repossessions and surrenders rose much more slowly than they had projected.)

To operationalize the methodology, BlackRock needed macroeconomic forecasts, and these were provided by the Central Bank (with the Troika

---

[6] We did not, however, think that they were correct in projecting that loan losses would continue on a large scale for decades.

team looking over our shoulder having a de facto veto – which they found no reason to employ). Baseline and stress cases were prepared. For once, I departed from my self-imposed practice of not intervening in a Central Bank macroeconomic projection, though only for the stress case. In my opinion, our financial stability specialists had chosen a stress that was too mild to be convincing to outsiders. I asked them to prepare a deeper stress involving in particular lower property prices than the base case, and this was used in the exercise. In the event, the actual trend in house prices and unemployment in the following year was close to the stress – much worse than the base case – so for credibility of the exercise it was just as well that we used a relatively severe stress case (though both recovered strongly later to beat the base case by 2012 in the case of house prices and 2015 in the case of unemployment).

BlackRock applied varying methodologies to the other sectors: commercial real estate, small and medium-sized enterprise (SME) lending, large corporates, household consumer lending. Certainly, they took the tough and sceptical line that was needed to ensure market credibility of the exercise, even if some of us wondered whether they took sufficient account of the traditional tendency for most Irish borrowers to honour their debts if they can. Once again, using Central Bank's in-house analytical capacity, we were able to explore alternatives and satisfy ourselves that BlackRock's results were defensible.

Translating the loan-loss estimates into the additional capital requirements which would be needed required more analysis, in this case carried out largely by Central Bank staff. The loan agreement with the Troika defined some new parameters which were going to influence the level of additional capital required. One parameter was the projected level of capital adequacy to be required of banks three years into the future (after the projected loan losses over that period had been accounted for), including a buffer intended to deal with losses that would not materialize until later. With intensified discussion of increasing global standards, and given the scepticism prevailing in the market about the Irish banks, the Troika insisted that a higher percentage of the banks' risk-weighted assets than we had set in 2010 (and much higher than the basic international standards) would have to be backed by risk-bearing capital.

Furthermore, the Troika insisted that the banks' loan-to-deposit ratio should also be reduced. In other words, they wanted the banks to become less reliant on potentially volatile funding from the financial markets and more reliant on stable sources of funding such as deposits. But we were worried about the loan-to-deposit ceiling, fearing it could lead to fire sales of loans, especially if the outflow of deposits continued.[7] For this reason, when it became clear that deposits were continuing to decline, we negotiated a waiver ensuring that declines in deposits after the date of the agreement would not be taken into account in assessing whether a bank had reached the target loan-to-deposit ratio. (However, this precaution did not fully prevent a deposit 'price war' from emerging during 2011 and 2012 as banks bid up rates in order to protect their customer deposit base.)

Asset sales by the banks could help reduce these ratios, and would also have the benefit, from the ECB's perspective, of generating cash that could enable the banks to reduce their indebtedness to the central banking system. At the European Commission, the Directorate General for Competition (DGCOMP) also wanted to see asset sales: it was part of their standard approach to the rescued banks. DGCOMP's thinking was that the state aid to banks should not distort competition; instead such banks should be required to shrink through divestment rather than using the aid they had got to maintain or expand their market share.

We recognized the need for asset sales: indeed AIB had already sold its sizable Polish subsidiary as a result of the capital adequacy requirement generated by PCAR2010. Selling the banks' assets at below their attainable value would mean further costs for the government: that had to be avoided. This was one of the aspects on which negotiations became somewhat heated; certain of the Troika negotiators adopted a tone which could only be described as imperious. In the initial programme negotiations they demanded specific time-bound disposal commitments, including certain specific asset sales by Irish banks to be completed by March 2011. The Irish side thought these particular sales were not desirable, and if demanded in the short time-scale proposed would entail heavy fire-sale losses (which would ultimately fall on the Irish government budget). Our approach – as in other similar tight corners that arose – was to keep cool and stand firm, not conceding any vital ground. What the Irish side finally committed to was only that each bank would create an asset sales strategy to be independently assessed for feasibility. The carefully negotiated wording would ensure that the pace of these sales was not forced.[8]

---

[7] The maximum loan-to-deposit percentage was set at 122.5 per cent, representing a compromise struck over the phone between myself and the head of the Troika team. By holding out for a higher figure, our negotiators allowed this to look like a concession, but in fact it was within the range of what we thought could be achieved without fire-sale losses.

[8] Over time, the Troika's interest in the proposal withered and it was quietly dropped.

How Much More Capital?

Despite the very significant additional capital needs announced in March 2010, and although at first well received by the financial markets, the PCAR2010 calculations had proved to be too vulnerable to further bad news. The Troika were right to convince us that a deeper stress, more thoroughly analysed, along with even higher capital standards, was needed to help restore the banks' abilities to fund themselves in the market.[9]

The results of the new capital and liquidity assessments were publicly announced in a detailed statement at the end of March 2011. While the scale of these PCAR2011 capital requirements tend to reflect badly on the previous year's stress test, it seems fair to note that only some of the capital needs arose from BlackRock's loan-loss projection methodology. Some was attributable to the higher percentage capital standard; some arose because of the higher haircuts on the later loan purchase tranches from NAMA; some reflected losses likely to crystallize from loan sales required by the loan-to-deposit ceiling; and some related to still-unfulfilled requirements from the 2010 exercise. The continued overshooting fall in property prices was an additional factor that had not been fully envisaged the previous year.

The important thing was that these estimates needed to convince the markets. The figure of €24 billion, announced as additional capital needed, was high enough for this purpose. The evident complexity and comprehensiveness of the exercise also helped. And the degree of transparency and the level of detail that was provided by the Central Bank in announcing the results of the exercise also helped make it a success.

The projected losses were high, meaning that the government would have to assign substantial resources for recapitalizing each of the major banks.[10] Only Bank of Ireland was in any position to raise capital from the market – and in the end it raised only a fraction of what was needed from that source. Given the high rates of interest at which the government was – at that point – borrowing from the Troika, and the likelihood that it would see little or no additional return from investing in banks it already fully owned, this was a worry. However, the banks did have some assets they

---

[9] Nevertheless, with the economic downturn not yet fully concluded, and in particular with a continued steep fall in property prices overshooting their equilibrium, it would have been unwise to accept the Troika's urgings that we conduct yet another stress test the following year 2012, and we resisted that successfully.

[10] Anglo was now sufficiently well capitalized with PNs; this reflected the pessimism of the forecasts made by their management when they learnt the previous September that Anglo was being wound down.

could sell, and some remaining subordinated debt holders who would be obliged under the circumstances, especially given the new resolution legislation that had been enacted the previous December, to exchange their debt for equity in the bank.[11] As a result, the need for additional cash capital from the state was well below the €24 billion announced as additional capital needs by the stress test and less than a half of the €36 billion that had been pencilled-in during the programme negotiations. Furthermore, it was accepted by the Troika that some of this capital could be in the form of so-called contingent capital securities (CoCos), which would yield a good dividend to the state while being available for conversion to equity in case of need.[12]

In 2008, the government had guaranteed the liabilities of banks in which it had no ownership; after the mid-2011 capital raising all of those banks were wholly government-owned, or almost so, except for Bank of Ireland, in which the government's equity stake was 15 per cent.[13]

A Belated Bail-in?

Even though the government's cash outlay for the 2011 bank capital injection was much less than had been feared, it was still a huge sum for the political system to absorb, particularly as many statements had been made in the election campaign promising to burn bondholders; to refrain from giving the banks a penny more; and so on.[14] Could the ECB be persuaded to reverse their view on burden sharing with senior bondholders of the failed entities Anglo and Irish Nationwide Building Society (INBS)? There were still a few billions of unredeemed unguaranteed senior bonds remaining in those two banks.

Given that these two banks had lost a multiple of their capital and were being kept solvent only with PNs that had been provided to them by the

[11] The banks had already aggressively restructured some of their subordinated debt at progressively steeper discounts over the previous couple of years, thereby achieving loss-sharing with those bondholders.

[12] A form of risk-bearing capital, these conditional convertible bonds carried a high rate of interest (remunerating the government) but would convert into equity if the bank's capital fell below a threshold percentage.

[13] Despite having controlling stakes in most of the banks, the government committed to a relationship framework promising, in particular, to stay out of operational matters, thereby protecting against politicization of the banking system.

[14] In particular, the impression given in Eichengreen (2015) that the entire EU–IMF loans were absorbed by the banking losses is quite misleading. Most of the banking recapitalization had already been injected back in 2010; at most a quarter of the programme loans can have been used for this purpose.

government and kept afloat with emergency liquidity assistance (ELA) from the central bank, could legislation compliant with the Irish constitution have been enacted with the effect of placing the holders of the senior bonds at the back of the queue behind the government and with little prospect of being paid? The government had been warned off any such action during the original negotiations with the Troika, but it had made no promises in this regard for the future.

Already in January I had explored Brian Lenihan's willingness to reopen the question of imposing losses on the unguaranteed debt of Anglo and INBS. He, however, had dismissed such ideas, in view of the known opposition of the finance ministers of the G7 countries (as reported earlier).

I told the new Minister for Finance, Michael Noonan, that I held out hope that attitudes of Troika lenders – including eventually the ECB – might change, allowing the possibility of bail-in of these bonds. This hope strengthened as the announcement of the results of the 2011 stress test approached – especially when Axel Weber, outgoing president of the Bundesbank, publicly expressed himself in favour of a bail-in of these bonds.[15]

To my surprise, the matter culminated suddenly following a poorly conceived gambit. In the draft speech prepared for the stress test results announcement, the Department of Finance included a tentative statement indicating that legislation imposing losses on the senior bonds of Anglo and INBS might be introduced 'if necessary'.[16] For two reasons, this seemed to me to be a somewhat flat-footed approach. First, any such action should be undertaken without prior notice to the market, especially if there are powerful voices opposing it. Second, instead of presenting the Troika with a fait accompli, Department of Finance officials had shared the draft text with Troika staff in case the speech as drafted might prevent

---

[15] 'Holders of Irish bank bonds should take losses instead of the government footing the bill for their bailout [Weber] said.' (Reuters, March 31).

[16] The relevant sentences in the draft were: 'As regards Anglo Irish Bank and Irish Nationwide, there is no immediate need for additional capital. The Government will, however, having consulted with the external partners, legislate if necessary to allow for burden sharing again on a cooperative and orderly basis with bondholders in those institutions if possible. We will act with due care and in close consultation with all the appropriate partners, having regard to the market situation, and the need to have regard to financial stability impacts in Ireland and abroad.' About €0.7 billion of Anglo's unguaranteed senior debt had already been repaid earlier in 2011. The amount of unguaranteed senior debt left in Anglo at that stage was €3.1 billion (about €1 billion of which due later in 2011, and €1.2 billion in January 2012), and in INBS €0.6 billion (not due until June 2012).

a favourable statement from the Troika endorsing the results of the stress test exercise. Admittedly, absence of a supporting statement from the ECB in particular would have been taken by the markets as a criticism and could have triggered renewed bank depositor panic, but asking for clearance of such a tentative policy intention was asking for push-back.

As it happened, several members of the ECB Governing Council shared Axel Weber's sympathetic view to a senior bondholder bail-in (especially when I pointed out to them that the relevant bonds were that day being traded in the market at between 60 and 65 cents in the euro, reflecting significant doubts as to whether they would be paid when they matured later that year or in 2012). But Weber's influence was limited by his impending resignation, and a majority were opposed, fearing the knock-on effect on bank funding markets in Europe as well as the prospect of having to finance a further outflow of deposits from Irish banks. Without a majority in favour, Jean-Claude Trichet could not endorse the government's proposed draft. The ECB would not make a statement welcoming the Irish government's decisions: to welcome the statement would have implied endorsement of a policy of bail-in. Michael Noonan was so informed, and – at the very last minute before making the speech – he decided to change the text.[17]

Although all was not yet lost (the new text did not rule anything out), the chances of a bondholder bail-in receded further. Indeed, despite my encouragement, nothing effective was subsequently done on this. Instead, focus shifted to the equally large question of how the huge ELA indebtedness of Anglo to the central bank could be dealt with on a long-term basis.

CONTINGENCY PLANNING

Bad though the situation of the Irish economy in general and Irish finance in particular had become, it was necessary to consider whether things could get worse and if so what was the best way of dealing with them. From 2008 right through to 2012 the global, euro area and Irish financial systems had

---

[17] Noonan recounted to the Oireachtas Banking Inquiry how he was warned by Trichet that day that, were the government to bail-in bondholders, 'a bomb would go off in Dublin.' Although I believe that it was chiefly ECB concerns about spillover effects to other countries' bank funding, more than solicitousness about Ireland, that mainly informed Trichet's warnings (he does not recall using those precise words to Noonan), I am sure that no threat was intended. Trichet also spoke to (new) Taoiseach Enda Kenny that afternoon by telephone from Shanghai, but there seems to have been some misunderstanding on that call as Trichet thought he was speaking only to the Taoiseach's 'chef de cabinet'.

hit unprecedented turmoil. Who could confidently rule out a further deterioration?

Given what had been said about the lack of preparedness of the Irish administration before the crisis, it would have been at the very least fool-hardy to neglect consideration of a number of remote contingencies. Among the unlikely but possible scenarios we were already mulling by mid-2010 were issues of sovereign default and debt restructuring; the possibility that the ECB would refuse additional needed ELA for the Irish banks, forcing them to suspend payments and triggering the government's guarantee; and even more extreme eventualities in which Ireland was no longer a member of the euro area, or in which the euro area had suffered a break-up.

This contingency planning was ramped up in 2011 and 2012, and there was collaboration with other official agencies in the state as appropriate. To the extent that issues of wider common interest in the euro area were involved, delicate inquiries were explored with other national central banks at an appropriate level.

In each case, comparable historical experiences, legal powers, practical first steps, and longer-term goals needed to be considered. Contingency planning exercises needed to involve a small but sufficient number of experts: enough to create a cadre of experts able to respond quickly if the contingency materialized, but not so many as to hamper the Central Bank's continuing work to deliver on the intended path.[18]

The initial presumption, that sovereign default or exclusion from the euro area for Ireland was highly undesirable, was reinforced by these exercises. The best mitigants we could envisage or prepare for were far from satisfactory. The staff participating in these exercises learnt much about various nuts and bolts in unfamiliar parts of central banking; to that extent the work was useful. Fortunately, the persistence and effectiveness of the national and European authorities' efforts to avoid such contingencies bore fruit and the threats receded.

PUTTING ANGLO TO REST

The exceptional growth of indebtedness of the Irish banks to the central banking system in the final months of 2010 had been both an indication of

---

[18] During this period, amusingly I once found myself sitting at an event in Washington next to an executive of the banknote printing firm De la Rue. I carefully made my excuses and left, hoping that no one had drawn any unwarranted conclusions from observing our brief conversation.

the loss of market confidence in Ireland and the source of concern to the ECB.

The ECB's concern was not just over whether it would eventually be paid back. There were other policy and legal concerns also. For one thing, it would be difficult to bring back normal monetary policy operations in the euro area with liquidity allocated in response to an auction, instead of at a fixed price, if several banks, having nowhere else to go because they lacked the confidence of the market, were induced to bid up aggressively the ECB's policy rate. The result could be a decoupling of the policy rate from the money market rates available to other unstressed banks. This would impair the effectiveness of monetary policy in steering the market cost of funds across the euro area.

Rebuilding the capital of stressed banks could help remove this obstacle to the effective functioning of monetary policy. But more capital might not be enough, and other ways of speeding a reduction in the indebtedness of banks that had become dependent on central bank funding were continuously being devised in Frankfurt. One example was a possible new ECB facility for stressed banks, providing exceptional funding renewable on a six-monthly basis; this plan was roundly rejected: by hawks as an unwarranted innovation and by doves as providing insufficient certainty to the debtor. None of these draft schemes would have been beneficial to Ireland; they were largely seen off by Central Bank diplomacy.[19]

Legal concerns were also to the fore, especially in regard to ELA. The legal arrangements for ELA in the Eurosystem had been devised for circumstances where a single bank was in trouble, and where a temporary advance of funds (at a penalty interest rate and against collateral) by the national central bank could be tolerated. In the last months of 2010 ELA in Ireland had grown to quite unprecedented levels, not only at the failed banks Anglo and INBS, but throughout the system. As previously indicated, the acronym ELA stood for 'emergency liquidity assistance', and my attempts to reword it as 'exceptional liquidity assistance' could not extinguish the formal position that ELA must be short term in nature. As ELA to Anglo/Irish Bank Resolution Corporation (IBRC) entered its third year, the undefined duration 'short-term' was coming under increasingly critical

---

[19] Some would have reduced the Central Bank's surplus income; others would have made it more costly or difficult for the banks to access central bank funding. Additional costs could have been passed-on to the banks' customers. By increasing the cost to those banks of securing liquidity such measures would have further squeezed credit availability and might have induced more precipitate and harsher treatment by the banks of their non-performing borrowers.

scrutiny. Besides, as it wound down, Anglo/IBRC's legal status as a bank would likely become unsustainable, at which point it could no longer be granted ELA.

With the gradual restoration of confidence and with the sale of assets as effectively mandated in the programme, the over-indebtedness of the going-concern banks to the central banking system could be expected to correct itself. Meanwhile, in order to reduce their dependence on ELA, the ECB pressed in early 2011 for an alternative solution: these banks should create new bonds under the government's guarantee and use them as collateral in the ECB's normal financing operations.[20] I was not an enthusiast for this device (first proposed, I believe, in a different context by Axel Weber) as it smacked of sweeping a problem under the carpet – especially when uncertainty was raised over whether the credit risk associated with such lending would remain with the Central Bank of Ireland or be pooled as in fully normal operations. Still, these drawbacks were not decisive and the device would help remove the stigma of ELA from the continuing banks.

Dealing with the ELA of the failed banks Anglo and INBS was another matter. These entities were in a wind-down mode and not taking new business. But they owed the Central Bank huge sums, secured against their assets, including the promissory notes that had been injected by government during 2010 to ensure that they satisfied formal solvency requirements and could thus be considered for ELA. The ELA facilities were renewed on a fortnightly basis and this renewal was subject to an explicit governing Council non-objection procedure. There was no prospect of these two failed banks raising cash from normal operations to repay the ELA.

If continuation of ELA were to be refused by the ECB Governing Council, where would the government get the cash to honour its undertakings in regard to the ELA? This consideration also suggested to some that continuation of ELA might be misconstrued as tantamount to central bank lending to the government itself.

Evidently, this whole situation needed to be put on a long-term basis from the point of view of banking, economics and law.

---

[20] For which the government guarantee would make them eligible. In recognition of the EU–IMF programme, the ECB had agreed in December 2010 that, even if the Irish government did not retain an investment grade rating, its guarantee would continue to be sufficient for eligibility in ECB lending. Some at the ECB held this up as a major concession to Ireland, even though it was never needed, because only one of the rating agencies ever lowered Ireland's rating below investment grade.

The complexities of the situation were illustrated by 'tap and swap', the name given to a sequence of unsuccessful attempts by some Troika staff to find a solution through financial engineering. Some of these proposals involved additional borrowing by the government from the ESM; some would have entailed exchanging Anglo's PNs for government bonds and then having Anglo swap these to the continuing banks in return for their hard-to-sell loan assets. When spelled out, none of these proposals stood up to financial scrutiny from the Irish side. While some might have helped the continuing banks, they risked worsening the state's finances, without necessarily offering a long-term solution to Anglo's funding costs. The same applied to other promising-sounding ideas including the potential purchase of Irish bank NPLs by the ECB or the ESM.

One requirement of the Troika programme turned out to simplify matters somewhat. Troika staff seemed to feel it improper that none of the six locally controlled banks had been closed in the crisis. This smacked to them of policy inaction (even though the main reason was that closing any of the guaranteed banks during the two years of the original guarantee would have triggered a sizable cash call on the government). To demonstrate progress, the Troika proposed that the failed banks Anglo and INBS would be merged, and their remaining deposit liabilities, along with eligible assets, sold to the highest bidding continuing bank.[21] This transaction had the effect of concentrating all of the ELA into one 'gone-concern' bank (IBRC), and this new bank would be free of the complications of deposit liabilities.[22]

Bringing ELA to an End

Resolution of the ELA problem got the highest priority from the middle of 2011. The short summary of how this was resolved is that, after Anglo/

---

[21] The merger of EBS into AIB was part of the same move. Unprompted, the Irish side would not have embarked on the AIB–EBS merger: it complicated AIB's management challenges without achieving any material efficiencies: it was an example of the kind of low-cost concession made to the Troika team, thereby providing space for robust opposition to more damaging proposals. Preservation of Permanent-Trustee Saving Bank (PTSB) (ex-Irish Life and Permanent [ILP]) as a stand-alone entity was also put into question by some of the Troika people, but eventually that rationalization was not pursued, the desirability of having an additional competitor being the decisive factor.

[22] A piece of central banking trivia refers to the peak level of ELA for the Irish banks. This spiked to a record €84 billion at the end of the first day of the deposit transfers when, because of in-process transfers, ELA had not yet fallen in the continuing banks, whereas it had temporarily increased in the two gone-concern banks.

IBRC was liquidated, the Central Bank's claim on IBRC was converted into very long-term government bonds in a way that, for complicated reasons, resulted in very low financing costs to the government. The importance of this issue and its complexity warrants a closer look at the details.

With the extended duration of ELA to Anglo/IBRC the subject of increasingly intensive pressure from the ECB, it was evident that ELA could not be extended much further. The ELA – more than €40 billion of it – represented, through the PNs on which it was secured, the bulk of the burden arising out of the initial government guarantee.

It was important to remind outsiders that this was a burden which, on the recommendation of the Central Bank, the government had assumed in September 2008 in order to contain the emerging financial instability which the Central Bank had itself failed to prevent. The least the Central Bank could do was to facilitate, as far as was legally possible, the financing of this burden. It would be ironic and counterproductive for the Central Bank to risk financial instability by making the servicing of this debt more costly than it need be.

When put to them in these terms, this reasoning was accepted by other governors. The eventual acquiescence of the Governing Council of the ECB in the complex arrangements that were devised to resolve the situation likely reflected their acceptance of this perspective. They may also have been uneasily conscious of the ECB's role in pressing the government in 2010 and 2011 to facilitate the repayment to bondholders of a smaller volume of unguaranteed debt of Anglo and INBS.

If there was universal willingness to find a solution, there was nevertheless no obvious way to meet the technical and legal objections that might be raised. Some potential solutions attractive to the ECB were unacceptable because they presented sizable costs or risks to Ireland. Great care had to be taken by Dublin to ensure that one unsustainable arrangement would not be replaced by another with hidden costs or risks for us, whether financial or in terms of public acceptance. There was great reluctance in Frankfurt to endorse any easy money solution which, though legally and economically sound as a central banking measure, might indirectly undermine the foundations of the ECB's operations. Many possible solutions were blocked by the conservative interpretation of the ECB's legal statutes by ECB lawyers.

The PNs were themselves unusual instruments. I had suggested to Brian Lenihan as far back as the spring of 2009 that capital deficiencies at the banks could be filled with some form of government bond or note, and not necessarily with cash. When the deficiencies began to crystallize in Anglo at the end of 2009, he decided to pursue this approach. With Irish government debt still rated AA, there could be no regulatory objection to this approach. But the Department of Finance's lawyers were even more ambitious: could they not devise an instrument which would be accepted as capital, but would not show up in Eurostat's official measure of government debt, and at the same time would be eligible as collateral for the ECB's normal monetary policy operations? This was the reason for the unusual characteristics of the PNs as finally designed: the annual instalment payments, without any final payment of principal; and the non-transferability of the instrument, except to the Central Bank.[23] Nevertheless, despite all the ingenuity, this failed to convince Eurostat or the ECB. The PNs were included in measured government debt for 2010 and were not eligible as collateral for normal ECB borrowing (though they could be used as collateral for ELA). Furthermore, it was soon painfully evident to the government that the annual PN payments were exceedingly large, not having been spread out over a sufficient number of years to suit a financially stressed government.

The first annual instalment payment of the PNs (€3.4 billion) was made in cash on the due date in March 2011. But the following year it seemed right, despite having no agreed solution to the ELA problem yet, to take unilateral action to slow the cash obligations of the government. Accordingly, the Irish government, with the formal agreement of IBRC, decided to pay the end-March 2012 instalment in kind, specifically in a new government bond of equivalent value. Reacting to this unexpected demarche from Ireland, the ECB pushed back immediately and vigorously, insisting that IBRC's ELA should fall by the full value of the instalment and refusing to allow IBRC to present this new bond as collateral for normal borrowing. This threatened to create an awkward confrontational impasse, but – with mere hours left before a default threatened – the stand-off was

---

[23] Each PN was a promise that the government would pay a fixed sum every year for a term of years (originally ten, but later extended) to the undercapitalized bank – Anglo, INBS or EBS. The annual payment and the number of years combined to give the PN a theoretical value sufficient to bring each bank into compliance with the capital adequacy requirements. (The theoretical value took account of the market yield on Irish government securities, with the result that the PN effectively baked-in some of the crisis-level yields.) The PN could not be transferred to any other entity, except the Central Bank. Despite the fact that the PN had no stated face value and no stated interest rate, Eurostat (rightly) treated it as a debt of the government. The ECB also correctly found that the PN did not satisfy the normal eligibility requirements (basically because it was not transferable and also because it did not have a stated face value).

resolved by IBRC using the new bond as collateral with another Irish bank to borrow the cash to pay down its ELA.[24]

The excitement over the March 2012 instalment highlighted the need to find a lasting solution to ELA and to the PNs. The ECB was growing increasingly insistent that this large emergency lending (and to a state-owned bank) must be brought to a close. But the government was still not in a position to produce cash on this scale; besides, paying the annual instalments in cash would not be politically sustainable. The government lobbied other member states, seeking and receiving political support of all of the most important countries in its attempts to find a solution.[25]

But central banks are independent. It took many months of central banking policy negotiations led by myself and our well-networked Deputy Governor Stefan Gerlach, and of technical discussion led in the Central Bank by the unflappable Director of Financial Operations Maurice McGuire and at the Department of Finance by the astute Second Secretary Ann Nolan, to land on a comprehensive package that would meet all of the requirements. These were only the leaders; a large team of dedicated legal, financial and economic experts at the Central Bank devoted long hours to the design, as did teams in the Department of Finance and the NTMA.

The arrangement finally arrived at followed exploration of many alternatives before we managed to hit on a solution which could sufficiently satisfy all legal, financial and political concerns. The basic plan was to put IBRC into liquidation: that act would end ELA. Instead of being the provider of regularly renewed ELA (amounting to just under €40 billion at that point), the Central Bank would now be a creditor in the liquidation and entitled to seize its collateral – effectively most of the remaining assets of IBRC. But the Central Bank did not want to end up holding non-standard, non-transferable PNs. Even less did it want to become the owner of the residual loan assets of IBRC. Accordingly the government had agreed to exchange the PNs held by the Central Bank of Ireland for government bonds and to have NAMA exchange the claim on IBRC's loan assets for NAMA bonds.

---

[24] The repo was provided by Bank of Ireland, the unusual transaction having been approved by an extraordinary general meeting of that bank. Funding from NAMA's accumulated cash balances bridged the gap until the EGM could be held. Ultimately, this bond was acquired by the Central Bank in the aftermath of the IBRC liquidation and subsequently sold at a very large profit reflecting the declining interest rates on Irish government bonds in 2014–15.

[25] Here Minister Noonan's cordial relationship with German Federal Minister of Finance Schäuble cannot have hurt.

The precise terms on which the exchange of PNs for government bonds would be made were the subject of close legal and financial examination. A key difference between the PNs and the new bonds was that the latter were transferable and as such could be considered a much more acceptable asset to be held on the books of the Central Bank.

Instead of carrying a fixed interest as is normal for long-term government bonds, we opted for floating rate notes (FRNs).[26] (We had to show that the proposed formula for the rate of interest on the FRNs gave them a sufficiently high yield to have a present value equal to the ELA debt that the PNs had secured.[27]) The advantage of having floating rates was that it insulated the Central Bank of Ireland from the risk that rising interest rates could impose heavy accounting losses, potentially eroding its capital reserves and triggering external pressure for the government to recapitalize it. (This risk has not materialized: instead the interest rate on the bonds has fallen.) The scheme was thus designed to be fail-safe regardless of whether interest rates increased or fell.

To protect financial stability, it was desirable that the bonds have a very long maturity.

A potentially important issue that had to be resolved if the ECB were to acquiesce in the transaction was how long the Central Bank could hold the FRNs.[28] The most decisive constraint here came from the insistence by ECB lawyers that, as Irish government obligations which had been acquired by the Central Bank following seizure of collateral, the FRNs could not be held to maturity: they must be disposed of over time. Although we were not convinced by the legal arguments, it became evident that this point would have to be conceded. The final compromise came when the Bank agreed to sell the FRNs 'as soon as possible, provided

---

[26] These differ from fully conventional bonds in that the interest rate tracks short-term money market rates. Such instruments are commonly traded in financial markets, though not at such long maturities. Indeed, by choosing a floating rate we created by far the largest block of very long-term floating rate bonds in the global financial market.

[27] Such calculations are not exactly rocket science, but ECB staff insisted that our calculations be validated by an independent firm. This inevitably entailed a further costly outlay in consultancy fees.

[28] One problem here was the Agreement on Net Financial Assets (ANFA), which placed a ceiling on each national central bank's (NCB's) holding of investment assets. The FRNs would push our investments well above that ceiling. For a while it seemed that we might be able to use ('borrow') part of the ceiling of some other NCBs who had chosen not to use their allocation fully; in the end this route proved not to be necessary as the ANFA ceilings evolved quantitatively over time.

conditions of financial stability permitted', and undertook in any event to sell at least in accordance with a predetermined schedule.[29]

Despite its complexity, this arrangement had all to be prepared in great secrecy.[30] In February 2013, the months of planning and debate, some of it fraught, and all of it calling for a demanding combination of financial economics; central banking law and practice, and multidimensional negotiation skills, finally reached the point where ECB Executive Board member Jörg Asmussen, who had begun to take the lead in the discussions on the ECB side, could confirm to me that each of the key participants in the debate seemed to be satisfied: all of the obstacles seemed to have been removed. In Dublin the government immediately prepared to introduce the necessary legislation as soon as the Governing Council had heard and noted without objection the final plan on the afternoon of 6 February.

At the last moment, there was a wobble when Bundesbank President Jens Weidmann raised a final doubt. Unfortunately the liquidation plans had now leaked to the media, and the Irish side spent an uncomfortable night having had to proceed with the liquidation not knowing for certain whether or when the financing side would be settled. But on the following morning the Governing Council did find time to return to the matter in an urgent fashion. Having pinpointed the source of the remaining difficulty, a small technical modification (not necessarily to the disadvantage of Ireland) was hastily hammered out during a break in the meeting.[31]

---

[29] The ECB staff caution was understandable given the scale of the operation. Indeed, the total value of Irish government bonds being held by the Central Bank after the transaction was so large that, when it came to the ECB's 2015 public sector asset purchase programme (the so-called quantitative easing [QE]) it briefly seemed that the Central Bank's FRN holdings might crowd out any Irish purchases under QE. This was because the ECB decided on a ceiling on its holdings of 33 per cent of each country's bond issues. Happily, the rule was applied only to debt in the maturity range being purchased under QE (i.e. between 2 and 30 years), and thus disregarded most of the FRNs as they still had residual maturities of greater than 30 years. In a way, albeit for entirely different reasons, it was as if Ireland already had its own version of QE.

[30] Although I had first contemplated a liquidation solution as far back as December 2010 (even going so far as to sound out ECB Executive Board member Jürgen Stark at that time for his initial reaction), at the Central Bank we explored many possible alternative approaches. The simplest plan was to consolidate the ELA into a very long-term loan to IBRC from the Central Bank of Ireland of €40 billion for 40 years; we prepared a full draft loan agreement along those lines. But, apart from liquidation, all options that we suggested failed to satisfy the objections of ECB lawyers, given their interpretation of the Treaty prohibition of monetary financing.

[31] The modification was to make the minimum sales schedule more explicit. For the economic welfare of Ireland as a whole, what counted was the *net present value* of future payments to the eurosystem, and how they might be affected by future events. For the

The patch worked: neither Weidmann nor anyone else registered any formal objection. It was, as Mario Draghi explained at that day's press conference (in a phrase much relished in Dublin), 'unanimously noted.'[32]

The financial engineering of the IBRC PN transaction, designed as it was to make full use of the legal and economic powers of central banking, was interesting to construct and satisfactory in its operation.

All sides benefitted. The central banking system benefitted through the elimination of ELA, through being insulated from the complexities of managing the loan assets which were part of the collateral, and through the replacement of the idiosyncratic PNs by fully transferable government bonds.

Above all, the financing arrangements also reduced the net costs to Ireland of the losses by many billions.[33] The main source of this gain came from the government being able to postpone the heavy payments due on the PNs and to refinance the debt in due course at much lower interest costs when financial market conditions were more favourable. The long maturity of the bonds ensured that the timing of their refinancing would not be predetermined independently of financial stability conditions. Having a long maturity also maximised the net gain to the government's finances from a fall in interest rates.

Because of the interaction between FRN interest payments, capital gains on the sale of the FRNs and the Central Bank surplus income, the net cost to government of servicing the debt fell sharply. The obligation to dispose of the bonds as soon as possible was no longer onerous for Ireland when interest rates fell over the following two years.

Eurosystem, what mattered (according to one legal interpretation) was the *date* by which the repayments would be concluded.

[32] The Irish side left little or nothing on the table in these discussions, one reflection being that for at least five years after the transaction the ECB felt the need to mention 'serious monetary financing concerns' about the IBRC legacy assets still being held by the Central Bank of Ireland in each of its Annual Reports. I did not share these concerns.

[33] Different approaches are possible in arriving at a precise estimate of how many billions were saved. Relative to the worst possible 'do-nothing' alternative of simply continuing to credit all PN instalments as debt repayments not affecting Central Bank's net profit (as would have been the natural way to account for them) the net gain to Ireland as calculated in 2018 comes out at more than €15 billion (net present value). In addition to the contribution to the Central Bank's net interest income, this calculation includes the sizable benefit of the fall in government bond yields. That there was so much to be saved is mainly due to the huge loan losses actually recorded by Anglo and INBS. It also reflects the pessimistic loss estimates that had been announced by Anglo management in September 2010 and in particular the high interest rates that had to be embedded in the valuation of the new PNs injected into Anglo following that announcement.

That the Central Bank financing of the bank debt-related repayments –
including those which had been effectively insisted upon by the Troika –
was eventually put onto a firm long-term and low-cost arrangement was
a key element in ensuring debt sustainability and allowing Ireland to exit
safely from the programme. The net advantages were somewhat camou-
flaged by accounting conventions, but were of comparable financial importance to the reduction, decided in July 2011, in interest rates on the
programme borrowings.[34]

Of course a much larger prerequisite for exit was delivery of the needed
scale of fiscal adjustment.

DELIVERING THE FISCAL ADJUSTMENT

Indeed, the fiscal measures needed to bring the public finances back to
balance were very large. So large as to have raised questions already at the
outset of the programme as to whether it would work in terms of macroeconomics. Clearly the fiscal adjustment would have a knock-on effect
through expenditure multipliers damping aggregate demand. These were
taken into account in our programme negotiations and built into the
macroeconomic forecasts. But were these projections reliable?
Fortunately – and unlike the situation in Greece and, to a lesser extent,
other countries – the answer is yes. While macroeconomic aggregates in
Ireland did undershoot the forecasts during 2011–13, they did so only by
the same percentage as the euro area as a whole underperformed expectations. The adverse multiplier effects must therefore have been broadly in
line with what was built into the programme.[35] Good programme design
from this point of view was essential – and it had been delivered. By 2015,
the final year for which forecasts had been provided in the original programme documentation, aggregate personal consumption expenditure
(a better proxy for spending aggregates for Ireland than GDP) had caught
up with the programme projection; unemployment beat the projection,
and total employment fell short by just 0.7 per cent (Figure 10.1).

Doubts as to the sustainability of the programme negotiated
in November 2010 centred more around the financial conditions: high

---

[34] In due course, further savings for the government were made by the decision of the
European lenders to permit early repayment of the more expensive IMF borrowings; most
of these were repaid during 2014–15 and the remainder in 2017.

[35] I don't know why the macroeconomic forecasts were better for Ireland than for other
programme countries. I certainly made no attempt to second-guess the Central Bank's
macroeconomic forecasters.

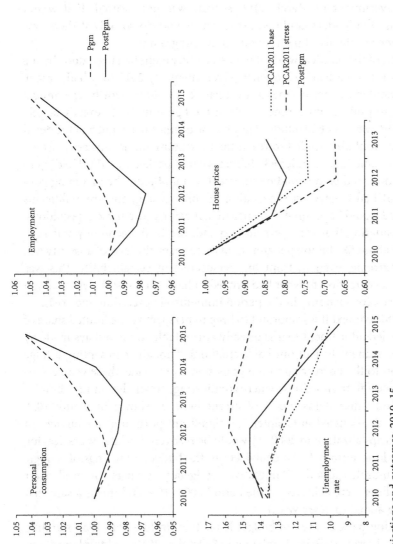

Figure 10.1 Projections and outcomes, 2010–15.

'Pgm' is the projection contained in the December 2010 programme documents. 'PostPgm' is the 'actual' i.e. latest IMF forecast after the end of the programme 2014/15.

'PCAR2011 base and stress' are the assumptions built into the Central Bank's March 2011 bank stress test.

Source: IMF Post-programme review documents CR1618 for 2013; CR1734 for 2014–15.

interest rates, uncertainty about the recapitalization needs of the banks, and the long-term solution for the ELA indebtedness of Anglo. As I told the representatives of the Labour and Fine Gael parties, when they were negotiating their coalition agreement in advance the formation of the new government in March 2011, success was not assured. If it wasn't working, the lenders could adjust it, but would do so only if there was adherence to the fiscal path set out in the programme.

Much of the political work of the fiscal adjustment had been done by the outgoing Fianna Fáil/Green Party government. By 2010 they had already implemented austerity measures relative to 2008 worth an annual €15 billion off the government deficit; the figure in 2011, already largely baked-in, was over €20 billion. They had also announced much of the detail of what would be needed to reach the maximum annual austerity, which actually came to just under €30 billion when it peaked in 2014. Holding to this announced path would be sufficient. Undoubtedly the incoming government had created an expectation of some easing, and the politicians involved would have some challenge in managing down these expectations.

Considering that total personal expenditure in the economy was running at about €84 billion per annum in these years, the level of austerity was quite extreme, even if, from the perspective of sustainability, this was merely a correction to what had proved to have been insufficient taxation and excessive spending in the period immediately preceding the crisis.

(In this context it is important to keep in perspective the limited share of the needed adjustment that is directly attributable to the outlays made by the government to bail out bank creditors. Though representing a huge addition to the borrowing in the years they were made, these were essentially one-off transactions, whereas adjusting down the annual flow of deficit on other items was a recurrent item, as shown in Figure 10.2. Indeed, as discussed in Chapter 7, a significant portion of the outlays on bank recapitalization in 2009–11 would be recovered in later years, leaving a likely long-term net cost equivalent to the budgetary savings of a single fifteen-month period. Cumulative budgetary savings of well over €150 billion were achieved in the period 2008–15 – and this is a sum that is being added to every year.)

Looking back at the pre-budget letter that, in line with long-standing practice, I wrote to Brian Lenihan on 18 October 2010, and thinking about how budgetary policy was subsequently conducted, I feel that both his government and the following one did better in adhering to the overall deficit figures than in developing and communicating a strategic approach to the choice of taxation and expenditure strategies. I had suggested that

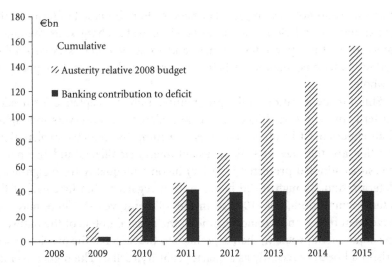

Figure 10.2 Scale of austerity compared to bank creditor bailout, 2008–15.
Note: IBRC is not treated as part of government sector; ignores deficit reducing guarantee fees etc. post 2013.
Source: Authors' calculations based on an update of Smyth and Barnes (2013).

each budgetary measure should be assessed by reference to two main touchstones: 'first, does it contribute to a return towards what were sustainable and acceptable tax and spending structures during the period of high and balanced growth of the 1990s [I had 1996 specifically in mind as a period of possibly optimal balance] or, if not, does it represent a definite improvement in the economic and social efficiency of fiscal structures?' I added, 'the package as a whole should be assessed for its fairness'.

The fiscal adjustment of 2011–13 would have been better balanced, better accepted, and more politically sustainable if the measures introduced had been chosen and publicly defended in terms of such a strategic framework. That strategic framework could also have addressed many structural obstacles to economic performance that persist in the Irish economy, including restrictive professional practices that raise costs and damage the public good.[36]

Instead, we have seen a clamour for the reversal of some measures now called temporary (such as the add-on to income tax known as universal social charge [USC], and perhaps the altered pay schedules for new entrants into some public service professions) that were intended as

[36] Instead, measures such as the capital gains and corporation tax reliefs introduced on property acquired between 2011 and 2014 suggest that the new government couldn't shake the idea that property speculation was an essential ingredient in a successful recovery.

corrective and not as stop gaps. Fairness is often discussed in terms of the regressivity of individual measures (such as water charges; or the emergence of distinct pay rates for new and existing public service staff in certain functions) instead of being assessed in the context of policy as a whole.

Still, for the duration of the programme, public acceptance for needed austerity measures was higher than expected by many observers and higher than experienced in other countries.[37] Among the possible explanations for this are the way in which the automatic stabilizers and the policy measures adopted protected (relative) income inequality from significant deterioration (though it did better in that regard in the first half of the adjustment period 2008–10 than in the following years). There may also have been better understanding among the general public of the nature of the adjustment problem, thanks perhaps to the fact that the previous fiscal crisis had been as recently as a quarter century earlier. The higher average education levels in Ireland relative to those in the other stressed countries may also have helped, as indeed may the more extensive personal knowledge that most Irish people have – through friends and relatives employed by internationally exposed firms at home and abroad – of the workings of the international economic system and the constraints it imposes on small countries. A full discussion of the politics of the fiscal adjustment would bring us too far afield (cf. Hardiman et al. 2017).

In any event, budgetary policy held firm in regard to the overall deficit, coming in at or better than the targets set in the EU–IMF programme, thereby rebuilding international trust and ultimately giving the government the luxury of choosing whether it should exit the Programme on schedule at the end of 2013 or opt for some form of precautionary arrangement for a further year or two.

There was quite a debate on the latter option. Some of the Troika and some Irish officials leaned towards a precautionary arrangement. Some euro area creditor country governments favoured a clean exit to show that at least some adjustment programmes were working. But what was best for Ireland?

---

[37] Nevertheless, there were some demonstrations. For example, Occupy Dame St, the Dublin instance of the worldwide protest movement, established themselves on the Central Bank's plaza on 8 October 2011, erecting a substantial village of tents and shacks. Recognizing that the entirely peaceful protest was legitimate and, to an extent, justified, I declined to facilitate their removal over the following months. Eventually, the occupation began to melt away until by early March there were only a few overnight residents and the Garda Siochána (police) suggested it was time to remove the encampment.

I myself thought that a clean exit was preferable, though the balance of advantage was not certain. That being so, it seemed right for the Central Bank not take too overt a stance on the question of exit. When the balance of national advantage had been clearly in favour of applying for a programme, the Central Bank had not hesitated to steer the previous government firmly in that direction. But the circumstances were quite different now: either course of action seemed defensible. My analysis, communicated to the minister, was that there was some risk in going ahead without the safety net, but that this was strongly offset by the upside risk of a successful clean exit. Besides, even if there were unexpectedly adverse developments, given the time frame and the procedures involved, it was unlikely that the sums made available through a precautionary arrangement would in fact be drawn down.

The government made the right choice and the country exited the programme on schedule.[38] The market reaction was favourable; the economy continued to strengthen. The Irish macro-financial crisis was over.

Quite strong employment growth persisted over the following years, passing the previous peak in 2018; unemployment (measured according to the usual International Labour Organization definition) declined steadily, falling below 6 per cent by 2018 compared with 16 per cent six years before. Already by late 2015 the spread on 10-year Irish government bonds over German bunds had slipped below half a percent (50 basis points). Having overshot on the way down, property prices made a partial recovery, reducing the incidence of negative equity among homeowners.

But the crisis would not be soon forgotten. It had caused a prolonged and sharp reduction in living standards and squeezed public services. Lengthy periods of unemployment and over-indebtedness were among the factors that heightened stress and anxiety for many (as documented in Whelan et al. 2016). Emigration had jumped. And scars would persist for years.

* * *

The main lessons learnt from Ireland's experience with the EU–IMF programme were by no means new. They can be summarized as the need for decisiveness, determination and home-grown detail. The actions had to err on the side of decisiveness to convince both the official lenders and the markets that the problems of financial imbalance were really coming under

---

[38] Also influenced, no doubt, by the view of the German government that a successful on-schedule exit of Ireland would be a positive signal for the prospects of wider economic recovery in the euro area.

control. Determination to deliver on what was promised had to drive implementation. And the detail of what was promised had to be largely home-grown if it was to stick.

While detailed conditions had been set out already in the Memorandum of Understanding signed in 2010, many further implementation details had to be hammered out during the course of the programme. The Irish negotiation tactics contrived to convey an impression of complaisance while carefully choosing the grounds on which to wrest important concessions from the Troika where necessary. Differences between the Irish and Troika negotiators were largely resolved behind closed doors and without grandstanding. Undesirable or impractical proposals from the Troika were mostly headed-off.[39] With much more at stake than the lenders, the Irish negotiators left little on the table in these detailed mid-course negotiations. The big initial defect in the programme, namely the onerous financial conditions, was closed.[40]

The supposed loss of sovereignty in all of this was greatly exaggerated. The outgoing government's shrewd and democratically correct decision to defer the promised bank recapitalization pending the results of the General Election was one signal illustration of this. And the new government's ability to make significant compositional changes in the fiscal adjustment (though not in its overall magnitude) was another. Accessing the official loans in practice gave the Irish government much more freedom of action than was otherwise available. The sovereign loss of freedom of action, such as it was, arose from the loss of market access, and not from the recourse to the official lenders.

Still, the crisis has left a legacy of debt, disrupted public services, interrupted employment records and much else. There is no point in pretending that all is healed.

---

[39] A good example of our ability to derail undesirable Troika proposals related to their pressure to remove the prohibition in the Central Bank's 2013 draft Code of Conduct on Mortgage Arrears preventing a lender from moving a defaulting borrower off a tracker mortgage as part of a debt restructuring. While we did remove the prohibition, we introduced other language which in practice had the same effect as an outright prohibition. (This is a different, though similar, issue to the tracker scandal discussed in Chapter 5.)

[40] The improved financing terms (the lower interest rates and longer terms of the European part of the Troika loans from mid-2011, retained despite early repayment of the more costly IMF part from 2014; and the funding arrangements for the IBRC PNs in 2013) recalls and can be compared with earlier Irish official debt settlements with the UK, in particular the 1925 Agreement on Ireland's post-Treaty liability in relation to the Imperial debt (FitzGerald and Kenny 2017) and the 1938 settlement of the land annuities dispute at the end of the 'economic war' (O'Rourke 1991).

PART IV

TAKING STOCK

11

The European Decade of Bank Failure

In focusing on Ireland's banking woes we should not lose sight of the wider context of bank distress in Europe and the startling fact that twenty or more European countries have suffered systemic banking failures in the decade from 2007 to 2017. The list is not confined to small countries like Cyprus and Iceland, though in these countries, as in Ireland, the weakness of the banking system was on a scale that precipitated the collapse of international market confidence in the finances of the country as a whole. Germany, the UK, France and Italy, to take the largest countries, each had significant failures, with the government stepping in to bolster bank capital. Fulfilling their classic role as lenders of last resort to illiquid but solvent banks, and sometimes going beyond that, most central banks provided extensive emergency liquidity, albeit in some cases only for very short periods, and often in a covert manner, at least at first.

If the causes and aetiologies of these crises were diverse, the policy responses were just as varied. The willingness of public authorities to stabilize banking through emergency liquidity and to bail out creditors of failing institutions varied from country to country and over time.

Within the euro area, the division of responsibilities between the union as a whole and national authorities came into focus. This applied to the supervision of banks, to the provision of emergency liquidity, to recapitalization and to closure and resolution decisions.

The inadequacies of national supervisory authorities had been thrown into sharp relief, leading to a reopening of the question of whether bank supervision should be centralized in the European Central Bank (ECB). Provision of emergency liquidity was also a national responsibility, but this decentralization too came under scrutiny. There were many calls for the mobilization of the financial muscle of the euro area as a whole to underpin the recapitalization of failing banks and to enhance the credibility of the statutory deposit guarantees. Finally, there was a perceived need for a centralized function for resolving failing banks in an orderly manner.

These debates raged for several years in the crisis while on the ground policy actions were taken that can seem lacking in consistency. Gradually a number of centralizing decisions were taken, most conspicuously the Single Supervisory Mechanism (SSM) and Resolution Board (SRB).

In the end, a new, albeit fragile, consensus had emerged, both in Europe and more widely, around an approach which envisages bail-in of wholesale creditors.

Application of such an approach in Ireland would have avoided budgetary outlays to make bank creditors whole, and, if applied in compliance with a Europe-wide rule-book, would not have incurred the kind of reputational damage that would have resulted from unilateral bail-in of the creditors of banks that had fuelled several years of transitory prosperity in Ireland. We will never know whether such an approach, had it been applied from the start on an international basis, would have increased or reduced the severity of the crisis in Europe as a whole.

Bail-in under the Bank Recovery and Resolution Directive (BRRD) greatly reduces the size of the common resolution fund that could be needed, and also removes some of the pressure on deposit guarantee funds. It is generally accepted that the process of centralization ('completion of the Banking Union') is not over. But the degree to which further centralization, including the provision of emergency liquidity, can be expected, or is needed, remains unclear.

CAUSES: MANY TRIGGERS, COMMON VULNERABILITY

The resonant list of failing European banks that needed government assistance to survive is impressive, ranging from the mighty British Royal Bank of Scotland, to the oldest bank of all, the Monte dei Paschi di Siena, founded in 1472, to the trio of Icelandic banks, too small to matter much in the wider European context, but whose failure was fatally damaging to that country's economy.

As varied as the banks that failed have been in size, history and business models, there has been equivalent variety in the immediate triggers of systemic crises in different countries. For example, the US structured finance market, much discussed in the early days of the crisis, with the complexities of originate-to-distribute and the slicing and dicing of securitized packages of loans, was at the root of several bank failures in Germany (Landesbanken, Hypo RE) and Switzerland (UBS). But this was not the only cause of bank failure in Europe. Banks in the UK and in Spain were (like those in Ireland) brought low by too much lending into the national real estate markets. Sovereign default was the main cause of needed bank recapitalizations in Greece. The Greek default also contributed significantly to the failures in Cyprus, though one of these was also associated with inappropriate tycoon financing. Unrestrained lending to tycoons connected with bank insiders was an important factor in the Icelandic failures and in that of the sizable Portuguese Banco Espiritu Santo. A more general syndrome of banker over-reach can be identified in the failures of over-ambitious growing banks in Belgium, Germany and the UK, for example, as well as in Ireland. Finally, the protracted period of weak economic growth proved fatal to a number of Italian banks.

How can the simultaneous emergence of so many disparate crises be explained? The answer is unlikely to lie in a coincidental convergence of different triggers. Instead it is almost surely the emergence of vulnerabilities common to all of these countries (and others besides). The specific culprit must be the growth of financialization. This global trend was characterized in particular by three correlated changes: the scale and speed of flows, high leverage and over-reliance (by bank directors, investors and regulators) on imperfect analytical risk-management tools. The latter, though sophisticated, have proved to be not at all as precise as was implicitly assumed by those who relied on them.

It is not therefore surprising that each country found it extremely difficult to get a good estimate of the 'hole' in the banks' accounts, i.e. the likely capital deficiency. Indeed, this has been a perennial problem with banking crises. Furthermore, though it is often assumed by the cynical that things will always be at least as bad as the worst estimate to date, experience, both in the past decade and earlier, shows that this is not the case. Instead, the usual pattern has been that the loss situation is underestimated at first, but then overestimated. Thus, when a troubled bank comes to the attention of the authorities, the true situation is generally worse than they think at first; but observers tend to become too pessimistic and project more further deterioration than actually occurs.

The US experience of 2008–9 is illustrative of this typical sequence of complacency followed by undue pessimism. After a series of over-optimistic statements by prominent US public officials and private bankers in the summer of 2008, the sudden bankruptcy in September of Lehman Brothers – with total assets of $639 billion and a derivatives portfolio of about $35 trillion – came as a shock. It was seen by market participants as potentially unleashing a tsunami of knock-on credit losses directly related to contract failures. That alarm was partly self-fulfilling in that it was a significant driver of the global recession (which did indeed worsen loan losses worldwide). But it surely exaggerated the actual risks from the Lehman failure. Ironically, the eventual creditor losses in the Lehman's bankruptcy (about $200 billion according to Bernanke 2015), though vast in terms of an individual firm, were equivalent to just about one week of global economic production.

In Iceland the swing in opinion also happened very quickly. The first concerns about the Icelandic banks in 2007 and 2008 elicited a number of soothing commentaries by experienced and distinguished observers, but immediately after the bankruptcy of Lehman, deep pessimism prevailed and the Icelandic banks lost access to funding. It was true that the banks were deeply insolvent and that the Icelandic government's financial resources were not sufficient to fill the hole. Even though only depositors of branches within Iceland were bailed out by the Icelandic government, the needed gross injection of funds equalled 44 per cent of GDP (though much of this was recovered, as explained in Chapter 7).

The move from optimism to pessimism was much slower in Spain. Pessimism about the state of the smaller Spanish banks peaked only in 2012. Before then the Spanish authorities had been denying the existence of any serious problem. In this case too, though, the problem proved to be less serious than thought at the peak. Accordingly, the Spanish authorities ultimately drew well under half of the €100 billion that they had applied for from the European Stability Mechanism (ESM) in June 2012 for the purpose of recapitalization of Spanish banks.

Ireland's experience in this respect is thus far from unusual. Though the fiscal cost of recapitalizing the banks was much higher than the government had estimated when Anglo was being nationalized in early 2009, little of the Troika's November 2010 estimate of an additional €36 billion recapitalization was ultimately needed to meet the eventual net losses, given the billions the government had already poured in by then.[1]

Not unrelated to the difficulty of narrowing the range of possibilities when it comes to estimating the financial hole is the tendency for corrective action with respect to a failing bank to be delayed too long. Ideally, awareness by the regulatory authorities of capital adequacy problems at a bank would trigger corrective action before the market has lost

---

[1] As we saw in Chapter 7, the final net fiscal cost will be well within the – admittedly wide – €50 billion range which I had suggested to a parliamentary committee hearing back in May 2009.

confidence. However, in practice during the crisis this was not typically the case. This was painfully obvious in the systemic liquidity freeze of September–October 2008, when many banks – including solvent ones – in Europe and elsewhere were squeezed by the paralysis of the short-term money markets. Even when, as increasingly became the case when the euro area crisis deepened, quite a lot of information was available pointing to undercapitalization or possible balance sheet insolvency, politics and a bureaucratic bias towards inertia often stood in the way of decisive corrective action.

THE ROLE OF PUBLIC AUTHORITIES IN BANK CRISIS MANAGEMENT

To maintain a sufficient flow of liquidity in the economy to enable continued functioning of the economy's normal payments and short-term credit system, central banks in Europe had to consider extraordinary steps, especially in 2008 and, in a few countries, in the following years. By pouring exceptional quantities of liquidity into the emergency in October 2008, the ECB and the Bank of England joined the US Federal Reserve and others in stabilizing the global liquidity situation. Extensive collateralized liquidity provision to support stressed banks continued in the euro area for several years (with national banking system recourse to central banking liquidity exceeding 100 per cent of GDP in some cases). Without these actions, banks would not have been able to satisfy the payments instructions of their customers.[2] Liquidity was made available to be borrowed at low interest rates by banks which were able to post sufficient collateral of the usual quality.

But more was needed. The central banks had to decide whether to lend even to banks that did not have what would normally be considered adequate collateral. This lender of last resort function of a central bank is vital in a systemic crisis, but it is also understood to be fraught with risks and longer-term consequences, even if it is limited to banks whose balance sheets suggest that they are solvent. In addition to the generally accommodating liquidity policy, emergency liquidity assistance (ELA) was granted at least for short periods to banks in several European countries.

There are policy alternatives to ELA. Governments may not have the ready cash to substitute for the central bank but, by providing guarantees, insurance or bonds, they can improve the creditworthiness of the bank and

---

[2] Honohan (2017) covers some of this ground in greater detail.

enable it to fund itself in the markets again. The quid pro quo for the government may be an ownership stake in the bank, or a guarantee or insurance fee. Inasmuch as any such intervention involves appreciable risk of loss, we can think of it as a bailout. Just which category of investor is bailed out depends on how the intervention is structured.

A quite different alternative is a financial restructuring of the failing bank, for example by transferring its deposit claims and sufficient assets to another bank (leaving the rest to be liquidated), or by reducing the claims of some of its creditors, for example by converting them into equity. This we can call a bail-in. In the USA, where failure among its numerous small banks has been a relatively frequent occurrence, bail-in was long the preferred option, even for quite large banks, though not the very largest. In contrast, at the outset of the crisis, European countries did not have an adequate legislative framework to accomplish bank restructuring quickly. Using normal company insolvency procedures is too slow to prevent a disorderly collapse of all but the simplest bank's operations.[3]

For a decade from 2007 not a year passed without one of these techniques being applied in some notable European case.

There was some reluctance in the early months of the crisis to provide ELA or other forms of bailout. Soon after the tough bail-in stance adopted by the US authorities in respect of Lehman Brothers, though, there was a sharp shift towards a more liberal approach on both sides of the Atlantic. Reluctant to risk further market instability by imposing losses on senior creditors, European governments (including those of Germany, the UK, France, Spain, Switzerland and the Netherlands, to mention the largest) were, as we have seen, already engaging in bailout on a large scale as early as September and October of 2008, including the injection of substantial government resources into the capital of certain banks, ensuring that their creditors were made whole.[4]

By 2013, though, European policy had toughened. First Cyprus, and later Greece, experienced administrative controls on deposit withdrawals as ceilings were placed on the banks' access to central bank funds. And

---

[3] The liquidation of some small Irish credit unions, all of whose customer deposits were fully covered by the €100,000 ceiling of the Deposit Guarantee Scheme, was effected without disruption. That cannot be said of Lehman Brothers.

[4] Sizable parts of most of these injections will not be recovered. Note the difference between an injection of funds into a bank through liquidity provision by the central bank and an injection of capital by the national government. The former does not increase the bank's buffer against loan losses because its liabilities (to the central bank) increase one-for-one with the new funds. The latter does change the bank's net asset position, inasmuch as the loss-absorbing buffer of capital has increased.

some senior creditors began to be bailed-in ahead of the new EU BRRD legislation (effective from 2016) mandating private sector bail-in ahead of the use of public funds in resolution. (The bail-in of some junior creditors had already begun in Ireland by 2010.)

It is worth looking a little more closely at how ELA and bail-out or bail-in policy evolved in Europe during the crisis.

Advantages and Drawbacks of ELA

ELA is the rescue option that most obviously involves the central bank. The lending being collateralized, the risk of credit loss to the central bank is supposed to be low – much lower than may be involved in the other forms of bailout. Prompt provision of liquidity is easy for the central bank, whereas it does not have sizable capital reserves to enable it to absorb losses.

Given inadequate accounting and supervisory information about many of the stressed banks, decisions on ELA during the crisis have had to be taken without full information on the true capital position of stressed banks.

ELA is not necessarily incompatible with bail-in should that prove necessary if the banks turn out to be balance sheet insolvent: collateralized lending can provide a breathing space while the authorities determine the appropriate resolution plan. Note, though, that, even if the collateral is good, provision of ELA to a bank that is truly balance sheet insolvent will allow the most pessimistic or well-informed creditors to get their cash out, leaving a heavier loss to be incurred by the more loyal or less informed depositors – and to the deposit guarantee fund. Still, provision of ELA does carry some credit risk for the central bank: if the bank fails and the low-quality collateral offered in return for the loan turns out to be no good, the central bank will take a loss. Any such loss will feed back indirectly into the government's budget and/or to inflation. This can take the central bank well outside its mandate. And the sums can be large.

The national government can step in to indemnify the central bank against credit losses, thereby augmenting the democratic legitimacy of the credit risks being taken. Some bailouts during the crisis involved packages jointly arranged between central bank and government, for example in Switzerland and the USA. (Such joint arrangements are not so easy to construct for the euro area given the multiple sovereign jurisdictions involved and the restrictions of the EU Treaty, a point to which we return later.) Because of the credit risk, and because too easy an ELA policy encourages and rewards imprudent bank practice, ELA is not granted lightly. But the central bank does have a mandate to avoid financial disruption, and should not shy away from the risks involved in extending liquidity if a bank of systemic importance is otherwise going to be unable to meet its obligations. And none of the European central banks has actually made a net loss on ELA.

Evolution of ELA Policy in Europe

The approach of European central banks to the provision of ELA in the crisis oscillated from reluctance, through liberality and then to a seeming reversal with two entire national banking systems left for extended periods with administrative controls on deposit withdrawals.

There has also been an evolution in the degree to which ELA decisions are made transparent – much more so now than before.

How to make sense of this oscillation? The changes partly reflect an evolving understanding of the relative costs and benefits of liberal and restrictive approaches to liquidity in a crisis – especially perspectives on the dangers of contagion, but they also reflect contrasting circumstances.

The initial decision by the Bank of England to refuse emergency liquidity when Northern Rock was unable to refinance itself in the rapidly deteriorating money market conditions of September 2007 was soon reversed, but disclosure of the ELA (which, at £50 billion, was far larger than any sum ever previously provided in such assistance) led to depositor panic and lengthy lines outside the offices of the bank.[5]

If the Northern Rock experience made some central banks cautious about ELA, the potential side effects of a failure to finance a bank run were evident in the case of Lehman Brothers. The US authorities stated that they lacked legal powers to provide the liquidity assistance that would have been needed to prevent the sudden bankruptcy of that firm in September 2008. Even though they acted swiftly to ensure payments continuity in respect of other financial firms in the following weeks, there was a sharp increase in the risk premia demanded by lenders of all sorts – as indeed the authorities apparently foresaw (Bernanke 2015). The failure or inability of the US authorities to provide ELA to Lehman is seen by many as having generated large economic costs worldwide (see the discussion by Cline and Gagnon 2013; also Ball 2018).

---

[5] Mervyn King, who was governor of the Bank of England at the time, has proposed a sweeping change to central banks' approach to the provision of ELA (King 2016).

The weeks following the Lehman failure saw sizable – but covert – use of the provision of ELA including to Belgian, Netherlands, German and UK banks (i.e. in the more prosperous parts of Europe), though (as we have seen) not in Ireland. These loans were repaid over the following weeks and months, but were succeeded by large emergency loans to Irish, Greek and Cypriot banks.

But there was a swing back to restriction, first in Cyprus (2013) and then (as mentioned in Chapter 3) in Greece (2015). The Greek case demands a closer look. Limitation of Greek ELA in the summer of 2015 followed the Greek government's decision to hold a referendum recommending refusal of the terms of the conditions demanded by official lenders for an extension of their lending to Greece.

The ECB Governing Council thus found itself in a position in which it was being asked not to object to large additional emergency loans needed to enable the Greek banks to meet the renewed surge of deposit withdrawals which would inevitably follow the referendum announcement.[6] Failure to approve this lending would inevitably trigger administrative restrictions on deposit withdrawals, resulting in considerable economic disruption. Even those ECB decision-makers willing to find a way to avoid such an outcome were left with no room to manoeuvre. After all, the collateral for such lending would be in effect promises from a government that was seeking public support for a course inevitably leading to default. The scenario was too far outside the agreed criteria for emergency lending to allow for this gap to be finessed; the required shift in policy was too great, and the time available for discussion too short. As a result, ELA provision was capped and deposit withdrawals in Greece were tightly constrained for many months thereafter.[7]

In this case, and the rather different case of Cyprus, the national banking systems were subject to prolonged administrative controls restricting the withdrawal of depositor funds. While economic performance of Greece and Cyprus following the introduction of these administrative controls was

---

[6] Because of Greece's low credit rating, Greek banks did not have enough collateral with sufficiently high credit rating to be eligible as collateral in normal Eurosystem operations, hence the heavy use of ELA. Orphanides (2017) has an interesting discussion of the origins of collateral rules in the ECB, arguing that the use of ratings was a mistake from the outset.

[7] Some observers interpreted the ECB's decision as an attempt to influence the Greek government and the referendum. While some influential persons seem to think that the ECB should use its monetary instruments to lever better fiscal and other policies in member countries, that would be an abuse of its power. In fact, the ECB is careful to provide quite different legal justification for its policy decisions with respect to Greece.

not good, the economic damage caused seems to have been less than was foreseen by many commentators at the time of their introduction.

By 2017, the existence of viable alternatives meant that the ELA request of Banco Popular Español could be safely refused by the ECB, pitching that bank into a resolution involving bail-in.

There has been much discussion of how soon the provision of ELA should be publicly disclosed, given the risk that such an announcement might actually back-fire by triggering the wider loss of confidence it was intended to avoid (as with Northern Rock). Some of the ELA of 2008 was kept secret for many months; in other cases the provision of ELA was either announced or strongly suspected. Temporary secrecy in such public policy actions may sometimes be socially beneficial, but prolonged lack of transparency sits uncomfortably with today's notions of democratic government. Besides, lack of transparency can foster unwarranted suspicion, aggravating perceived risk. And maintaining secrecy may prove to be impossible. The more recent experience, relating to Greece and Cyprus, suggests that a strategy of proactive and comprehensive communication about the crisis management plan offers the best prospect of a quick return to stability.

Given the lack of legislative and administrative preparedness for the crisis in 2008–10, extensive recourse to ELA was an inevitable component of the best available policy response in the European countries where it was employed. When granted to a solvent firm, the direct social costs of liquidity provision even to a significant bank are small; the anti-contagion benefits can be considerable. Still, this needs to be tempered by concern for the moral hazard created by too-liberal an approach. (Thus, for example, coordination between the central bank and the financial regulator needs to ensure that there are appropriate consequences for the controlling insiders of the assisted bank so that management incompetence is not being bankrolled.)

Bail-in versus Bail-out

Emergency liquidity is intended for solvent banks. A failing bank will generally require additional capital or a restructuring of its liabilities if it is to be brought back to solvency and to having a sufficient buffer of capital to satisfy the regulatory requirements for it to resume operations as a safe and sound entity. If private shareholders are not willing or able to inject capital to make up for the losses incurred (which may well be the case if the recoverable value of the bank's assets has fallen below its liabilities), the burden must fall elsewhere. Hence the question of bail-in or bail-out.

(Recall that, as we are defining the terms here, bail-in entails losses being imposed on debt holders of the bank, whether in the form of a straight haircut, or through a debt-to-equity conversion, or just through the normal process of liquidation. Bail-out means that the government injects funds or guarantees to make all of the creditors whole.)

When it comes to deciding how to allocate the direct financial losses entailed in a bank failure among potential stakeholders, it would of course be useful for the authorities to know in advance the size of the hole in a failing bank's balance sheet. As we have seen, this is rarely possible. Poor information from the outset about the balance sheets of the banks has hampered good decision-making. Almost a decade after the first signs of the crisis, the 'size of the hole' question continues to throw up surprises (for example in the case of Banco Popular Español in 2017).

Successive decisions in different countries regarding the distribution of the losses have differed sharply, partly reflecting the evolution of thinking on the part of some of the main policymaking entities (European Commission, ECB, IMF).

In the early phase 2008–11, European policy was driven in part by a perception that bail-in of bank creditors even in a weak country could destabilize the wider European bank funding market through a contagion effect increasing the cost of bank funding, thereby increasing the cost and limiting the availability of credit to the economy, with a knock-on effect on economic activity. Although equity holders were typically diluted, governments succumbed to the old temptation to socialize at least part – usually a large part – of the remaining losses.

With the growing scale of potential losses, the feasibility of bailout by the government began to come into question in some European countries. Recapitalization of a large failing bank with public funds can stress the sovereign's debt sustainability; and if the sovereign is weakened, this may drag other banks down too through a variety of channels (ownership of sovereign debt, exposure to arbitrary taxation, etc.). Even if bailout of uninsured creditors is not contemplated, the sovereign's debt sustainability might be threatened if it has backstopped a deposit guarantee fund which is insufficiently capitalized. All of these problems moved from the hypothetical to reality during 2010–11 (cf. Cline 2014; Dübel 2013; Philippon and Salord 2017).

Although bank failures were widespread, the aggregate quantity of funds needed for recapitalization could not have challenged the debt sustainability of the European Union as a whole. However, even where official sector European funds were employed in recapitalizations, as in Ireland,

Greece and Spain, for example, the funds were channelled via national government borrowing, thereby weakening the national public finances in the borrowing countries.

Evolution of Bailout Policy in Practice

Bailout has taken various forms in the recent crisis, each different in its benefit to different stakeholders and in its likely ultimate impact on the government's finances. Gradually, practice has shifted from predominant bail-out (in late 2008) towards a degree of bail-in (from about 2013).

The injection of funds – cash or other instruments – in return for an equity stake or subordinated debt protects more senior creditors, while diluting existing shareholders: the degree to which dilution occurs depends on the price of the equity. In some cases (such as Anglo Irish Bank), the failing bank was fully nationalized and the shareholders not compensated. In other cases (for example Royal Bank of Scotland [RBS] in the UK; Fortis in Belgium) shareholders retained significant value.[8]

A more complicated recapitalization case is Greece, whose banks were not only weakened by the deep slump from 2009, but also experienced heavy losses in the sovereign debt restructuring of 2012 (see Zettelmeyer et al. 2013). However, in contrast to the direct holders of Greek government debt, Greek bank creditors were made whole; most shareholders retained significant value.

An alternative approach is to provide no cash but instead a government guarantee of creditors, as at first in Ireland. Typically guarantees have required a premium payment by the covered bank: even if the guarantee scheme shows a profit in the end, it may have benefited both the creditors and the shareholders ex ante.

A third mechanism potentially bailing out creditors is for the government to underwrite or insure the value of a stressed bank's problem assets or to acquire the assets. Asset insurance schemes of one sort or another were used in the UK, Switzerland and the USA. If under-priced, insurance amounts to a subsidy or bailout of the creditors; in the countries mentioned, no significant losses were made on such schemes.

Asset management companies purchasing problem assets of stressed banks have been an important component of the policy approach in

---

[8] Almost ten years on, the market price of the government's equity stake in the large RBS was not yet high enough to repay the initial investment; other equity injections have had varying return experiences.

Germany, Spain, Switzerland and, of course, Ireland. Unlike the other three countries, the German government-guaranteed asset management company acquired the assets of Hypo RE and some other banks from 2010 at 'book' prices that were well above market, implying a subsidy or bailout of the bank creditors.[9] This is in contrast to the Irish asset management agency National Asset Management Agency (NAMA) and the Spanish one SAREB (Sociedad de Gestión de Activos Procedentes de la Reestructuración Bancaria), which acquired comparably large portfolios of assets in 2010–12, but at prices that were closer to market – a fact that explains why NAMA can now even look forward to the prospect of ultimate net profit. The Swiss asset management company set up to deal with assets from UBS also made a profit.

Denmark's policy in early 2011 was an outlier in that the authorities bailed in senior creditors of two small banks, Amagerbanken and Fjordbank Mors. Bank ratings were revised downwards in the aftermath of the bail-in and observers commented on an increase in the cost of funds at that time to other Danish banks (cf. FT 23 May 2011 www.ft.com/content/281c7f70-855f-11e0-ae32-00144feabdc0).

By 2013 policy had hardened in response to popular revulsion against the extensive use of public funds in European countries to bail out creditors who were on average much wealthier than the average, and included creditors from outside the paying country or even outside Europe as a whole.

This hardening was reflected in the treatment of the Cypriot banks. One of the two main banks (Laiki) was closed and uninsured depositors had to take their place in the liquidation. The other bank (Bank of Cyprus) remained open and began to manage continuing business transferred from the first bank. However, for this bank also, uninsured depositors suffered a costly debt-to-equity swap.[10]

Spain and Italy also experienced heavy bank losses, but these were not fully recognized before 2013 (Spain) and 2016 (Italy). By that time, the

---

[9] The European Commission estimated that, together with a government capital injection, the amount of state aid resulting from the portfolio acquisition totalled more than 20 per cent of Hypo RE's pre-crisis risk-weighted assets (Buder et al. 2011).

[10] The handling of the Cypriot case was something of a fiasco not only because of the abortive suggestion of the Eurogroup that small depositors would be bailed in (despite being covered by the national deposit insurance scheme), but also because of the controversial decision to sell the Greek branches of the largest Cypriot banks to a Greek bank just before the resolution of Laiki, with the result that the creditors of the Greek branches were made whole, in effect at the expense of the other creditors, including uninsured depositors at the branches in Cyprus (for competing views, see Xiouras 2016 and Demetriades 2017).

hardening of attitudes in European institutions against the bailout of subordinated debt had contributed to the speed with which European legislation was reformed (in the BRRD of 2014), to ensure that the essential economic functions being performed by stressed banks could be maintained by efficient mechanisms of resolution involving bail-in of wholesale creditors and without the significant use of public funds. The new European law on banking resolution, which came into effect in 2016, proscribed further bailouts of subordinated debt. However, the bail-in of some subordinated debt in failing Spanish and Italian banks proved to be politically controversial when it was suggested that much of the bailed-in debt may have been mis-sold to retail customers, as the banks worked to build their capital to the higher levels being mandated by regulators since the crisis began.

The resolution of the sizable failed Portuguese bank Banco Espiritu Santo (later called Novo Banco) during 2014–16 entailed bail-in of senior bondholders as the new European resolution framework was coming into effect. Controversially, this was implemented by the Portuguese authorities in an unorthodox way that did not treat all bondholders equally (though the authorities argued that there were objective differences between the classes of bonds differently treated).

Bail-in under the New European Resolution Framework (BRRD)

In 2017, a medium-size Spanish entity, Banco Popular Español, was the first case to be resolved by the European Single Resolution Board (SRB) under the BRRD. Even after bailing in debt, the valuation of the remainder of the business was so low that it was sold to a large Spanish bank for a nominal €1.

The BRRD resolution policy reforms are designed to ensure that following the normal hierarchy of claims, without government bailout, is viable both politically and in terms of the ability of the financial markets to absorb such action.

Essentially this is being done by making a clear ex ante differentiation between the kinds of customer accounts whose interruption would disrupt their ability to make the payments needed for conducting normal non-financial transactions, and as such might deserve protection, from liabilities which are more akin to investment assets, and to ensure that there are sufficient of the latter to absorb any plausible losses in bankruptcy. (Another part of the process involves improving resolvability of banks for example through the preparation of progressively more detailed 'living wills' intended to streamline the resolution process and to avoid interruption of essential functions.)

The general idea of BRRD is that the bailout of large holders of senior debt should be avoided in isolated banking failures, and the legal and regulatory regime in place should allow that to happen without damaging externalities.

Still, there is always the fear of the unknown: that bail-in of bank liabilities in a systemic crisis could trigger a wider failure of payments and interruption of economic activity, as well as potentially an unwarranted sharp increase in risk aversion. This fear is one of the reasons why governments have been willing to incur the fiscal costs of bailout in the case of some systemically important failures.

Indeed, it is possible to argue that the BRRD approach could be so destabilizing as to result in a worse outcome than the pre-existing regimes which made bailout more likely. According to such an opinion (argued, for example by Goodhart and Avgouleas 2016), bailout would be socially optimal even though it absorbs valuable public resources.

I do not share that view, though I admit that one has to be careful. On the whole, I think that what evidence there is suggests that financial systems are resilient to well understood and predictable policy responses to unexpected shocks. Certainly when the scale of losses to be absorbed is as high as it was in Cyprus, Iceland and Ireland (relative to available resources) it is hard to argue that assuming all of the losses was, or would have been, socially optimal.

Given the scale of modern finance and its cross-border nature, the size of a systemic bailout can easily result – and has often resulted – in distorting increases in taxation and cutbacks in needed public spending programmes. It is not only in the rare cases where the cost is sufficiently large to trigger a doom-loop of unsustainable debt that the balance of advantages (and the question of which public authority should bear the costs of bailout) needs careful evaluation.

Open-ended commitments to bailout, such as blanket guarantees, should be avoided in such circumstances. After all, it is not only the socialization of private costs that is at issue here, but also the moral hazard generated by the practice of bailouts blunting the risk-aversion of bankers and their financiers and thereby increasing the likelihood of future crises.

The BRRD sets out clear, and perhaps overly rigid, rules for bail-in. In particular, the rule that bail-in must reach 8 per cent of total assets (not risk-weighted) before public rescue or resolution funds are relied on is undoubtedly demanding. This may be a transitional problem in that it will be less challenging to put into practice when additional explicitly loss-absorbing liabilities are fully in place in each bank, but it could create unnecessary problems in the interim.

Despite the adoption of the BRRD, residual reluctance of several European governments to implement the spirit of the new rules in full cannot be ignored. The much discussed 2017 decision of the Italian authorities to bail out creditors of two failed banks in the Veneto region (at a cost of €17 billion) exemplifies this reluctance.[11] It may be that a politically viable equilibrium has not yet been fully achieved in this area.

HOW MUCH CENTRALIZATION?

The new European approach to bank resolution was only one of the major reforms, together known as the Banking Union, brought to the table during 2012–14. Weak bank supervision, lax regulations, especially in respect of capital adequacy, and a lack of preparedness to deal effectively with failing banks had clearly contributed to the costs of the financial crisis. Public authorities around the world recognized the need for extensive reforms.

The key period of detailed negotiation and planning here was early 2013, during the Irish presidency of the EU, and Irish officials, including many experts from the Central Bank, can take some credit for the speed and effectiveness of the legislative accomplishments of those years, especially in the areas of bank resolution, capital adequacy and supervision.

The distinctive feature of the euro area's post-crisis banking reforms was that each area involved a transfer of authority to the centre from national agencies. The European SRB and the SSM were created de novo (the latter as an arm of the ECB). They complemented, for the euro area, the regulatory function of the European Banking Authority, which had been established at the beginning of 2011, and which now presided over the implementation of tighter capital adequacy regulations (for the EU as a whole).

Despite all of this centralization, a significant number of elements that deserve to be centralized remain at a national level. Two of these elements, emergency liquidity and the recapitalization of banks at risk of failing, were prominent in the Irish case, and I will return to them later.

---

[11] The Italian government was able to do this because the SRB decided that formal resolution under the BRRD was not warranted for these banks. This meant that BRRD did not apply and enabled the Italian authorities to wind them up under pre-existing Italian legislation.

Probably the most discussed of the gaps in centralization relates to deposit insurance. Because national governments are still required to provide the backstop to deposit guarantee funds, the risk that, as happened in Cyprus and Iceland, failure of a large bank failure would overwhelm the government's finances undermines the credibility of this mandatory deposit guarantee system. Accordingly, it is incoherent for the EU as a whole to delegate the provision of the deposit guarantee to the national level. It is not just that to do so leaves open the danger of a national depositor run triggered by fears that the deposit guarantee scheme would not be able to meet its promises. (Indeed it should kept in mind that it is not the small insured depositors, but the large uninsured depositors and other creditors that present the main destabilizing threat to the liquidity of a banking system.)[12] In addition, it makes the location decision for any sizable bank depend heavily on the financial strength of the host national government, thereby undermining the single cross-border market in banking.

It has been dispiriting to observe the reluctance with which many of the centralizing reforms have been adopted. Creditor countries were consumed by the fear that each proposed centralization represented an attempt to raid their national savings to fill a hole created by bank failure in other countries. Such fears were often stoked and validated by wholly unrealistic schemes envisaged in debtor countries, such as the idea that some European fund would buy the outstanding stock of non-performing bank loans at face value, thereby absorbing the embedded losses.

Further centralization is being considered by the European Commission, which has been quite effective in pushing forward the reform agenda over the years. It has, for example, already made proposals for a centralized European Deposit Insurance Scheme and is talking about a centralized backstop funding arrangement for resolution, centralized sovereign bond-backed securities and legislation to require higher levels of loan-loss provisioning by banks. And there have been many other serious and well-thought out proposals covering wider financial and fiscal reform issues in Europe addressing many opportunities for better risk-sharing. The interest in such ideas from senior politicians has fluctuated and has not yet reached the level that would ensure implementation.

[12] The net contribution of deposit insurance schemes to financial stability has long been controversial. Jerry Caprio and I summarized the arguments for and against in World Bank (2001). For a recent update, see Anginer et al. (2014).

I am inclined to think that what has been achieved already covers the most important steps for improving the safety and soundness of the banking system, namely centralized supervision and the bail-in rules of the BRRD. Both of these greatly reduce the likelihood and scale of any need for future recourse to national budgets for bailing out bank creditors.

A full discussion of the remaining centralizing financial reform ideas would take us too far into a rapidly flowing debate (see for example Bénassy-Quéré et al. 2018). Let me merely address two elements that became live topics for Ireland in the crisis, namely direct European recapitalization of stressed banks and emergency liquidity.

Direct Recapitalization and the SSM

The idea of using European funds to recapitalizing weak banks directly rather than lending the relevant national government the money to do so is one which has not been fully realized, but which has had a catalytic effect in creating Europe's Single SSM.

The Irish case was central to the debate. As mentioned, the uncertain overhang of potential further bank losses represented a significant drag on market confidence in the Irish public finances even after the bailout. Direct recapitalization of the banks by the ESM instead of the loan they made for that purpose to the Irish government could have helped. By removing the threat of further losses being incurred by the government, it would have boosted confidence, speeding the government's return to access at reasonable interest costs to the private financial markets, and stimulating investment and consumption decisions that would have brought forward the economic recovery. Furthermore, properly structured, it could have been highly profitable to the ESM. This was a missed opportunity.

The reluctance of creditor countries to back direct recapitalization is understandable given the lack of trust which prevailed during the worst of the crisis. For example, one obvious obstacle to mutualization in the context of a multi-country monetary union is the danger that one country could use its sovereign legislative power to grab resources from the banks driving them into insolvency in the knowledge that creditor losses would be largely paid for by the other countries participating in the mutualization of banking risk. One way of limiting that threat is to transfer the supervision and control of banking to the multinational level.

Indeed, it seems that such reasoning was decisive in making a final push towards the creation of the SSM. According to Wieser (2018), who was well placed to observe the international political discussions around this issue, the final trigger for establishing the SSM was the need to overcome the objections of some Eurogroup members to permitting direct recapitalization of failing banks by the ESM (see also Véron 2016). Indeed, this linkage is reflected in the wording of the communique issued by the euro area heads of government at their summit at the end of June 2012. And expectations were high in Dublin when that communique explicitly linked help for Ireland to the creation of a direct recapitalization tool.[13] These expectations were not to be realized – at least in that form.

Ironically, although the creation of the SSM was triggered by the desire to unlock direct recapitalization of banks, little progress has been made on the latter. Yes, direct recapitalization by the ESM has been possible since December 2014, but it is permitted only under very restrictive conditions.[14] The Irish interest in using direct recapitalization had faded by the end of 2014, given the restored confidence in Ireland's fiscal and overall economic situation. More widely, while government funds can still be envisaged for precautionary recapitalization of banks not thought to be actually failing or likely to fail, the need for government funds to be used in bank recapitalization is reduced by the BRRD's reliance on the alternative of bail-in for failing banks.

But the SSM is in itself a good idea. Already discussed in the early days of euro area design, a single supervisor offers many other advantages, including a reduced degree of political interference over the previous fragmented arrangements for bank supervision (Honohan 1991).

A key advantage of the SSM is that integration can help go some distance towards removing politics from the enforcement of bank supervision. It can also bring greater emotional detachment to the process of

---

[13] According to the euro area summit statement of 29 June 2012: 'When an effective single supervisory mechanism is established, involving the ECB, for banks in the euro area the ESM could, following a regular decision, have the possibility to recapitalize banks directly. This would rely on appropriate conditionality, including compliance with state aid rules, which should be institution specific, sector-specific or economy-wide and would be formalised in a Memorandum of Understanding. The Eurogroup will examine the situation of the Irish financial sector with the view of further improving the sustainability of the well-performing adjustment programme' (www.consilium.europa.eu/media/21400/20120629-euro-area-summit-statement-en.pdf). Out of a 300-word communique, it was striking that 24 referred specifically to Ireland. It suggests an awareness that the fiscal burden of Ireland's bank recapitalization had not yet been adequately dealt with by Europe.

[14] For example, direct recapitalization is permitted only if the relevant member state is unable to do the recapitalization itself 'without very adverse effects on its own fiscal sustainability'.

supervision, removing the rose-tinted national spectacles that have sometimes been worn by national supervisors. It should also lever the diversity of supervisory experience and aptitude across Europe to provide multiple cross-checks on bank soundness, while not limiting bank behaviour into a straitjacket.

It is too early to make a definitive assessment of how well the SSM is doing in achieving these improvements. Certainly, it got up and running remarkably quickly and has made its mark in a number of high-profile cases.

It seems to have escaped the worst of a number of potential pitfalls. There was always the danger that the process of setting up the SSM could disrupt the 'business as usual' of supervision. The huge tasks of transferring knowledge to the centre, and of building new communications channels between national supervisors and the central team, might have been too great a distraction. Process might have overwhelmed product in an interim period with the result that some problems remained undetected, hidden by the dust kicked up by the creation of the new structure. Even though the principles of supervision remained the same, creation of the SSM certainly implied an operationally challenging process of change in the organization and working methods of bank supervision in Ireland.

However, the SSM does not seem to have become unduly bogged-down in overly complex layering of decision-making structures. Moving decisions to the centre and away from national authorities in what can be a very sensitive area created the risk of potentially divisive clashes between broad European and national interests; still, these have been finessed without fatal damage to the integrity of the supervisory system. All in all, the SSM's first years must be accounted a reasonable success.

Emergency Liquidity: Centralized or a National Responsibility?

Since so many things have been centralized in the banking union, what about emergency liquidity (ELA)? Drawing on the euro area payments system (Trans-European Automated Real-time Gross Settlement Express Transfer system [TARGET]), a national central bank can provide emergency liquidity to a solvent but illiquid bank against lower quality collateral unless (as we have seen) the ECB Governing Council objects.[15] ELA is still a responsibility of the national central bank (NCB); only if a stressed bank

---

[15] The role of national central banks is constrained by the Treaty. They are primarily concerned with delivering the mandate of the Eurosystem, but each NCB may, depending

has collateral satisfying the ECB's relatively strict eligibility requirements will it be able to access ECB liquidity directly.

The debate on whether ELA should remain as a national responsibility or be centralized is instructive in that it overlaps with wider issues about financial risk- and burden-sharing in the euro area. Indeed, the ELA debate can be thought of as a microcosm of those issues.

One obvious reason for the Governing Council to object to the provision of ELA on a large scale is if the additional liquidity created were to be so large as to influence the overall monetary policy stance for the area as a whole. Despite the large amounts of ELA extended at different times by the Irish and Greek national central banks, the fact that liquidity was being provided in unlimited amounts to any banks against eligible collateral during the crisis meant that the total volume of liquidity in the system was not a policy target at the time, and thus even large provision of ELA did not interfere with overall monetary policy.

Nevertheless, ELA provision in one member state could be a concern for the rest on other grounds. On the scale it reached in Cyprus and Greece, as well as Ireland, and considering that the funds being provided by the lending national central bank were in effect being drawn from the rest of the system, a large default could imply credit risk for the other NCBs if the ELA collateral provided by the failing bank turned out to be of lower value than had been supposed. To be sure, there were protections here. ELA was not to be given to an insolvent bank, it should be short term in nature and must be collateralized, even if the collateral was not eligible in the normal ECB lending operations. The bank supervisors (the SSM after 2014) were consulted on the question of solvency, and the collateral assessed and valued at a steep haircut relative to face value. Still the risk of a chain of default running right through the NCB and imposing losses on the rest of the system was always a spectre in the background for Ireland, Greece or Cyprus. (ELA granted by other central banks in the crisis was relatively smaller.) In each of the countries that made heavy use of ELA in the crisis for more than a few weeks, the notion that ELA credit risks were entirely a matter for the NCB concerned contained a strong element of fiction. At the end of 2010, the Central Bank of Ireland had capital and reserves amounting to just 0.8 per cent of its total assets and less than 4 per cent of its ELA exposure. In effect, leaving ELA as a national responsibility does not prevent a degree of involuntary risk-sharing across countries.

on its national legislative mandate, perform other functions, provided the ECB Governing Council does not object by a two-thirds majority.

The long-drawn out saga of Anglo Irish Bank made the Governing Council determine a tighter control over the granting of ELA for future cases. More explicit strict rules were drawn up which had the effect of making the requirement for a supermajority (two-thirds majority) redundant. Now the Governing Council took a more active role in influencing the allowable quantity of ELA granted to the banking systems of Cyprus and Greece. Even though ELA was still a national responsibility, the ECB had de facto limited its scale, thereby limiting the potential for involuntary risk-sharing.

The provision of ELA can seem like a bargaining situation between (on one side) a mendicant NCB, confident of the stressed bank's solvency and trying to avoid contagion to the rest of the national banking system, and (on the other side) the members of the Governing Council, some of them suspicious, others disengaged.

Decisions on ELA do need to be informed by information about local market conditions. But ELA is not simply a matter of local or national concern. After all, with a resolution regime that ensures continuation of essential intermediation services to each national economy, decisions on ELA can be taken without any danger of the kind of side effects that made its provision a matter of vital national importance for Ireland in the crisis.

Instead, the Governing Council, with its de facto veto over ELA provision, and with its access (through the SSM as supervisor) to solvency information, should take the additional step of acknowledging its clear responsibility in relation to financial stability and liquidity provision by establishing a centralized ELA.

* * *

After a zig-zag course in managing the crisis, Europe has built an elaborate, albeit incomplete, banking union structure. To what extent would such a structure, had it been in place, have prevented or smoothed the crisis? It is probably futile to speculate on whether or to what extent an SSM created a decade earlier than it was would have reined-in the Irish banks, obviating their failure. The new capital adequacy rules would have increased the buffer of shareholder funds to absorb losses (and might possibly have had some function in discouraging risk-taking on the scale that occurred). Had the BRRD been in effect in September 2008, the Irish government would not have been at liberty to provide a guarantee in the terms that were then used.

Reflecting the multi-country context, the new resolution mechanisms of the European Union are complex, and in some respects not fully articulated. But they promise to create a more rational, predictable and socially acceptable regime for dealing with bank failure. It stands alongside the

SSM bank supervision mechanism as a signal reform that offers some prospect of improvement relative to the – for some countries disastrous – supervisory inadequacies and hand-to-mouth policy response to bank failure that Europe saw in the past decade.

Given the slow pace of non-performing loan clean-up, it is not surprising that equity markets remain somewhat unconvinced about the capitalization of European banks. Adherence to a coherent resolution regime is one of the essential elements for redressing this situation.

The main elements of the policy framework needed for a coherent approach to crisis management and resolution are in place, preventing society at large from having to shoulder the burden of private banking losses in order to ensure smooth continued functioning of the payments and credit system. At the same time, enough emergency liquidity and bailout powers are still present to ensure that a severe panic can be halted.

There should be more. The promised banking union has not yet been completed, with a common deposit guarantee scheme still on the drafting table and with the funding of the common resolution authority still in the early build-up phase. The reluctance to use collective resources directly to fund precautionary recapitalization on mutualized basis (instead of routing such moneys through the budget of what may be stressed national governments) is another shortcoming, blocking what would seem the obvious route to further strengthening of loss absorbing capacity of European banks. And the procedures of the competition authorities of the European Commission designed to prevent government-assisted restructurings from distorting competition can – and have – sometimes unnecessarily complicate the resolution process.

Ideally, the need for such measures in the future will be reduced by the parallel efforts that have been made to improve safety and soundness of the European banking system through better supervision, not least in dealing with the still exceptionally high level of loan arrears (including in Ireland, but not only there), and especially through general increases in required capitalization of banks (even though here too more could be done). Several European regulatory authorities are going beyond capital requirements and adopting macro-prudential rules, such as those introduced in Ireland during 2015, limiting banks' exposure to types of credit contract that have been associated in the past with subsequent losses. It is unlikely that loss-absorbing or capital instruments will be so heedlessly mis-sold to retail customers as may have been the case in some countries in the past. Attention is also being focused on the vulnerabilities created by excessive exposure of banks to the debt of financially weak governments.

12

The Irish Economy in Boom and Bust

'Thuas seal agus thíos seal'

'Good times alternating with bad times'[1] is an appropriate summary of overall economic performance during Ireland's century of independence.

Indeed the whole period has been a game of two halves; falling population and income stagnation characterized the first fifty years, while the second half-century has seen Ireland's average living standards converge towards the frontier of international experience. Superimposed on these secular trends, Ireland has experienced four major macroeconomic crises, two in each half-century, which may be described as home-grown, even though each of them was influenced by external developments (cf. Ó Gráda 2011; O'Rourke 2017).

The so-called 'economic war' of the 1930s occurred during the international Great Depression and was the result of a calculated reopening or renegotiation of the 1922 Treaty understanding regarding certain debt-servicing liabilities vis-à-vis the British government (the land annuities). The withholding of these payments by the Irish government triggered a trade war which had severe consequences, especially for the vital agriculture sector.

The mid-1950s balance of payments crisis, seemingly caused by Dublin's reluctance to track interest rate increases in London, has already been touched on earlier (Chapter 1). This resulted in capital outflows that triggered a fiscal contraction resulting in an employment slump and soaring emigration.

---

[1] The full proverb, thought of as subversive of a static hierarchy, says 'Ní huasal ná íseal ach thuas seal agus thíos seal', which translates as 'It's not a question of nobles and plebs, but sometimes up and sometimes down.'

THE TWO CRISES

Turning to the second, more successful half-century, two deep national macroeconomic crises, each following suddenly after a change of exchange rate regime, have defined the working life of my generation of Irish economists. Separated by a decade and a half of growth and rapid recovery, the two crises are often spoken of in the same breath, sometimes to say that they were but variants of the same problem; sometimes to highlight the differences.

Both crises were exceptionally severe; indeed it is debatable as to which was worse. Although five years in, the most recent one looked likely to claim this dubious honour, the steady recovery from mid-2012 makes the comparison with that of the 1980s a close call.

Should Ireland, once bitten (the 1980s), have been sufficiently shy to avoid the problems of the past decade, or were the circumstances really sufficiently different to explain and justify the policy errors that were made?

In comparing the two events, it is the similarities that jump out. Both events were driven by spending in the boom phase that exceeded the economy's ability to generate output that could pay for what was spent. Both episodes saw an almost reckless disregard for the fiscal consequences of structural decisions. In both cases, an international downturn contributed to exposing the domestic imbalances and made recovery more difficult. In the 1980s it was the combination of the deflationary policies in the USA (Volcker) and the UK (Thatcher); in the 2000s the Global Financial Crisis.

Both episodes saw macroeconomic policy errors based on exaggerated reliance on bowdlerized versions of simplistic paradigms. There was a naïve caricature of Keynesianism in the first instance; a credulous adoption of intensive financialization in the second.

The macroeconomic adjustment of the economy in both cases also displayed common features. Recovery each time required a re-balancing of the public finances using both tax increases and spending cuts. Improvements in wage competitiveness were also a central element in the adjustment process on both occasions. This was helped in the 1980s by the new weakness of the currency regime relative to that of the largest trading partner (the UK), and by the ability, exercised in 1986, to make a significant but one-off unilateral devaluation, an option that was not available in the euro area.

All in all, the experience of the past decade can be seen as yet another example of the start-and-stop pattern of the hare-and-tortoise metaphor used in a 2002 article by Brendan Walsh and myself to describe the previous half-century of Irish macroeconomic evolution.

But, despite the important similarities, it is important not to neglect some important differences between the two episodes.

One clear difference was in the main driving force of boom and bust. As far as the earlier crisis is concerned, it was fiscal profligacy in the late 1970s – motivated by the desire to counter the surge in unemployment that had followed the first oil crisis – that un-balanced the public finances and resulted in a soaring government debt ratio. Fiscal policy was stabilized only following a protracted period of high interest rates, unemployment and emigration. This is a clear contrast with the recent crisis, where the boom was driven by unsustainable but unconstrained bank credit expansion, though in the later stages the public finances also became too relaxed.

The second crisis affected an economy that had become much more dynamic and more at risk of volatility, likely due to the increased globalization of the Irish economy and in particular in its reliance on international finance. The Irish economy since the mid-1990s has had a higher trend growth than in the 1980s, but this seems to have come with a larger amplitude of boom-and-bust fluctuation.

Accordingly the dynamic of the two crises was quite different. The second crisis happened faster and resulted in a deeper loss of output and employment: the build-up of output and employment was steeper, the collapse more severe and the recovery faster.

Some of the difference is due to the degree to which the pre-crisis economy had become structurally distorted before the crash. The economy in 2007 was arguably much more distorted than that of 1981. In the earlier episode, the fiscal expansion had been relatively broad-based, whereas in the 2000s the heavy emphasis on the construction sector had skewed the sectoral pattern of economic activity and the sources of tax revenue, and left households and enterprises with over-large property-related indebtedness.

Let us look in a little more detail at a number of similarities and differences as between the two episodes both with regard to causes and the evolution of the main macroeconomic aggregates.

Causes

One should always distinguish between proximate and underlying causes in considering major conjunctural disturbances.

(a) *Proximate causes.* For proximate causes we can easily accept the important commonality and the main distinction between the two events. Both were caused by the emergence of multi-year overspending: the distinction lying in the fact that the 1980s followed a period of mainly public sector overspending, whereas it was private overspending that mainly teed-up the recent crash, though towards the end of the boom public overspending was also present.

The government over-spending of the late 1970s is generally and rightly traced back to the winning general election manifesto of 1977. Motivated by a desire to reduce unemployment by means of a fiscal expansion, this heralded a post-austerity splurge, following the sharp fiscal contraction that had corrected emerging imbalances in 1975. The expansive policies of 1977–81 put in place higher public sector pay rates and ambitious spending programmes that were politically difficult to dismantle when they proved unaffordable.

In the 2000s the cause lay of course in the property construction and house price boom, fuelled by easy credit provided by poorly managed and inadequately supervised banks competing for market share using funds sourced from abroad.

With tax revenue greatly but temporarily increased during the 2000s boom, the government had eventually succumbed once again to the temptation to increase pay and social benefit rates and generally increase staffing of public services to levels that would prove unsustainable. For the tax system was quite pro-cyclical. Capital gains tax generated revenues mainly in boom times. The property transactions tax known as stamp duty generated soaring revenues only when property market activity was high and especially when property prices were high. And even Ireland's low rate of corporation profits tax yielded substantial revenue when firms were making profits, i.e. in the boom. And, with a couple of brief interruptions (in the early 1990s and early 2000s) it was a long boom, during which the government took advantage of this boom-time revenue to reduce income tax rates (as well as increasing public spending). The share in total tax revenue of just the three cyclical taxes mentioned increased from 8 per cent in 1987 (at the trough of the previous crisis) to 30 per cent on the eve of the crisis. By 2009, the share had fallen back to 16 per cent and the government had stumbled into another public finance crisis.

(b) *Underlying causes.* But why did these policy errors emerge? Here the relevance of Keynes' observation that policymakers are often in thrall to some defunct theoretician is evident.[2] In both the 1970s and the early

---

[2] 'The ideas of economists and political philosophers, both when they are right and when they are wrong are more powerful than is commonly understood. Indeed, the world is ruled by little else. Practical men, who believe themselves to be quite exempt from any

2000s, Irish governments fell foul of bad ideas falsely distilled from simplistic versions of prevailing orthodoxies.

Thus, in the 1970s an oversimplified and deformed version of Keynesianism was used to justify a government spending-led growth spurt which was intended to generate self-sustained revenue expansion. This was an attractive idea in general and vague terms, but demanded quantification before being implemented. It should have become clear with even back-of-the-envelope calculations that, taking any reasonably realistic values for the size of the relevant multipliers and other parameters in such a small and open economy, the expansive government deficit was never going to be closed: the policies were wildly wrong.[3]

In the 2000s, in contrast, the government was lulled into complacency by an apparently crass belief in untrammelled financialization. This financialization generated excessive private spending, reflected in a growing balance of payments deficit and in outflows of investment in property acquisition abroad. This temporarily misled policymakers into an expansive fiscal stance that seemed sustainable, when in fact it too was building up unsustainable commitments financed by insecure and transient revenue sources. The resulting public and private sector balance sheet exposures ultimately destabilized the economy.

Evolution of the Main Macro Aggregates

Both recessions were extremely deep and protracted. Still, there are noteworthy differences in timing and in the dynamics of such indicators as (a) employment, (b) unemployment, (c) household incomes, (d) asset prices and (e) the public finances.

(a) *Employment.* The most obvious broad measure of economic dislocation in any recession is the contraction of labour demand. In both crises firms responded to shrinking demand by contraction and closure; employment in government and publicly funded services also contracted, reflecting the fiscal adjustments.

Figure 12.1 superimposes the evolution of aggregate employment in each of the crises. It displays how the economy of the 2000s had a higher trend employment growth rate than the 1980s, and a larger amplitude of

intellectual influences, are usually slaves of some defunct economist' (Keynes 1936: 383–84).

[3] See Ó Gráda (2012) for a vivid table showing how badly the plan for 1977–81 missed its unrealistic targets.

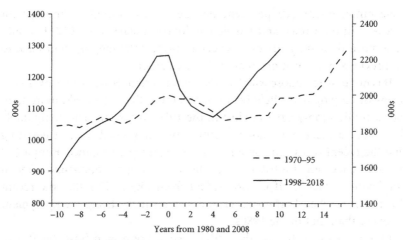

Figure 12.1 Total employment, 1970–95 and 1998–2018.
Source: Central Statistics Office.

fluctuation around that trend, with the cycle faster both in the boom and the bust phase.[4]

In the 1980s slump, the adverse shock to employment produced an overall fall of about 7 per cent over seven years. The 1980 peak in employment was not achieved again until 1993. There is a striking contrast across the gender divide. Most of the employment decline related to men for whom the decline was not fully reversed until 1996. The numbers of women at work also fell, but by a much smaller percentage and this was soon reversed. In effect, the secular trend increase in female labour force participation in those decades meant that the number of women at work suffered only a temporary setback.

The peak-to-trough fall in male employment between 2007 and 2012, at almost 23 per cent, was much faster and steeper than in the 1980s.[5] The fact that male employment bore the brunt of this shock can be attributed to the way in which the pre-crisis economy had become so unsustainably skewed towards construction, which remains a male-dominated sector in terms of employment. Female employment also fell sharply in the more recent period, but again much less so than

---

[4] These numbers (like those of Figure I.1) use the International Labour Organization definition of employment. Data for the alternative national 'principal economic status' definition show a broadly similar pattern albeit with a somewhat smaller amplitude of fluctuation.

[5] Based on quarterly series, not seasonally adjusted.

male employment (10 per cent decline peak-to-trough). Employment recovery in both male and female employment started in 2012. It would take more than six years of recovery to bring total employment back to its previous peak of more than a decade earlier.

It is not easy to choose which of the two experiences was worse overall in terms of employment. Relative to maintaining the 1980 peak, more than half-a-million job-years were lost in the 1980s recession. The comparable figure for the recent recession was almost two million job-years, suggesting that the recent recession had a much worse jobs performance. But part of the difference here is attributable to the much steeper boom-time surge in employment 2004–7. It is also evident from Figure 12.1 that the recent downturn reached bottom faster and saw a much stronger employment recovery than that of the 1980s.

In employment terms, then, the recent boom-and-bust event was sharper but shorter than the earlier one. To choose between the employment performance in the two crises requires a decision on the relative weights to be attached to amplitude and duration. In addition, though the longer term sequel needs to be kept in mind: a repetition of the rapid employment growth of the 1990s is hardly to be anticipated for the 2020s.

(b) *Unemployment.* With migration as an important balancing mechanism, trends in unemployment in Ireland do not always closely track those in employment. One very striking regularity which has persisted through both crises is the close manner in which the dynamics of Irish unemployment have tracked those of the UK (and less so those of the countries that became part of the euro area) (Figure 12.2).

The surge in unemployment rates was higher in the 1980s, despite the smaller dip in employment (Figure 12.3). Having hovered for years around 4 to 5 per cent, unemployment had moved much higher during the first oil price crisis of the mid-1970s, and the recovery of the late 1970s was moderate. Unemployment rates then surged again to record levels in the early 1980s against the background of the contemporary recession in UK. Indeed, after a brief recovery in the late 1980s, unemployment rose again into 1993; although it fell steadily thereafter, it did not fall to 5 per cent again until the last year of the century.

In contrast, the 2008 crash had been preceded by six or seven years of continuous full employment (as indicated by a measured unemployment rate of around 4 per cent). Despite the contemporary global financial crisis and the euro area crisis, Irish unemployment rates in

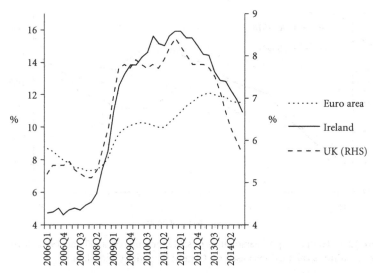

Figure 12.2 Unemployment rates: Ireland, the UK and euro area, 2006–14. Per cent of labour force; seasonally adjusted.
Source: Eurostat.

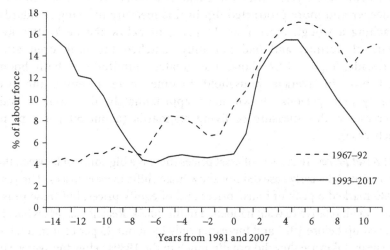

Figure 12.3 Unemployment in two cycles, 1967–92 and 1993–2017.
Source: Central Statistics Office.

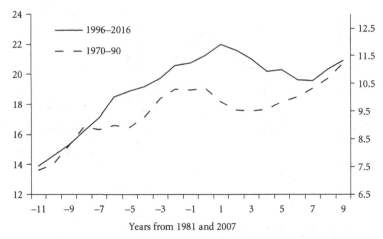

Figure 12.4 Real per capita personal disposable income, 1970–90 and 1996–2016.
Source: Author's calculations based on Central Statistics Office data.

the recent crisis peaked slightly below 1980s levels at 16 per cent and, helped by stronger labour market developments in the UK, started to turn down from 2012, dropping below 6 per cent by 2018, much faster than in the earlier episode.

(c) *Household income.* Real per capita personal disposable income fell by about 8 per cent in the earlier downturn, but had recovered all of that drop seven years after the peak. The more recent crisis showed a deeper and more protracted dip in this measure of living standards, reaching a trough more than 11 per cent below the peak after five years of decline, and had not fully matched the peak even after a decade. Figure 12.4 shows the greater amplitude of both boom and bust in average household income more recently; the two twenty-year periods shown have approximately the same overall increase in this measure of living standards (about 50 per cent in each case).

(d) *Asset prices.* In respect of asset prices there is a big contrast between the two crises. The early case did not show huge shifts in asset prices. The year 1980 marked a peak of house prices and of equity prices; but these peaks were small relative to what happened in the 2000s. Real house prices hardly moved up before 1977 and thereafter only by about 25 per cent in total to the peak. Likewise they did not dip much in the 1980s below the average of the previous decade.

The amplitude of the asset price boom and bust was much larger in the 2000s. Even though house prices began their rise in the late 1990s from a much higher plateau in real terms than that of the 1970s, the subsequent house price bubble was much larger than in the 1970s, with *real* house prices rising by 265 per cent in Dublin between 1996 and 2007.[6] The fall was also very sharp: peak to trough nationwide it is estimated that residential property prices fell by 55 per cent, and by more than 60 per cent in Dublin.

Nevertheless, five years after the 2007 peak, house prices bottomed out well above their fifty-year average in real terms. The failure of real house prices to fall back to long-term historical averages raises questions that are hard to answer. Has the low nominal interest rate regime permanently lifted equilibrium house prices? Are real costs of construction permanently and unavoidably higher? Or are prices still elevated relative to their likely long-term trend?

Equity prices also fell sharply from 2007, much more than had happened in the 1980s. The decline in bank shares in particular was irreversible. There had been corporate bankruptcies in the 1980s, especially of long-established firms that had begun to struggle in the face of international competition within the European Common Market. But nothing on the scale of what was recently seen. Having roughly doubled in the boom, the share price of the two main bank shares fell to almost nothing in the bust.

The much more sizable asset price movements in the recent crisis, combined with the scale of private borrowing (which had contributed to the price movements) resulted in the grossly unbalanced private sector portfolios which we have discussed and which triggered a sequence of losses of confidence on the part of investors.

What about the international risk-sharing dimension (cf. Kalemli-Ozcan et al. 2014)? As one of the most globalized economies in the world, including foreign ownership of business enterprises, and through the heavy reliance on foreign funding of the property and construction bubble, one might expect the adverse effects of the 2000s crisis to have been felt to a considerable extent by foreign financiers. But the most globalized sectors by far were (and are) those dealing with export-oriented manufacturing and internationally traded services; these sectors suffered relatively little in the crisis. As discussed, the foreign owners of

---

[6] This came on top of a steady recovery in house prices over the previous decade at a rate about 4 percentage points higher than consumer price inflation.

five of the top ten domestically focused Irish banks, and the considerable foreign-owned share of the equity of other leading Irish banks, all suffered the loss of effectively all of their investment. Holders of sub-ordinated bank debt also absorbed heavy losses as we have seen. But the remainder of the foreign financing of the boom was in the form of deposits and senior debt which were protected. All-in-all therefore, the degree of private risk-sharing through the financial markets was less than might be expected in such a globalized economy.

(e) *Public Debt.* The contrast in the dynamic pattern of public debt between the two crises is remarkable. The 1980s crisis was characterized by a slow but steady accumulation of debt until the political logjam was broken and decisive corrective fiscal action was taken. Indeed, debt had not yet got seriously out of line when the crisis began to be tackled, albeit too tentatively, in 1981. It is relevant that most debt was domestic and in local currency. This contributed to limiting fears of default, and indeed permitted successive governments to defer decisive adjustment until the debt ratio had crept up to the vicinity of 120 per cent of GDP (though for GDP see Box 12.1).[7]

In the more recent case public debt was low and falling until just before the crisis was identified. Then it started growing rapidly (even before the banking debt was taken onto the books). In fact, public debt jumped to roughly the same peak proportion of GDP as had been recorded in the 1980s, but did so from a much lower recent base and much faster: increasing by a factor almost five in just five years. The debt at that stage was almost all foreign and, of course, none in a 'domestic currency'. As discussed earlier, it was the sudden and belated international awareness of the scale of banking losses being crystallized onto the government's debt during the third quarter of 2010 that resulted in a rapid loss of financial market confidence in Ireland.

The evolution of financial market confidence, as measured by spread on long-term government bonds, is shown in Figure 12.5. The difference between the two patterns shown is striking. Already from the mid-1970s, spreads on Irish government bonds (over those of Germany) were as high or higher than generally observed in the recent crisis. Of course in the 1970s investors were concerned about

---

[7] The distinguished commentator Rüdiger Dornbusch was one of the few to suggest that a default could be needed, but already by the time he was writing (1988) the corner had been turned and growth was beginning to take care of debt sustainability concerns.

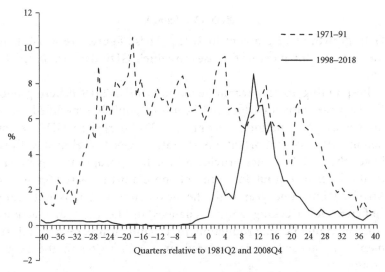

Figure 12.5 Irish long spread over bunds, 1971–91 and 1998–2018.
Source: International Financial Statistics (line 61) and European Central Bank.

BOX 12.1 **The GDP Measurement Problem**

The reader may have noticed how little mention has been made of Gross Domestic Product (GDP) in the preceding comparison of macroeconomic performance, despite it being the usual summary metric of a country's economic performance.

In fact, as already mentioned in Chapter 2, Ireland's macroeconomic statistics have been increasingly hard to track in recent decades. Not only have the monetary statistics relevant to the domestic economy been swamped by the activities of offshore finance through the International Financial Services Centre (a factor which may have helped mask the scale of the domestic credit excess), export and GDP data – and for the past decade or so GNP data also – have been very hard to interpret because of the unusual prominence of multinational corporation (MNC) activities influencing them.

Thanks to the ingenuity of lawyers designing tax-efficient corporate structures for these firms, this problem has got completely out of hand in the past few years, as is illustrated by the reported

BOX 12.1 (cont.)

GDP growth of 26 per cent in 2015.[8] These figures are worse than meaningless for most of the uses to which GDP data are normally put.

Responding to the recommendations of a 2016 expert group, the Central Statistics Office has begun to publish a modified series known as gross national income (GNI*) to replace GDP as the denominator of important policy ratios. GNI* – almost a third lower than GDP – does provide a broadly appropriate adjustment to the level of output for some of the distorting activities of the MNCs, taking one year with the next. However, it is not really sufficient for tracking annual changes in the economic activity truly attributable to production in Ireland. More refined adjustments are needed, as I proposed in a submission to the expert group.

A further question mark must be raised over the failure of the international statistical standards to make ex post adjustments for embedded bank loan losses in the investment data during the construction boom. The problem arises because of the way in which the net interest income of banks is normally used as an estimate of the added value of the banks' intermediation activities. If the banks are going to make losses, some of the interest should be subtracted as it will eventually be offset by these losses. Bank loan losses are normally sufficiently small for this problem to be manageable by current statistical practice. But when, as in the boom years in Ireland, the net interest income received by banks is not going to be anywhere near enough to cover the loan losses that will eventually occur, neglect of these future losses results in a substantial overstatement of the true value of the banks' activities in those years. According to standard methodology, the net interest is fully credited to GDP in boom years. But the subsequent loan losses suffered by the banks in later years are not subtracted from GDP for *any* year. Instead (in line with standard international practice) they are treated as unforeseen capital losses, not to be recorded in the current account of the National Accounts from

---

[8] The continued strength of Ireland's MNC sector during the crisis was a contributor to the recovery, but the extent to which it contributed risks being exaggerated because of these data issues (cf. Brazys and Regan 2017).

BOX 12.1 (cont.)

which GDP is drawn (cf. Figure 12.6, which provides a schematic calculation). The implication (for Ireland and for other countries which experienced large loan-losses) is that recorded GDP for the boom years is considerably larger than it would have been if the banks had correctly foreseen and provided for future loan-losses. And there has been no compensation for that overstatement in the GDP of the later years in which the losses were booked.

Interpreting the full fiscal impact of the role of the bank credit driven employment and income boom of the first years of the new millennium requires an equal degree of care. The boom generated sizable amounts of tax revenue, but these were not only transient (could not have continued when the boom turned to bust) but could also be thought of as having been eaten up by the direct costs of the bank bailouts. (A rough calculation suggests that excess tax revenues from the bubble were €25 to 35 billion – approaching the net cost of the guarantee.)

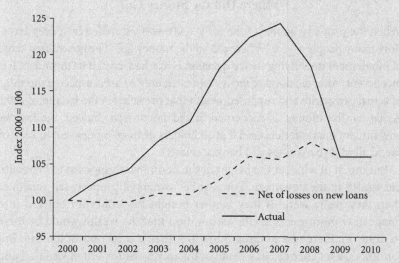

Figure 12.6 Actual and hypothetical GDP, 2000–10.
The hypothetical shows what GDP would have been if realistic estimates of new loan losses had been provided at the outset.
Note: Indicative loan losses are subtracted in each year from 2001 to 2008: Specifically, the sums subtracted (in billions of 2004 euros) are: 1; 1½; 2½; 3½; 5½; 6; 7; 4.
Source: Author's estimates.

exchange risk as well as default risk; the fact that the former had been eliminated by euro membership made the confidence crisis in the financial markets much shorter in the more recent period.

WINNERS AND LOSERS

Where Did the Money Go?

When the property bubble of the early 2000s was succeeded by a deep recession, many people asked: 'Where did all the money go?' The generalized sense of puzzlement underlying such a question is justified, even if its formulation is incoherent. After all, flows of *money* represent only a partial aspect of the surge of actual prosperity and supposed wealth that prevailed in the Ireland of 2006. As far as 'the money' is concerned, it did not vanish. Indeed, the famous government guarantee ensured that all holders of Irish 'money' got to keep or spend all of it (banknotes and bank accounts).

But much of what, at the height of the boom, was supposed to be wealth did vanish in the downturn. For a while, owners of property felt wealthier than they really were. If they neither bought nor sold, nor entered into financial commitments on the assumption that the wealth would be there to draw on, there was nothing more to it than a brief optical illusion. But for others, a lot changed as a result of the mismeasurement of wealth. Land and buildings bought with the proceeds of borrowing proved to be less valuable than the price paid for them.

The big swings in asset prices and in the numbers in and out of work mean that there was a spread of winners and losers in the recent cycle on a much larger scale than in most twenty-year periods. Whether one became a winner or (more likely) a loser overall in the boom-and-bust depended on where one was positioned in the economy in terms of employment and assets and what decisions one took.

The *property market* was the most conspicuous venue for winners and losers. In respect of the buying and selling of real estate property there was something like a zero-sum game: the sellers of land when prices temporarily surged into bubble territory received a windfall gain; the buyers suffered a windfall loss.[9] As usual, the winners along this dimension were those who sold high or bought low (the latter including some foreign-owned funds). But some could afford to lose more than others: many of those who had borrowed to buy property at the height of the boom were plunged into negative equity.

There were also many short-term beneficiaries of the boom, and losers in the bust, who had not bought or sold property, and they were broadly distributed across society. Some people lost in the bust only what they had gained in the boom, but that was not always the case. Some of those who had gained in the boom held onto their gains. And some of those who lost in the bust had not made much gain in the boom.[10]

The *job market* was a second major source of gains and losses. In the boom, building workers and suppliers of building materials earned their keep: no doubt their wages and profits were a bit higher during the boom than they might otherwise have been, and fewer of them would have migrated to Ireland for employment. Indeed wages and profits in the economy generally were lifted in the boom. Among those who suffered were those who lost their jobs and those entering the job market without success in the downturn years.

The third main theatre in which the reshuffling of society's financial resources in boom and bust as between different categories of households took place was the *government's budget*. The government had financed quite a lot of its growing spending in the middle of the first decade of the twenty-first century with windfall tax revenue coming from the property taxes, value-added tax (VAT) and other taxes temporarily inflated thanks to the boom. Public servants' salaries were increased, as were social welfare payments. Income tax rates continued to be shaved down.

[9] It could be argued that other beneficiaries were those who bought property before it became so expensive and managed to finance their borrowings at the tracker rates that subsequently fell so low, thanks to the bust.

[10] Although the equity market does not account for a large fraction of Irish household wealth, another category of losers, small but strongly affected, comprised households (mainly older, retired, hitherto prosperous people) dependent on dividends from bank shares to maintain their standard of living.

All of this public largesse – and more – was going to have to be cut back when the boom ended. And it was, leaving previous beneficiaries puzzled as to just why this comfortable era had come to an end. Tax rate increases and cuts in the salaries of public servants and others post crisis also hit household welfare (even though some of these setbacks only reversed previous recent gains).

From one perspective it is possible to see a degree of symmetry between the accumulated tax revenue generated from the bank credit driven boom and the debt subsequently assumed by the government from the banks when the boom turned to bust.

The government did not – could not – undo all of the distributional impacts of the boom and bust.[11] Yes, the state could – and did – step in to provide some protection for households impoverished in the downturn. But such action was inevitably limited.

Many households fell into more than one of these categories of fortune or misfortune. Many households were winners along one dimension and losers on another.[12]

Inequality

How did all of this churning between winners and losers affect vertical inequality of income and wealth? While measures of inequality in the distribution of income are multidimensional and defy simple generalizations, the main consistent message from the available data seems to be that redistributive policy limited the market-driven fluctuations in inequality.[13] This was also true in the crisis of the 1980s.

Thus, while the boom periods seem to have been accompanied by relatively little change in overall summary measures of income or earnings inequality, the adjustment periods show increases in *earnings* inequality which have been significantly offset by redistributive public policy resulting in little change in the inequality of *disposal income*.

---

[11] The state did of course step in during 2008 to guarantee bank creditors; but this was not so much for the purpose of protecting those creditors, but more for fear of the national consequences of not doing so (a judgement discussed in Chapter 7).

[12] Some of the complexity of the issues is illustrated by the work of sociologists Whelan et al. (2016), who have sought to identify the groups who on average experienced the greatest increase in economic stress in the downturn. Along the income scale they identified levels between the 15th and 65th percentiles as the worst affected. Households with mortgages, those with children or dependent on social welfare in the downturn were other groups with higher economic stress, especially for those in the age group 35 to 65.

[13] See, for example, Callan et al. (2018), Madden (2014) and Nolan (2012).

Even if income inequality did not deteriorate much in the downturn, this cannot conceal the fact that, just as both boom periods experienced sharply declining absolute poverty, the proportion of the population experiencing *absolute* poverty increased during 2007–13 (as it had during 1980–7), reflecting rising unemployment and falling incomes.

And, although the adjustment periods clawed back some of the boom-time increase in the slice of the cake going to the top 1 per cent, the overall trend in the share of that very small group has been strongly upward since the 1980s.

Of course, an even more progressive public policy could have sought to reduce income inequality in the adjustment period so that the burden of adjustment fell more on those better able to bear it. Nevertheless, the fact that government policy prevented any significant deterioration in the relative distribution of disposable income represents a noteworthy common feature of the both crisis episodes.

Less is known about how the distribution of wealth changed. As Ireland emerged from the recent crash, measured inequality in the distribution of net wealth was relatively high compared with other EU countries. (For example, in the ECB's household finance and consumption survey from about 2014, Ireland ranks third out of twenty-one countries on the Gini index of net wealth.) This fact reflects the number of households in negative equity at that time. It is also relevant to note that the growth in bank mortgage lending in the boom years reached further down the income distribution than before, with the bottom three quintiles receiving 40 per cent of the lending by 2007, up from 15 per cent in 1994 (Lydon and McCann 2017); many of these loans fell into negative equity.

But it is not just a question of society ending up with a less equal vertical distribution of net wealth than it started. There were also shifts between different categories of households, notably when classified by the age of the head of household. Horizontal wealth and income inequality as between different age groups increased. Some age groups were worse hit than others, especially those who moved into their mid-20s – typical age for the first house purchase – around 2004–6.[14] Thus, a legacy of the boom and bust is an asset-poor generation of which many will never fully recover the same degree of financial autonomy with which they began their working lives at the start of the millennium.

---

[14] Gerlach-Kristen and Merola (2013) explore the higher incidence of saving ratios among middle-aged households.

COUNTERFACTUALS

A coherent formulation of the 'where did it all go' question asks an explicit counterfactual: how would the economy have done if prudential regulatory policy had effectively restricted the banks from going overboard with the granting of credit?[15]

While we cannot hope to calculate how each category of household would have fared under this counterfactual, given the complex structure of winners and losers, we can at least attempt to model how the macro-economic aggregates would have performed.

I will not pretend to have precise figures on how aggregate income and employment would have panned out in the counterfactual scenario of no property bubble, but the broad outlines are clear. The counterfactual Irish economy would have grown much more slowly than actual in the period up to 2007, and much faster in the post-crisis years. Furthermore, the counterfactual would have seen lower wages, lower tax revenue and less government expenditure during 2003–7. The global financial crisis would still have knocked the economy, but it would have fared much better in 2009–12 and beyond in the counterfactual scenario because austerity driven by the fiscal crisis would have not been needed. Employment in construction would never have got so large and would therefore not have shrunk so much. Far fewer houses would have been built.

Thomas Conefrey and I recently attempted to quantify these effects using the Economic and Social Research Institute (ESRI) model HERMES. Thus we superimposed on that model a counterfactual constant real house price from 2000 to 2007 and simulated the macroeconomic consequences. If this simulation can be believed, the counterfactual would have seen about 130,000 fewer houses being built in the seven years. With this lower construction activity and its knock-on effects through the economy, total employment would have been about 60,000 (or about 3 per cent) smaller by 2007, and (despite migration) the unemployment rate would have ended 2007 more than 2 percentage points higher than actual. Incomes would have been much lower too, with per capita personal consumption running about 8 per cent lower than actual in 2007. Taxation

---

[15] This is our second counterfactual experiment. Chapter 2 considered what Ireland might have looked like outside the euro area both in the pre-crisis phase and in crisis manage-ment. The present experiment, asking what might have happened to Ireland within the euro, but with bank lending constrained, is closer to that examined in a formal model for four peripheral countries by Martin and Philippon (2017), whose results for Ireland are consistent with our discussion here.

and government spending would both have been lower, but the government would have run a modest deficit adding about 12 percentage points to the debt ratio by 2007.

Heading into the global recession, then, the Irish economy would have been smaller, with more moderate wage rates and a somewhat higher government debt and deficit. It would have been better placed to absorb what was coming. Ireland would have been hit by the global recession, of course, but recovery would not have been held back by the implosion of a bloated construction sector, by the collapse in tax revenue and by excessive debt. And the government would not have lost the confidence of the financial markets.

Lacking the banking shock and the need for sharp budgetary cutbacks from 2008, the Irish economy, though starting smaller, would have been hit much less hard by the global and euro area crises. Public services would not have seen the sharp cutbacks that have occurred and there would not have been the legacy of household and firm over-indebtedness as well as the heavier burden of public debt.

Without these burdens, it is plausible that Ireland would have done at least as well as the average post-2008 performance of other euro area countries in the five years of crisis. If so, it can be calculated that by 2013, living standards would have been about 15 per cent above their actual level, and employment about 8 per cent higher. It is plausible that those gaps would persist for many further years.

The boom and the bust both damaged the economy. The boom, and the decisions that were taken during it, meant that Ireland had to adjust down from living standards that could never have been sustained, with sizable and capricious shifts in the distribution of wealth. Despite the path of recovery, the economy still markedly underperforms relative to what could have been achieved had the property bubble been curtailed.

Post-crisis Counterfactuals

Turning to post-crisis macro-management, the natural counterfactual question to ask is whether a slower fiscal adjustment might have yielded a better overall economic recovery for Ireland.

Whatever about other countries, with Ireland's gross government debt soaring to 120 per cent of GDP by 2012 (and recalling how flattering Ireland's economic structure makes that particular metric), and with much punditry at first about the apparent attractions of a sovereign default or debt restructuring, Ireland's unilateral ability to run a more relaxed fiscal stance was extremely limited.

Could fiscal adjustment have been slowed sufficiently to reduce the employment loss without this simply postponing an inevitable adjustment and potentially making the long-run effect of the needed adjustment even worse?

In my view, the answer is no.

To slow the fiscal adjustment would clearly have entailed a higher rate of primary deficit, thereby contributing to the accumulation of debt. This would have had an adverse medium-term effect on the cost of borrowing. And the impact on overall capital formation and saving in the economy would also have been negative.

While the overall fiscal stance of the euro area was undoubtedly too tight, it is much harder to argue that this was the case for Ireland, given the necessity to return quickly to being able to finance itself in the markets. In the range where Ireland has found itself, it is simply not the case that fiscal contractions are self-defeating: corrective action does work. In fact the deficit ratio was reduced substantially and, in due course, the debt ratio was placed on a downward trajectory.

True, debt-financed counter-cyclical spending is in many circumstances an important policy tool. The empirical growth impact of higher debt burdens is not as great as has sometimes been claimed. And both optimal and safe transitory levels of national debt are surely not insensitive to the medium-term prospect for interest rates.

But simple calculations suggest that a more relaxed fiscal adjustment would not have increased employment and incomes by much, and would likely have left Ireland unable to demonstrate a sustainable debt profile.

Even if the official lenders had permitted a more relaxed deficit reduction plan, could a path close to full employment have been maintained during the programme period at the cost of a more gradual adjustment of the deficit and accumulation of more debt? That too must be doubted: after all, more than nine-tenths of the peak-to-trough employment fall of 389,000 had happened in the three years *before* the programme came into effect.[16]

Even if a more relaxed overall fiscal stance had been possible, broad-based demand management could not have prevented all of the sharp fall in employment – almost half of them construction jobs – in the first three years of the downturn 2008–10. A general expansion of demand would

---

[16] Unemployment had reached 15.7 per cent by the time of the programme; it peaked just a little higher at 16.0 per cent about a year later.

have struggled to re-employ all of the workers who had lost their jobs as a result of this combination of a sectoral shock (construction) with an externally driven macroeconomic demand contraction.

Any scholar wishing to show that a significantly better aggregate fiscal adjustment path, in terms of the attained output and employment path, than the one actually negotiated by one Irish government – and implemented by its successor – in the EU–IMF programme of 2010 thus has their work cut out for them. Indeed, a case could be made for a faster fiscal adjustment; the confidence-sapping effect of the tentative and gradual adjustment strategy employed during 1981–7 was certainly not a model to be emulated.

Whatever about the precise choices made by government as to where the savings or extra tax revenue would come from, the overall scale of 'austerity' was thus arguably neither too little nor too much for ensuring the maximum availability of employment and incomes in Ireland.[17]

Of course, had there been appetite for more official risk-sharing and a higher level of overall demand in the euro area, things would have been better. But that is another story.[18]

Ireland Relative to Others

How should Ireland's economic collapse and the subsequent recovery be rated in comparison with other affected European countries? One way of looking at this is to take snapshots of how deep the recession was peak-to-trough and by how much had each economy recovered a decade after the crisis began in 2007. Once again taking total employment as the best summary indicator, Figure 12.7 shows that Ireland was among the six countries with the deepest slump peak-to-trough, the others being Greece, Spain and the three Baltic States.[19] Ireland subsequently recovered

---

[17] I cannot resist noting that the new government in 2011 looked as if it still couldn't shake off the idea that property speculation was an essential ingredient in a successful macroeconomic recovery. It was willing to forgo future tax revenue to pump-prime such speculation towards the bottom of the market through reliefs from corporation tax and capital gains tax on property acquired between 2011 and 2014, provided the property was held until 2021 (later revised to 2018 when land hoarding had become a problem).

[18] This would be a federal-type story in which international political solidarity and standing mechanisms for redistribution in Europe would have to be much greater than they are today. Ireland and the other stressed economies would have benefitted from the stabilizing effects of risk-sharing. In my opinion, in such a Europe Ireland would also have to be a sizable net contributor in helping to achieve convergence in living standards.

[19] Of course different countries are affected to differing degrees in such dimensions as population growth and secular trends in female participation, so an in-depth study of this aspect would not simply rely on total employment.

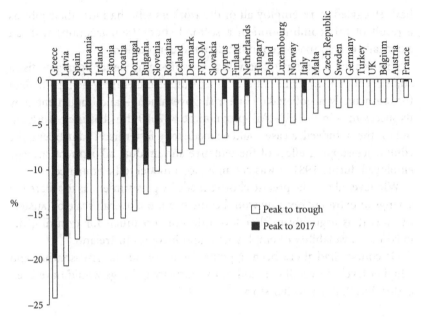

Figure 12.7   Fall in numbers employed from 2007 peak to trough and to 2017, European countries.
Source: Eurostat.

more of its losses than any of the others apart from Estonia. Indeed, there are four other European countries, Portugal, Croatia, Bulgaria and Romania, which, while not having fallen as far, were showing employment by 2017 further below peak than Ireland. (It is worth noticing that these underperformers include both countries that were in the euro area and several that are not, or joined only after the crisis.) Poor performance of the Russian economy, still an important trading partner for many Central and Eastern European countries, is likely a factor for some of these countries.

The timing of the decline and recovery differs quite a lot from country to country. Although most of the affected countries saw peak employment in late 2007 or 2008, some reached the trough much faster than others. The three Baltic States (and the UK – which saw only a moderate fall in employment) started to turn in 2010, though the recovery was slow in Latvia and Lithuania (which have both been experiencing population decline for a quarter century). As we have seen, most of Ireland's employment decline had occurred by 2010, though there was some further drift until mid-2012. But the sharp employment decline in Portugal, Spain and Greece continued into 2013 (Figure 12.8).

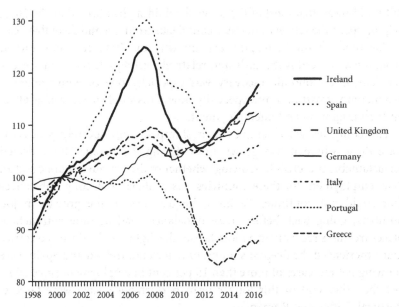

Figure 12.8 Numbers at work: Selected EU countries, 1998–2017.
Source: Eurostat.

The case of the UK is especially interesting given the close banking relationships between Ireland and Britain, and the extent to which, as mentioned, innovation in bank lending (tracker mortgages and high loan-to-value mortgages) seems to have been introduced into Irish banking largely by way of Britain. That country also experienced a property price boom in the early 2000s, though not involving construction on anything like the scale of Ireland. Britain's faster recovery partly reflects the fact that the property boom was not as extensive, but it also reflects the sharp depreciation in the pound sterling in the early months of the crisis, which helped boost UK competitiveness. The UK economy has a quite different sectoral productive structure to that of Ireland, and it is note-worthy that labour demand remained much stronger there in the early years of the crisis, with labour productivity strikingly weak.

Two factors could be important in explaining why Ireland reached its trough relatively early. One is the early fiscal correction initiated by the Irish government already during 2008. Certainly front-loading the fiscal adjustment will not have helped slow the fall in employment in 2009 and 2010.[20]

---

[20] If one can call it front-loading, seeing that the deficit in that year was still a remarkably wide 14 per cent of the GDP – or 11 per cent if bank recapitalization costs are ignored.

But it did mean that most of the heavy fiscal lifting had been done by 2011, helping speed the return of investor confidence from the middle of that year.

The other factor in helping explain why the Irish economy turned around when it did is the early and relatively strong UK economic recovery. The UK economic recovery was especially one of employment – productivity growth was unexpectedly slow. This surely had a sizable effect on Irish migration and unemployment.

The countries where employment slumped most severely post-crisis were those where it had grown most during the boom. This reflected unsustainable pre-crisis borrowing, whether of the private or public sector. Peak employment for these countries was artificial, reflecting imbalances that could not continue. Taking a longer view of the growth in job numbers, going back before these imbalances had become entrenched, places Ireland's recovery in a more favourable light. Of the dozen countries that experienced the deepest slumps, only Iceland, Ireland and Spain were showing net increases of more than 15 per cent in employment since 2001. (At the other end of this longer term performance scale were Greece, Portugal, Latvia and Romania.)

Thus, peak-to-trough, Ireland's employment collapse was in relative terms severe (and much worse, for example, than that in Italy or the UK), and recovery was slow. But taking into account the previous boom, the net position of Ireland a decade and a half into the new millennium was a good deal better than that of neighbouring UK, or indeed Germany, both of which had contained employment decline in the slump, but grew only gradually during the both the pre-crisis and recovery years.

* * *

By analogy with Aesop's fable, it was the tendency of the Irish economy to stall from time to time, while at other intervals displaying a healthy rate of progress, that led Brendan Walsh and I to refer (almost two decades ago) to the Celtic Hare rather than the geographically dubious Celtic Tiger coined as a comparison of Ireland's late 1990s growth with that of the so-called East Asian Tiger economies.

Despite the recurrent crises, net progress has been substantial, as the economy migrated from its dependence on agriculture with relatively low overall labour market participation (as was the case in mid-century) to today's high employment and high productivity economy.

Though economically damaged, Ireland emerged from each of the earlier crises with some new strengths. The 1938 settlement with Britain at the end of the 'economic war' was strikingly favourable to Ireland.

The events of the mid-1950s created the political preconditions for the decisive movement towards openness to foreign investment and foreign trade that heralded the progressive second half-century.

When the fiscal challenges of the 1980s were finally brought under control, a pent-up growth potential (reflecting already expanded provision of education, and the benefits of EU-financed infrastructure spending, among other elements) was unleashed for the 1990s, bringing full employment to Ireland for the first time and in a way that was based on competitive efficiency.

The most recent crisis threatened at one stage to be far worse than any of the previous ones (at least since independence). The recent crisis must still be considered the worst from many perspectives. Its start was certainly more abrupt: it had the steepest peak-to-trough fall in employment for example, though that was after an exceptionally steep run-up. The decline in gross and net wealth was also almost surely more severe in the recent episode – though once again this followed a large run-up. The larger amplitude of the swings reflects the greater exposure of an economy as globalized as Ireland to swings in external financing conditions. However, corrective action was earlier and more effective in the recent episode, helping the economic recovery to be faster than had been feared and faster than in the 1980s. Because of the sharp shifts in asset prices and the scale of household borrowing, averages conceal extremes. The share of households experiencing severe household economic distress as a result of the boom and bust may well therefore have been greater this time. If a case could still be made for considering the earlier crisis as worse overall it would have to be based on the more protracted decline in employment and household incomes, the persistence of high unemployment, and the fact that the decline did not follow as steep – and evidently unsustainable – a prior boom.

Fiscal policy could have been more progressive in both recoveries, but it did limit the worsening of aggregate disposable income inequality as conventionally measured. That is not to say that it prevented a complex pattern of winners and losers, especially in terms of wealth, in the past decade and a half. There was no practical way of fully unwinding these gains and losses, which for many households will have lasting consequences. All in all, the likely persistence of these significant recent wealth redistributions inclines me to conclude that, despite the relatively rapid aggregate economic recovery, the 2003–13 boom and bust probably had worse welfare effects than any previous episode.

Rightly or wrongly, the liberal market economy, with which we have operated in Ireland and which has been a powerful driver of aggregate income growth, is also prone to generating arbitrary redistributions. It is a system in which it is left to individuals to assume and manage risks, not all of which will yield the hoped-for results. Government policy can insulate against some of these losses, but not all. For the losers, it is little comfort to be told that this is a system within which large and ultimately sustained improvements in living standards have been achieved in Ireland over the last six decades. Indeed, it is not a system whose unmediated outcomes always rate highly in fairness terms. That is why government safety nets are so important. But it is a more effective system than any other that has been devised, and that is why it is established in the Irish Constitution and its laws.

For the average household, taking the boom with the bust and recovery together, Ireland comes out as one of the better performing European economies on average in the years of the new millennium, despite the ups and downs.

A decade after it began, a legacy of damage from the last crisis still affects many parts of society; it is too soon to make a definitive evaluation of how well Ireland is positioned for coping with the many new challenges that have already appeared on the horizon. Still, there is reason for optimism from the unemployment figures and from the arrangements that have so contained the cost of servicing the huge debt accumulated by the government.

The boom before any crisis tends to display subtle differences from what has gone before. It is these differences that can blind policy-makers to the vulnerabilities that are building. In the recent crisis oversimplified approaches to assessing fiscal vulnerability and a formulaic and credulous approach to bank solvency and bank credit risk created problems that are still being worked through. Although the denouement revealed the source of the problem to be relatively obvious, pinpointing the behavioural flaws (in the activities of lenders, regulators and borrowers) that prevented enough of them from fore-seeing the risks and mitigating them has been less easy. The tendency to overlook fundamental similarities between situations of emerging vulnerability on the grounds that 'this time is different' was well exemplified in the Irish policy behaviour in the early 2000s – barely fifteen years since Ireland had emerged from a deep macroeconomic crisis with shared underlying commonalities, despite evident, but ultimately superficial, differences.

13

Lessons Learnt

FOR ONE SMALL COUNTRY

Like many other small countries, but more than most, Ireland has depended on international trade in goods and services for advancing its prosperity. Migration, both outward and inward, has been a hallmark and gauge of the fluctuations in Ireland's prosperity. As one of the most globalized economies on the planet, the way in which Ireland has dealt with its international economic relations has been crucial. Banking and finance has been central to this engagement.

Over the past several decades, Ireland has experienced a convergence of average living standards towards the highest levels achieved worldwide. But there have been some severe setbacks, most of which had financial failings, whether governmental or private, at their heart. The most recent crisis of 2008–13 has been the most dramatic.

This experience offers lessons for financial sector policymakers of the future in small open economies.

Ireland's mixed experience with each of the several exchange rate regimes that it has adopted over the century of the state's existence strongly suggests that it is not the choice of regime that matters as much as the quality of the accompanying policies and the extent to which they take account of the differing demands of different regimes. Ireland's fraught experience in the second decade of the euro area does not imply that the decision to join was a mistake: the poor record reflects weakness of macroeconomic and prudential policy.

Fixed exchange rate regimes generally last until a sufficiently large shock, whether coming from abroad or home-grown, hits the system so hard that it cannot sustain the peg without imposing damaging costs on the economy. Ireland was an exception in 1979 when it abandoned the sterling link to join the Exchange Rate Mechanism (ERM) on what were essentially political grounds. Given the scale and speed of international capital movements these days, it is doubtful that any unilaterally fixed exchange rate can be sustained indefinitely.

But the euro area is different. It is the adoption of a currency not under national control. This changes the range of possibilities for a member country. The very large shock that hit Ireland in 2008 would have made any normal fixed exchange rate impossible to sustain. But euro area liquidity was available, preventing a currency collapse and almost certainly a disorderly wave of bank failures in 2008–9.

One can imagine better decisions being taken by Ireland at the time of the guarantee at end-September 2008, but nothing that could have been done at that stage would have prevented the meltdown that subsequently occurred: it was too late for that. Thereafter the challenge was to contain the banking collapse while moving to correct the alarming fiscal imbalance that had emerged when tax revenue shrank at the ending of the property price and construction bubble.

A key part of the attempt to deal with the banking loan losses was the establishment of the National Asset Management Agency (NAMA). Its design avoided many pitfalls. The aggregate loan-loss stress projections made at the time of the first NAMA purchases had to be tough in order to be credible. But the government's finances were too fragile at that stage to overdo the additional capital requirements. Besides, no matter how well capitalized the banks, they could not recover their ability to function in the market if the sovereign was thought considered unsustainable. Thus it proved impossible to restore banking or fiscal credibility without outside help.

Adjusting the fiscal and competitiveness imbalances that had built up during the property price and construction bubble was going to take time, a process that could, in a different currency regime, have been partly short-circuited by devaluation. The contrasting case of Iceland illustrates how that would have been different. Sharp cuts in real wages there meant that the spike in unemployment was of shorter duration than in Ireland.

To cope, Ireland (like Iceland) had to have recourse to official lending, and (as in Iceland) this gave some protection from the exaggerated fears of the international financial markets and gave more space for an orderly fiscal adjustment.

Thus, early entry into an EU–IMF programme was the key to correcting the financial and economic slide. Still, the high interest rate and lack of a risk-sharing element cast doubt on the viability of the initial programme.

Euro area arrangements for dealing with the emergence of financial and fiscal stress in a member country fell short of what should be economically and politically possible within such a large and integrated area. There should have been more innovation in the form of risk-sharing arrangements (for example, direct recapitalization of failing banks; economic recovery-indexed loans to government) to prevent euro membership from aggravating rather than easing national adjustment to major shocks, as has happened in Greece. The same could have happened in Ireland, as witness the doubts about sustainability that existed at the time the EU–IMF programme was negotiated.

Fortunately, Ireland seized the fat from the fire with the lowering of interest rates on the European loans and on the servicing of the legacy debt from Anglo Irish Bank. Combined with the fiscal adjustment, these were sufficient to enable the government to exit the programme on time and recover national financial self-reliance. But it would have been better if these ex post financing fixes had not been needed.

Our experience has clearly shown that the crisis management role of central banks is much more demanding than their role in maintaining price stability and calls on the use of a wider range of tools. The European Central Bank (ECB) and the Central Bank of Ireland both eventually exploited their legal powers to the full. New institutional and legislative arrangements, notably the Single Supervisory Mechanism, and the new laws governing bank resolution, offer the prospect of better preparedness for future banking failures. But these efforts would have been more effective if supplemented by a more coherent effort on the part of Europe's political structures. The lack of trust between creditor and debtor countries, and the insufficiently effective use by the European Commission of its power of initiative, meant that the crisis of the euro area was deeper and lasted longer than was necessary.

Every country needs a well-functioning banking system. It provides the mechanism for making payments and other elements of the life-blood of the economy. Ireland's banking system displayed considerable stability in the twentieth century, albeit without obviously contributing as strongly to Ireland's economic growth and development as financial systems have been seen to do in many other countries. Indeed the long period of banking stability may have lulled policymakers into a false sense of security. Certainly the banking regulators allowed excesses to cumulate to the point where they could threaten the solvency of the Irish state.

Financialization helped drive a couple of decades of strong growth in Ireland as in many other countries. In the end, though, the exaggerated faith of many in the risk-management capability of financial firms was exploded by the dramatic failures of 2008, and the crash also exposed far too many incidents of sharp practice and illegality in financial firms. A tightening of prudential regulation, especially with regard to higher capital and liquidity requirements, followed.

And there were penalties, though mainly for firms. As in other countries, it has proved difficult for the relevant authorities to secure convictions for offences associated with the banking abuses that led to the heavy losses. The legal and quasi-legal process of sanctioning individuals even for non-criminal breaches can be extraordinarily time-consuming. Still, several senior Irish bankers have been jailed for criminal offences. But, despite being suggested by me on more than one occasion over the years, there is as yet no Irish statutory offence corresponding to 'reckless management of a bank' such as was introduced in the UK in 2014. And the continued evidence of sharp practice by banks in Ireland seeking to find ways of profiting from customer inertia or innocence suggests that cultural short-comings remain in the system – a deficiency for which no obvious solution has emerged.

Though adequately recapitalized by mid-2011, the banks continued to be very slow in dealing with non-performing loans (NPLs). They were penny-pinching in their reluctance to make realistic deals with over-indebted borrowers. As a result, bringing the problem of NPLs under control took much longer than hoped for. The public authorities sought to balance the interests of distressed borrowers and the functioning of the banking system with reforms to personal insolvency legislation, a code of conduct for lenders on dealing with mortgage arrears and time-bound requirements to find sustainable solutions for NPLs. It remains unclear what additional policy measures could have been more effective in speeding things up.

That Ireland has now carefully implemented international agreements on prudential regulation has been verified by international assessments. Ireland has also innovated in areas where international rules were lacking. The methodological boundaries of capital adequacy reviews and stress testing were explored and extended in the 2011 assessment. There was innovation in the reforms to insolvency legislation and the regulatory pressure on banks in respect of NPLs contained bespoke features not known in international standards.

Looking to the future, the Central Bank designed a set of macro-prudential restrictions limiting the degree to which banks can grant high mortgages involving high loan-to-value and loan-to-borrower-income ratios. Such measures can work, at least for a while. The intention to introduce such restrictions was announced in October 2014 after an eighteen-month period of rapid price bounce-back in Dublin, giving rise to public fears of a new bubble. Dublin house prices stabilized over the following eighteen months, though they continued to increase thereafter.

Ireland experienced a somewhat faster macroeconomic recovery from the crisis than the other most stressed euro area countries. This can be attributed to a degree of underlying dynamism in the economy, to the persistence of the government in pursuing credible adjustment policies, and to the pragmatic response of the general public who, though angry with the damage that elites had done, were well informed and realistic about what the best solutions for the country could be.

Despite the policy failings, public opinion has been resilient in a number of dimensions. Accurately enough, more than 50 per cent of the general public surveyed periodically (in the 'Eurobarometer' surveys) had recognized the economic situation in Ireland as 'very bad' by mid-2009, a percentage which increased to more than 80 per cent by the end of 2010. But confidence in the economy returned fairly steadily over subsequent quarters and by late 2015 fewer than 10 per cent described the situation as 'very bad', with 60 per cent finding it to be 'good'.

And the experience did not turn Irish people against the euro. Already by mid-2016, a higher proportion of Irish respondents was once again more favourable to the European economic and monetary union than in any other EU country apart from Luxembourg.

The focus of Irish officials in managing Ireland's financial system and macroeconomy was to ensure a speedy return to conditions such as those that had delivered healthy prosperity in the 1990s. But there could have been greater recognition that times of crisis are also times of opportunity to make needed changes in aspects of economy and society. Ireland's political, business and administrative elite had been shocked and demoralized by the unexpected emergence of crisis. They only gradually recovered their self-confidence. Perhaps this explains why more was not done in this respect, but the government's bandwidth seems to have been too narrow to forge consensus around significant change at the same time as deciding on and achieving the needed, but painful, fiscal adjustments. Indeed, almost as soon as this had been accomplished, Ireland once more faced a complex and far-reaching challenge in the form of Brexit. Slower-moving and different in character from the banking and fiscal crisis, Brexit will once more call on the commitment and imagination of Irish policymakers if the adverse impact is to be minimized.

The recovery was faster than many expected, and generated resources that could be harnessed by the government to deal with the many problems facing society. But the recovery did not and could not wholly undo the relative gains and losses that had been generated by the boom and bust. Losers outnumbered and outweighed winners. Those who lost jobs or were unable to find their first jobs; those who had borrowed heavily to buy homes; those who had been relying on the – previously stable – dividends from bank shares to maintain them in old age; these were losers who were largely uncompensated. Those who sold property or bank shares at the top of the market were winners. Gains and losses are inherent in the market economy to which society has subscribed. But the scale of mispricing generated in the boom turned too much of economic life into a casino. Activities which had come to be regarded as conventional were revealed to be highly speculative.

And it gets more complicated: when the banks, largely state-owned at the height of the crisis, were struggling to finance themselves in the market, they were paying much more for the marginal funds than they were receiving from borrowers on tracker rates: from one perspective, one could say that many of the tracker rates were being subsidised by the government (which had also bailed out most of the banks' creditors).

As illustrated by the discussion in Chapter 5 of the obstacles to devising a top-down scheme of relief for over-indebted borrowers, it is not clear what viable government measures could have unwound or compensated all of the unexpected and unusual redistributions that occurred. Nevertheless, the crisis has created new inequalities cutting across the familiar sources of variation in prosperity, and in a way which generates results that do not feel fair to most people.

The banks' treatment of borrowers, both distressed and performing, has also fallen short of the standards society is entitled to expect. Partly this is due to their having expanded the scale and scope of their lending in a poorly controlled manner and well beyond their capacity to manage in an effective way. Vague contracts, poorly documented loans and countless administrative and system errors contributed significantly both to the slow and ineffective resolution of mortgage arrears and to the high profile tracker mortgage scandal. But both of these were also greatly aggravated, I think, by the attitude to customers inculcated by a long-standing sense of corporate entitlement by the banks operating in Ireland. If they needed more revenue, then they could, and would, generate it. While such an attitude is inconsistent with the Central Bank's codes, enforcement of these is inevitably slow, given the requirements of due process, and has not yet been effective in reforming these cultural shortcomings.

The emergence and retention of high margins on mortgage lending, made possible because of the lack of competition from new entrants, is part of the same syndrome. Before I stood down at the end of my period in office, the extensive and persistent tracker review was under way and new rules restricting a bank's ability to alter standard variable rate mortgages without sufficient cause were also being introduced. But full success on this front cannot be claimed.

As to international fairness, it is easy to find fault with the distribution of the costs of the crisis as between different European countries. Still, despite setbacks, the end result for Ireland was better than seemed likely at the end of 2010, given the financing arrangements that were finally put in place for the government's indebtedness arising from the crisis. Ireland hoped and tried for more, but it is easy to see why governments of our European and international partners will not consider the overall outcome for Ireland to be unfair. As we were constantly reminded by them, the boom years had filled the nation's coffers; it was not to be wondered that international partners would expect the nation to pay at least some of the bills. The ECB, exaggerating the risks to the system as a whole, made some tactical errors in insisting on the bonds of failed Irish banks being paid at a time (2011) when bail-in would have been possible and safe – and would have improved market discipline in the funding of European banks. But other decisions of the ECB can be interpreted as having eventually enabled Ireland to claw back the outlays involved in that episode.

Should the Irish side have negotiated with the lenders in a more publicly aggressive manner? Fighting words might have been cathartic, and might have played well on national media. Evidence from other countries suggests that such an approach was unlikely to be more effective in securing better conditions. In fact there were numerous robust conversations behind closed doors, some of them involving officials (including at the Central Bank) as well as others where Irish ministers were taking the lead. These were generally sufficient to communicate matters of substance and political pressure points. With less at stake on their side, Troika negotiators were generally willing to concede on points of contention regarding the policy conditionality as long as the main lines of the agreed policy adjustment were maintained. My view, shared I think by most of the participants, is that the terms of the assistance received and the policy conditionality accepted were, in the end, as good as could have been negotiated. Despite our hopes and efforts for better terms, bluster and public threats would not have helped.

* * *

FOR THE BANKING UNION

Banks in the Currency Union

Relative to the size of the economy, Ireland's banking crisis was much more severe than that of other European countries apart from Cyprus and Iceland. Nevertheless, significant bank failures, imposing serious fiscal and economic costs, affected some twenty European countries in what has been the decade of European bank failures. It is important not to forget that countries other than Ireland also displayed supervisory and regulatory weaknesses, and often responded to the emergence of crisis with a mixed bag of half-baked solutions, with national policy inertia inhibiting needed corrective action.

The crisis revealed a neglected gap in the architecture of the currency union, namely the role of poorly managed and supervised banks as transmitters and amplifiers of shocks. Failing banks severely weakened the public finances in Cyprus and Spain as well as in Ireland, and added materially to the growing debt burden in several euro area countries. On the other hand, market doubts about sustainability of the public finances could manifest themselves in bank runs – most notoriously in the Greek referendum crisis of June 2015, but also after the hamfisted October 2010 Merkel–Sarkozy Deauville accord on how private sector bail-in should be handled.

Pre-crisis, location decisions of banks within the euro area were insensitive to the scale of the national economy and the depth of the national government's pocket. It was only when the crisis broke that investors started to worry about the scale of the banking systems of Ireland and Cyprus, for example, when it seemed that repayment of some bank debt would depend on the condition of the public finances.

It is in respect of these banking issues that the euro area has moved most decisively to fill the architectural gap. The increased capital requirements (in line with Basel III) help restore market confidence. The Single Supervisory Mechanism has established a centralized supervisory regime that collects much more information from banks, both on-site and off-site, and is more willing than most national pre-crisis regimes to flex its muscles when it detects banks that are not robust to potential stresses. The resolution legislation (Bank Recovery and Resolution Directive [BRRD]) provides a more orderly and predictable framework for ensuring the bank losses are largely absorbed in the private sector. There is even a mechanism for using European funds for direct recapitalization of a failing bank if use of national government funds would be destabilizing (though this is unlikely to be much used given the bail-in procedures of the BRRD).

It is essential that these initiatives are kept operational and fully enforced. Together, they should greatly reduce the destabilizing potential of banks and provide a better framework for dealing with banking problems that arise. This will enhance the quality of European policy response to future banking confidence and solvency problems. No longer will we see poorly planned ad hoc guarantee schemes; emergency liquidity granted to banks with embedded but not yet evident losses; and pressure on governments from their peers to bail out wholesale financiers of failing banks.

Banking union is still incomplete. A centralized European deposit insurance scheme is needed to remove an important remaining potential destabilizing coupling between banks and their national government. Bank holdings of national government debt can also be destabilizing, as was seen in the cases of Greece and Cyprus: several proposals seek to create alternative ways of providing banks with access to the safe assets they need to do business, without undermining national governments' ability to finance part of their operations with debt held by banks and other financial intermediaries. As has been the pattern to date, these proposals have stalled because of perceptions that they would ultimately result in debt mutualization to the disadvantage of some creditor countries.

Monetary Policy

Establishing its credibility as an inflation fighter was an important early task for the ECB. But it pursued this goal to the exclusion of wider economic policy considerations which, when the crisis hit, should have figured more centrally in its policy deliberations. Instead, the ECB's monetary easing in the first years of the crisis was less whole-hearted than that of the other leading central banks. Limiting the scope of its response to the financial market disruption, it underestimated the feedback loops that were taking hold in Europe as the deterioration in the government's finances fed through to household and corporate spending and on to banks and around again.

Depending on ECB policy, more than one potential equilibrium configuration of financial market prices could have been achieved in the crisis: a bad equilibrium, with high risk-premia on most government bonds reflecting the fear of euro break-up; and a good equilibrium based on confidence that there would be no break-up. At first, the aversion to any steps that could lead to an international transfer within the euro area meant that the ECB's measures were too tentative to steer the euro area economy into the good equilibrium. Only after Mario Draghi convinced markets that the tools the ECB had available within its mandate would be sufficient to 'preserve the euro' did the market move away from the bad equilibrium. Now, especially after the introduction of quantitative easing (QE) in 2015, the effective removal of those risk premia has moved the system to a better equilibrium without entailing any international transfers of wealth.

The statutory prohibition on monetary financing of the government was over-interpreted with the result that, even when the need for further easing was fully evident by 2012, all other avenues, including negative interest rates, had to be explored before a consensus was reached that outright purchases of government bonds would be embarked on.

In the future, monetary policy for a currency union must not be hijacked by fundamentalist dogma.

Risk-Sharing

More generally, the crisis has focused attention on the limited scope for risk-sharing in the euro area. This of course is seen as 'a feature rather than a bug' by creditor countries which were convinced to create the system only on the understanding that it would not be a 'transfer union'.

We have seen how, when pressures arise in some euro area member states, their banking system has the capacity to draw liquidity from the system as a whole. The kind of response familiar from Latin American crises, with devaluations and inflationary surges, is absent. But the flip side of the lack of a national currency is that it removes devaluation as an adjustment mechanism (reducing real wages and the real value of indebtedness denominated in the national currency).

National governments should have anticipated these adjustment difficulties and chosen policies that were less likely to expose them to such pressures. Creation of the euro embedded a higher penalty for bad macro-economic and banking policies, and it is the failure of several governments to respond to this heightened risk that generated the crisis. The net benefits of the euro were lower than expected because of this unresolved political economy trap.

While some integration of risk-pricing in private equity markets was observed following the creation of the euro area, the degree of private risk-sharing of country-specific shocks in the face of the financial crisis was limited. National governments took much of the stress and, because their access to financing was not unlimited, the needed adjustment of their fiscal deficits had adverse multiplier effects on the affected national economies. Over-zealous fiscal adjustment from 2010 in less stressed countries that did have some fiscal headroom was also a negative factor. How much more financing would have been optimal and the extent of additional government debt restructuring there should have been over and above the limited amount settled for Greece in 2011–12 is a question that cannot be answered here.

As far as the banking losses in the more severely affected countries and the Greek government debt are concerned, a single-minded policy either of default/bail-in or of collective socialization at the European level might have allowed a speedier and less costly recovery from the crisis than the compromise middle course that was adopted in Europe.

Better intergovernmental risk-sharing mechanisms should be created in the euro area going beyond the existing mandate of the European Stability Mechanism (ESM), and that this can be done without creating undue moral hazard. Political discussions around such mechanisms are likely to continue to be fraught, not only because of the divergent cultural and historical perspectives on these matters of the elites in different countries (cf. Brunnermeier et al. 2016) but also because there has been no correlation between average national living standards and crisis-proneness.

Role of National Central Banks

When the euro was originally designed it seemed to me that maintaining the national central banks in the Governing Council with one vote each was an unnecessary concession to those sceptical about the new regime. In normal times, a technocratic monetary policy committee can do an effective job of maintaining euro area price-stability. No need to insist on national representation or on retaining national central banks at all.

But, conditional on price stability, the ECB is mandated to support economic policies of the Union. The experience of a deep crisis with asymmetric shocks hitting different countries in sharply different ways, and the continued sovereignty of member states reveals that national interests need to be interpreted to and defended at the ECB by each national central bank. And the constraints and other implications of euro membership for national policies need to be communicated to national governments and parliaments in a way that can be done convincingly and effectively only by national central banks to the extent that they are seen as loyal to national interests.

Thus, while the transfer to the ECB of additional tasks previously conducted by national central banks (including bank supervision, already in place, and emergency liquidity, not yet transferred) is to be welcomed, the degree of economic policy integration in the EU is not yet close to the point where the abolition of national central banks could be safely envisaged.

* * *

It is not only in Ireland that passive and libertarian pre-crisis financial sector policies created the conditions that allowed the distortions to build to such a disastrous level. The resulting crisis constrained the resources available to government and to society at large. Financial stability has now been restored and, though government debt is much higher than it was at the outset, its servicing costs have been contained.

Banking and financial market conditions in Ireland and other advanced economies both in Europe and elsewhere were disrupted during the crisis in ways that were unprecedented in recent history. Some policy decisions were taken in the heat of the moment by poorly prepared and frightened decision-makers. This is certainly the case for the Irish banking guarantee. Ireland was not the only country whose financial authorities took hasty decisions they came to regret. In Europe, the international failure to deal adequately with the Greek debt overhang in 2010 falls into the same category. Other mistakes, such as the too-early move to fiscal consolidation, and the ECB interest rate increases of 2011, are explicable as being based more on a determination not to repeat the inflationary errors of the 1970s than on a coherent analysis of the costs and benefits of a less constrained policy.

In the end, though, the euro and the ECB survived a major test in the crisis of 2010–13. The crisis revealed the limitations of its institutional architecture. Its survival can be attributed to a few decisive and far-reaching actions based on out-of-the-box thinking, such as the creation of what ultimately became the ESM, with its large capacity for medium-term international stabilization finance in Europe, and the ECB's suite of asset purchase programmes including the outright monetary transactions (OMT). Survival of the euro in a future crisis could depend on policy-makers' preparedness and willingness to embark on comparably innova-tive measures.

Wider political problems confront the EU. Brexit and the absorption of immigrants, among other matters, have added to the centrifugal pressures that emerged during the financial crisis to turn the focus of national policymakers inward. The historic momentum towards greater integration in Europe has slowed or even reversed. The financial crisis clarified the need for more centralization of financial regulation and risk-sharing and much better governance structures in Europe. Although the monetary and financial structures of the euro area have been strengthened, not as much has been achieved as is needed. The wider challenges of the EU are likely to inhibit or delay further progress, though it may continue to be possible to do more within the euro area than on the wider canvas of the EU.

The experience of individual member states in coping with the monetary and banking dimensions of the crisis varied. Ireland was one of the most severely affected countries in the crisis. It received liquidity assistance from the ECB, but this was, for a time, done grudgingly, in an atmosphere of suspicion and alarm, and on conditions that looked unfavourable. In the end, though, treatment became more favourable. Both Ireland and the system survived the test and emerged better prepared institutionally for the next crisis.

Seemingly relegated in the 1990s to the role of a price level thermostat in a world of only moderate macroeconomic fluctuations, central banks the world over have been thrust by the turbulence of the new millennium into the forefront of active stabilization. Their mandates, explicit or implicit, have broadened, and their potential for doing good or ill is clearly larger than it once seemed.

In managing crises, and in guarding against the emergence of future crises, the Irish experience illustrates the proposition that central banks need to be much more active than was conventional in the past, both in regard to their macroeconomic function and in the supervision of banks (where that is also part of their responsibility). Clarity and persistence in pursuing attainable goals consistent with the legal mandate must be the hallmark. At the same time, they have to respect the limitations of their mandates: they cannot arrogate to themselves the role of government, but have to work with government.

For some observers, the policy reaction to the crisis was disappointingly conservative. They deplore the missed opportunity to turn the upheaval to strategic advantage, by undermining power structures that stand in the way of a more egalitarian and sustainable economic development. A more radical approach to economic and social policy than has been pursued by Ireland can certainly be imagined. But the global history of failed central bank activism outside of its normal mandate tells us that it is usually a mistake for the central bank to be placed in the vanguard of such an approach. Populist measures such as tight interest rate ceilings and direct lending to small businesses by central banks have a long record of failure to achieve stated objectives and large damaging side effects. The central bank will best promote economic welfare by providing financial stability (as well as seeking to ensure good conduct by the providers of financial services) as a backdrop to the conduct of governmental economic and social policy.

On the whole, Ireland has prospered in the era of globalization. Benefits have accrued to most sections of society. But, although public policy has helped contain the rise in income inequality to a greater extent in Ireland than elsewhere, the resources of the nation have not been deployed as effectively as they might to spread the fruits of national prosperity more widely. Long-standing weaknesses in the provision of social housing and healthcare are only the most salient of many shortcomings that would be within the capacity of Irish government to correct. Some of this could entail a radical governmental strategy; but the chief contribution of the central bank will still be the relatively conservative one of protecting the restored financial stability as a platform that helps ensure that society does have the resources to tackle such challenges effectively.

A consequence of this stability focus is that central bankers will tend to appear conservative. Such conservatism in the narrow realm of their mandate is, however, very different to being reactionary (as some central bankers have been: seeking to use their power to thwart the aims and policy of governments). Instead, apparent conservativism (in this narrow sense) can be consistent with being a trusted advisor even to a government pursuing radical economic policies.

The future of finance may be quite different from what we see today. The way in which money and finance are organized may change quite significantly over coming decades, with the blockchain only one of the innovations likely to be influential in this regard. Technology makes it likely that commercial banks will no longer be the monopoly providers of the payments system, and credit flows too may benefit from innovations that are at present only embryonic. But money will always need a social regulator. The role of the national central bank will change, not diminish.

Understanding Ireland's chequered experience can help central bankers of the future devise safe courses through this changing environment.

References

Adelino, Manuel, Antoinette Schoar and Felipe Severino. (2016). 'Dynamics of Housing Debt in the Recent Boom and Great Recession'. NBER Working Paper No. 23502. Cambridge, MA: National Bureau of Economic Research.

Anginer, Deniz, Aslı Demirgüç-Kunt and Min Zhu. (2014). 'How Does Deposit Insurance Affect Bank Risk? Evidence from the Recent Crisis'. *Journal of Banking and Finance* 48: 312–21. (World Bank Policy Research Working Paper 6289).

Aron, Janine and John Muellbauer. (2016). 'Modelling and Forecasting Mortgage Delinquency and Foreclosure in the UK'. *Journal of Urban Economics* 94(C): 32–53.

Baker, Terry, John FitzGerald and Patrick Honohan, eds. (1996). *Economic Implications for Ireland of EMU*. Dublin: Economic and Social Research Institute.

Baldursson, Fridrik Mar, Richard Portes and Eirikur Elis Thorlaksson. (2016). 'All's Well That Ends Well? Resolving Iceland's Failed Banks'. CEPR Discussion Paper DP11185. Washington, DC: Center for Economic and Policy Research.

Ball, Laurence M. (2018). *The Fed and Lehman Brothers: Setting the Record Straight on a Financial Disaster*. New York: Cambridge University Press.

Ball, Laurence, Joseph Gagnon, Patrick Honohan and Signe Krogstrup. (2016). *What Else Can Central Banks Do?* Geneva Reports on the World Economy 18. Geneva: International Center for Monetary and Banking Studies and London: Centre for Economic Policy Research.

Barnes, Sebastian and Diarmaid Smyth. (2013). 'The Government's Balance Sheet after the Crisis: A Comprehensive Perspective'. Irish Fiscal Advisory Council Working Paper.

Barry, Frank. (2017). 'The Irish Single-Currency Debate of the 1990s in Retrospect'. *Journal of the Statistical and Social Inquiry Society of Ireland* XLVI: 71–96.

Bastasin, Carlo. (2012). *Saving Europe: How National Politics Nearly Destroyed the Euro*. Washington, DC: The Brookings Institution.

Bénassy-Quéré, Agnès, Markus K. Brunnermeier, Henrik Enderlein, et al. (2018). 'Reconciling Risk Sharing with Market Discipline: A Constructive Approach to Euro Area Reform'. CEPR Policy Insight No. 91. London: Centre for Economic Policy Research.

Benediktsdottir, Sigridur, Jon Danielsson and Gylfi Zoega. (2011). 'Lessons from a Collapse of a Financial System'. *Economic Policy* 26(66): 183–235.

Benediktsdóttir, Sigríður, Gauti B. Eggertsson and Eggert Þórarinsson. (2017). 'The Rise, Fall, and Resurrection of Iceland: A Post-Mortem Analysis of the 2008 Financial Crisis'. Brookings Papers on Economic Activity, Fall, 191–308.

Bernanke, Ben S. (2015). *The Courage to Act: A Memoir of a Crisis and Its Aftermath.* New York : W. W. Norton.

Blayney, John and Tom Grace. (2004). *Report on Investigations into the Affairs of National Irish Bank Ltd. and National Irish Bank Financial Services Ltd.* Dublin: Stationery Office.

Blinder, Alan S. (2009). 'Making Monetary Policy by Committee'. *International Finance* 12(2): 171–94.

Blustein, Paul. (2016). *Laid Low: Inside the Crisis That Overwhelmed Europe and the IMF.* Toronto: Centre for International Governance Intervention.

Bova, Elva, Marta Ruiz-Arranz, Frederik Toscani and H. Elif Ture. (2016). 'The Fiscal Costs of Contingent Liabilities: A New Dataset'. IMF Working Paper WP/16/14. Washington, DC: International Monetary Fund.

Brazys, Samuel and Aidan Regan. (2017). 'The Politics of Capitalist Diversity in Europe: Explaining Ireland's Divergent Recovery from the Euro Crisis'. *Perspectives on Politics* 15(2): 411–27.

Brunnermeier, Markus, Harold James and Jean-Pierre Landau. (2016). *The Euro and the Battle of Ideas.* Princeton, NJ: Princeton University Press.

Buder, Matthäus, Max Lienemeyer, Marcel Magnus, Bert Smits and Karl Soukup. (2011). 'The Rescue and Restructuring of Hypo Real Estate'. *Competition Policy Newsletter* No. 3, 41–4.

Buiter, Willem H. (2009). 'What Can Central Banks Do?' In *Maintaining Stability in a Changing Financial System.* Proceedings of the 2008 Jackson Hole Symposium. Kansas City, MO: Federal Reserve Bank of Kansas City, 495–633.

Callan, Tim, Maxime Bercholz and John R. Walsh. (2018). 'Income Growth and Income Distribution: A Long-Run View of Irish Experience'. Budget Perspectives 2018/03. Dublin: Economic and Social Research Institute. https://doi.org/10.26504/bp201903

Calomiris, Charles W. and Charles M. Kahn. (1991). 'The Role of Demandable Debt in Structuring Optimal Banking Arrangements'. *American Economic Review* 81(3): 497–513.

Calvo, Guillermo, Alejandro Izquierdo and Ernesto Talvi. (2006). 'Sudden Stops and Phoenix Miracles in Emerging Markets'. *American Economic Review* 96(2): 405–10.

Caprio, Gerard Jr. and Patrick Honohan. (1999). 'Restoring Banking Stability: Beyond Supervised Capital Requirements'. *Journal of Economic Perspectives* 13(4): 43–64.

Caprio, Gerard Jr. and Patrick Honohan. (2015). 'Banking Crises: Those Hardy Perennials'. In Allen N. Berger, Philip Molyneux and John O. S. Wilson (eds.), *The Oxford Handbook of Banking*, 2nd edn. Oxford: Oxford University Press, 700–20.

Cardiff, Kevin. (2016). *Recap: Inside Ireland's Financial Crisis.* Dublin: Liffey Press.

Carswell, Simon. (2011). *Anglo Republic: Inside the Bank that Broke Ireland.* Dublin: Penguin Ireland.

Casey, Ciarán Michael. (2018). *Policy Failures and the Irish Economic Crisis.* London: Palgrave Macmillan.

Chamley, Christophe, Laurence J. Kotlikoff and Herakles Polemarchakis. (2012). 'Limited Purpose Banking: Moving from "Trust Me" to "Show Me" Banking'. *American Economic Review: Papers and Proceedings* 102(3): 1–10.

Chopra, Ajai. (2015). 'The ECB's Role in the Design and Implementation of Crisis Country Programmes: Ireland and Beyond'. In *The ECB's Role in the Design and Implementation of (Financial) Measures in Crisis-hit Countries.* Luxembourg: European Parliament. www.europarl.europa.eu%2FRegData%2Fetudes%2FIDAN% 2F2015%2F569963%2FIPOL_IDA(2015)569963_EN.pdf&usg=AOvVaw2ZQZu7C-Qu1sGhHAGWM6g3

Cline, William R. (2014). *Managing the Euro Area Debt Crisis.* Washington, DC: Peterson Institute for International Economics.

Cline, William R. and Joseph E. Gagnon. (2013). 'Lehman Died, Bagehot Lives: Why Did the Fed and Treasury Let a Major Wall Street Bank Fail?' Peterson Institute for International Economics Policy Brief 13–21. https://piie.com/publications/policy-briefs/lehman-died-bagehot-lives-why-did-fed-and-treasury-let-major-wall-street

Cole, Harold, Daniel Neuhann and Guillermo Ordoñez. (2016). 'Debt Crises: For Whom the Bell Tolls'. NBER Working Paper 22330.

Collins, Michael. (1991). *Banks and Industrial Finance in Britain 1800–1939.* London: Macmillan.

Commission of Inquiry into Banking, Currency and Credit. (1938). *Reports.* Dublin: Stationery Office.

Comptroller and Auditor General (Ireland). (2016). *National Asset Management Agency's Sale of Project Eagle.* Dublin: Government Publications. http://audgen .gov.ie/viewdoc.asp?DocID=2338

Comptroller and Auditor General (Ireland). (2017). *Annual Report 2016.* Dublin: Government Publications.

Connor, Gregory, Thomas Flavin and Brian O'Kelly. (2015). 'Restructuring and Recovery of the Irish Financial Sector: An Economic Case History'. Maynooth Economics Working Paper N259-15. http://eprints.maynoothuniversity.ie/6076/7/ N259-15.pdf

Cooper, Matt. (2012). *How Ireland Really Went Bust.* Dublin: Penguin Ireland.

Coyle, Diane. (2015). *GDP: A Brief but Affectionate History.* Princeton, NJ: Princeton University Press.

Creaton, Siobhan and Conor O'Clery. (2002). *Panic at the Bank.* Dublin: Gill and Macmillan.

Daly, Gavin and Ian Kehoe. (2014). *Citizen Quinn.* Dublin: Penguin Ireland.

Daly, Paul. (2019). 'The Administrative State Inside and Outside the Irish Courts'. In Niamh Hardiman and David M. Farrell (eds.), *Oxford Handbook of Irish Politics.* Oxford: Oxford University Press.

Darling, Alistair. (2011). *Back from the Brink: 1000 Days at Number 11.* London: Atlantic Books.

De Grauwe, Paul and Ji Yuemei. (2013). 'Self-fulfilling Crises in the Eurozone: An Empirical Test'. *Journal of International Money and Finance* 34: 15–36.

Demetriades, Panicos. (2017). *A Diary of the Euro Crisis in Cyprus: Lessons for Bank Recovery and Resolution.* London: Macmillan.

Donnery, Sharon, Trevor Fitzpatrick, Darren Greaney, Fergal McCann and Mícheál O'Keeffe. (2018). 'Resolving Non-Performing Loans in Ireland: 2010–2018'. *Central Bank of Ireland Quarterly Bulletin* 2018/2: 54–70.

Donovan, Donal. (2016). 'The IMF's Role in Ireland'. Washington DC: IMF Independent Evaluation Office. BP/16–02/04.

Donovan, Donal and Antoin E. Murphy. (2012). *The Fall of the Celtic Tiger*. Oxford: Oxford University Press.

Dornbusch, Rüdiger. (1989). 'Credibility, Debt and Unemployment: Ireland's Failed Stabilization'. *Economic Policy* 8: 173–209.

Drea, Eoin. (2013). 'The Bank of England, Montagu Norman and the Internationalization of Anglo-Irish Monetary Relations, 1922–43'. *Financial History Review* 21(1): 59–76. DOI:10.1017/S0968565013000231.

Drea, Eoin. (2015). 'The Impact of Henry Parker-Willis and the Federal Reserve on the Institutional Design of the Irish Currency Act 1927'. *The Historical Journal* 58(3): 855–75. DOI:10.1017/S0018246X14000466

Dübel, Achim. (2013). 'The Capital Structure of Banks and Practice of Bank Restructuring'. CFS Working Paper 2013/04. Frankfurt: Center for Financial Studies. http://nbn-resolving.de/urn:nbn:de:hebis:30:3-324811

Eichengreen, Barry. (2011). *Exorbitant Privilege*. Oxford: Oxford University Press.

Eichengreen, Barry. (2015). *Hall of Mirrors: The Great Depression, the Great Recession, and the Uses-and Misuses-of History*. Oxford: Oxford University Press.

Eichengreen, Barry, Andrew K. Rose and Charles Wyplosz. (1996). 'Speculative Attacks on Pegged Exchange Rates'. In Matthew B. Canzoneri, Wilfred J. Ethier and Vittorio Grilli (eds.), *The New Transatlantic Economy*. Cambridge: Cambridge University Press, 191–228.

Everett, Mary, Joe McNeill and Gillian Phelan. (2013). 'Measuring the Value Added of the Financial Sector in Ireland'. *Central Bank of Ireland Quarterly Bulletin* 2013/2.

Feldstein, Martin. (1997). 'EMU and International Conflict'. *Foreign Affairs* 76(6): 60–73.

FitzGerald, John. (2018). 'National Accounts for a Global Economy: The Case of Ireland'. *Economic and Social Research Institute Quarterly Economic Review*, June.

FitzGerald, John and Sean Kenny. (2017). '"Till Debt Do Us Part": Financial Implications of the Divorce of the Irish Free State from the UK, 1922–26'. *Lund Papers in Economic History* 166.

Foley-Fisher, Nathan and Eoin McLaughlin. (2016a). 'Capitalising on the Irish Land Question: Land Reform and State Banking in Ireland, 1891–1938'. *Financial History Review* 23(1): 71–109.

Foley-Fisher, Nathan and Eoin McLaughlin. (2016b). 'Sovereign Debt Guarantees and Default: Lessons from the UK and Ireland, 1920–38'. *European Economic Review* 87: 272–86.

Geithner, Timothy F. (2014). *Stress Test: Reflections on Financial Crises*. New York: Crown.

Gerlach-Kristen, Petra and Rossana Merola. (2013). 'Consumption and Credit Constraints: A Model and Evidence for Ireland'. *Economic and Social Research Institute Working Paper* 471.

Goggin, Jean, Sarah Holton, Jane Kelly, Reamonn Lydon and Kieran McQuinn. (2012). 'Variable Mortgage Rate Pricing in Ireland'. *Central Bank of Ireland Economic Letters* 2012/2.

Goodhart, Charles and Emilios Avgouleas. (2016). 'A Critical Evaluation of Bail-ins as Bank Recapitalisation Mechanisms'. In Douglas D. Evanoff, Andrew Haldane and George G. Kaufman (eds.), *The New International Financial System: Analyzing the*

Cumulative Impact of Regulatory Reform. World Scientific Studies in International Economics, 48. Singapore: World Scientific, 267–305.

Gopinath, Gita. (2018). 'Rethinking Macroeconomic Policy: International Economy Issues'. In Olivier Blanchard and Larry Summers (eds.), *Rethinking Macroeconomic Policy 4*. Cambridge, MA: MIT Press.

Gourinchas, Pierre-Olivier, Thomas Philippon and Dimitri Vayanos. (2016). 'The Analytics of the Greek Crisis'. *NBER Macroeconomics Annual* 31: 1–81.

Haldane, Andrew G. and Vasileos Madouros. (2012). 'The Dog and the Frisbee'. *Proceedings of the Economic Policy Symposium at Jackson Hole*. Federal Reserve Bank of Kansas City, 109–59. www.bis.org/review/r120905a.pdf

Hall, F. G. (1949). *The Bank of Ireland 1783–1946*. Dublin: Hodges Figgis.

Hardiman, Niamh, Spyros Blavoukos, Sebastian Dellepiane Avellaneda and George Pagoulatos. (2017). 'Austerity in the European Periphery: The Irish Experience'. In Emma Heffernan, John McHale and Niamh Moore-Cherry (eds.), *Debating Austerity: Crisis, Experience and Recovery*. Dublin: Royal Irish Academy.

Heffernan, Emma, John McHale and Niamh Moore-Cherry. (2017). *Debating Austerity: Crisis, Experience and Recovery*. Dublin: Royal Irish Academy.

Holton, Sarah, Jane Kelly, Reamonn Lydon, Allen Monks and Nuala O'Donnell. (2013). 'The Impact of the Financial Crisis on Banks' Net Interest Margins'. *Central Bank of Ireland Economic Letters* 2013/1.

Honohan, Patrick. (1991). 'Monetary Union in Europe'. In Rory O'Donnell (ed.), *Studies in European Union: Economic and Monetary Union*. Dublin: Institute for European Affairs, 49–85.

Honohan, Patrick. (1993). *An Examination of Irish Currency Policy*. Dublin: Economic and Social Research Institute.

Honohan, Patrick. (1994). 'Costing the Delay in Devaluing, 1992–93'. *Irish Banking Review* Spring, 3–15.

Honohan, Patrick. (1997). 'Banking System Failures in Developing and Transition Countries: Diagnosis and Prediction'. Bank for International Settlements Working Paper 39, January. www.bis.org/publ/work39.htm

Honohan, Patrick. (2000). 'Ireland in EMU: Skateboard or Straitjacket?' *Irish Banking Review* Winter, 15–31.

Honohan, Patrick. (2006). ''To What Extent Has Finance Been a Driver of Ireland's Economic Success?' *ESRI Quarterly Economic Commentary* December, 59–72.

Honohan, Patrick. (2010). 'The Irish Banking Crisis: Regulatory and Financial Stability Policy 2003–8'. A Report to the Minister for Finance by the Governor of the Central Bank. Dublin 2010. www.bankinginquiry.gov.ie/Preliminary_Reports.aspx

Honohan, Patrick. (2014). 'Brian Lenihan and the Nation's Finances'. In Brian Murphy, Mary O'Rourke and Noel Whelan (eds.), *Brian Lenihan: His Times and Trials*. Dublin: Irish Academic Press, 64–82.

Honohan, Patrick. (2015). 'Some Lessons Learnt from the EU-IMF Program'. In *Ireland: Lessons from Its Recovery from the Bank-Sovereign Loop*. European Departmental Paper 15/1. Washington, DC: International Monetary Fund, 24–32. www.imf.org/external/pubs/cat/longres.aspx?sk=43361.0

Honohan, Patrick. (2017). 'Management and Resolution of Banking Crises: Lessons from Recent European Experience'. PIIE Policy Brief 17–1. Washington, DC: Peterson Institute for International Economics.

Honohan, Patrick. (2018a). 'Could Performance-linked Lending Have Helped in the Euro Crisis? Could It Still?' In Robert Shiller, Jonathan D. Ostry and James Benford (eds.), *Sovereign GDP-Linked Bonds: Rationale and Design*. (A Voxeu.org ebook) London: CEPR Press.

Honohan, Patrick. (2018b). 'Real and Imagined Constraints on Euro Area Monetary Policy'. PIIE Working Paper 18–8. Washington, DC: Peterson Institute for International Economics.

Honohan, Patrick and Charles Conroy. (1994). *Irish Interest Rate Fluctuations in the European Monetary System*. Dublin: Economic and Social Research Institute.

Honohan, Patrick and Jane Kelly. (1997). 'The Insurance Corporation Collapse: Resolving Ireland's Worst Financial Crash'. *Administration* 45(3): 67–77.

Honohan, Patrick, Domenico Lombardi and Samantha St Amand. (2019). 'Managing Macrofinancial Crises: The Role of the Central Bank'. In David Mayes, Pierre L. Siklos and Jan-Egbert Sturm (eds.), *The Oxford Handbook of the Economics of Central Banking*. Oxford: Oxford University Press.

Honohan, Patrick and Gavin Murphy. (2010). 'Breaking the Sterling Link: Ireland's Decision to Enter the EMS'. Institute for International Integration Studies Discussion Paper 317. Trinity College Dublin.

Honohan, Patrick and Cormac Ó Gráda. (1998). 'The Irish Macroeconomic Crisis of 1955–56: How Much Was Due to Monetary Policy?' *Irish Economic and Social History* 25: 52–80.

Honohan, Patrick and Joseph E. Stiglitz. (2001). 'Robust Financial Restraint'. In Gerard Caprio, Patrick Honohan and Joseph E. Stiglitz (eds.), *Financial Liberalization: How Far, How Fast?* Cambridge: Cambridge University Press, 31–59.

Honohan, Patrick and Brendan Walsh. (2002). 'Catching-up with the Leaders: The Irish Hare'. *Brookings Papers on Economic Activity* 2002/1: 1–79.

Hourigan, Niamh. (2015). *Rule-Breakers: Why Being There Trumps Being Fair in Ireland*. Dublin: Gill and Macmillan.

Hourigan, Niamh. (2017). 'Austerity, Resistance and Social Protest in Ireland: Movement Outcomes'. In Emma Heffernan, Niamh Moore-Cherry and John McHale (eds.), *Debating Austerity*. Dublin: Royal Irish Academy, 111–24.

Independent Evaluation Office. (2017). *The IMF and the Crises in Greece, Ireland, and Portugal*. Washington, DC: International Monetary Fund.

International Monetary Fund (IMF). (2015). 'Assessing Reserve Adequacy: Specific Proposals'. Washington, DC: International Monetary Fund. www.imf.org/external/np/pp/eng/2014/121914.pdf

James, Harold. (2012). *Making the European Monetary Union*. Cambridge, MA: Belknap Press.

James, Harold. (2017). 'Extraordinary Measures for Ordinary Times'. *Project Syndicate*. 3 August. www.project-syndicate.org/commentary/post-crisis-decisionism-carl-schmitt-by-harold-james-2017-08.

Jónsson, Ásgeir and Hersir Sigurgeirsson. (2016). *The Icelandic Financial Crisis: A Study into the World's Smallest Currency Area and Its Recovery from Total Banking Collapse*. London: Palgrave Macmillan.

Jordà, Òscar, Björn Richter, Moritz Schularick and Alan M. Taylor. (2017). 'Bank Capital Redux: Solvency, Liquidity and Crisis'. Federal Reserve Bank of San Francisco Working Paper 2017-06.

Kalemli-Ozcan, Sebnem, Emiliano Luttini and Bent Sørensen. (2014). 'Debt Crises and Risk-Sharing: The Role of Markets versus Sovereigns'. *Scandinavian Journal of Economics* 116(1): 253–76.

Kay, John. (2015). *Other People's Money: Master of the Universe or Servant of the People?* London: Profile Books.

Keena, Colm. (2018). 'The €2.75 m House, the Multimillion AIB Debts and the Link to a Galway Family'. *Irish Times* 26 March.

Kelly, Robert, Paul Lyons and Conor O'Toole. (2015). 'Mortgage Interest Rate Types in Ireland'. *Central Bank of Ireland Economic Letters* 2015/9.

Kelly, Robert, Yvonne McCarthy and Kieran McQuinn. (2012). 'Impairment and Negative Equity in the Irish Mortgage Market'. *Journal of Housing Economics* 21(3): 256–68.

Keynes, John Maynard. (1930). *A Treatise on Money*. London: Macmillan.

Keynes, John Maynard. (1936). *General Theory of Employment Interest and Money*. London: Macmillan.

King, Mervyn. (2016). *The End of Alchemy: Money, Banking, and the Future of the Global Economy*. New York: W. W. Norton.

Kinghan, Christina, Paul Lyons, Yvonne McCarthy and Conor O'Toole. (2017). 'Macroprudential Measures and Irish Mortgage Lending: An Overview of Lending in 2016'. *Central Bank of Ireland Economic Letters* 2017/6.

Klein, Michael W. and Jay C. Shambaugh. (2012). *Exchange Rate Regimes in the Modern Era*. Cambridge, MA: MIT Press.

Laeven, Luc and Fabián Valencia. (2012). 'Systemic Banking Crises Database: An Update'. IMF Working Paper 12/163.

Lane, Philip R. (2011). 'The Irish Crisis'. In Miroslav Beblavy, David Cobham and L'udovit Odor (eds.), *The Euro Area and the Financial Crisis*. Cambridge University Press, 59–80.

Lane, Philip R. (2013). 'Capital Flows in the Euro Area'. *European Commission Economic Papers* 497.

Lane, Philip R. (2015). 'The Funding of the Irish Domestic Banking System during the Boom'. *Journal of the Statistical and Social Inquiry Society* XVIV: 40–70.

Lane, Philip R. (2018). 'Macro-Financial Stability and the Euro'. Lecture at the Central Bank of Ireland/IMF Economic Review Conference *The Euro at 20* (26 June). http://centralbank.ie/news/article/macro-financial-stability-and-euro-governor-philip-r-lane

Leahy, Pat. (2013). *The Price of Power*. Dublin: Penguin Ireland.

Lee, John and Daniel McConnell. (2016). *Hell at the Gates: The Inside Story of the Irish Financial Downfall*. Dublin: Mercier Press.

Lucey, Brian C, Charles Larkin and Constantijn Gurdgiev, eds. (2012). *What if Ireland Defaults?* Dublin: Orpen Press.

Lunn, Peter D. (2013). 'The Role of Decision-Making Biases in Ireland's Banking Crisis'. *Irish Political Studies* 28(4): 563–90.

Lydon, Reamonn and Fergal McCann. (2017). 'Income distribution and the Irish mortgage market'. *Central Bank of Ireland Economic Letters* 2017/5.

Lydon, Reamonn and Tara McIndoe-Calder. (2017). 'The Great Irish (De)leveraging 2005–14'. European Central Bank Working Paper 2062.

Lydon, Reamonn and Niall O'Hanlon. (2012). 'Housing Equity Withdrawal, Property Bubbles and Consumption'. Central Bank of Ireland Research Technical Paper 05/RT/12.

Lyons, Tom and Richard Curran. 2013. *Fingers: The Man Who Brought Down Irish Nationwide and Cost Us €5.4bn.* Dublin: Gill.

Madden, David. (2014). 'Winners and Losers on the Roller-Coaster: Ireland, 2003–2011'. *Economic and Social Review* 45(3): 405–21.

Martin, Philippe and Thomas Philippon. (2014). 'Inspecting the Mechanism: Leverage and the Great Recession in the Eurozone'. *American Economic Review* 107(7): 1904–37.

McCann, Fergal. (2017a). 'Mortgage Modification in Ireland: A Recent History'. *Central Bank of Ireland Economic Letters* 2017/16.

McCann, Fergal. (2017b). 'Resolving a Non-Performing Loan Crisis: The Ongoing Case of the Irish Mortgage Market'. Central Bank of Ireland Research Technical Papers 10/RT/17.

McCarthy, Yvonne. (2014). 'Dis-entangling the Mortgage Arrears Crisis: The Role of the Labour Market, Income Volatility and Housing Equity'. Central Bank of Ireland Technical Research Paper 2/RT/2014.

McDonald, Frank and Kathy Sheridan. (2008). *The Builders.* Dublin: Penguin Ireland.

McGinley, Michael. (2004). *The La Touche Family in Ireland.* Dublin: The La Touche Legacy Committee.

McGowan, Padraig. (1990). *Money and Banking in Ireland.* Dublin: Institute of Public Administration.

Medina Cas, Stephanie Peresa and Irena Peresa. (2016). 'What Makes a Good 'Bad Bank'? The Irish, Spanish and German Experience'. European Commission Discussion Paper 36.

Meenan, James. (1970). *The Irish Economy since 1922.* Liverpool: University of Liverpool Press.

Mian, Atif and Amir Sufi. (2014). *House of Debt: How They (and You) Caused the Great Recession.* Chicago: University of Chicago Press.

Mody, Ashoka. (2018). *Eurotragedy: A Drama in Eight Acts.* Oxford: Oxford University Press.

Moynihan, Maurice. (1975). *Currency and Central Banking in Ireland.* Dublin: Gill and Macmillan.

Murphy, Brian, Mary O'Rourke and Noel Whelan, eds. (2013). *Brian Lenihan: In Calm and Crisis.* Dublin: Merrion.

Murphy, Gareth. (2015). 'Address at the Irish Funds Symposium'. Dublin, 9 October 2015. www.centralbank.ie/news/article/address-by-director-of-markets-supervision-gareth-murphy-at-the-irish-funds-symposium

National Asset Management Agency. (2016). *Response to the C&AG Special Report on Project Eagle.* www.nama.ie/fileadmin/user_upload/documents/C_AG_Report/NAMA_-_response_to_the_CAG_Special_Report_on_Project_Eagle_-_14_Sept_2016.pdf

Nolan, Brian. (2012). 'Updating Top Incomes Shares for Ireland 2000–2009', WID. world Technical Note, 2012/6. http://wid.world/document/wid_methodology_notes_2012_6_ireland/

Nyberg, Peter. (2011). *Misjudging Risk: Causes of the Systemic Banking Crisis in Ireland* Dublin: Government Publications. www.bankinginquiry.gov.ie/

Ó Broin, Leon. (1982). *No Man's Man: A Biographical Memoir of Joseph Brennan.* Dublin: Institute of Public Administration.

O'Clery, Conor and Siobhán Creaton. (2002). *Panic at the Bank: How John Rusnak Lost AIB $700 Million.* Dublin: Gill and Macmillan.

Ó Gráda, Cormac. (1993). *Ireland: A New Economic History 1780–1939.* Oxford: Oxford University Press.

Ó Gráda, Cormac. (1995). 'Money and Banking in the Irish Free State'. In C. H. Feinstein (ed.), *Banking, Currency and Finance in Europe between the Wars.* Oxford: Oxford University Press.

Ó Gráda, Cormac. (2002). 'Should the Munster Bank Have Been Saved?' In David Dickson and Cormac Ó Gráda, *Refiguring Ireland.* Dublin: Lilliput, 316–41. http://hdl.handle.net/10197/487

Ó Gráda, Cormac. (2011). 'Five Crises'. Central Bank of Ireland T. K. Whitaker Lecture, 29 June 2011. UCD Centre for Economic Research Working Paper Series WP 11/12.

Ó Gráda, Cormac. (2012). 'The Last Major Irish Bank Failure before 2008'. *Financial History Review* 19(2): 199–217. Earlier version available at: http://researchrepository.ucd.ie/handle/10197/2672

Oireachtas. (2016). *Report of the Joint Committee of Inquiry into the Banking Crisis.* Dublin: Stationery Office. https://inquiries.oireachtas.ie/banking

Ollerenshaw, Philip. (1987). *Banking in Nineteenth Century Ireland: The Belfast Banks 1825–1914.* Manchester: Manchester University Press.

O'Malley, Terry. (2018). 'Did the Dunne Judgment Lead to More Mortgage Defaults?' *Central Bank of Ireland Economic Letters* 2018/1.

Ó Riain, Seán. (2014). *The Rise and Fall of Ireland's Celtic Tiger: Liberalism, Boom and Bust.* Cambridge: Cambridge University Press.

O'Rourke, Kevin. (1991). 'Burn Everything English but Their Coal: The Anglo-Irish Economic War of the 1930s'. *The Journal of Economic History* 51(2): 357–66.

O'Rourke, Kevin Hjortshøj. (2016). 'Independent Ireland in Comparative Perspective'. In Tom Boylan, Nicholas Canny and Mary Harris (eds.), *Ireland 1916–2016: The Promise and Challenge of National Sovereignty.* Dublin: Four Courts Press.

Orphanides, Athanasios. (2017). 'The Fiscal-Monetary Policy Mix in the Euro Area: Challenges at the Zero Lower Bound'. MIT Sloan Research Paper No. 5197–17. https://ssrn.com/abstract=2965805

Philippon, Thomas. (2016). 'The Fintech Opportunity'. NBER Working Paper 22476.

Philippon, Thomas and Aude Salord. (2017). 'Bail-ins and Bank Resolution in Europe'. Geneva Reports on the World Economy Special Report. Geneva: International Center for Monetary and Banking Studies.

Promontory Financial Group. (2016). *RBS Group's Treatment of SME Customers Referred to the Global Restructuring Group.* A Report under Section 166 of the Financial Services and Markets Act 2000). London: Financial Conduct Authority. www.parliament.uk/documents/commons-committees/treasury/s166-rbs-grg.pdf

Rajan, Raghuram. (2011). *Fault Lines.* Princeton, NJ: Princeton University Press.

Rajan, Raghuram. (2018). 'Liquidity and Leverage'. Speech to the American Economic Association Annual Meeting. https://faculty.chicagobooth.edu/raghuram.rajan/research/papers/AEA AFA Talk Liquidity and Leverage.pdf

Roche, William K., Philip J. O'Connell and Andrea Prothero, eds. (2016). *Austerity and Recovery in Ireland: Europe's Poster Child and the Great Recession.* Oxford: Oxford University Press.

Rose, Andrew K. (2000). 'One Money, One Market: The Effect of Common Currencies on Trade'. *Economic Policy* 15(30): 8–45.

Ross, Shane. (2010). *The Bankers: How the Banks Brought Ireland to Its Knees.* Dublin: Penguin Ireland.

Salz, Anthony. (2013). *An Independent Review of Barclays' Business Practices.* The Salz Review. London: Barclays PLC.

Schuker, Stephen A. (1976). *The End of French Predominance in Europe. The Financial Crisis of 1924 and the Adoption of the Dawes Plan.* Chapel Hill, NC: The University of North Carolina Press.

Tooze, Adam. (2018). *Crashed: How a Decade of Financial Crises Changed the World.* London: Allen Lane.

Tucker, Paul. (2018). *Unelected Power: The Quest for Legitimacy in Central Banking and the Regulatory State.* Princeton, NJ: Princeton University Press.

Turner, Philip. (2017). 'Did Central Banks Cause the Last Financial Crisis? Will They Cause the Next?' London School of Economics Financial Market Group Special Paper 249.

Véron, Nicolas. (2016). 'The IMF's Role in the Euro Area Crisis: Financial Sector Aspects'. BP/16–02/10. Washington, DC: IMF Independent Evaluation Office.

Whelan, Christopher T., Helen Russell and Bertrand Maître. (2016). 'Economic Stress and the Great Recession in Ireland: Polarization, Individualization or "Middle Class Squeeze"'? *Social Indicators Research* 126(2): 503–26.

Whelan, Karl. (2009). 'Garrett Fitzgerald and Senior Bonds'. Blogpost IrishEconomy.ie 30 August 2009.

Whelan, Karl. (2014). 'Ireland's Economic Crisis: The Good, the Bad and the Ugly'. *Journal of Macroeconomics* 39B, 424–40.

Whitaker, T. Kenneth. (1979). 'Central Bank and Government 1967–76'. Central Bank Archive.

Whitaker, T. Kenneth. (1980). 'Ireland's External Reserves'. *Journal of the Institute of Bankers in Ireland* LXXXII(1): 38–49.

Wieser, Thomas. (2018). 'Interview with FT Alphachat's Jim Brunsden and Alex Barker'. 2 February. www.ft.com/content/adfa67d3-e2b2-4a15-8041-0a2128bccec6

World Bank. (2001). *Finance for Growth: Policy Choices in a Volatile World.* Oxford: Oxford University Press. https://mpra.ub.uni-muenchen.de/9929/1/MPRA_paper_9929.pdf

World Bank. (2008). *Finance for All? Policies and Pitfalls in Expanding Access.* Oxford: Oxford University Press. https://siteresources.worldbank.org/INTFINFORALL/Resources/ . . . /FFA_book.pdf

Xiouras, Costas. (2016). 'Handling of the Laiki ELA and the Cyprus Bail-in Package'. In Alexander George Michaelides and Athanasios Orphanides (eds.), *The Cyprus Bail-in: Policy Lessons from the Cyprus Economic Crisis.* London: Imperial College Press.

Zettelmeyer, Jeromin, Christoph Trebesch and Mitu Gulati. (2013). 'Greek Debt Restructuring: An Autopsy'. *Economic Policy* 28(75): 513–63.

Index